Confidence Game

How a Hedge Fund Manager Called Wall Street's Bluff

by Christine S. Richard

Bloomberg News

"Christine Richard's Confidence Game *is an insightful, timely, and fascinating high-speed drive into the often difficult-to-penetrate world of short sellers, with its particular focus on Bill Ackman and his campaign against monoline insurance giant MBIA."*

> SCOTT B. MACDONALD
>
> SENIOR MANAGING DIRECTOR
>
> ALADDIN CAPITAL LLC AND COAUTHOR OF *SEPARATING FOOLS FROM THEIR MONEY*

"How to head off the next crash? Listen to the dissidents now. Christine Richard's deeply researched and deftly written account of Bill Ackman's high-stakes struggle with a leading pillar of a now-collapsed system is the right book at the right time, and a mesmerizing read."

> DEAN STARKMAN
>
> EDITOR
>
> "THE AUDIT," THE BUSINESS SECTION OF THE *COLUMBIA JOURNALISM REVIEW*

"Bill Ackman's battle with MBIA will be remembered as one of the great epics of Wall Street history, and no one followed the story more closely than Christine Richard."

> BETHANY MCLEAN
>
> COAUTHOR OF *THE SMARTEST GUYS IN THE ROOM*

"Finally, a financial crisis book with a hero. It's a compelling morality tale of how one man uncovered a massive fraud and then fought tenaciously to show the world he was right. Richard had unparalleled access to the major players in this saga—from venal executives to incompetent regulators—and she weaves the threads of complex financial shenanigans into a page-turning

narrative. Ackman emerges as the Don Quixote of financial markets: you will root for him and a happy ending."

FRANK PARTNOY

AUTHOR OF *F.I.A.S.C.O.*, *INFECTIOUS GREED*, AND *THE MATCH KING*

"Confidence Game *is a lesson for all investors on the value of independent and exhaustive research. It's also a riveting story.*"

TODD SULLIVAN

CREATOR OF VALUEPLAYS.NET AND A REGULAR CONTRIBUTOR TO THE STOCKTWITS BLOG NETWORK AND SEEKING ALPHA

CONFIDENCE GAME

CONFIDENCE GAME

HOW A HEDGE FUND MANAGER CALLED WALL STREET'S BLUFF

Christine S. Richard
Bloomberg News

WILEY

John Wiley & Sons, Inc.

Published by John Wiley & Sons, Inc., Hoboken, New Jersey.
Published simultaneously in Canada.

For general information on our other products and services or for technical support, please contact our Customer Care Department within the United States at (800) 762-2974, outside the United States at (317) 572-3993 or fax (317) 572-4002.

Wiley also publishes its books in a variety of electronic formats. Some content that appears in print may not be available in electronic books. For more information about Wiley products, visit our web site at www.wiley.com.

Library of Congress Cataloging-in-Publication Data:
Richard, Christine S.
    Confidence game : how a hedge fund manager called Wall Street's bluff / Christine S. Richard.
        p. cm.
    Includes bibliographical references and index.
    Summary: "Confidence Game tells the story how hedge fund manager Bill Ackman's warnings regarding bond insurer MBIA's credit rating went unheeded as Wall Street careened toward disaster"— Provided by publisher.
        ISBN 978-0-470-64827-8 (cloth)
1. Municipal bond insurance—History—21st century. 2. Securities industry—Credit ratings—21st century. 3. Wall Street (New York, N.Y.)—21st century. 4. Global Financial Crisis, 2008-2009. I. Title.
    HG4538.52.R53 2010
    368.8'7—dc22   2010001831

Printed in the United States of America
10 9 8 7 6 5 4 3 2

For Dean

Contents

Preface

OR NEARLY 10 YEARS, I covered the bond market as a Wall Street reporter, first at Dow Jones and later for Bloomberg News. It was a period of enormous growth and innovation in the credit markets. As the expansion peaked, Wall Street manufactured billions of dollars of debt every day, astonishing amounts of it considered triple-A or virtually risk-free. For a while, this was accomplished with true financial innovation. Later, the process was corrupted by delusion and dishonesty.

Of all the stories I covered, there was one that never seemed to go away: the battle between a company called MBIA and a hedge fund manager named Bill Ackman, who was obsessed with that company's practices.

What is MBIA? It stands for Municipal Bond Insurance Association. For years it was the largest of a handful of extraordinarily profitable companies that together guaranteed more than $2 trillion of debt issued by entities ranging from the Cincinnati school system to a shell company in the Cayman Islands. Insurance transformed lower-rated bonds into triple-A-rated securities. Business boomed, giving MBIA some of the highest reported profit margins of any publicly traded company in the United States—even higher than Google and Microsoft.

If there was something about this business that was too good to be true, few people had any reason to point it out. Then in late 2002, Ackman, who ran a hedge fund called Gotham Partners, issued a research report titled *Is MBIA Triple-A?* in which he questioned just about every aspect of MBIA's business. Before he made his views public, Ackman bet against the company by purchasing derivative contracts called credit-default swaps, which would make his fund billions of dollars if MBIA filed for bankruptcy.

Ackman's research report was the opening shot in what became a long and bitter Wall Street feud between him and MBIA. From the start, MBIA was determined to silence Ackman's criticism, and he was no less determined to see MBIA leveled. Ackman was investigated at MBIA's urging by Eliot Spitzer, then New York's attorney general, and the Securities and Exchange Commission (SEC) followed suit.

For more than five years, the hedge fund manager questioned nearly every aspect of MBIA's business, bringing his research to the attention of rating companies, regulators, reporters, and investors. He cornered the chief executive officer (CEO) of PriceWaterhouseCoopers, MBIA's auditors, at a charity function, broached the issue with a bullish equity analyst at a funeral, and wrote to board members of Moody's Investors Service, warning them they could be held personally liable for inaccurate ratings. Eventually, Ackman turned the tables on MBIA, getting regulators to probe MBIA's business practices.

Big names have dominated the headlines during the credit crisis. Bear Stearns was the first major financial institution to collapse. American International Group required a $180 billion government rescue, a larger commitment in inflation-adjusted dollars than the Marshall Plan that rebuilt Europe after World War II. Lehman Brothers was the financial failure felt around the world.

Before all of this happened, another crisis played out. Little known outside of Wall Street, MBIA made hundreds of millions of dollars a year selling its triple-A credit rating. At the same time, it boasted to analysts and investors that it insured bonds on which it saw no chance of loss.

In the lobby of MBIA's headquarters in Armonk, New York, visitors were greeted by a large photo of sunlight pouring through trees. The image is one you might expect to see on an inspirational greeting card—the sunlight, a symbol of some higher power. "We help our clients achieve their financial goals by providing AAA credit protection," read the message alongside the photo. The sanctity of MBIA and the permanence of its triple-A credit rating were articles of faith on Wall Street.

Brash, blunt, almost neurotically persistent, Ackman was the perfect foil to the bond insurance business. Even among his friends and colleagues, Ackman is known for being a font of not-always-welcome forthrightness. He will tell people straight out that their hairstyle is unflattering or they ought to consult with his nutritionist about losing some weight. Ask him about his candor, and he says he gives people honest advice and that's a rare thing in this world.

The first time I spoke with Ackman was December 9, 2002, the day he issued his report on MBIA. "The more I looked, the more I found," he told me, and he just kept finding more. We spoke about MBIA and bond insurance on and off for more than five years.

Persistence had its price. Eventually, nearly every analyst who covered the company refused to take my calls. But MBIA was intriguing. I found the line that summed up the intrigue and contradiction of MBIA in a presentation Ackman made to Moody's Investors Service: "Management integrity has been compromised to uphold the 'no-loss' illusion." Someday, I thought, this conflict over a triple-A-rated company that was not as safe as it appeared would make a great story, one that might prove bigger than Ackman and MBIA.

How was it that MBIA could write insurance on hundreds of billions of dollars of debt and yet tell its investors that it guaranteed only bonds on which it expected to pay no claims? In an article for *Bloomberg Markets* magazine called "The Insurance Charade," Darrell Preston and I exposed part of the secret by looking into various public projects that weren't supposed to be obligations of the taxpayer. Yet when the insured bonds issued to finance these projects threatened to default, taxpayers were called on to cover the losses. MBIA had a nearly perfect track record in the municipal bond market because it wasn't the real insurer of the debt: Taxpayers were.

So what would eventually shatter this no-loss illusion? Bond insurers expanded into the structured finance market, the epicenter of Wall Street innovation. In this market, where all types of loans and securities were bundled into new securities, the game was not rigged in MBIA's favor.

In writing *Confidence Game*, I was able to draw from a wealth of source material that is contemporaneous with the events described in the book. Ackman gave me a CD-ROM containing every e-mail he had written or received that mentioned MBIA as well as years of appointment calendars and access to an office filled with more than 40 boxes of documents he'd collected in researching MBIA. He encouraged colleagues, advisers, and friends to talk with me and spent hours answering my questions. Ackman waived attorney-client privilege with Aaron Marcu, the attorney who represented him in the New York attorney general's investigation of Gotham Partners, so that Marcu could speak with me. Under several Freedom of Information requests, I obtained thousands of pages of testimony taken during Spitzer's and the SEC's probe of Gotham. (I have made several of the full transcripts available at confidencegame.net)

MBIA ultimately decided not to comment for the book or respond to any questions. For the most part, the views of MBIA management, as well as credit-rating company analysts, sell-side analysts, regulators, and MBIA investors, are represented through their public statements. Eric Dinallo, the New York state insurance superintendent who spoke with me about his efforts to stabilize the bond insurers beginning in 2007, was a helpful contributor to the book.

When Ackman bet against MBIA in the summer of 2002, bond insurance and triple-A ratings were unquestioned because they had to be above reproach. Too much depended on the ratings being right. By 2008, MBIA CEO Jay Brown acknowledged that somehow the bond insurer had become "the lynchpin supporting the global financial system."

"Bond insurance was almost like a religious institution in a kingdom that was totally inscrutable," said Richard Blumenthal, Connecticut's attorney general, who launched an investigation of credit ratings and bond insurance in 2008. This was a land in which financial sector debt—at $17 trillion—had grown from about 15 percent of gross domestic product in 1976 to 120 percent in 2008. This explosion of debt transformed Wall Street into a place of extraordinary wealth, where even those far down in the ranks came to expect multimillion-dollar bonuses. Almost no one on Wall Street wanted the music to stop.

Of course, Ackman took on this sacred institution knowing that he stood to make his investors billions of dollars if he was right. That was reason enough for many to view him as a villain. It turns out that Ackman had more than a bearish position on MBIA. He had a stake in the system being wrong. That makes his story an extraordinary vantage point from which to view the approaching credit crisis. As a result, he did something that few people were willing to do as irrationality continued to build in the credit markets: He raised questions and demanded answers in a era when too many people were silent.

So the story begins with the title of Ackman's controversial 2002 research report and a question that many people found impudent and even dangerous: "Is MBIA Triple-A?"

CHRISTINE S. RICHARD

March 2010

Acknowledgments

THIS BOOK WOULD not have been possible without the support of Bloomberg News's editor-in-chief, Matthew Winkler. Every good story is about conflict, Matt tells reporters. I hope this one doesn't disappoint.

Mary Ann McGuigan, my editor at Bloomberg Press, provided guidance and encouragement. I also want to thank JoAnne Kanaval and Yvette Romero at Bloomberg Press and Laura Walsh, Todd Tedesco, Sharon Polese, and Adrianna Johnson at John Wiley & Sons, who picked up and ran with the project in its final stages. Anita Kumar, Mike Novatkoski, and Nick Tamasi in Bloomberg's library helped with the research, tracking down documents with their usual lightning speed. Jennifer Kaufman provided invaluable expertise proofreading the page proofs.

Bloomberg News's reporters and editors are a continual source of inspiration, and their excellent work on the credit crisis is cited throughout this book. I want to particularly thank Jody Shenn, who added to an already considerable load by taking on the bond insurance beat when I went on leave. My team leader at Bloomberg, Alan Goldstein, was extraordinarily patient with my leave of absence at a time when reporters were much in demand to cover stories on the credit markets.

Emma Moody, my editor at Bloomberg News during long days covering the bond insurance crisis, was a rock of composure and good spirits. Bob Burgess and Jonathan Neumann helped shepherd two award-winning stories on the bond insurers through the editing process. The late Fred Weigold edited a *Bloomberg Markets* article on the collapse of the bond insurers. His broad smile and booming laugh were a constant reminder that reporting can be the best job in the world. Mark Pittman, a Bloomberg reporter who was battling to make the Federal Reserve more accountable when he died in late 2009, proved to me that reporting can be the most important job in the world.

Bill Ackman's openness and optimism are key ingredients of this book, and I am grateful to him for sharing both with me over the last few years. He gave me a story to tell amidst all the financial gloom and doom that is in many ways about the importance of free speech, persistence, and staying positive.

Many thanks also are due to the people who agreed to be interviewed for the book, especially those who participated against their better judgment. Roy Katzovicz, Pershing Square's chief legal officer (and an excellent storyteller), is just one who springs to mind. Joelle Dellis and Bethany Norvell at Pershing Square cheerfully fielded numerous requests to track down documents.

Of the many helpful sources I called on in my reporting on the bond insurers, three stand out for their patience and willingness to share their insights: Ed Grebeck, Dick Larkin, and Matt Fabian.

One of the privileges of being a reporter is to learn from other people every day. Doug Noland, who warned about the problems in the credit markets for more than a decade as an analyst at David W. Tice & Assoc., convinced me that debt was the great, unrecognized story in America. Glenda Busick and Carol Hayes, two women in Brevard County, Florida who took on the formidable combination of Wall Street and the "good old boys" of local government, were an inspiration. Glenda's book on her experiences, which she wrote and published on her own time and at her own expense, is a testament to the hard work required of citizens in a democracy.

Finally, thanks to my family. My daughter, Sophie, encouraged me countless times with words, notes, and drawings when it felt like I'd taken on an impossible task. My greatest debt is to my husband, Dean Richard, who has cheered me on since I was twenty years old, and without whom nothing would be possible.

Chapter One

The Meeting

In our minds, our franchise is the ultimate money-back guarantee, the "Good Housekeeping Seal of Approval."

—GARY DUNTON, PRESIDENT OF MBIA, 2001

A S THE TAXI PULLED AWAY from Grand Central Station on a late November afternoon in 2002, Bill Ackman was bracing for a fight. The 36-year-old cofounder of a hedge fund called Gotham Partners had been summoned to a meeting with Jay Brown, the chief executive officer of MBIA Inc. MBIA's general counsel wouldn't say what Brown wanted to discuss, but Ackman had a suspicion. Gotham had placed a bet against the company that could make the fund $2 billion if MBIA filed for bankruptcy. The hedge fund planned to issue a critical research report questioning the bond insurer's triple-A rating.

Ackman had already described the situation in an October 2002 letter to his investors. "Our newest and largest [short] investment is on an extremely highly levered, yet triple-A-rated financial institution, which we believe has inadequate reserves, undisclosed credit-quality problems, aggressive accounting, and substantial unconsolidated indebtedness contained in off-balance-sheet special-purpose vehicles," he wrote. Ackman explained that the position had the potential to generate a return of approximately five times the fund's total assets if it was successful.

Though little known outside of Wall Street circles in 2002, MBIA ranked as one of the top five financial institutions in the country, as measured by outstanding credit exposure, along with Citigroup, Bank of America, and government-sponsored mortgage lenders Fannie Mae and Freddie Mac. Using its triple-A credit rating, MBIA had turned nearly half a trillion dollars of securities into investments that rating companies apparently considered as safe as U.S. Treasuries. Bonds issued by a water and sewer authority in Mississippi, debt backed by loans on used cars to people with a history of not paying their bills, and complex pools of derivatives held by a shell company in the Cayman Islands all became top-rated securities under the Midas touch of an MBIA guarantee.

Moody's Investors Service, Standard & Poor's, and Fitch Ratings—the credit-rating oligopoly—all assigned MBIA's bond-insurance unit a triple-A rating. Using computer models and historical default data, analysts at the rating companies had determined that MBIA could weather another Great Depression and still meet all of its claims.

Ackman was not convinced.

MBIA held just $1 of capital for every $140 of debt it guaranteed. Although the company claimed it underwrote risk to a so-called "zero-loss" standard, its past performance hadn't been free from error. The high leverage meant MBIA had virtually no margin of safety. The company's underwriting, transparency, accounting, and track record all had to be beyond reproach. Ackman, a money manager known for his intensive research, thought he saw problems with every one of these issues.

Earlier that day, Ackman had met for lunch with Michael Ovitz, the founder of Hollywood's Creative Artists Agency and a longtime investor in Ackman's fund. As they worked their way through six different versions of toro, the Japanese fatty tuna delicacy, Ackman asked Ovitz's advice about the upcoming meeting with Brown.

"It sounds like a very Japanese meeting," said Ovitz. In other words, he said, "Just shut up and listen."

———

ACKMAN'S TAXI STOPPED on Third Avenue outside the building where MBIA's attorneys, Debevoise & Plimpton, have their offices. Together with Gotham's general counsel, David Klafter, and one of the firm's analysts, Greg Lyss, Ackman headed for the security desk in the lobby. The group was sent upstairs, where Ackman told the receptionist they were there for the meeting with Jay Brown. She pointed Ackman toward a closed conference room door just behind the reception desk. Opening it, he found Brown seated at a conference table with a dozen other men. The conversation in the room came to an abrupt halt. "Hi," he said. "I'm Bill Ackman. I'm here to . . ."

"Wrong meeting," one of the men said as he jumped up to close the door. Ackman returned to the reception area, convinced he'd just interrupted a tired and frazzled-looking Brown in a meeting with his crisis-management team. The Gotham group was shown to another conference room and told to wait.

———•———

ACKMAN COFOUNDED Gotham Partners in 1993 with David Berkowitz, increasing the hedge fund's assets from $3 million to more than $350 million by 2001. The firm was small, with just nine employees. Ackman and the fund's analysts sought out companies with securities that were mispriced or misunderstood by the market. In MBIA's case, the market believed in the permanence of the company's triple-A rating. If it didn't, then the bond insurer's ability to write new business would have disappeared overnight.

Ackman had placed his bet against MBIA principally in the credit-default-swap market. Credit-default swaps, or CDS contracts, are derivatives that allow parties to buy and sell protection against a default on a security. The contracts are essentially life insurance policies on companies. The protection buyer—in Wall Street parlance—makes regular payments over the life of the contract to the protection seller, who promises to make a lump sum payment to the insurance buyer if a security defaults. The cost of the insurance rises and falls minute by minute based on the market's perception of the company's credit quality. Default protection on a company with a triple-A rating, which MBIA had in 2002, could be purchased cheaply because the risk of default was perceived to be de minimus.

Blythe Masters, a 26-year-old Trinity College graduate working at JPMorgan in 1995, is often credited with having invented CDS contracts. The contracts were created as a way for commercial banks to reduce their exposure to corporate borrowers. By purchasing protection against a default, the bank took on a position that would offset losses if a borrower defaulted.

The market for CDS contracts, which didn't exist before the mid-1990s, totaled $2.2 trillion by the end of 2002. Outstanding contracts hit $62 trillion by the end of 2007. Ackman was not seeking protection against MBIA filing for bankruptcy; he was betting that the chance of the company defaulting on its bonds was more likely than the market believed. In addition to shorting tens of millions of dollars of MBIA stock, Ackman bought protection against a default on $2 billion worth of MBIA debt. He had also set up two additional funds, Gotham Credit Partners I and IA, to hold CDS contracts on MBIA. Investors in these funds could earn nearly 40 times their money, or a 4,000 percent return, if MBIA filed for bankruptcy. Of course, investors would lose their entire investment if perceptions about MBIA's triple-A rating remained unchanged and unchallenged.

Ackman's bet was spectacularly contrarian. He was wagering on the collapse of a company that the rating companies had awarded their highest triple-A rating and that everyone else was counting on.

Indeed, MBIA's reason for being was to take the worries out of the debt market. MBIA's president, Gary Dunton, summed it up in the company's 2001 annual report: "In our minds, our franchise is the ultimate money-back guarantee, the 'Good Housekeeping Seal of Approval.'"

The company was started in the early 1970s by a young man named Jack Butler, who had worked on Wall Street for Franklin National Bank, picking municipal bonds for the bank's portfolio. One winter afternoon in 1967, as Butler was driving back from a ski weekend in Vermont with Jim Lopp, an investment banker, the pair hit on an idea: If you took the time to understand how the municipal bond market really worked, you could find plenty of municipal bonds on which the risk of default was practically zero. Butler bought such bonds all the time. Selling insurance on bonds that would never default sounded like a good business.

Butler and Lopp had worked together on a deal in Omaha, Nebraska, several years earlier that became their blueprint. The mayor of Omaha wanted to raise millions of dollars to build a sewage-incineration plant. The process was experimental, however, and taxpayers didn't want to foot the bill if the project didn't work. The sewage-incineration plan was designed to blast the sewage into a solid substance, which could then provide fuel to blast the next batch of sewage into more fuel. To finance the plan, the mayor, Lopp, and Butler came to an agreement. Lopp would underwrite the bonds, Butler would buy them, and the mayor would see to it that the project was bailed out if something went wrong.

In fact, the plant didn't work. As Butler remembers it, the headline in the local Omaha newspaper read "Ten Million Dollar Toilet Doesn't Flush." But the mayor made good on his promise, and the taxpayers bailed out the bondholders.

The municipal bond market was less risky than it appeared, Butler realized. The credit ratings on many municipal bonds didn't take into account the understanding between investors and public officials, such as Omaha's mayor, that bonds used to fund public projects wouldn't default.

Then came the spark of inspiration. If a smart investor could find bonds that were safer than they appeared, an even more astute businessperson could create a business guaranteeing these bonds. The bond-insurance business was simple: In exchange for receiving an upfront insurance premium, the bond insurer agreed to cover all interest and principal payments over the life of the bond if the issuer defaulted. As long as the bond insurer maintained its triple-A rating, the bonds remained triple-A. The beauty of bond insurance, Butler saw, was that the bond insurer didn't need capital to buy the bonds. The bond investor put up the capital. The insurer would collect the insurance premium up front in exchange for guaranteeing the bonds and would invest the premiums over the long term.

That's not to say bond insurance required no capital. To enter the business, Butler had to prove to regulators that the company had the wherewithal to make good on its guarantees. That meant setting aside some fraction of the amount of each bond it guaranteed. But how much? To determine the amount, Butler hired George Hempel, an economist who had studied municipal bond defaults during the Great Depression. With Hempel's help, Butler figured out how much capital a municipal bond–insurance company would have needed to weather the Depression. Although a large number of municipalities missed bond payments at the height of the Depression, most paid bondholders back, with interest, after just a few years. That meant a bond insurer didn't really need to pay claims so much as advance money for brief periods during times of extreme financial distress.

Still, it was a business that required extreme caution. "It has to be underwritten to a no-loss standard, otherwise the leverage is deadly," says Butler.

Butler and Lopp toyed with other business ideas, including manufacturing hollow golf balls. In the end, they went with municipal bond insurance. Bulter founded MBIA. Lopp, who died at age 51 of a heart attack on the tennis court of his vacation home in the south of France, started up Financial Security Assurance, another bond insurer.

————

FIFTEEN MINUTES AFTER Ackman and the others from Gotham were shown to the conference room, Brown appeared with MBIA's general counsel, Ram Wertheim, whose first question to the Gotham group was whether it planned to record the meeting. Ackman told him no, then asked Wertheim whether he and Brown planned on making a recording. They did not, Wertheim said.

Brown wasted no time getting to the point. He had been in the insurance industry for years, and no one had ever questioned his reputation, Ackman remembers Brown saying, "No one has ever gone to my regulators without my permission."

Ackman asked Brown whether he disputed any of the assertions Ackman had made about MBIA. Brown was aware of the issues in Ackman's report from questions he had received from a Wall Street equity analyst with whom Ackman had shared his findings.

"This isn't about the facts; it's about process," Ackman recalls Brown saying. "You're a young guy, early in your career. You should think long and hard before issuing the report. We are the largest guarantor of New York state and New York City bonds. In fact, we're the largest guarantor of municipal debt in the country. Let's put it this way: We have friends in high places."

In a follow-up letter to Ackman after the meeting, Wertheim reminded Gotham what was at stake: "MBIA is a regulated insurance company that operates in a regulated environment and acts in a fiduciary capacity for the benefit of our many constituencies—principally our policyholders, our customers, including the numerous states and municipalities that rely on bond insurance, and our stockholders but also our employees, our community, and the other people who rely on the vitality of the markets that we support. . . . MBIA's credibility and reputation in the market, and its triple-A ratings, are critical to our continued ability to service these constituencies."

In the meeting, Brown compared Gotham to Enron, which had been accused of manipulating California's electricity market. Was Gotham seeking to manipulate perceptions about a regulated insurance company by taking positions in the unregulated CDS market? Brown also asked Ackman how long Gotham planned to hold its CDS position on MBIA.

Ackman explained that for the hedge fund to make money on its CDS position, it was going to have to be correct in its criticism of MBIA. Ackman told Brown that the CDS market was not liquid enough for Gotham to easily trade in and out of such a huge position.

Wertheim asked to see a copy of Gotham's report before it was published so MBIA could check Gotham's facts. Ackman countered that it was considered inappropriate for analysts to give advance copies of research reports to companies but again offered to discuss any findings at the meeting.

The meeting ended abruptly. As the men filed out of the room, Ackman reached out to shake Brown's hand. "I don't think so," Brown said, refusing to extend his hand.

When Ackman, Klafter, and Lyss stepped back out onto Third Avenue, Ackman's first call was to Aaron Marcu, a lawyer with Covington & Burling, who had been advising Gotham on its research. "We left the meeting thinking we were going to be sued," Ackman told me years later.

Ackman's second call was to Paul Hilal, an investor in one of the Gotham Credit Partners funds and Ackman's friend since the two were undergraduate roommates at Harvard in the late 1980s. Ackman related the high points of the brief meeting: Brown's refusal to discuss Gotham's report, the apparent paranoia about whether Gotham was recording the conversation, the warning, the refusal to shake hands. Years later, Brown told the *Wall Street Journal* that he remembered refusing to shake Ackman's hand, though he recalled saying nothing that should have been interpreted as a threat.

Hilal had been hearing about MBIA for months. He and his girlfriend had spent a week with Ackman and his wife, Karen, at a beach house the Ackmans rented in Watch Hill, Rhode Island, during the summer of 2002. "Bill did what he always does on vacation," Hilal says. He read financial statements. That week his reading consisted of years of MBIA quarterly filings. "Every once in a while, you'd hear Bill exclaim, 'Oh, my God, this is such bullshit,'" Hilal recalls. "What he was reading about was another layer of hidden leverage or messed up accounting at MBIA. The tone was a combination of surprise but also glee: 'I can't believe it's this good.'"

Chapter **2** *Two*

The Short Seller

A closed mouth gathers no foot.

—BILL ACKMAN'S HIGH SCHOOL YEARBOOK EPITHET, 1984

B ILL ACKMAN'S INTEREST in MBIA started with an interest in triple-A ratings. Earlier in 2002, he'd made a substantial sum by shorting the stock and purchasing credit-default swaps on a company called the Federal Agricultural Mortgage Corporation, better known as Farmer Mac. The company was chartered by the U.S. government to create a secondary market for farm loans, and this government connection caused investors to view Farmer Mac as a triple-A-rated company. In fact, the company never sought to obtain a credit rating because the market perceived it to be triple-A and its bonds traded like other top-rated agency bonds at very tight spreads to Treasuries.

Ackman had originally gotten the idea of looking into Farmer Mac from Whitney Tilson, who heads up the hedge fund T2 Partners and who had been friends with Ackman since they were undergraduates at Harvard in the 1980s. Tilson suggested Ackman consider buying shares in the company. When Ackman reviewed the company's financial statements and later met with the company's chief executive officer

(CEO), he decided to short it instead. Before Ackman's involvement, Farmer Mac was rarely mentioned outside of trade publications such as *Progressive Farmer* and *Pork Magazine.* Ackman's research landed the company on the front page of the *New York Times* business section after he spoke with reporter Alison Leigh Cowan about his findings. Ackman churned out a series of reports on the company provocatively titled "Buying the Farm," Parts I, II, and III. He didn't mince words: "Gotham believes that the company is in precarious financial condition and could face severe financial stress."

For months, Ackman was a thorn in Farmer Mac's side. During one of the company's investor conference calls, Farmer Mac executives explained that their reason for not obtaining a credit rating was that the company did not want to pay the cost. In response, Ackman offered to pay for Farmer Mac's rating. His offer was rebuffed.

After Ackman issued his first report on the company, Farmer Mac's shares plummeted and premiums on its credit-default-swap (CDS) contracts jumped. Then the Senate Agricultural Committee asked the U.S. Government Accountability Office to look into the issues raised in the reports. The company responded by accusing Ackman and the *Times* of orchestrating a negative campaign to drive down its shares and asking the Securities and Exchange Commission (SEC) to investigate the *Times* reporter, Alison Leigh Cowan.

In July 2003, after MBIA prompted the New York attorney general's office to investigate Gotham Partners, Tilson was called to testify about Ackman's research efforts and, in particular, about his use of the press to spread his message. "Bill spent a number of hours walking [the *New York Times* reporter] through Farmer Mac's filings, the 10-K and 10-Q documents going back many years," Tilson said about one marathon meeting with Cowan, which he also attended. Ackman spent hours showing the reporter "problems, things that he believed the company was trying to hide." Investigators asked Tilson how long the meeting lasted. "Eight, maybe twelve hours," he replied.

Ackman's fund netted about $80 million on its Farmer Mac position. Shortly after his Farmer Mac win in the spring of 2002, Ackman asked Michael Neumann, a salesman on Lehman Brothers' credit desk who had sold him the contracts on Farmer Mac, if he could think of another triple-A-rated company that might not merit its lofty rating. Neumann told Ackman he was skeptical of the bond insurers. The largest bond insurer was MBIA Inc.

Ackman called MBIA and requested the previous five years of annual reports. Later, when he began to read Jay Brown's letter to shareholders in MBIA's 2001 annual report, it didn't take long for him to spot the first red flag. In the letter, Brown addressed the issue of so-called special-purpose vehicles (SPVs), which are created by companies to finance assets off of their balance sheets. The SPV purchases assets such as mortgages from a sponsor or parent company and sells debt to finance the purchase. The SPV is considered legally separate from the company that created it and is considered "bankruptcy remote," meaning that if the parent company filed for bankruptcy, the SPV would be unlikely to be dragged into the parent company's bankruptcy. Investors began to raise questions about the use of SPVs after Enron Corporation's off-balance-sheet debt contributed to its collapse because the risk had not actually been transferred.

"During the past several months, there has been a fair amount of public debate on issues such as balance-sheet transparency, special-purpose vehicles, risk management, accounting conflicts, and quality of earnings," Brown wrote in MBIA's annual report. "As you might expect, we have spent some time staring in the mirror." The result of this reflection, Brown told shareholders, was that investors would find expanded disclosure on the company's approximately $8 billion of special-purpose vehicles in that year's 10-K.

Ackman searched MBIA's public filings and found no previous mention of the SPVs to which Brown had alluded. The apparent deception caused Ackman to look deeper. He began a research process that involved reading thousands of pages of SEC filings, conference-call transcripts, and rating-company and analysts' reports.

What Ackman really wanted was a face-to-face meeting with MBIA executives. In August 2002, Ackman got the chance. Robert Gendelman, a friend and at that time an investment adviser at Neuberger Berman, one of the largest holders of MBIA stock, agreed to arrange a meeting.

Several days before his visit to MBIA, Ackman e-mailed a senior insurance executive who had once worked with Brown, seeking his opinion on the executive. "He is smart and top notch," the acquaintance wrote back. And that's important because "business is dangerous, like picking up dimes in front of a steamroller."

Ackman and Gendelman made the short trip by car to MBIA's headquarters an hour north of Manhattan in the leafy Westchester suburb of Armonk. Gendelman introduced Ackman to MBIA executives as a money manager who had done a lot of research on the company.

MBIA welcomed him. The question of whether Ackman had a long or short position on MBIA never came up.

The meetings, which began around 10 in the morning and ran well into the evening, started in Brown's office. Acquaintances describe Brown as a very private person. He is also a self-made man, who sometimes told colleagues about the years he spent driving a truck before he completed college. A graduate of Northern Illinois University who had majored in statistics, Brown rose through the ranks of Fireman's Fund Insurance, starting with the company as an actuarial trainee when he was 25, eventually becoming its CEO.

Brown later advised Xerox Corporation on the sale of its insurance unit, including Crum and Forster, a 150-year-old insurer based in Morristown, New Jersey, which had huge exposure to asbestos claims. Asbestos was the miracle building material of the 1960s and 1970s. In the 1980s, however, doctors discovered that the mineral, named after the Greek word meaning "inextinguishable," lodged in the lungs of workers, remaining there for years and causing cancer and other fatal respiratory diseases. By the late 1990s, the insurance industry was bracing for asbestos-related workers' compensation claims of more than $250 billion.

Brown's ability to dispose of this toxic exposure at a profit to Xerox earned him a reputation as a dealmaker. Brown, who had served on MBIA's board since the mid-1980s, joined MBIA as its CEO in 1999 after the company's longtime president and CEO, David Elliott, suddenly stepped down. After assuming the top spot, Brown purchased more than $7 million of MBIA's shares using his own money. "He is a tough, tough man who is deceptively gentle in his demeanor," James Lebenthal, a longtime MBIA board member, said of Brown.

In his meeting with Brown at the company's headquarters that August, Ackman took notes, jotting down Brown's description of MBIA's two core businesses. "Structured finance is analyzable, understandable," Ackman noted as Brown explained the business of insuring asset-backed securities, bonds backed by everything from credit-card bills to mortgages and even other bonds.

Bankers often use the analogy of a waterfall to explain how asset-backed-securities holders are paid. Each month, payments on mortgages or credit cards flow into a trust that has issued various securities to fund the purchase of the loans. The cash is used to pay the highest-rated asset-backed-securities holders first before the overflow spills down to the next highest-rated level of securities holders and so on. Defaults on the underlying loans reduce the amount of cash available to pay securities holders. As a result, the lower down in the waterfall, the riskier the securities and the higher the yield the trust must pay to get investors to buy these junior, or subordinate, securities.

Brown explained that insuring public finance securities required a completely different approach. "It's illogical and not analytical. It's a moral commitment." The federal government wouldn't let a state go broke, Brown explained. Debt issuers below the state level, such as counties, cities, and towns, always have "someone above who can help out," Ackman's notes read. "When you went that last step, public finance resolves around a moral obligation," Brown told him.

Ackman met later that day with MBIA's chief financial officer, Neil Budnick, and the two discussed the company's so-called "zero-loss" underwriting policy. The former Moody's Investors Service analyst told Ackman that it was crucial that MBIA back only those bonds on which it expected to take no losses. MBIA risked losing its triple-A credit rating on losses of as little as $900 million, Budnick said. In other words, if MBIA was required to make payments on just 0.2 percent of the nearly half a trillion dollars of bonds it had insured, it risked losing its triple-A rating.

By the time Ackman met with Mark Gold, who oversaw MBIA's structured finance business, it was nearly 7 p.m. The fund manager from Neuberger Berman was long gone, and the building was nearly deserted on that summer evening. Ackman talked with Gold about the company's business of guaranteeing collateralized-debt obligations (CDOs), a business that Budnick described as "booming."

CDOs were Wall Street's favorite new asset class. The securities are built out of pools of securities rather than pools of loans. Otherwise, CDOs work on the same waterfall principle as simpler asset-backed bonds. MBIA was backing lots of CDOs at what it called "super-senior levels," the most senior or highest levels of a CDO securitization. These super-senior exposures were considered better than triple-A because they had a greater cushion to absorb losses than what the rating companies believed was necessary to achieve triple-A performance.

Gold gave Ackman a history of the CDO business, including a description of a groundbreaking transaction called "BISTRO." The CDO was created by JPMorgan as a way to lay off the credit risk of a pool of loans it held on its balance sheet.

In his notes, Ackman took down the nickname Gold told him people in the industry gave to BISTRO: "Bank for International Settlements Total Rip

Off." The Bank for International Settlements is an organization headquartered in Basel, Switzerland, that was created to promote global financial stability. One of its ongoing projects has been to create bank capital guidelines. BISTRO gamed those guidelines by converting long-term lending risk into a series of credit-default contracts that required less capital.

These CDS contracts had become the preferred way for banks to hedge their exposure to CDOs. Most of the CDOs MBIA guaranteed were insured through CDS contracts. In doing his research, Ackman found that insurance companies were prohibited from dealing in derivatives such as credit-default swaps. He asked Gold about this restriction during their meeting.

"Financial guarantors can't write swaps," Gold agreed. That's why MBIA had set up LaCrosse Financial Products, which Gold called "an orphaned subsidiary." LaCrosse, a shell company with nominal assets that was owned by an apparently unaffiliated charity, sold credit-default swaps, and MBIA guaranteed LaCrosse's obligations. The orphaned subsidiary allowed MBIA to indirectly participate in the CDS market apparently without breaking the law. Ackman had asked Neil Budnick about LaCrosse, which was disclosed in a footnote in MBIA's annual report, during their meeting earlier in the day, and he was surprised when the chief financial officer said he'd never heard of LaCrosse. Ackman found this particularly striking when Gold said later in the day that the company had seen "huge growth" and "remarkable volume" in its super-senior CDO business through LaCrosse.

Gold told Ackman that the performance of the CDO guarantees had been disappointing. MBIA wasn't paying claims on its super-senior guarantees, but CDOs weren't proving as stable as the financial models had predicted. Because the contracts were in derivative form, accounting rules required that the guarantees be marked to market, or valued each quarter based on the current market price. Because the CDOs were considered even safer than the highest-rated securities, the premiums MBIA received to insure the securities were tiny. That made the volatility of super-senior CDOs even more of a concern, Gold explained.

Ackman ended his visit to MBIA with his suspicions confirmed. In the car on the way back to the city, he called his business partner, David Berkowitz. The pair had started Gotham together nearly 10 years earlier after graduating from Harvard Business School. "It's even worse than I thought," Ackman told him.

AFTER THE MEETING AT MBIA, Ackman wanted to increase his wager on MBIA. He called Lehman Brothers in August 2002, looking to buy huge amounts of CDSs on MBIA, Michael Neumann, the CDS salesman at Lehman, later told the New York attorney general's office when it investigated Gotham's activities in 2003. "We're very interested in this trade," Ackman told him. "We're really interested in buying big size." But Neumann struggled to find enough parties willing to sell protection on MBIA to meet Ackman's demand.

"In our market, $5 [million] to $10 million is a typical trade, and he was expressing interest in multiple hundreds of millions," Neumann told the attorneys. "It wasn't unheard of, but it was unusual. It was our first request for MBIA in that size."

As Ackman continued to buy, the price rose. At the beginning of 2002, it cost around $35,000 per annum to buy protection on $10 million of MBIA debt. By late summer, the price topped $200,000 a year.

Then, in August, Neumann tapped into a substantial seller. The mystery seller allowed Gotham to increase its position to hundreds of millions of dollars of contracts. This newfound supply of credit-default protection on MBIA also caused the price of buying CDSs on MBIA to fall to around $100,000 per annum and sent a reassuring message to the market about MBIA's financial health. Ackman suspected that the counterparty on the other side of many of his trades was MBIA. The company later confirmed that it sold CDS contracts on itself.

"Frankly, it's a very crazy thing to do," Ackman told attorneys at the Securities and Exchange Commission after the SEC launched an investigation of Gotham several months later.

After all, MBIA was selling protection against its own bankruptcy filing. Who would buy an insurance policy that by definition required the policyholder to collect from a bankrupt company? Wall Street brokers would have agreed to arrange such a transaction only if MBIA put up collateral to make sure that it could pay out in the event of a default.

The real reason MBIA was selling protection on itself, Ackman suggested to regulators, was to drive down the price of its CDS contracts and create an impression of stability. Conversely, the SEC would question whether Gotham was trying to undermine confidence in the company by bidding up the contracts.

"Every once in a while, spreads would go out, and we would step out of the market because we didn't want to pay these high prices," Ackman explained to the SEC. "Those are the times we believe they would step in to sell it, so it would come back down, and then we would start nibbling again."

———

AMONG THE FIRST PEOPLE Ackman talked to after his meeting with MBIA executives in August was Henny Sender, a reporter at the *Wall Street Journal*. Ackman spent several months talking to Sender about MBIA's expansion beyond municipal finance, its off-balance-sheet debt, and the guarantees on CDOs it was writing by the billions. But when Sender's article appeared in early November 2002, it was as much about Ackman as it was about MBIA.

The market for credit-default swaps could be extremely thin, sources told the *Journal*, and an investor taking even a small position in a company could easily push the premiums one way or the other. The *Journal* estimated that Ackman's $1 billion position against MBIA might have cost as little as $15 million.

"This is a company built on faith," Ackman told the *Journal*. "[MBIA] depends on the markets believing that it has the resources to back all its claims." MBIA's president, Gary Dunton, along with analysts from Fitch Ratings and Standard & Poor's, said the credit-default-swap market— and, by extension, Gotham—had it wrong. The company was as secure as it had ever been. The shares fell in response to the article but rebounded the next day.

Disappointed in the *Wall Street Journal* article, Ackman began to write a research report that would lay out all of his concerns about MBIA. In preparing the report, Ackman approached the New York State Insurance Department (NYSID). His first tip that MBIA's regulators might have been in over their heads came when he called to set up a meeting with the official responsible for overseeing the financial-guarantee companies. "Auto," said the person answering the phone. MBIA, with credit-market exposure nearly the size of Citigroup, was overseen out of the same division that regulates insurers that cover fender benders and stolen cars.

Ackman and David Klafter, Gotham's general counsel, met with officials at the insurance department on November 6, 2002. They talked to the group about MBIA's expansion into the CDS business despite a New York state prohibition against insurers engaging in derivative transactions. Officials asked several times during the meeting, "Are you sure they're using insurance company capital to guarantee credit derivatives?" He also told the officials that he didn't believe the company was marking its derivative contracts to market, another violation of state insurance law.

When Ackman returned to the office that afternoon, he received a call from the NYSID asking him to come back the next day to give his presentation to a wider group of regulators. "We believe that our analysis was taken seriously and is being considered at the highest levels of the insurance department," Ackman wrote in a November 10 e-mail to his hedge fund investors.

Ackman told them that he'd obtained an estimate of where the CDOs MBIA had guaranteed were trading. "Late last week, we received bid, offer, and mid-market prices from Deutsche Bank on MBIA's CDO and synthetic CDO portfolio balances, which were disclosed in detail for the first time," Ackman wrote. "The mid-market prices indicate that MBIA has a mark-to-market loss of $5.4 billion in its portfolio as of August 31, 2002," Ackman wrote. "The company, however, has shown only an extremely modest loss on this portfolio in its filings."

Ackman was also determined to get Morgan Stanley analyst Alice Schroeder on his side. Voted the top insurance analyst two years running by *Institutional Investor* magazine, Schroeder, author of *The Snowball: Warren Buffett and the Business of Life* (Bantam, 2008), was known as Buffett's favorite analyst. Buffett once described her as the only Wall Street analyst whose work he bothered to read. The dinner she hosted at Berkshire Hathaway's annual meetings was *the* ticket of the year for fans of Buffett, who made an appearance to speak to Schroeder's guests.

"While 'turning' a bullish analyst is going to be difficult, we can be pretty convincing and it's therefore worth the energy," Ackman wrote in the November 10 e-mail message to investors in Gotham Credit Partners. He left Schroeder a voice-mail message asking for a meeting to discuss his views on MBIA. But her return voice message was not encouraging: "I have no interest in being part of a market-manipulation scheme."

Undaunted, Ackman called Byron Wien, then Morgan Stanley's well-known stock market strategist, asking Wien to vouch for Ackman's credibility to Schroeder. Schroeder says her willingness to meet with Ackman was not the result of a call from Wien but followed from the advice of a Morgan Stanley lawyer. She recalls Ackman mentioning that New York Attorney General Eliot Spitzer, who had recently announced a settlement with the major investment banks over conflicted Wall Street research, would "take an interest in an analyst who willfully overlooked important information about a company" when assigning a rating to the stock. "We were ignoring him at our peril" was the idea that Ackman wanted to convey, Schroeder says.

Morgan Stanley's lawyer advised Schroeder to meet with Ackman, to have others present, and to document the meeting. It was important that the analysts not appear to be downgrading a stock because they were pressured to do so, Schroeder says. "We will meet with you," Schroeder answered Ackman in an e-mail. She added, "Our main concern is not MBIA but rather the implications of what you're saying for the credit markets as whole."

The meeting was held on November 12 at Morgan Stanley's office, with Schroeder, Vinay Saqi, the lead analyst on MBIA, and members of Morgan Stanley's structured finance team attending. Ackman brought along Gotham analyst Greg Lyss and general counsel David Klafter.

"Bill came in bearing an armload of stuff, talking a hundred miles an hour," Schroeder says. "There was the obvious part, that [MBIA was] overleveraged, and we agreed with that." But there was a list of other issues, "a many-headed hydra" of other issues, not all of which Morgan Stanley analysts agreed were problems, Schroeder says.

Lyss, who later would be called in to give testimony in the New York attorney general's investigation of Gotham, was asked for his impressions of the meeting during his testimony. "I remember the Morgan Stanley analysts agreeing that this is a bad business model, the financial guarantee business," Lyss said.

Regulators also asked Klafter what the investment bank analysts had to say after hearing Ackman's presentation. "Something along the lines of 'You just have to have confidence in them because if you don't have confidence in them then the whole business doesn't work; the model doesn't work,'" Klafter recalled.

Ackman updated his investors after hearing back from Schroeder, who had called Jay Brown to check out Ackman's insights. Schroeder called "to tell me that she had spoken to MBIA, had verified a number of our assertions, and had lost confidence in management after hearing the company's answers to her questions," Ackman wrote in an e-mail dated November 14, 2002. "She also believes that the entire guarantee industry is at risk of failure because she believes the company's practices are widespread."

Schroeder can't recall telling Ackman that she had lost confidence in management. "It sounds self-serving," she says. The business of bond insurance was another matter, she says. "It was a kind of Mad Hatter world. The 'rating agencies' had the power to decide whether this business model was viable or not. It didn't matter if they were 50 times or 2,000 times leveraged."

A few days later, on November 14, 2002, Morgan Stanley released a report warning MBIA investors about Ackman. "There is potential for additional headline risk in the near-term, given one investor's bearish play on the company's stock and its credit," wrote Saqi and Schroeder, citing the *Wall Street Journal* article on Gotham. It's possible Gotham may be preparing a research report on MBIA, which, for the near term, casts "a cloud over MBIA's stock price as well as other stocks in the space."

Ackman remained upbeat. He was convinced Schroeder would issue a negative report on MBIA. "I got the sense from Alice that she does not want to 'scoop' us," Ackman wrote to investors after the Morgan Stanley report was released. "That said, I think she wants to be a close second."

———•———

ACKMAN'S UNWILLINGNESS TO mince words was evident long before he came to Wall Street. "He's not a critical guy, but he has a point of view," says Michael Grossman, a friend of Ackman's from high school. The two grew up in the prosperous suburb of Chappaqua, New York, with the children of executives from IBM and Wall Street. "There was a lot of type A in the mix. It was an affluent, competitive place," Grossman recalls.

Grossman describes Ackman as a "force of nature" at the Horace Greeley High School, where he graduated fourth in his class in 1984. Tall, with prematurely gray hair, Ackman stood out. "When Bill came into a room, you knew he was there." That was even before one got wind of his personality. "Bold. Sharp. Brash. Blunt," Grossman says. "Some people loved him, some found him abrasive." Grossman gave Ackman the epithet that appeared in his high school yearbook: "A closed mouth gathers no foot."

The sentiment sprung partly from Grossman's frustration with Ackman as a partner on the tennis team. "If there were a film of us playing tennis, it would show him talking and me ignoring him," says Grossman. "He'd say to me, 'You just missed a forehand volley into the net.' He'd reprimand himself, too, if he missed a shot. He would talk to me literally after every point. He paid compliments, too, even to himself."

Ackman doesn't remember being an annoying tennis partner, though he recalls that the pair made it to the New York state quarterfinals.

Years later, watching Ackman play out his very public and vocal battle with MBIA, Grossman recognized the teenager who refused to keep his opinions to himself. "He says what he thinks. He has always said what he thinks. There's not a lot of nuance. Either it's true or it's not," Grossman says. "I think actually he's mellowed."

After high school, Ackman followed in his sister Jeanne's footsteps, entering the freshman class at Harvard in 1984. After graduation, Ackman worked for two years in his family's commercial-mortgage business, then called Ackman Brothers & Singer, before returning to Harvard to attend business school.

Harvard did nothing to soften Ackman's sharp edge. As the co-captain of the Harvard Business School's rowing team in the early 1990s, Ackman defended the team's controversial decision to row with dollar signs painted on their oars and on the back of their shirts. "I think it's a snobbish, superficial symbol that represents wealth and greed and is a very narrow interpretation of what business represents," Eve Stacey, the Harvard women's team captain, said of the dollar signs in an interview with the *Wall Street Journal*.

"Let's face up to what Harvard Business School represents," Ackman argued in a commentary in the *Harbus News*, the student newspaper, after spectators booed the Harvard Business School team at the Head of the Charles races. "We spend 90 percent of our studies at HBS pursuing the maximization of the dollar."

At Harvard, Ackman met David Berkowitz, an MIT-educated engineer. Ackman told Berkowitz that he found his comments in class insightful and convinced his classmate to work with him in picking stocks. He urged Berkowitz to read *Margin of Safety: Risk Averse Value Investing Strategies for the Thoughtful Investor* by Seth Klarman, who graduated from Harvard Business School a decade before Ackman and went on to run his own highly successful hedge fund called the Baupost Group.

"Being a value investor usually means standing apart from the crowd, challenging conventional wisdom, and opposing the prevailing investment winds," Klarman wrote. "It can be a lonely undertaking."

Despite having no professional money-management experience, the pair began scouting for investors even before graduation. It took a healthy amount of gumption for Ackman, then 26 years old, and Berkowitz, 32, to ask millionaires and billionaires to trust them with a piece of their fortunes.

The first potential investor they tried was Marty Peretz, the editor-in-chief of the *New Republic* magazine, who had been Ackman's thesis adviser when he was an undergraduate at Harvard. Ackman and Berkowitz drove from Boston to Peretz's summer house on Cape Cod to pitch him the idea, and Peretz became their first investor with a $250,000 commitment. Ackman and Berkowitz got $500,000 from the father of a Harvard Business School classmate. Ackman's future mother-in-law, Marilyn Herskovitz, who sold high-end real estate in Manhattan, recommended the pair to a client who ended up investing $1 million. "One investor," Ackman says, "sold meat balls to Pizza Hut."

Ackman's father, Larry, who urged his son to get experience before starting a fund, initially refused to invest. Just before they launched the fund, Ackman's father relented and wrote a check.

They set up shop in a windowless office in the Helmsley Building, which they leased from brokerage firm Furman Selz, and Ackman wasted no time getting to know influential investors. When Bernard Selz, the financier and philanthropist, got into the elevator one day with Ackman and Berkowitz, Ackman immediately introduced himself. "You should call me sometime," Selz said politely before stepping off the elevator. As soon as Ackman got back to his office, he was on the phone with Selz's secretary setting up an appointment.

The two fund managers drew the spotlight in the mid-1990s when they participated in the bidding for the public company that owned the mortgage on New York's landmark Rockefeller Center. It was a heady time for Ackman, then just 28 years old. There was the morning Ackman and Jerry Speyer, a founding partner of real estate giant Tishman Speyer, emerged from an all-night strategy session in a diner to grab a predawn copy of the *New York Times* and read that their supposed partner in the deal, Mitsubishi Estate, had decided to default on the Rockefeller Center mortgage.

And there was the time Donald Trump called. "Goldman Sachs is trying to steal Rockefeller Center, Bill. We've got to do something about it," announced Trump, who had never spoken with Ackman before. When Trump suggested a meeting at Ackman's office, the young man quickly offered to make the trip to Trump Tower. "I didn't want him to see that we worked out of shared office space," Ackman says.

In July 1996, a group led by Goldman Sachs and David Rockefeller, the philanthropist and grandson of the founder of Standard Oil, took control of the complex for $1.2 billion in cash and assumed debt. Gotham didn't walk away with Rockefeller Center nor did it team up with Trump, but the fund made a fortune for its investors, selling its stake to Goldman at a large profit. The fund was up 50 percent that year. Confirming that he had arrived at an early age, *Crain's New York Business* included Ackman on its "Forty Under 40" list in 1999 for his work on Rockefeller Center.

Ackman also caught the attention of executives at Leucadia National Corporation, a publicly traded investment holding company whose secretive owners, Joseph Steinberg and Ian Cumming, regularly make *Forbes's* list of the wealthiest Americans. Leucadia would co-invest with Ackman in multiple deals over the years.

Ackman had a way of leaving an impression. Laurel Touby, the founder of mediabistro.com, a networking site for journalists, met Ackman in 2000 when she was seeking to raise money for her company. Ackman, who eventually invested $750,000, could be charming but also manically critical. "He had a way of bludgeoning with his intelligence," Touby remembers. During one Media Bistro board meeting, Ackman's barrage of questions about Touby's business plan left Touby in tears. "That many questions just makes you feel inadequate," she says.

Yet Touby also remembers Ackman out of the blue asking her during a meeting if she was single. When she told him she was, Ackman remarked that not only was he going to invest in her company but he would help her find a husband. "He just personalizes things in a way you don't expect," Touby says.

By the start of 2002, Ackman had experienced a long run of good fortune: He was happily married to the former Karen Herskovitz, a landscape architect he'd met when they were both graduate students at Harvard; he had two young daughters, a close circle of family and friends, his own firm, and an apartment in the Majestic Building, overlooking Central Park.

But these were unsettling times. Trust in corporate America and in Wall Street were at all-time lows. Stocks had been dropping since the spring, with the Dow Jones Industrial Average sinking back below levels not seen since the wake of the September 11 terrorist attacks. WorldCom had just settled an SEC investigation into a $9 billion restatement. Federal regulators had accused Enron Corporation of using bogus orders to run up the cost of power in California before the company imploded in an accounting scandal. The head of the Securities and Exchange Commission, Harvey Pitt, had resigned after criticism that he was subverting enforcement efforts. And New York Attorney General Eliot Spitzer had turned *Institutional Investor's* annual All-American Research Team awards dinner into a dressing-down session, telling the evening's award winners that their top rankings served to confuse small investors about their stock-picking abilities, which were verifiably lackluster.

In November 2002, the month that brought his unsettling confrontation with the CEO of MBIA, the ground for Ackman was shakier, too. Ackman and Berkowitz had received a number of requests from investors to redeem money. Some were spooked by Gotham's concentration of holdings in illiquid assets, such as Gotham Golf, a private company that owned a string of golf courses. The Ziff family, one of Gotham's largest investors, planned to pull its money out at year's end.

Ackman expected to bring a new investor into the fund, which would allow Gotham to avoid selling a disproportionate share of its liquid, publicly traded securities to cash out departing investors. Gabriel Capital hedge fund manager Ezra Merkin told Ackman he was willing to invest $50 million in exchange for a 15 percent stake in Gotham's management company. Ackman and Merkin were in the final stages of working out a deal.

There was one other moving piece. Ackman and Berkowitz had entered into a deal to merge one of their struggling investments, Gotham Golf, with First Union Real Estate Equity and Mortgage Trust, a Cleveland real estate investment trust that Ackman took control of in the late 1990s. They wanted to use cash-rich First Union as a platform for making private-equity investments, separating Gotham's long-term investments from Gotham's holdings of public securities. They also expected to use First Union cash to repay a loan that Gotham's hedge fund had extended to the golf course company.

The cash generated by that transaction would help smooth the way for meeting redemptions. The only stumbling block to the proposed merger was a lawsuit by First Union preferred stockholders, who wanted to be cashed out ahead of the merger. Gotham's advisers at one of the top merger and acquisitions law firms in the country, Wachtell, Lipton, Rosen & Katz, were confident the deal would go ahead despite the lawsuit. In fact, everyone at Gotham was counting on it.

Chapter 3 Three

The Question

Just bear in mind that the goal is to make the stock fall and the credit spreads widen. It's no more complicated than that.

—JAY BROWN, MBIA's CHIEF EXECUTIVE OFFICER, DECEMBER 2002

ON NOVEMBER 21, 2002, the day of Bill Ackman's meeting with Jay Brown and MBIA's general counsel, attorneys for Gotham Partners and First Union gathered at the New York Supreme Court in lower Manhattan. They were expecting to hear that the lawsuit seeking to block the merger of First Union and Gotham Golf had been dismissed. They were in for a surprise. There was a new face in the courtroom. Jerome Tarnoff (with the law firm Morrison, Cohen & Singer) had joined the team representing the First Union preferred shareholders.

Better known for his work in municipal bonds and family law, Tarnoff wasn't familiar to First Union's and Gotham's lawyers on the mergers and acquisitions circuit. He was also a force in New York politics, having served as vice chairman of the New York County Democratic Party for more than 30 years. Tarnoff was certainly an influential figure in any courtroom in a state where judges are selected by the party leadership.

Tarnoff greeted the judge warmly and took a seat directly opposite the judge's bench, positioning himself in front of the plaintiff's table rather than behind it with the other lawyers.

In July 2002, lawyers for First Union and Gotham had filed a motion to dismiss the preferred shareholders' suit, arguing that it had no merit. Judge Charles Ramos had appeared to support Gotham's view and enjoined any discovery proceedings until the decision to dismiss was finalized. Gotham's camp viewed Ramos's decision as a clear sign that he saw the preferred shareholders' case as a nuisance suit. The Gotham and First Union lawyers turned up in court on November 21 expecting Ramos to sign dismissal papers.

But on that day, the day on which Tarnoff joined the plaintiff's team, the preferred shareholders seemed to have the judge's ear for the first time since the suit was filed. They contended that Ackman was effectively liquidating First Union so that the cash could be used to bail out a bad investment. Now Judge Ramos was voicing similar concerns about the health of Gotham Golf: Was the golf business "a pig in a poke"? Was the company "going into the crapper"? No dismissal papers were signed that day.

Ackman joined the others in court the next day as the First Union hearings got under way. The scene in the courtroom that day and throughout the week-long session was bizarre. Tarnoff said nothing during the proceedings, but he assumed expressions of surprise and indignation when witnesses for the defense, including Ackman, testified. He often threw his arms up in a gesture of frustration and let out a disbelieving "Phish" in response to their testimony.

The First Union and Gotham Golf merger had been scheduled to close on December 12, but Judge Ramos issued a temporary restraining order on December 6, dashing any hope that the merger would go through by the end of the year and give Gotham the cash it needed to redeem investors without selling a disproportionate share of the fund's liquid assets. Gotham and First Union planned to appeal, but that could take months and Gotham didn't have that kind of time. All of Ackman's carefully orchestrated plans came crashing down.

When I called Tarnoff in 2009 to ask him whether MBIA may have somehow intervened in the case, Tarnoff replied by asking me what the letters M-B-I-A stand for. It was a surprising question given Tarnoff's expertise in municipal finance and MBIA's dominant share of the municipal bond guarantee business.

When I asked if his presence in the courtroom was intended to sway the judge's decision, Tarnoff told me, "Whoever said that has a perverted opinion."

As for the gestures and eye rolling during the proceedings, he said, "This is a ridiculous inquiry!" Then he hung up abruptly, ending the interview. My calls to Ramos's office were not returned.

When First Union's attorneys took depositions as part of the appeal process, lead plaintiff George Kimeldorf was asked about the preferred shareholders' last-minute decision to add Tarnoff's law firm, Morrison Cohen, to their legal team.

"I was told that their senior attorney, Mr. Tarnoff, had some acquaintance with the judge. And I believe I was told that they were good attorneys," Kimeldorf responded.

ACKMAN SOON LEARNED that getting people to listen to his concerns about MBIA's top rating would be tough going. At a birthday celebration in late November at the home of Greg Lyss, the Gotham analyst, Ackman met Richard Cantor, a former bond insurance analyst for Moody's Investors Service. It would be "unthinkable" for an analyst to downgrade MBIA, Cantor told Ackman. Analysts assigned to cover the company approach it that way, he added. "The triple-A rating is just something an analyst inherits."

Ackman witnessed that resistance firsthand at Standard & Poor's (S&P) in a meeting that had been arranged at the suggestion of Leo O'Neill, the president of S&P. Ackman met O'Neill at the Harvard Club in September, where O'Neill was speaking at a symposium. "What would happen if an analyst came to S&P and said that a company it rated triple-A didn't deserve its top rating?" Ackman asked when O'Neill took questions from the audience after his talk. "We'd take it very seriously," O'Neill answered from the podium.

"It's not a hypothetical. It's real," Ackman told O'Neill privately after the presentation.

"Is it Fannie Mae?" O'Neill added, dropping his voice.

When Ackman said it wasn't, O'Neill told him to call his office so they could set up a meeting.

The meeting was well attended. Howard Mischel, Dick Smith, and David Veno, the bond-insurance analysts, were summoned, along with the firm's chief credit officer, the head of public finance ratings, the head of structured finance ratings, and S&P's general counsel. But as Ackman gave his presentation on MBIA to the assembled group, his sense was that no one was taking him seriously, as several of the analysts continually looked at their watches.

Ackman was undeterred. He turned his full attention to writing a detailed report on MBIA. During the first week of December 2002, the report was e-mailed back and forth numerous times among lawyers and various Gotham employees. "We want to stay far, far away from libel, slander, etc., and make clear what's fact and what's opinion," Ackman wrote in an e-mail to Lyss and David Klafter.

Ackman, David Berkowitz, Klafter, and Lyss had been vetting the report for days, trying to clarify complicated ideas, labeling what was fact and what was Gotham's opinion. "Last version," Ackman wrote, eliciting an immediate response from Lyss: "I assume you mean latest."

The revisions continued. "There must be some mistake," Lyss wrote to Ackman. "We've been chopping and chopping, yet this draft is 59 pages long."

Another week passed. The weekend before the release of the report still found Ackman, Klafter, and Lyss in the office going through the report line by line, noting the source for each statement from more than a dozen boxes of material Ackman had amassed.

After taking a last look at the report, Aaron Marcu, an attorney at Covington & Burling, e-mailed his thoughts to Ackman: "There will be a serious counter-attack by MBIA, as I'm sure you know, and I would imagine that the First Union surprise is part of it. Still, as long as your response is focused on the facts of the report and MBIA's anticipated failure to dispute them, you will maximize the chances (although not guarantee) that the press reports will be about MBIA and not you. Good luck."

Finally, Gotham Partners released the 66-page report shortly after 11 a.m. on December 9, 2002. *Is MBIA Triple-A? A Detailed Analysis of SPVs, CDOs, and Accounting and Reserving Policies at MBIA Inc.* The report didn't leave much ambiguity about the answer to the question it was posing. "In light of MBIA's enormous leverage, the company's credit quality, underwriting, transparency, accounting, and track record must be beyond reproach," the report stated. "Were the insurance company downgraded by even one notch (from AAA to AA+), even the company acknowledges its business could be materially impaired."

The Gotham report pointed out that MBIA was levered 139 to 1. The company had guaranteed principal and interest payments on bonds totaling $764 billion and had $5.5 billion of shareholders' equity, the excess of a firm's assets over its liabilities. Ackman explained in the report how losses of just $900 million—a sliver of the $764 billion in outstanding MBIA-insured debt—could lead to the company being downgraded.

Problem credits are larger than investors realize, the report said, because MBIA hadn't publicly disclosed how many bonds had been restructured to prevent a default. These transactions, Gotham stated, may only serve to defer losses into the future.

The Gotham report noted an unusal reinsurance transaction that had allowed MBIA to avoid booking a loss on a hospital's bonds after the health-care organization filed for bankruptcy. Under these reinsurance contracts, several insurers agreed to reimburse MBIA for its losses in exchange for guaranteed reinsurance business in the future. To Ackman, the deal looked much more like a loan than reinsurance. If it were accounted for as a loan, then MBIA would have had to take a large loss. The predictability of MBIA's earnings was one factor that supported its triple-A rating. We "believe that this mechanism is not in fact reinsurance but rather a loss-deferral, earnings-smoothing device," Gotham stated.

MBIA's special-purpose vehicles (SPVs) were featured prominently in the report. Although the company never disclosed what assets it funded through the SPVs, Gotham had been able to identify about half of the $8 billion in loans. Companies selling assets to the SPVs included Onyx Acceptance Corporation, which made loans to credit-impaired borrowers to purchase used cars, and American Business Financial Services, a company that originated home-equity loans in the subprime market.

Gotham also pointed out that MBIA was now entering into credit-default-swap (CDS) contracts as a way to guarantee collateralized-debt obligations (CDOs), despite a New York state prohibition on bond insurers backing derivatives. "LaCrosse transforms obligations that MBIA cannot guarantee directly into ones it believes it can guarantee indirectly," the report said. A statement in MBIA's most recent filing with the New York State Insurance Department, saying the company has not entered into any transactions classified as derivative instruments, "obscures the company's true credit derivative exposure," the report said.

Ackman also disclosed the mark-to-market estimate he obtained for MBIA's credit derivative contracts. "We are at a loss to explain the enormous gap between dealer mid-market pricing, which shows the company with a $5.3 [*billion*] to $7.7 *billion* pre-tax loss, and the $35.5 *million* loss reported by the company."

MBIA was ballooning its exposure to CDOs—adding $30 billion of guarantees in nine months—and underestimating the risk, the report said. Bonds referenced in CDOs are more likely to suffer from adverse selection because banks may use CDOs to offload risk to credits they're worried about, Ackman wrote. As a result, CDOs are more likely to be packed with higher-risk credits than a random portfolio of bonds, he explained.

The credit-rating companies also were underestimating correlation risk, the report said. Although an earthquake in California doesn't increase the chance of an earthquake occurring in Florida, bond defaults tend to be contagious and closely correlated in times of economic stress. That makes CDOs, which mingle various types of loans across different geographic regions, vulnerable to the same pressures.

In fact, the whole bond-insurance industry might be vulnerable to faulty statistical models that rely on the past to predict the future, Ackman argued in the report. These models estimated that MBIA faced just a 1-in-10,000 chance of confronting a scenario that would leave it unable to meet all its claims. Yet historical data–based models considered the 1987 stock market crash an event so improbable that it would be expected to happen only once in a trillion years, Ackman explained. "The recent stock market bubble and its collapse are good reminders that the 'unthinkable' and the 'unpredictable' occur more often than expected," Ackman wrote.

Ackman also pointed out that MBIA was dangerously reliant on its own triple-A credit rating. Without the top rating, MBIA wouldn't be able to write new business, Ackman said. MBIA's investment portfolio would fall in value after a downgrade because it was packed with bonds guaranteed by MBIA itself. The assets in the SPVs, some of which were insured by MBIA, would fall in value while investors—who provided financing to the SPV through the commercial paper and medium-term note markets— would demand a higher yield or perhaps shun the securities altogether if they carried a lower rating. "An actual or perceived downgrade of MBIA would have fairly draconian consequences for the company and create substantial drains on the company's liquidity," Ackman concluded.

"The self-reinforcing and circular nature of the company's exposures makes MBIA a poor candidate for a triple-A rating."

The report sent MBIA's shares tumbling nearly 4 percent on the day it was released.

MBIA issued a press release within minutes of the report's publication. The report "is not independent, objective research but rather a negative advocacy piece by a hedge fund that has shorted MBIA stock and has also taken a speculative position in derivatives on MBIA-insured debt," the statement said. "Many of the points raised in the Gotham report are patently wrong and demonstrate a clear lack of understanding."

The Gotham press release landed on my desk at Dow Jones. I called Ackman to request a copy of the report. It was rare to find anyone on Wall Street willing to publicly criticize a company. But Ackman was bursting with comments: "The more I looked, the more I found," he told me.

Equity analysts rushed to discredit the report. "We believe the Gotham report mixes and matches in such a way to as to prey upon post-Enron fears," Joshua Shanker, an analyst with Blaylock & Partners, said in a report.

Not everyone, however, was critical. Several days after the report was released, Ackman received an e-mail from a former senior MBIA executive. "I commend the authors of the December 9 research on MBIA," the e-mail began. "It is extremely well documented for the arcane sector of the financial-guaranty insurance and hopefully has been well received for its many revelations."

The following day, Brown took the podium at a Keefe Bruyette & Woods insurance conference at Le Parker Meridien Hotel in New York, where Ackman, Berkowitz, and Paul Hilal were in the audience. "Some people who have looked at our company for the first time this year were surprised to find out that we lend to—that we provide credit guarantees to—a wide variety of different types of institutions," Brown began. "This is not new. It's not new news."

In fact, Brown told the group, even he had been skeptical of the bond insurance business initially: "I took a look at the business model and said, 'My God, how can this business model possibly work?'" Brown said. "It's called risk selection, and our goal is to do it right all the time."

Someone in the audience asked Brown whether the Gotham report contained factual errors. "Yes, I probably should comment about the Gotham report," he answered. "The company plans to respond to the inaccuracies shortly," but "let's step back and ask, what do we have here? Well, we have a lot of old news. MBIA is very complicated. We are an insurance company, so we take on a fair degree of risk in proportion to our claims-paying ability. All insurance companies do. That's the nature of the business."

Then Brown asked the audience to consider whether a hedge fund should be able to take a position on a company and later benefit from publicly bashing the firm. "I don't think it's right; maybe it's legal."

Still, Brown insisted, MBIA had no objections to Ackman's issuing research. In fact, MBIA sent the report directly to hundreds of its investors so they could read it, he said. "If you want to speak to Mr. Ackman and his associates, I'm sure he is here," Brown said, causing a slight stir in the audience as people looked to see if Ackman would identify himself. "He probably has more to say about the company," Brown continued. "I think it's a very healthy situation for somebody to identify issues or potential issues about our company," he told the group. "Just bear in mind that the goal is to make the stock fall and the credit spreads widen. It's no more complicated than that."

Ackman and Berkowitz returned to the office relieved. Brown didn't sound as if he planned to sue them. Hilal remained at the conference for lunch and scrambled to grab a seat at the same table as Gary Dunton, MBIA's president. Hilal wanted to ask Dunton about Gotham's report, but before he got the chance, someone else at the table brought it up. "It's surprising how few inaccuracies there were," Dunton said of the report. Hilal leaned in closer to listen amid the clinking of silverware and the din of conversation. "It all comes down to how you think the future is going to play out," Dunton told the group.

<hr/>

ACKMAN MADE SURE Moody's Investors Service, the leading credit-rating company, received a copy of Gotham's report. "My goal is for you to consider the seriousness of the issues we have raised, and for you to arrange a meeting with appropriate senior personnel at Moody's, including the analysts responsible for covering the company," Ackman wrote in an e-mail on December 11, 2002, to John Rutherfurd, Moody's chairman and CEO. He attached the MBIA report and a copy of a speech titled "Charlie Munger on the Psychology of Human Misjudgment."

Munger, Warren Buffett's long-time investment partner at Berkshire Hathaway, lectured Harvard students in 1995 on the mental blocks that lead to business mistakes. Munger told the students that an inability to accept new ideas when those ideas require people to displace hard-won conclusions constituted "a superpower in error-causing."

"The human mind is a lot like the human egg, and the human egg has a shut-off device," Munger told the students. "When one sperm gets in, it shuts down so the next one can't get in. The human mind has a big tendency of the same sort." This inability to accept new ideas had stymied even the most brilliant physicists, Munger said. It literally took a new generation of thinkers who were "less brain-blocked by previous conclusions" to move the field forward.

If Rutherfurd had read the speech, then he might have noted some advice in it for Ackman as well: "If you make a public disclosure of your conclusion, you're pounding it into your own head," Munger told the Harvard audience. "Many that are screaming at us aren't convincing us, but they're forming mental change for themselves, because what they're shouting out [is] what they're pounding in."

"Thank you for the report," Rutherfurd wrote back. "I will read at least the executive summary over the weekend."

On December 16, a week after the publication of the Gotham report, Morgan Stanley issued its second report relating to MBIA since the firm's analysts met with Ackman. This one was titled *Gotham's Concerns— Warranted or Not?*

Analysts Alice Schroeder and Vinay Saqi also make a surprising point about MBIA and its competitors. "Ultimately to invest in this industry, we believe investors need to address the business-model question for themselves," they wrote. Morgan Stanley had concerns about the model, they added, "however, our rating and valuation, of necessity, reflect the fact that investors (not to mention those whose paper is being guaranteed) have been willing to accept financial guarantors as a viable business model, because only those who do will buy the stocks and, therefore, set a price for them."

Morgan Stanley's response to the Gotham report laid out a dilemma that would have far-reaching implications not just for MBIA but also for the credit markets and the U.S. economy. Could the models being employed across Wall Street—not only to establish MBIA's triple-A rating but also to set the ratings on trillions of dollars of securities—be relied on to safeguard the financial system?

From the perspective of a stock market investor, the answer was simple: "The business model question is one investors must take a position on and move on," the analysts wrote. The answer wasn't as simple for the credit-rating companies. By assigning the bond insurers triple-A ratings, the rating companies ultimately determined whether or not the bond insurers had a business. "We do not expect the rating agencies to do an immediate 180-degree as the result of a report such as Gotham's," wrote the analysts. One reason: "The rating agencies are an explicit participant in the guarantors' business model, and, in effect, are now in the awkward position of passing judgment on themselves."

Ackman's startlingly high estimates for MBIA's mark-to-market losses on CDOs were cited in the Morgan Stanley report. "Because of the gap between MBIA's mark-to-model loss and the loss estimate other market participants have cited, this is the area that concerns us the most," the analysts wrote. Growth in MBIA's business of guaranteeing CDOs "has been explosive," they noted.

MBIA responded to the Morgan Stanley report the same day. For the company to pay a single dollar covering a loss on a CDO, defaults on investment-grade bonds would have to be more than 2.5 times historical maximum default rates, the company said. Such a situation would be "an extremely unlikely catastrophic event, approaching a global meltdown of corporate credit."

———

GOTHAM PARTNERS FACED a meltdown of its own in the days after the MBIA report was issued as Ackman and Berkowitz worked frantically to save the First Union deal. In a series of meetings, some lasting late into the night, Ackman and Berkowitz tried to come up with a settlement offer for First Union preferred shareholders. In the end, the preferred shareholders would not settle. Ackman and Berkowitz were not able to salvage the deal with First Union.

The decision to wind down Gotham's main funds followed a meeting with Paul Roth, one of the top hedge fund attorneys in New York, and Joel Press, then a senior partner at Ernst & Young LLP, who was considered by many to be the dean of hedge fund accounting. The alternative to winding down the funds was to redeem the investors who asked for their money back in November. That would leave the remaining investors with a disproportionate amount of their capital in illiquid investments. Roth advised against it. The funds had experienced a material event with the halted merger of First Union and Gotham Golf. Every investor now would likely want to redeem, given the uncertainty created by the temporary restraining order. The news about the planned merger's undoing had come just a few weeks after the redemption deadline. It would be unfair to leave some investors with illiquid assets while using up the funds' liquid investments to cash out other investors. Press advised the hedge fund to write down to zero its investment in and loan to Gotham Golf.

Ackman and Berkowitz decided to wind down the funds, liquidating the assets over time to maximize the return of capital to all investors. The hedge fund managers would need time to sell assets such as the Maxwell House Coffee factory, a 25-acre site on the Hoboken waterfront; a stake in Hallwood Realty Partners LP; a legal judgment against the government of Nicaragua; and Memorial Properties, LP, a mausoleum in Short Hills, New Jersey. The pair immediately began to sell Gotham's publicly traded securities, including shares of Pre-Paid Legal Services, a holding that David Berkowitz had championed.

Speculation around Gotham that the First Union merger may have been scuttled because of Gotham's aggressive attack on MBIA was fraying Berkowitz's relationship with Ackman. Berkowitz preferred to remain out of the limelight, even in good times, whereas Ackman actively courted the press. It was Berkowitz, however, who took the first blow in what would become a string of negative articles about the fund.

Whitney Tilson, the hedge fund manager who oversees T2 Partners, spotted the article first as he was reading the *New York Times* on a Sunday morning just before Christmas in 2002. Pulitzer Prize–winning business commentator Gretchen Morgenson's column that week was titled "It Still Pays to See Who Did the Research." It described how Gotham began to liquidate its Pre-Paid Legal shares several weeks after posting a positive research report on its Web site that said the fund held more than 1 million shares.

At the request of TheStreet.com, Berkowitz had written the report, which was posted on the Web on November 19, in response to an avalanche of negative commentary on TheStreet.com about the company. TheStreet.com would not publish Berkowitz's 26-page report, but it did publish the executive summary, which provided a link to the full report.

Morgenson's article explained that the hedge fund had sold more than a quarter of its Pre-Paid shares beginning around the second week of December while the upbeat report remained on Gotham's Web site. The article, which included a graph of Pre-Paid share sales titled "Cheering and Selling," suggested that New York Attorney General Eliot Spitzer's work in cleaning up dishonest research wouldn't be complete as long as tactics such as Berkowitz's went unchecked. The article didn't mention that Gotham began to sell the shares of Pre-Paid and its other liquid securities only after Judge Ramos's preliminary injunction blocked the First Union and Gotham Golf merger and led to Gotham's decision to wind down its funds.

When Tilson called Ackman to alert him to the article, Ackman explained that Gotham had been selling everything it could, including the Pre-Paid shares, after the decision was made to wind down the fund. Berkowitz still thought the stock was a "buy," Ackman added, telling Tilson: "We were so busy dealing with the First Union thing and dealing with investor redemptions—and things were going absolutely haywire—that we just weren't focused on what was on our Web site."

"I was horrified," Tilson later told the New York attorney general's office when it investigated Ackman. "You feel for anybody that has their reputations dragged through the mud on the front page of the business section of the *New York Times*."

"What was it about the article that made them look so bad?" an attorney wanted to know.

"It said that they wrote favorably about Pre-Paid. The stock went up a couple of bucks and they sold it."

"Isn't that what happened?" the lawyer asked.

"Well, I guess partial truth can be as misleading as outright fabrication," said Tilson.

Gotham pulled the plug on its Web site after Morgenson's article appeared. Less than a week later, Ackman and Berkowitz announced to investors that they were winding down their main funds. "After much deliberation and in light of recent partnership events, we have decided that it is in the interest of all partners for us to wind up the investment activities of Gotham Partners, LP, Gotham Partners III, LP, and Gotham Partners International Limited and distribute the proceeds from an orderly sale of assets pro rata to all partners."

Ackman closed by saying, "It has been a pleasure managing Gotham for nearly 10 years through very good times and the recent difficult period."

FOR THE GOTHAM managing partners, the years of success were fading away, replaced by a newfound notoriety. "I think the folks at Gotham are sincere about MBIA," Alice Schroeder wrote in an e-mail message to Whitney Tilson. "However, I think an outsider might perceive them as not objective and possibly as trying to manipulate the market simply because of the aggressive way they market their ideas."

People frequently try to convince analysts to upgrade their ratings, and it is something analysts learn to ignore, Schroeder said. She called it "unique in my career as an analyst" to be on the receiving end of a campaign to downgrade a stock. "The problem is that Gotham itself would be the prime mover for the event that makes their short call work. It is pretty obvious how that leaves them open to charges of market manipulation."

"One of my cardinal principles is that the writer should not become part of the story," Schroeder wrote. "No matter how outrageous I might think something is, if nothing changes after I write about it, let it be. It's a mistake to go on a crusade. We are not saving underprivileged children or curing cancer. [Gotham Partners is] on a mission and they believe the guarantors have to be stopped before they blow up the credit markets. Fair enough. But the feeling that 'nobody gets it but me and I've got to convince them' should be a warning sign, not a call to action."

If the idea isn't strong enough to move the market, that's a sign its time has not come yet, wrote Schroeder. Instead of "going around and getting in everyone's face," they'd be better off to let the idea "percolate."

The credit-default-swap market showed no concern about the issues raised in the Gotham report. "MBIA is ratcheting tighter," Mike Neumann, the CDS broker at Lehman Brothers, said in an e-mail to Ackman several weeks after the report was issued.

This narrowing of MBIA CDS spreads—an indication that the market was less nervous about MBIA—was frustrating to Ackman, Neumann later told lawyers at the New York attorney general's office during its investigation of Gotham. The overall credit market was improving, Neumann explained, and MBIA was outperforming the market.

Ackman told Neumann he felt the market's response was a slap in the face. The point that Ackman seemed to be missing, Neumann told the attorneys, is that the credit derivatives market "has every reason to want MBIA to be a successful, thriving company. I think Bill hadn't factored into his analysis [the possibility] that the market would just ignore what he said, even if he was right."

The lawyers asked Neumann to elaborate.

"If what he wrote was right, it would really create a disaster," said Neumann. "This is not just my opinion. I've discussed this with many people. It would be a disaster if MBIA did default because, for example, they have a lot of municipal bonds that they insure." Many investors holding MBIA-insured bonds are allowed to hold only triple-A-rated paper, he added.

"You're counting on the market to just be completely 100 percent rational," Neumann remembered telling Ackman, "but even if you're right, the market's not going to do what you want it to. It may turn out that only the history books tell you you're right 10 or 20 years from now."

Chapter 4 *Four*

Backlash

I won't tell you not to be paranoid, because paranoia may serve you well, but here, I would have to say, you are, in effect, in the restaurant business, where you spend a lot of time in the kitchen, therefore, you have to be prepared for some heat.

—ALICE SCHROEDER, E-MAIL TO BILL ACKMAN, 2003

EVEN BEFORE IT STARTED, Bill Ackman and his partner, David Berkowitz, knew that 2003 was going to be a tough year. After a decade of building Gotham Partners, the pair faced months of liquidating a fund, selling assets, and returning money to investors. Their only active investment would be the credit-default-swap (CDS) contracts on MBIA held by the Gotham Credit Partners funds.

"While you can consider your investment in Gotham Credit Partners to be a hedge against a bear market or other economic collapse, our goal here is to make you money no matter what the general state of the economy or market," Ackman wrote in an e-mail to investors in late December 2002. Investors in the funds included Leucadia National Corporation; Jack Nash and Leon Levy, who founded the highly successful Odyssey Partners hedge fund; Ezra Merkin, the managing partner of hedge fund Gabriel Capital; Marco

Kheirallah, a founder of Banco UBS Pactual in Rio de Janeiro; T2 Partners, Whitney Tilson's hedge fund; and Ackman's father, Larry.

Gotham had taken down its Web site, but during the first week of January, Ackman talked to David Klafter, Gotham's general counsel, about reactivating it so that the fund's reports on Federal Agricultural Mortgage Corporation (Farmer Mac), Pre-Paid Legal, and MBIA could be made publicly available again. Klafter worked on a new disclaimer that included a laundry list of reasons the firm might change its investment position without explanation or notice. The tone was defiant: "Gotham has First Amendment rights to comment and express opinions on topics of public importance, including MBIA's and Farmer Mac's credit quality and related topics." But the disclaimer was never used because the Web site wouldn't be activated. Events were about to take a turn for the worse.

On January 8, 2003, a front-page article by Henny Sender in the *Wall Street Journal's* Money and Investing section chronicled the decision by Gotham Partners to wind down its main funds. The article was a fall-from-grace story. It began with a description of Ackman addressing a group of students at Harvard Business School several months earlier on how to start a hedge fund, and it quipped he might return to lecture on how to close a fund. It described how Ackman and Berkowitz were trapped by a strategy of illiquid investments including Gotham Golf. They were described as "publicity hungry," and the research reports on MBIA, Farmer Mac, and Pre-Paid Legal were depicted as attempts to salvage disappointing returns. Gotham's demise, the article concluded, highlighted the perils of hedge fund investing.

Ackman's criticism of MBIA was now completely eclipsed by Gotham's own problems. "The MBIA story was incredibly complicated to convey in a newspaper article," Klafter recalls. "An easier story was about the hotshots who stumbled."

The morning the article ran, Ackman received an e-mail from Morgan Stanley analyst Alice Schroeder: "On the issue of Gotham itself, I had no idea of anything going on internally, but it has no impact on my opinion of your research, which stands on its own. Anyone intelligent will feel the same, although not everyone is intelligent."

Schroeder continued: "I won't tell you not to be paranoid, because paranoia may serve you well, but here, I would have to say, you are, in effect, in the restaurant business, where you spend a lot of time in the kitchen; therefore, you have to be prepared for some heat."

"We are not dropping the ball on MBIA," Ackman wrote back. "They have worked hard to do this to us, and they have succeeded. Some day the facts will make it our turn."

It would be years before that day would come. After the markets closed on January 8, 2003, the news agency Reuters ran a story saying New York Attorney General Eliot Spitzer was looking into Gotham's activities, citing a source familiar with the matter. Michael J. Burry, who heads up Scion Capital LLC, a California hedge fund, forwarded the article to Ackman by e-mail with a brief note: "How incredibly ridiculous."

Some people close to Ackman, such as his friend Whitney Tilson, thought it was time for Ackman to defend himself in response to the accusations regarding Pre-Paid Legal. In an early morning e-mail the following day, he told Ackman, "I think you're getting terrible advice to sit quietly, say nothing, and hope this blows over. Your good name is getting dragged through the mud. I'm hearing people say, 'Jeez, those Gotham guys are sleazy,' or 'Jeez, those Gotham guys are so stupid. How could they have let this happen?' Neither of these statements is true, yet by remaining silent, you are signaling to the world that they *are* true. Otherwise, why wouldn't you defend yourself? Silence implies that you have something to hide, feel guilty about. Yes, the media attention will blow over, but the damage to your reputation will not unless you act now."

Tilson suggested that Ackman draft a letter explaining Gotham's position, telling the world that the fund had not blown up but was liquidating. Be clear that the fund still stands behind its research, he told Ackman, and that it sold Pre-Paid because it needed to meet redemptions and that it was not part of a pump-and-dump scheme. Put the Web site back up. Let everyone read the research, Tilson advised. "This really looks bad—promoting PPD [Pre-Paid Legal] while you sold it, which is what this looks like—and this is the reason Spitzer is going after [stock analysts Jack] Grubman and [Henry] Blodget. Do you really want your name to be seared into people's memories alongside theirs for eternity?" Grubman, a Salomon Smith Barney telecom analyst, and Blodget, a Merrill Lynch technology analyst, were implicated in Eliot Spitzer's investigation into misleading Wall Street research that was used to drum up investment-banking business.

Ackman forwarded Tilson's e-mail to his lawyer Aaron Marcu at Covington & Burling: "Please explain to me what is wrong with this logic, that is, not talking to the media but putting out a press release. I know that it's likely to create more news, but I just want to consider everything at this point."

Marcu balked. "Issuing a public statement will certainly lead to more press, which at a very minimum will repeat the allegations and make the story look like it is a growing scandal," Marcu answered. The MBIA and Farmer Mac research will stand on its own, said Marcu, who was more worried about Pre-Paid Legal. Gotham would have to say it was okay for the hedge fund to be selling its Pre-Paid shares while still touting the stock on its Web site, Marcu continued, "which definitely would increase the attorney general's taste for you." It was not clear at this point that Spitzer would pursue the fund, but he was certainly considering it, if the Reuters article was any indication.

"Talking to folks like Mr. Tilson here may make you feel better or like you're defending yourself," Marcu wrote, "but it will ultimately only raise the risks of further press damage and inflaming the attorney general."

Press coverage of Gotham's doings showed no signs of abating. Later that day, January 9, 2003, Ackman got a call from Henny Sender, the reporter at the *Wall Street Journal* who had written on Gotham's CDS position on MBIA. The *Journal* planned to run another article on Gotham, Sender told him. This one would say that Spitzer was investigating the hedge fund. "Do you have any comment?"

It was clear to Ackman that the press knew more than he and Berkowitz did about Spitzer's interest in Gotham. Sender knew Gotham was being investigated before the subpoena arrived at Gotham's offices. An MBIA spokesman gave Sender the name of a contact in Spitzer's office with whom she could confirm the investigation, Sender told Ackman. Morgenson knew how many Pre-Paid shares the firm sold and when. "How does she know that we are selling the stock?" Berkowitz later asked prosecutors when he was called to testify in Spitzer's regulatory probe of Gotham in June 2003. "We didn't tell her. We didn't file with the [Securities and Exchange Commission]. How does she know?"

Berkowitz didn't get a response and didn't seem to expect one. "I am asking a rhetorical question. I know it's not my place to ask questions," Berkowitz told the prosecutors. "How does the [*Times*] reader know how she knows? I think when she asked me, I wouldn't confirm or deny that we had sold the stock. It's her word that we have sold it. She doesn't give a source."

"It was true, wasn't it?" the attorney interviewing Berkowitz asked. "She was right?"

"Yes," Berkowitz agreed. "She was right."

Ackman refused to be discouraged. The night before the *Wall Street Journal* ran its article about the Gotham probe, Ackman, his wife Karen, Paul Hilal, and Paul's girlfriend went to see *Catch Me If You Can,* a film about a con artist who is pursued by an FBI agent. "Maybe a bad choice given the circumstances," Hilal recalls.

After the movie, as they stood outside the theater on that cold January evening, Ackman's indefatigable optimism emerged. "This is going to be a good thing," Ackman told the group. "I'm going to meet Eliot Spitzer."

Ackman previously had sent the MBIA report to both Spitzer and the Securities and Exchange Commission (SEC) but hadn't heard back. Now Spitzer would hear him out. "I'm going to convince him that there's merit to what I have to say. This had to happen, so it's a good thing," Ackman told the group. He even suggested that someday, once Spitzer got to the bottom of the problems at MBIA, he and Ackman would appear together at a press conference. "He'll put his arm around me and say, 'Thanks, Bill.'"

Ackman's optimism contrasted starkly with the picture painted in the next morning's *Wall Street Journal*: "The New York Attorney General's office is looking into allegations that Gotham Partners Management Company, a once-high-flying hedge fund, acted improperly in connection with a bearish position in bond-guarantee firm MBIA Inc., say people familiar with the matter," the article began.

Extensive press coverage of the Gotham investigation followed. On January 19, 2003, the *New York Times* described Gotham's worsening troubles in a Sunday business section story. In it, Gretchen Morgenson and Geraldine Fabrikant chronicled Ackman's and Berkowitz's "startling comedown" from their "glittering client list, dazzling reputations, and smarts galore" to desperation after the Gotham Golf and First Union merger was scuttled. The article mentioned Gotham's unusually public investment strategy and how it had drawn Spitzer's attention. The reporters quoted from a recent letter Gotham had sent to its investors informing them that Gotham also had received requests for information from the SEC.

Ackman was convinced that MBIA's public relations firm, Sard Verbinnen, was getting hold of Gotham's letters and passing them along to the press. Ackman and Berkowitz had hired their own public relations firm, but the advice they were getting from their attorneys was to stay quiet. Michael Ovitz a friend of Ackman's and an investor who had been the target of negative press himself, seconded the advice on how Ackman should handle all questions from reporters: "N-O C-O-M-M-E-N-T!"

The smear campaign, as Ackman called it, was effective. Word appeared to be spreading far and wide. "I received a message from Mohamed al Moradi from the *Baghdad Times*," Ackman wrote to Gotham's then PR firm, Joele Frank Wilkinson Brimmer. "He hears that we are 'going bust.' It sounds like a joke, but my assistant thought he seemed real. I am not sure it makes sense to call back, but I sure am curious."

Although the newspaper articles brought a flurry of supportive e-mails from family, college friends, and other acquaintances, the coverage also elicited a certain schadenfreude among some of the hypercompetitive MBAs who populate Wall Street. After watching Ackman take the unusually independent path of setting up a hedge fund straight out of business school, Hilal says, some of Ackman's peers were gleeful about the negative press. "For some of his Harvard Business School colleagues working in the bowels of investment banks, it was good to see him fall," says Hilal. "Probably every week, someone would say to me, 'Fuck him; he had it coming.'"

As the pressure from the press continued, Ackman and Hilal took frequent late-night walks to the Hudson River to talk. Hilal sensed this was the one time Ackman let anyone see that he was worried. "Bill has a feeling of invulnerability," says Hilal. But it was clear to Hilal that his friend was concerned about the impact of all the negative publicity on his kids, his wife, and his father's business. The timing couldn't have been worse for what is a notoriously anxiety-producing ritual for well-off New York City parents: Ackman and his wife were making the rounds interviewing at private schools for one of their daughters. "It's no fun going around to nursery schools and having people think you're the next Dennis Kozlowski," Ackman says. The idea that Ackman and Berkowitz might go to jail was something Hilal thought about in darker moments.

There were light moments, too, though. Playing off David Berkowitz's name—the same as that of the Son of Sam serial killer who had terrorized New York City in the 1970s—Klafter joked that hardened inmates would fear sharing a cell with Berkowitz after reading about his crimes in the *Wall Street Journal*. "Oh no! Not him! Not David Berkowitz, *the hedge fund manager!*"

"It was a bit of gallows humor," Hilal says, but it helped keep their spirits up.

———•———

BY LATE JANUARY, the Spitzer investigation was broadening to include other hedge fund managers who had been publicly skeptical about MBIA and several other financial firms. One of these investors was David Einhorn, founder and president of the hedge fund Greenlight Capital. Ackman and Einhorn had struck up a friendship several years earlier after attending an "idea dinner" where investors shared information about and got feedback on investments.

In recent months, Ackman had shared his analysis of MBIA with Einhorn, who had meanwhile been unusually public in his criticism of another company called Allied Capital Corporation, a firm that provided debt and equity financing to midsized companies. Einhorn told the audience at an investment conference in May 2002 that he was taking a short position on Allied Capital because he was skeptical about the firm's accounting and disclosure practices. The stock dropped 10 percent on his comments. Einhorn later posted a research report on Greenlight's Web site detailing his analysis of the Washington, DC–based company.

On January 21, during his annual dinner for investors, Einhorn got a call from *Wall Street Journal* reporter David Armstrong. Armstrong asked Einhorn a series of questions about Allied Capital, MBIA, and Gotham. Before ending the conversation, the reporter asked him if he had heard from Spitzer's office or from the Securities and Exchange Commission. He wouldn't tell Einhorn why he thought he might.

After a tense evening, Einhorn returned home around 11:30 p.m. and found the *Wall Street Journal* story online. It described how Ackman, Berkowitz, Tilson, and Einhorn engaged in what appeared to be coordinated attacks on MBIA, Farmer Mac, and Allied Capital. Although the article didn't say that they broke any laws, it portrayed the group as a band of business school bullies turned loose on the financial markets. Gotham released a negative research report on MBIA and Tilson wrote a negative article on the bond insurer that appeared on several Web sites. Einhorn asked no fewer than 10 questions during a Moody's Investors Service conference call on the bond insurers shortly after Ackman's report was issued. Ackman, Tilson, and another Greenlight employee all asked questions during a Goldman Sachs conference call on bond insurance around the same time.

This fusillade of skepticism had angered company executives, the article explained. Farmer Mac told regulators that its problems began when Ackman turned up to interview its chief executive officer, appearing initially as an interested investor before launching into a battery of "hostile" questions. Allied Capital's complaints started with Einhorn's presentation in May, at which he suggested the company's stock as a good one to short.

Several days after the *Journal* article ran, Einhorn received a request for information from Spitzer's office titled "In the Matter of Farmer Mac." Subsequent requests for documents were titled "In the Matter of Gotham Partners." Tilson also got subpoenaed.

Within a few weeks, on February 7, 2003, an article appeared in the *Wall Street Journal* that described how Spitzer was directing his investigation toward Gotham's use of credit derivatives. Because the market for contracts on some companies' debt was quite thin, the article suggested that it would have been easy for a position such as Gotham's to cause the spreads to widen as the fund bought protection on hundreds of millions of dollars of debt. What the attorney general's office wanted to know, the article revealed, was whether the purchases themselves were aimed at creating the impression that the company was in financial danger. If that was the case, Gotham may have violated securities laws prohibiting market manipulation.

Then there was the issue of the Pre-Paid Legal report. Jim Cramer, the outspoken former hedge fund manager and founder of TheStreet. com, was livid over Berkowitz's Pre-Paid posting that appeared on TheStreet.com's Web site before Gotham decided to sell the shares. Andy Brimmer at Gotham's then public relations firm Joele Frank told Ackman in an e-mail that Cramer believed that Gotham should have known it was going to run into problems in the First Union case and could have anticipated that it would need to sell its Pre-Paid shares.

"When you play with Jim Cramer, you're playing with fire," Cramer wrote to Brimmer, who passed along the message to Ackman's lawyer, Aaron Marcu.

"Maybe suggest he take two lithium and calm down," Marcu advised Brimmer in his reply.

Cramer, a long-time friend of Eliot Spitzer, wrote about the Pre-Paid hullabaloo in a column on The Street.com on February 18, which began by asking, "What's the difference between the sales Ken Lay made in Enron and the sales Gotham Partners made in Pre-Paid Legal? I think there isn't any." He ended with this conclusion: "If you tell us you love a stock and subsequently sell it into your own hype, I don't want to know your excuse. I just want an investigation and a prosecution if the sales were made simultaneously with the hype. That's enough for me."

With pressure mounting, Ackman and his wife took a break from the months of stress, heading for the upscale resort of Las Ventanas al Paraíso, or "the windows to paradise." The hotel and spa is situated on the Baja peninsula in Mexico, nestled between desert sand dunes and the Sea of Cortez. It was the perfect place to get away from the stress of the investigation and the negative press.

Ackman didn't know it yet, but Ian Cumming, the chairman of Leucadia, one of the largest investors in the Gotham funds, had also come to Las Ventanas that week to recover from recent hip surgery. As Ackman and his wife made their way around the pool, guests dozed in the sun while "pool butlers" hovered, ready to spritz them with Evian water. The quiet was suddenly shattered as Cumming, who was stretched out in a lounge chair, recognized the hedge fund manager: "Ackman!" Cumming yelled from across the pool, "What the fuck is going on with you?"

Chapter **5** *Five*

The Worst
That Could Happen

Our no-loss underwriting standard—no losses under the worst probable scenario—is the most important discipline that we have as a triple-A-rated, credit enhancement company.

—GARY DUNTON, PRESIDENT OF MBIA, 2000 ANNUAL REPORT

FOR MORE THAN half a century, visitors to Moody's Investors Service's offices in lower Manhattan passed beneath a giant bronze frieze titled "Credit: Man's Confidence in Man." The 1950s work showed two heroic figures clasping hands over a stalk of wheat, a scythe, a wheel—symbols of a prospering economy. The willingness of one man to lend to another made that prosperity possible. Founded by John Moody in 1909, the company is one of the most influential in the world. Its assessments of borrowers' default risk determine how much companies and governments pay to access the debt markets and, in some instances, whether they borrow at all. Its ratings, a combination of letters and numbers that rank an issuer's risk of default, appear on almost every major bond issue sold around the world.

The highest rating category is triple-A, an indication that Moody's sees "minimal risk" of an issuer defaulting on its debts. The U.S. government is rated triple-A based on the revenue-generating capability of the world's largest economy and the Treasury's ability to increase taxes and even print money if it faces a shortfall. The lowest rating is C, which indicates "the bonds are in default, with little prospect for recovery of principal or interest." Typically, the lower a company's credit rating, the more it has to pay investors to borrow money.

Though criticized for missing risks at Enron and WorldCom, credit-rating companies make it possible for investors to sift through the billions of dollars of debt sold every week around the world. At a glance, investors can compare whether it's riskier to lend to the government of Indonesia or to Mattress Discounters.

By 2003, the credit-rating business was less about confidence in men or in the companies they ran than it was about models that attempted to predict the probability of loan defaults. Moody's and its only two serious competitors, Standard & Poor's and Fitch Ratings, were earning an ever-larger share of their profits from rating asset-backed securities (ABS). To create these securities, investment banks bundle hundreds and even thousands of mortgages, credit-card receivables, or other types of loans into special-purpose vehicles (SPVs), which sell bonds to finance the purchase of these assets. The key to assessing the credit of these securities is in modeling how the underlying loans will perform under various economic scenarios. The Holy Grail for Wall Street is finding ways to manufacture triple-A-rated securities out of higher-risk assets.

In many ways, the bond insurers were the template for the entire structured finance market. Bond insurers, like SPVs that sell asset-backed bonds, are essentially diverse pools of credit risk. The companies, like the lowest-risk piece of a securitization, were structured in such a way that they would receive triple-A ratings from Moody's and Standard & Poor's.

To get that top rating, bond insurers had to show the credit-rating companies that they could pay all claims on defaulted bonds in 99.99 percent of the scenarios generated by rating-company models. Gary Dunton, MBIA's president, described it this way in the company's 2000 annual report: "Our no-loss underwriting standard—no losses under the worst probable scenario—is the most important discipline that we have as a triple-A-rated credit enhancement company."

Read that again. "No losses in the *worst probable* scenario." At first glance, the statement seems to inspire confidence. It's also easy to misread it as: "No losses in the *worst possible* scenario." But there's a big difference. In the worst possible scenario, all the bonds MBIA guaranteed would default. Defining the worst probable outcome is a matter for statisticians.

The bond insurers and the credit-rating companies used so-called Monte Carlo simulations to determine how likely it was that a bond insurer would be unable to meet its claims. This modeling technique was named after the Mediterranean gambling city in Monaco because it relies on randomly generated numbers to create the different scenarios.

Monte Carlo simulations are like computerized crystal balls that generate thousands of versions of what the future might look like. In the case of the bond insurers, the model analyzed what would happen to the insurer's claims-paying resources under various economic scenarios. What if unemployment was 1 percent and home prices rose by 5 percent? Or what if unemployment was 10 percent and home prices were flat? What if defaults on credit-card bills hit 15 percent? Would a bond insurer be able to pay all the resulting claims?

Fitch's model for assessing the bond insurers' claims-paying resources tests the companies' portfolios under 500,000 different scenarios. The model uses so much computing power and takes so long to run that the analysts input all of the required data and push the start button as they are headed out the door for the evening. By the time they arrive back at work the next morning, they have their result.

If the portfolio was successfully constructed to a triple-A level of safety, then the Monte Carlo simulation would find that the insurer had enough capital to cover claims 99.99 percent of the time. In other words, a triple-A-rated bond insurer would fail the test only once in every 10,000 scenarios. It was a very reassuring-sounding outcome.

But was it? Models often rely on historical data to predict what is possible. Unfortunately, the past is not always a reliable guide to the future.

By 2003, CDOs were the hottest securities in the structured finance market, although not everyone was sure why. Frank Raiter, a former director at Standard & Poor's, testified at a congressional hearing in 2008 that he and many of his colleagues were baffled by the success of CDOs. "To a lot of us analysts that were outside the CDO area but were looking at it through the glass, intuitively it didn't make a whole lot of sense," Raiter said.

The business apparently made sense to the bond insurers, though. MBIA defended the business in a report it posted on its Web site shortly after Gotham released its report. The securities were a positive development because they allowed financial institutions and investors to transfer risk, the report said. For that reason, "CDOs are extremely beneficial to the global capital markets," MBIA asserted. "I feel strongly that if you don't like CDOs, you don't like MBIA," Jay Brown told attendees of the company's investor meeting that spring.

Most of the equity analysts covering MBIA liked the CDO business, too. Though sometimes they seemed hard-pressed to explain exactly why. "Potential losses are carefully monitored, new entrants are entering the business, and the rating agencies are confident that the business is sound," wrote Joshua Shanker, an analyst with Blaylock & Partners, in a February 2003 report. MBIA's expansion into backing CDOs "carries the aura of a good business," Shanker concluded.

When MBIA talked about CDOs, the statements were reminiscent of how it talked about its own business. "MBIA has structured its synthetic CDO transactions to withstand a very large number of investment-grade corporate defaults—typically about 7 times the average historical default rates and more than 2.5 times the historical maximum default rates—before losing a single dollar," MBIA said in its December report on CDOs. In the company's opinion, this level of defaults would be "an extremely unlikely catastrophic event, approaching a global meltdown of corporate credit."

That's why the Gotham report's estimate of MBIA's CDO losses was so shocking. The securities were supposed to be extraordinarily stable—just like the bond insurers themselves. When the New York attorney general's office launched an investigation of Gotham, it wanted to know if Bill Ackman's estimates were reasonable. MBIA had insisted that any estimate by an outsider who lacked knowledge of specific CDOs backed by MBIA was meaningless.

The attorneys investigating Gotham called in Boaz Weinstein, one of the credit-default-swap (CDS) traders Ackman spoke with to make his estimates. Weinstein, a University of Michigan philosophy major and Life Master chess player, who headed up credit trading for North America at Deutsche Bank in 2002, told investigators that Ackman's approach was reasonable: "I said that at best it would be a rough approximation, but that certainly you could get it in the ballpark."

Weinstein argued that CDOs that originated around the same time were similar. "These deals by nature have a tremendous amount of overlap," Weinstein explained. The same 100 companies were referenced in most deals, which meant the performance of the CDOs would be roughly the same.

Weinstein also told the investigators that any range of estimates would be wide but that Ackman had the right order of magnitude.

"Is there any reason the [Gotham report's] estimated $5.34 billion in losses couldn't be $3 billion just as easily? Or $8 billion?" one of the attorneys asked.

"I feel far more confident that it is $9 billion than $1 billion. None of them has a profit in them," said Weinstein. All of the CDOs were backed by pools of corporate credits that had defaulted at a higher rate than anticipated, he explained. You have to go back to the Great Depression to see a level of corporate defaults by investment-grade companies equal to the level that occurred over the last year, he told the attorneys. In fact, eight of the 12 biggest bankruptcies in U.S. history were filed over a 13-month period ending in December 2002. They included WorldCom, Enron, Conseco, Global Crossing, United Airlines, Adelphia, Kmart, and NTL.

Ackman had not identified Deutsche Bank in his report, and the attorneys asked why.

"I told my boss that a client wanted the data, and he agreed that we would provide it but not with attribution, because that might upset MBIA," Weinstein said. "They are one of the bank's biggest clients."

Lehman Brothers had even more reservations about helping Ackman with his estimate.

"I told [Ackman] we would never venture to mark to market MBIA's CDO portfolio," Michael Neumann, the Lehman broker who gave Ackman the idea to short MBIA, told investigators when he was called to testify in the Gotham investigation. "You really need to see the actual portfolio and see the names of the CDOs and stuff to know what the value is or to have an idea, and you'd never get to look at that."

And there would have been another problem in coming up with an estimate, Neumann explained. "Politically, MBIA is a client of Lehman's. There's no way we would agree to try to take a stab at it. Even if we could, even if somebody showed it to us, we wouldn't share it for somebody's report: 'Oh, yeah, it's worth 60 or whatever.'"

Neumann said he was surprised to learn that Ackman identified Lehman as the other bank providing him with data for the report. He'd given Ackman some estimates of CDO prices, but he said he didn't expect they'd be used to value MBIA's portfolio. Neumann had asked a couple of credit traders to give him estimates of where they would mark various CDOs, but the response wasn't encouraging. "Both of them rolled their eyes and said there's just no way they could give him any information he could use. It's too generic a question." Eventually, though, they came up with some very rough numbers. Neumann said he jotted them down on a sticky note and called Ackman, cautioning him that the data weren't very useful.

"Mr. Neumann, I'd like to show you what's been marked as Neumann Exhibit 2 and ask you if you've ever seen it before," the attorney said, Neumann looked over the document.

"This is an e-mail that I sent to him that, quite frankly, I forgot I sent," Neumann replied.

"This was not part of the Lehman production" to comply with the subpoena, the attorney said, noting for the record that the document was a November 12, 2002, e-mail. "Do you know why?"

"I didn't have a copy of this e-mail on my computer," Neumann said.

Among the thousands of documents Ackman produced in response to the subpoena from the New York attorney general was an e-mail he received from Neumann at 1:43 p.m. on November 12, 2002, that included a table of Lehman's estimated values for CDOs ranging from 30 cents on the dollar to 97 cents on the dollar.

It seems no one on Wall Street wanted to call attention to MBIA's losses.

———

APPARENTLY, MBIA ITSELF was having trouble valuing its CDO portfolio. When the company held its conference call to discuss fourth-quarter 2002 earnings on February 4, 2003, it reported a surprise $82 million writedown on its CDO guarantees.

The company that MBIA used for pricing its CDOs hired a new data vendor, and suddenly the CDO prices were much lower, CEO Jay Brown explained. "We couldn't make heads or tails of it," he added.

MBIA had made some other changes in the wake of the Gotham report, such as providing a more detailed earnings release. "That is not because there's a lot of new news," Brown said. "It's mainly because beginning exactly 90 days ago, when we appeared in the *Wall Street Journal* with a lot of questions, we've had more contact with our investor base and various analysts than we've had probably over the past two or three years."

During the call's question-and-answer session, analysts had more questions about the mark-to-market losses. "What are you really doing when you mark to market the portfolio?" asked Robert Hottensen from Goldman Sachs. "I'm still a little confused as to the linkage between actual credit losses and the change."

Brown explained that the company backed certain CDOs using credit-default-swap contracts, a derivative that is required under accounting pronouncement FASB 133 to be marked to market. It is "confusing," Brown reassured Hottensen. In fact, it's really quite counterintuitive. The company has to take a loss as the price of CDOs declines and the value of MBIA's guarantee on those securities consequently increases. The rule ignores the benefit to MBIA, which is able to charge more for its new CDO business, he explained. Meanwhile, the existing book of business is no riskier. "They're still triple-A and super triple-A," Brown said.

Not everyone bought that logic. Marco Kheirallah, an investor in Gotham Credit Partners and head of International Equities at Banco USB Pactual in Rio de Janeiro, frequently spoke with Ackman about MBIA. The company's tendency to muffle any hint of volatility or uncertainty was a warning, he believed.

"Financial schemes are like magic tricks," Kheirallah says. "They are about making people see what they're not really seeing."

IN EARLY 2003, in addition to preparing for upcoming testimony at the attorney general's office and at the Securities and Exchange Commission, Ackman was working to liquidate Gotham's holdings. He negotiated the sale of Gotham's stake in Hallwood Realty Partners to renowned shareholder activist and corporate raider Carl Icahn for $80 a share. As part of the agreement, Ackman and Icahn worked out a "schmuck insurance" arrangement under which Ackman would get half of the profits if Icahn sold his Hallwood stake within 18 months.

When Icahn asked Ackman if he had any other interesting investment ideas, Ackman launched into his argument for shorting MBIA and gave Icahn a copy of the Gotham report *Is MBIA Triple-A?* Ackman thought Icahn seemed interested.

Even with the investigation hanging over his head, Ackman kept trying to interest people in his MBIA research. "I never did get your thoughts on our report on MBIA," Ackman wrote to John Rutherfurd at

Moody's. It had been more than a month since Ackman first e-mailed him. "If you remember, you suggested that you would read at least the executive summary."

Rutherfurd's response was brief: "Noted," he wrote. "As mentioned to you, I am not involved in the rating of individual companies, nor will I comment on them."

Ackman appealed to Rutherfurd to reconsider. This is a "CEO-level issue for Moody's," he insisted.

It was a phrase he repeated when he wrote Stephen Joynt, the head of Fitch Ratings, a 15-page letter in March 2003. "MBIA is a CEO-level issue."

"Clearly, I am not writing to you as simply an unbiased good citizen," Ackman told Joynt. "Rather, I am writing after having done extensive research and having made investments on which we will profit if my analysis is correct."

The issues he'd spotted at MBIA needed high-level scrutiny, Ackman insisted. "CDOs are a particular concern, and the confusion and controversy over MBIA accounting for losses on these securities should be a red flag."

Quoting Warren Buffett, Ackman wrote: "Errors will usually be honest, reflecting only the human tendency to take an optimistic view of one's commitments. But the parties to derivatives also have enormous incentives to cheat in accounting for them." Buffett had explained in his most recent letter to shareholders that the valuation of derivatives affects earnings, which determine executive compensation. If there is no real market for the securities, then firms will begin to "mark-to-model," he added. "This substitution can bring on large-scale mischief" as "fanciful assumptions" make their way into the models, Buffett explained. "In extreme cases, mark-to-model degenerates into what I would call mark-to-myth."

Ackman also followed up on an overture he had made to Samuel DiPiazza, the chief executive officer of PriceWaterhouseCoopers, MBIA's auditing firm. In January 2003, at a charity dinner for the Initiative for a Competitive Inner City, Ackman had cornered DiPiazza. After spending a few minutes telling him about the MBIA report, Ackman dashed back to his office to retrieve a copy for him.

"I was curious as to your thoughts on the issues raised in the report," Ackman wrote to DiPiazza on February 21, 2003. DiPiazza responded but said he hadn't had time to review the report.

Three days later, Ackman e-mailed DiPiazza again, this time summarizing the report. He also stressed the important role the auditors played in supporting the view that MBIA was triple-A. "According to the rating agencies, they do not do their own investigation of the company's accounting; rather, they accept the auditors' statements as fact and determine their rating of the company based on this information," Ackman explained. Given the reliance of the rating companies on the auditors and the market's reliance on MBIA's triple-A ratings, "I do believe it is a CEO-level issue for PriceWaterhouse," Ackman wrote.

In all three e-mails, Ackman concluded with a version of the following: "MBIA has asked the attorney general and the SEC to investigate Gotham Partners in connection with our public release of the MBIA report on our [Web site]." MBIA also had hired a public relations firm to discredit Gotham, Ackman wrote. "I ask only that you not discredit the report based on stories about us that you read in the newspaper. While MBIA has attacked us and materially harmed our business and reputation, they have not identified any material factual errors in our report."

When Jay Brown wrote to MBIA's shareholders at the end of February as part of the company's annual report, he mentioned the Gotham report. "My views in this area are straightforward and consistent with the U.S. system of free and open capital markets," Brown wrote. "We encourage all investors to seek out all forms of research on both our company and our industry, whether flattering or critical."

Ackman, who was scheduled to testify several days later at the attorney general's office, was incredulous. While Brown claimed to be tolerant of critical opinions, MBIA was privately advocating for Ackman to be punished for publishing the report. "While no CEO likes to see his or her stock sold short, I believe this form of investing contributes to the robust nature of the American capital system," Brown concluded.

ON MARCH 3, 2003, the day before Ackman was scheduled to testify at the attorney general's office, he attended a Wall Street Hedge Fund Forum presentation at the McGraw-Hill building in midtown Manhattan. Eliot Spitzer was the guest speaker. Spitzer opened with a joke about every third hedge fund manager in the audience having a subpoena waiting under their seats. Then the good news: Unlike Wall Street research departments, Spitzer said, hedge funds aren't in need of a structural overhaul. They are, however, under increased pressure "to play games" as the market has fallen.

During the question-and-answer session that followed Spitzer's speech, he was asked whether his investigations of short sellers could have a chilling effect on investors expressing critical views about companies.

"We do not begin an inquiry unless and in fact we actually think that there is more than just somebody's desire to get back at somebody and to quiet somebody down," Spitzer replied. The attorney general's office doesn't open investigations until it has a "fair degree of well-founded evidence." In fact, most investigations conclude without seeing the light of day, he told the group. "Even with all these intrepid reporters around, they never know about it. And that's as it should be. Because, of course, it would be wrong for those investigations that begin and are closed without anything resulting to emerge and sully the reputations of people."

If the message Spitzer intended was "Read about yourself in the *Wall Street Journal* and you can be pretty sure we've got you," that wasn't the one Ackman took away from the evening. Instead, he focused on something else Spitzer said: "Short sellers have a critical role in our marketplace as long as—and here's the critical caveat—as long as it is not part of a scheme or artifice, as long as it is not part of a manipulation that is based upon the dissemination of deceptive information."

Chapter Six

The Trouble with Triple-A

Financed conduits supported by $1 trillion of asset-backed commercial paper were constructed on the basis of triple-A ratings that suggested—no, practically guaranteed—that the investments could never fail.

—BILL GROSS, PIMCO, NOVEMBER 2007

THE DAY AFTER Eliot Spitzer's presentation at the Wall Street Hedge Fund Forum in March 2003, Bill Ackman and his lawyer, Aaron Marcu from Covington & Burling, were having coffee in Starbucks across from the attorney general's office at 120 Broadway. Ackman was scheduled to begin testifying at 10 a.m.

Marcu and Ackman knew from press coverage that MBIA had complained about the Gotham report, though MBIA had never followed through on its statement that it would publicly identify errors in the report. The obvious question for regulators was whether Ackman had knowingly put false information in the report in an attempt to spread fear about the company and increase the value of his short position.

Ackman and his lawyer also knew from reading the *Wall Street Journal* that Spitzer was troubled by Gotham's use of the credit-default swap market to place its bets against MBIA and Farmer Mac. Was it possible that Ackman's intention in purchasing the CDS contracts was to cause a spike in prices and spook the market?

"I just want to remind you that you're here to answer questions. There is no need to volunteer anything," Marcu told Ackman. "You answer, and you wait for the next question."

The questions started at 10:15 a.m. in a room on the 23rd floor with a view of a brick wall. Roger Waldman, the assistant attorney general of the Investor Protection Bureau, introduced himself: "This examination is being conducted by the attorney general of the state of New York, pursuant to Article 23-A of the General Business Law, more commonly known as the Martin Act." Also present from Spitzer's Investor Protection Bureau were attorneys Marc Minor and Lydie Pierre-Louis.

The Martin Act, a New York statute passed in 1921, gives the attorney general broad powers to investigate financial fraud. The law gathered dust for decades after it was used to prosecute so-called bucket shops, which took small investors' money to make bets on stocks but didn't actually purchase securities and often went bust. Then an attorney in Spitzer's office, Eric Dinallo, dusted it off to use against some of the biggest firms on Wall Street.

Under the Martin Act, an investigation may be made public or kept secret, and suspects questioned under the Martin Act have no right to counsel. Although Marcu was permitted to accompany Ackman, he was permitted to advise him only on issues of attorney-client privilege. He could inform Ackman, for instance, if he believed that answering a question would cause him to reveal confidential communications between Ackman and his lawyers.

The Martin Act doesn't require the attorney general to prove that someone intended to commit a crime, only that the person has committed one. The low bar to conviction is seen as one reason Wall Street firms charged under the statute often agree to settle so quickly. There is a dearth of case law referencing the Martin Act, which creates uncertainty over exactly how far the attorney general's powers extend.

Waldman asked Ackman to provide details about his career history, his decision to short MBIA, his research on the company, and his meeting in Armonk with MBIA executives. He wanted to know who set up the meeting and whether Ackman represented himself as a short seller. "Before the meeting, had you established in your own mind some concerns about the company that you felt made it less attractive than the market was regarding it?" he asked.

The question opened the floodgates.

"Starting with the big picture, the company is leveraged about 140 to 1. And that was kind of a glaring number to me," Ackman said. "It does not leave much of what we call a margin of safety. You have to be right pretty much every time if you have that degree of leverage because even a small flaw could put you out of business." Then there was the company's claim in its annual report that it underwrote to a so-called 99.99 percent confidence level, according to Ackman. "That struck me as unusual."

MBIA was betting the entire company on a belief that a statistically unlikely event could not occur, Ackman said. Yet the stock market crash of 1987 was described at the time as a 27-standard-deviation event. That implies an event with a confidence level of 99.99—with 159 more 9's after it. "It's an unheard of kind of event," Ackman said. But it happened.

Over the next few years, financial firms around the world would lever up their balance sheets with huge amounts of assets that had only a remote chance of defaulting. "Frankly, in the financial markets, it seems like every three or four years we have what amounts to a multi-standard-deviation event," Ackman said.

Ackman also told Waldman that he believed that MBIA's expansion into the credit derivatives market was risky. "One of the things I was told early on in the credit derivatives business is that I may be trading with someone who has inside information. And that's something you need to be wary of because banks have much better access to information."

Waldman, who was keeping a running total, told Ackman he had listed nine issues.

"I've thought of some more," Ackman replied. Acquisition fees, the acceleration of premiums, changing the method of reserving. He described them all.

"Anything else?"

"I probably could go on."

And he did.

As the day wore on, Ackman showed no inclination to shorten his answers.

Waldman wanted to know if Ackman told MBIA executives during his meetings with them whether he was short the stock.

"The company excludes people whom they believe are potentially short sellers from their conference calls. You know . . . "

"Just answer the question, okay?" Marcu instructed Ackman.

"Do not do that again," Waldman said to Marcu.

"Excuse me?"

"Do not interrupt an answer again."

"Roger, I would like this examination to go forward and for us to finish sometime in my lifetime," Marcu answered.

Ackman was eager to get the conversation rolling again. "I was saying that the company excludes people they believe may be shorting. Everyone—other than someone they know is either an owner of the stock or an analyst—is excluded from the conference calls."

The questioning returned to Ackman's meeting with MBIA executives in August 2002. Ackman related what Jay Brown told him about the business of insuring bonds. "He really prefers the structured finance business over the municipal finance business because the municipal business, he said, is not really a financial business. You are not really doing traditional financial analysis," Ackman said. "He called it more of a moral commitment."

Marcu jumped in with a question: "Were those his words?"

"Yes. That's what he said," Ackman replied.

"Do you remember him using those words?" Marcu asked again.

"Yes," Ackman said. "And he said that as a result it was kind of hard to analyze."

The investigators didn't dwell on the issue, although it has profound implications for understanding bond insurance. The "moral-obligation" bond had been created by a young attorney named John Mitchell, who would later become Richard Nixon's attorney general and serve 19 months in prison for his role in the Watergate scandal.

During his final year of law school, Mitchell worked as a clerk for the New York law firm Caldwell and Raymond, where he was assigned to look into a federal plan to encourage the financing of affordable housing. Mitchell figured investors would balk at buying bonds to finance the construction of affordable housing if those bonds relied on the program's loans to high-risk homeowners for repayment. But surely those investors would buy the debt if they believed the government stood behind the bonds. Mitchell suggested that federal housing authorities, though not bound to buy the program's defaulted housing loans, pledge their intention to do so.

Mitchell later applied this concept to all types of debt, advising local governments on how to set up a bond-issuing authority that, in turn, secured a pledge from the government that it "intended" to help pay off the authority's debt if necessary. The issuance of these bonds didn't require a vote by local payers because the municipality was not pledging its full faith and credit to the repayment of the bonds.

The securities were dubbed "moral-obligation bonds," and they made Mitchell a wealthy man by the time he was 30. Municipalities seeking to raise debt beat a path to his door, turning Mitchell into the best-known public-finance lawyer in the country. Mitchell's innovation changed the public finance markets radically, making it possible for municipalities to issue much more debt. New York Governor Nelson Rockefeller, who used moral-obligation bonds to finance the construction of affordable housing in New York City in the 1960s, called Mitchell's creation "the greatest system ever invented." Mitchell's former law partner, William A. Madison, summed up the moral-obligation concept this way: "It was a—sort of like a gimmick."

In 1976, the state of New York outlawed the use of moral-obligation bonds after a Moreland Act Commission found the debt had contributed to the state's fiscal crisis the year before. The commission concluded that the sale of such bonds created "a dangerous and misleading illusion." It allowed politicians to put a growing and unrecognized burden on taxpayers, according to the report.

In a November 1984 interview in *Bond Buyer* magazine, four years before Mitchell died, he was asked to respond to critics' charges that moral-obligation bonds bypass the voters' right to a referendum on debt issues. His answer: "That's exactly the purpose of them."

Brown explained it to Ackman when they met in August 2002. "Public finance is illogical. A moral commitment," Ackman scrawled in his notes. "Once you get below state level, there is someone who can help out. Feds won't let a state go broke."

It was not a topic that interested the investigators.

Waldman asked Ackman to turn to page 23 of Gotham's report—*Is MBIA Triple-A?*—referencing the portion of the report that discussed the off-balance-sheet special-purpose vehicle (SPV) called Triple-A One Funding. It quickly became clear that Gotham's views on Triple-A One were a major focus of the investigation.

Triple-A One was an asset-backed commercial paper (ABCP) issuer set up by MBIA in an obscure but booming corner of the financial markets. It sold commercial paper to risk-averse investors such as money market funds and used the proceeds to purchase securities. Like a bank, Triple-A

One borrowed short-term funds and made longer-term investments. Unlike a bank, it wasn't regulated.

The market for ABCP would top out at around $1.2 trillion in 2007 before plunging by two-thirds as investors questioned for the first time the quality of the assets backing the commercial paper.

Ackman had cracked open the door on Triple-A One in his report. He listed some of the assets held by the SPV. They included mortgage loans to "credit-impaired borrowers" and used-car loans to subprime borrowers. MBIA had never publicly disclosed what was financed in its conduits.

Ackman had gone one step further and suggested this off-balance-sheet SPV could cause a run on MBIA.

Waldman asked Ackman to read from his report. "We believe this SPV's commercial paper creates significant liquidity risk for MBIA," Ackman read. "In the event of a decline in MBIA's actual or perceived credit rating, these CP buyers may withdraw their support of Triple-A One Funding, requiring the SPV to draw upon its outstanding bank liquidity lines."

A liquidity line is an arrangement under which a bank agrees to buy commercial paper in the event the mutual funds and corporate treasurers who usually buy the short-term debt reject it.

"How can the commercial paper conduit create a risk if the banks fund the liquidity lines?" Waldman wanted to know.

Ackman said that by reading an article in the December 2001 issue of a trade publication called *Financial Stability Review,* he learned that liquidity facilities often had "outs," or reasons a bank could cite for refusing to buy the commercial paper. MBIA didn't publicly disclose enough detail for outsiders to be sure what those outs were.

The questioning about Triple-A One continued into a second day. The transaction made for dizzying rounds of questions. While the cash flow from the loans held by Triple-A One supported repayment of the CP, MBIA insured the assets in case the loans didn't pay off. The banks provided the liquidity backup for the CP in case investors shunned the short-term debt. MBIA, however, insured the liquidity providers against taking any losses on the CP if they wound up having to purchase it.

"Where is this going to break down and why?" Waldman asked Ackman.

There might be circumstances under which the banks would be allowed to walk away from their obligations, Ackman said. He hadn't been able to find any disclosure on that, however.

"Would you mark this as Exhibit 5," Waldman said as he placed a report on the table.

It was a Standard & Poor's research report on Triple-A One Funding. The report, Waldman explained, described the conditions under which banks could stop providing support. But that didn't end the disagreement. Waldman pointed out that the SPV had to be insolvent for the banks to back out. So didn't this prove that Ackman was wrong and that the banks would remain on the hook?

Ackman disagreed. "I would say it implies that I'm correct," Ackman said. "Solvency is defined as assets exceeding liabilities."

Waldman fired back: "Solvency also can mean ability to pay when [liabilities] come due, as you well know."

"I think it doesn't have the ability without a guarantee from MBIA," Ackman said, referring to the MBIA insurance policy on the assets. The circularity of the arrangement was making it impossible to untangle the ownership of the risk.

"It has a guarantee?" Waldman asked.

"Right," Ackman said.

"I'd like to move on," Waldman replied.

While Waldman almost certainly had been briefed by MBIA's advisers on the SPVs, the details of how they worked seemed maddeningly elusive.

In November 2007, four years after Ackman and Waldman debated the risks of MBIA's SPVs, Bill Gross, founder and co-chief investment officer of PIMCO, wrote an editorial in *Fortune* magazine titled "Beware Our Shadow Banking System." The term was created by his PIMCO colleague Paul McCulley to describe the thousands of off-balance-sheet entities that engage in lending outside of the banking system with its capital requirements and regulatory oversight. "[The shadow banking system] has lain hidden for years, untouched by regulation, yet free to magically and mystically create and then package subprime loans into a host of three-letter conduits that only Wall Street wizards could explain."

Waldman and Ackman were bogged down in the workings of this as-yet-unnamed shadow banking system as they went round and round about Triple-A One Funding. The entity was a labyrinth of assumptions, interpretations, and contingencies. The few public references to the special-purpose vehicle were vague and almost certainly intended to be that way, yet it was only one of many such programs set up by financial institutions as off-balance sheet lenders.

"Financed conduits supported by $1 trillion of asset-backed commercial paper were constructed on the basis of triple-A ratings that suggested—no, practically guaranteed—that the investments could never fail," wrote Gross.

Ackman's report had briefly shone a light into the shadows. That was a dangerous thing to do because it was easy to be wrong. Information about many SPVs wasn't readily available; even when it was, the details were often open to interpretation. Waldman reminded Ackman that it was risky to tread in this murky territory. He wanted to know what Ackman's understanding of the law was regarding the release of research to the public on a company, particularly on a company an investor had shorted.

"My understanding is that as long as you do not knowingly disseminate false and misleading information, there is nothing wrong with sharing your views as an investor with anyone, positively or negatively. I got that from Mr. Spitzer. I was comforted by his remarks."

"That does not sound like Mr. Spitzer's view."

"I listened very carefully. Mr. Spitzer said, 'As long as you do not knowingly disseminate false and misleading information for the purpose of generating a trading benefit . . . we don't have a problem with that. However, if you do do that, we are going to pursue it aggressively.'"

During each break, including the lunch break when Ackman and Marcu headed for a sandwich shop in the lobby, Marcu reminded his client that he was there to answer questions, not to volunteer information. He wasn't optimistic that Ackman would heed his advice. "Bill rejected my advice more times than all of my other clients combined over the course of my entire career," Marcu remembers.

When questioning resumed, Waldman directed Ackman's attention to a letter collected as part of the investigation. In it, Ackman tells his investors that his lawyers have advised him there is nothing illegal or inappropriate about making Gotham's analysis of MBIA public. Marcu and Waldman were comparing various drafts of the letter when Ackman interrupted them.

"May I speak?"

"There's no question pending," said Waldman. "Do you wish to volunteer something?"

He did. "We live in America. Free speech is an important central tenet of living in America," Ackman said. "Someone may say something they believe to be true, which later turns out to be false. If they were held to a standard whereby they were subject to some violation of law as a result of that, I don't think anyone would ever make a public statement again. Certainly not about something as complicated as a public company, particularly this one."

He continued. "The capital markets benefit when money managers, who do their homework, share ideas. I worked incredibly hard to make this report accurate. Is it possible that there's a mistake in the report? Yes. Did I knowingly put something in the report that was false? No."

THE ATTORNEY GENERAL'S office had more questions about Triple-A One Funding that they put to Greg Lyss. The former Gotham analyst arrived at 120 Broadway to testify several weeks later with Marcu. Waldman and Marc Minor conducted his interview.

Lyss left Gotham after the fund cut back to only a few employees, but he had helped to put together the report on MBIA. It was Lyss who suggested changing some phrasing in the report to say that MBIA guaranteed Triple-A One Funding's commercial paper. It seemed obvious to Lyss from reading the company's filings that this was the case. MBIA later said it didn't guarantee the short-term debt. The question was important because the credit-rating companies would not assign MBIA a triple-A rating if it were on the hook to buy up billions of dollars of commercial paper in the event the securities were rejected by investors.

Lyss told Waldman there were situations in which the banks might not be required to make good on their commitment to provide liquidity. Language in MBIA's filings suggested to Lyss that MBIA might then be obliged to buy the commercial paper.

"Did you entertain any doubt about your interpretation?" Waldman asked.

"I can't recall," Lyss said.

"What about today? Any doubts?"

"I have no doubt about what I would conclude from reading this paragraph," Lyss said, pointing to the wording he had originally reviewed to determine whether MBIA had an obligation.

"Do you have any doubt today that there is a guarantee of commercial paper?" Waldman asked.

"I have a doubt today solely because the company said so," Lyss explained. "However, based on this paragraph, it would lead me to believe that they have guaranteed the commercial paper."

"You believe there is no other interpretation possible of this paragraph," Waldman said. "Is that right?"

"Well, apparently you have a different interpretation, which means it is possible to have a different interpretation," Lyss remarked.

Lyss and Waldman continued to debate the issue. Where did the banks' responsibilities end and MBIA's begin? Or did MBIA have any responsibility? Finally, Lyss summed up his views in lay terms. "I do believe that if Triple-A One Funding crapped out and they put it into bankruptcy and MBIA didn't make good on it and those commercial paper holders were stiffed, that would have a serious impact on MBIA's business," Lyss said. "You can't stiff one related entity and have it not affect the rest of your business."

———

BETWEEN DAYS OF TESTIMONY, Ackman attended Berkshire Hathaway's annual meeting with Whitney Tilson. The meeting, held in Omaha, Nebraska, has been called the Woodstock of Capitalism and generally draws more than 20,000 people. Warren Buffett and his partner, Charlie Munger, take the stage for hours to present their views on business and answer questions from the audience.

For Ackman and Tilson, attending the meeting had become a tradition. Berkshire shareholders and other investors queue up early in the morning to get a place in line at several microphones set up in the main auditorium. Ackman knew from experience that the overflow room, where investors watch the show on a large-screen TV, was his best shot at getting in a question, and Ackman had an important question he needed to ask.

When Ackman and Tilson arrived, there was no one in the overflow room, which assured Ackman of getting a turn for a question. When Buffett and Munger got around to taking questions from the overflow room, Ackman asked them to comment on the practice of insurance companies taking credit risks using credit-derivative contracts and to offer their thoughts about whether insurance companies engaged in this business should have triple-A credit ratings.

"The curse of the insurance business, as well as one of the benefits of it, is that people hand you a lot of money for writing out a little piece of paper," Buffett said. "What you put on that paper is enormously important. The money that's coming in, which seems so easy, can tempt you into doing very, very foolish things."

Buffett described how GEICO took in $70,000 for a few policies and lost $93 million paying claims. Such mistakes can wipe out a lifetime of earnings—a few cents gained when you're right and a fortune lost when you're wrong, Buffett said.

Ackman believed that was exactly what MBIA was doing with its collateralized-debt-obligation (CDO) business. The huge decline in the value of the CDOs MBIA had insured was proof, Ackman believed, that the bond insurer was massively underpricing risk.

Jay Brown had addressed Gotham's estimates in his letter to shareholders in the company's annual report that spring. "There was an 'analysis' performed by a hedge fund which suggested that our mark was miscalculated by several billion," Brown wrote.

Brown's rebuttal of the Gotham estimates left Ackman aghast. "The entire adjusted net premium we collected for our entire synthetic book was under $200 million," Brown explained. "This suggests to me that the 'analysis' methodology had another goal in mind."

Ackman read it again. And again. Just because MBIA had received only $200 million to assume the risk on tens of billions of dollars of CDOs didn't mean that the company couldn't end up paying billions of dollars in claims. It certainly didn't mean that the value of those securities couldn't have fallen by billions of dollars.

Buffett continued: "If you're willing to do dumb things in insurance, the world will find you. You can be in a rowboat in the middle of the Atlantic; just whisper 'I'm willing to write this,' and then name a dumb price. You will have brokers swimming to you—with their fins showing, incidentally," Buffett said, laughing.

Chapter Seven

Unanswered Questions

As long as [MBIA] is triple-A rated and sailing through unnoticed, this company is fine. The moment it's downgraded, it's no longer fine. The business is at significant risk.

—BILL ACKMAN, MAY 2003, UNDER OATH

BETWEEN APPEARANCES AT the attorney general's office during the early summer of 2003, Bill Ackman tried to keep the pressure on MBIA. He dialed in to the company's second-quarter conference call, hoping to ask some questions, but the line was never opened for him. "The company did not permit anyone other than analysts to ask a question on the recent quarterly conference call," Ackman wrote to Gotham Credit Partners investors in a May e-mail. "I did, however, receive a call yesterday from the chief financial officer, Neil Budnick, offering to answer my questions if I put them in writing."

Ackman's follow-up e-mail to Budnick contained 146 questions, starting with: "Why did MBIA ask the regulators to investigate Gotham Partners? Why did the company hire a PR firm and work to discredit Gotham in the media if it is truly Jay Brown's desire that shareholders seek out even critical points of view? Doesn't Brown realize that few others will be prepared to criticize MBIA in light of how aggressively the company has attacked Gotham?"

Ackman asked Budnick to explain Brown's comments in MBIA's 2002 annual report in which he dismissed Gotham's estimates of MBIA's collateralized-debt obligation (CDO) losses because the company had only collected $200 million in premiums. How did the fact that MBIA collected less than $200 million in premiums to guarantee these CDOs suggest to Brown that Gotham had "another goal in mind"? Ackman asked. "In my report, I stated my belief that the company had been underpricing its synthetic CDO guarantees. That the company has earned only $200 million shouldn't have anything to do with the mark-to-market calculation in light of the company's $45 billion or so of exposure at year-end. What am I missing?" The controversy over the market values of the CDOs could be settled if MBIA would just disclose the CDOs it guaranteed, Ackman suggested. "Would you do so? If not, why not?"

Ackman's questions continued for pages: Why have losses been so high on a series of securities backed by tax liens? How many securities insured by itself does MBIA own in its investment portfolio? When will it consolidate the off-balance-sheet conduits such as Triple-A One Funding? Why does MBIA collect fees to administer these conduits? Why did the number of insured bonds guaranteed by MBIA and rated below investment grade double in the last few quarters?

"I will probably have a few more questions for you after I hear back," Ackman said. Lastly, Ackman asked, "When should I expect to get a response to my questions?"

Ackman's first answer came not from Budnick but from MBIA's general counsel, Ram Wertheim. "I understand that you sent this e-mail at Neil's suggestion, who, based on your conversation, was expecting a 'few' questions," Wertheim wrote. It would take awhile for the company to decide whether it would answer the questions and in what format, he added.

Ackman didn't plan to wait. He wrote to his investors that he planned to issue the list of questions in a press release. "I think this format will accomplish our goal of shining sunlight on the problem," Ackman wrote in the May letter to Gotham Credit Partners investors. "To the extent the company does not answer our questions or gives inaccurate or nonresponsive answers, [their publication] will assist us greatly." But in a rare win for Ackman's lawyers, they convinced him not to publish the questions in a press release.

Meanwhile, Ackman had received expressions of interest from some of the Gotham Credit investors wanting to add capital to the bet against MBIA. None of the investors expressed any interest in selling their positions. "I currently plan to take in the new capital on a mark-to-market basis and reinvest in five-year swaps at current pricing of approximately 60 basis points," Ackman explained in a letter. At that level, the fund could buy protection against default on $10 million of MBIA debt for $60,000 a year. It was a chance to "average down" the cost of Gotham's previous investment by adding to the investment at a lower cost and to extend the term of the contracts further into the future. "So for each million, if MBIA defaults within the next five years, we earn 100 percent of our original $29 million of capital back," he explained.

A few weeks later, in June 2003, Ackman was back on the receiving end of questions about MBIA. Down at 120 Broadway, Waldman showed Ackman an e-mail Ackman had written to Alice Schroeder regarding MBIA that read "And most significantly, we believe they are in violation of the New York State insurance regulations." "Exactly what insurance regulations did you believe they were violating?" asked Waldman.

"Well, I am not a lawyer, but there is a fairly strict prohibition against insurance companies generally not guaranteeing—using insurance company capital to guarantee—derivatives," Ackman said. "I think there is actually an outright prohibition."

Ackman explained that MBIA got around this prohibition with a special-purpose vehicle (SPV) that's also known as "an orphaned transformer." It was orphaned because the equity was owned by a nominee or a charity rather than MBIA, and it transformed the business from one that MBIA couldn't do directly into one it apparently could do *indirectly*, he explained. This orphaned transformer did not have the financial wherewithal to actually pay counterparties in the event it needed to make good on a credit-default-swap contract, but MBIA insured all of the SPV's obligations so counterparties would be willing to trade with it. "The entity is called LaCrosse Financial Products— LaCrosse like the game," Ackman said.

"What about the company?" asked Waldman. "Did you ask MBIA about whether they were violating the law? Did you ask whether [the SPVs] were legal or not?"

"No."

"Why not?"

"I assumed they thought it was legal."

"What about the state insurance department?" asked Waldman. "Did you take your question to regulators?"

"We told the insurance department what [MBIA] was doing and their reaction was: 'Are you sure they're using insurance capital to guarantee credit derivatives through this entity? Or is it the holding company that's providing the guarantee?' They asked us this question multiple times."

Ackman told Waldman that he attempted to bring an insurance law expert to his first meeting with the insurance department. He had contacted Bonnie Steingart, an attorney at Fried, Frank, Harris, Shriver & Jacobson and the former general counsel for the New York State Insurance Department. According to Ackman, Steingart told him that she believed arrangements like LaCrosse Financial would not be legal under New York insurance law.

Steingart never got a chance to tell the New York State Insurance Department what she thought. After Ackman and Steingart spoke by phone, Ackman decided to retain her to represent Gotham. Indeed, plans were made on a Friday for Steingart to attend a meeting with Gotham at the insurance department the following week, Ackman told Waldman. All had agreed that her presence at the meeting would add credibility to Ackman's arguments. But the day before the meeting, Steingart called and canceled, Ackman explained.

"After consulting with some of her partners in the structured finance group, she said they would not let her represent us because Fried Frank did not want to represent someone whose interests were adverse to MBIA's, in light of the large amount of business the structured finance group does with MBIA," Ackman said during testimony at the attorney general's office. "So she declined to come to the meeting, and that was the last conversation we had with her about the subject."

Reached at her office in October 2009, Steingart said it was her recollection that Ackman had retained another firm. She said Fried Frank had never represented MBIA and wouldn't have refused to represent a party whose interests were adverse to MBIA's "MBIA was always fair game," she said.

It took another five years for Ackman to find a firm willing to represent him in meetings with the New York State Insurance Department.

CONVERSATIONS ABOUT REGULATING credit-default swaps had a way of getting cut short. In the 1990s, Brooksley Born, the head of the

Commodity Futures Trading Commission (CFTC), suggested bringing the credit-default-swap (CDS) market under the control of the commission. The CFTC already oversaw markets for futures and options, including those written on commodities such as pork bellies and corn. But Wall Street lobbyists, with the ideological backing of Federal Reserve Chairman Alan Greenspan, put up resistance. The Commodity Futures Modernization Act of 2000—buried in an 11,000-page budget bill and never debated—was passed the night before Congress recessed for Christmas in December 2000. It exempted credit-default swaps from federal oversight and from state gambling laws.

The CDS market had another near miss with regulation, also in 2000, when bond insurers sought permission to enter the market. That would have brought the CDS business under the umbrella of state insurance regulators. Credit-default swaps were, after all, very similar to the product companies such as MBIA and Ambac already provided—a promise to cover losses if a bond defaulted. Financial Security Assurance, the bond insurer founded by Jim Lopp, asked the New York State Insurance Department to opine on whether it could enter into CDS contracts as part of its insurance business. The answer was no.

Insurance was intended to provide protection against losses, regulators ruled. Although a company's bankruptcy filing almost certainly results in someone losing money, there is no way of knowing that the person holding a credit-default-swap contract actually suffered a loss, the regulators reasoned. So credit-default swaps weren't regulated— not as securities or gambling or insurance—and they proliferated at an astounding pace. Bond insurers got around the prohibition by setting up shell companies such as LaCrosse. American International Group (AIG) eventually sold protection on around $500 billion of risk through the credit-default-swap market. It conducted the business through a nonregulated unit called AIG Financial Products, headquartered in London. Wall Street was happy to deal with both the bond insurers and AIG because they appeared to be among the most creditworthy counterparties in the world.

As the questions at 120 Broadway continued, Waldman wanted to know how Ackman came up with his multibillion-dollar estimate for MBIA's mark-to-market losses on credit-default swaps. Ackman explained how the Wall Street dealers he contacted were able to provide a price range for CDOs based on the original ratings of the CDOs and the year the securities were sold, or their "vintage."

"For anyone interested in wine, it's kind of the same thing," Ackman explained to the lawyers. "Let's say the '82 Bordeaux was a really good year and the '92 Bordeaux is a really bad year. The same kind of thing holds true for CDOs."

The dealers gave Ackman an indication of the bids and the offers on various types of CDOs. The spread between the bids and offers was wide, suggesting great uncertainty about the price. So Ackman took a midpoint number to come up with his estimates, he explained. MBIA had to be using its own internal model—rather than market prices—for determining the size of its losses, Ackman said.

"Can you conceive of a situation in which mark to model would be a better indication of value than mark to market?" Waldman asked.

"I would say probably not."

"None? Suppose there are only three trades?" Waldman insisted.

"I would much rather rely on a trade of a comparable instrument than I would on any model."

"Suppose there is only one trade. Do you like that better than a model?" asked Waldman.

"Yes. If it is between a willing buyer and a willing seller. Yes. Absolutely."

"You don't think there could be any extraneous influence on the trade?" Waldman pressed.

"A lot less than there is on the models performed by management. MBIA has set aside only $10 million of reserves for losses against its entire $65 billion portfolio," Ackman told Waldman. "That's MBIA's best estimate."

"Ten million dollars out of $65 billion?"

"Correct. The dealers say the number [the mark-to-market losses] is closer to $5 [billion] to $7 billion."

"You're not suggesting, are you, that they should have a loss reserve—or are you—of $5 billion to $7 billion?"

"I'm saying that with respect to their synthetic CDO portfolio, they're hugely under-reserving," said Ackman.

"And one of the things auditors do, don't they, is analyze whether reserves for losses are adequate?" Waldman pointed out.

"No."

"They don't?"

"That's correct. They don't." Ackman replied.

"They just accept whatever the reserve is? No test, no nothing?"

"That's correct," said Ackman. "Basically what the auditors do is examine the processes that management uses to determine reserves and decide whether the process is reasonable or not."

"In this case, the process apparently does not include the mark-to-market methodology your dealers employed?"

"That's correct."

"Do you know who the auditors were?" asked Waldman.

"PriceWaterhouse."

Waldman wondered aloud if it ever gave Ackman pause that such a well-known accounting firm didn't insist on the valuation process Ackman was using.

"No, not at all," said Ackman. "Unfortunately, the auditors are not particularly good on the subject of reserves."

"Even if—for the sake of argument—your estimate of the bond insurer's losses are right, would it have any real impact on MBIA's ability to meet its obligations?" Waldman asked.

"It really depends," Ackman said. If these losses caused the credit-rating companies to rethink MBIA's triple-A rating, things could start to unravel, he explained. MBIA insures lots of the bonds it holds in its investment portfolio. These would be worth less if MBIA were downgraded. For that matter, bonds insured by other financial guarantors that MBIA held in its portfolio would also likely fall in value.

"I suspect that the circumstances in which MBIA would be forced to mark to market its CDO portfolio would be the same circumstances in which Ambac and FSA would be forced to mark to market their portfolios, which would in turn cause a downgrade of each of the respective companies," Ackman said. "MBIA buys insurance from Ambac, and Ambac buys insurance from MBIA, and so their fate is tied together." The company might find its counterparties on derivative transactions asking for more collateral if it were downgraded, Ackman said. A loss of the company's top rating also might cause investors in Triple-A One Funding's commercial paper to shun the securities at the next auction.

The large mark-to-market losses don't immediately cause a drain on the company's cash, Ackman explained. But a series of events, one event tripping the next, creates the problem. It requires one to think about MBIA within a broader context to see that risks become correlated when things go wrong in credit markets. The shield that protects MBIA is its triple-A rating. "As long as this thing is triple-A rated and sailing through unnoticed, this company is fine," Ackman said. "The moment it's downgraded, it's no longer fine. The business is at significant risk because the entire enterprise depends on that triple-A rating—their investment portfolio, their ability to revolve their commercial paper, their ability to borrow money, collateral for derivatives. It is one connected nexus of . . . "

But the attorneys cut Ackman off there and moved on to other questions.

OTHERS WERE CALLED to testify as well. On May 8, 2003, hedge fund manager David Einhorn of Greenlight Capital arrived at the Securities and Exchange Commission (SEC) in Washington to give testimony in the Gotham investigation.

Investigators were trying to find some connection between Einhorn's very public short position on Allied Capital and Ackman's critical research and trading in the securities of MBIA and Farmer Mac (the Federal Agricultural Mortgage Corporation). Had the pair somehow worked together to undermine confidence in the companies? Or to manipulate the companies' securities?

"Have you ever met regularly or irregularly with a group of fund managers that would include Whitney Tilson and Bill Ackman?" asked the SEC attorneys. "Have they ever compensated you for providing them with an investment idea? Are there any other relationships between you and Greenlight and Mr. Ackman and Gotham Partners?"

Several years later, in a book about his experiences as a short seller, Einhorn recalled the uncomfortable interview. The temperature in the basement room where he testified felt like it was 85 degrees on that early May morning, Einhorn recalled. "The environment was unsettling. It was supposed to be that way," Einhorn wrote. "Perhaps the austerity foreshadowed what might happen if your case didn't go well."

The interview, however, turned up no untoward connections between the hedge fund managers, and Einhorn was not called back for questioning in the afternoon.

David Berkowitz also was called to testify at both the SEC and the attorney general's office. Berkowitz and Ackman had parted ways earlier that year. While Ackman continued to sell off Gotham's assets and oversee the Gotham Credit Partners fund, Berkowitz moved on to another firm where he managed money for a wealthy family.

At the attorney general's office, Berkowitz answered questions about Pre-Paid Legal, about the decision to wind down the main Gotham funds, and about the MBIA report. As the hours of testimony dragged on, the questions seemed to be going nowhere.

"Mr. Berkowitz, to the best of your knowledge, have you or Gotham Partners ever received anything in the way of compensation—money or otherwise—from a reporter in exchange for information related to a story that the reporter would be working on?" Marc Minor, one of Spitzer's attorneys, asked.

"No," Berkowitz replied.

"Were you in the practice of using reporters to get information about a company that you otherwise were not able to get?"

"No," Berkowitz said.

Minor seemed determined to uncover some plot involving reporters. He pulled out what he called "Exhibit 35," a Bank of America research report that appeared to have been faxed to Berkowitz from the *Wall Street Journal*.

"Do you recall receiving this document?" Minor asked him.

"No," Berkowitz said.

"The underlining in the body of the document—are those your underlinings?"

"I am a bit neater in underlining," Berkowitz responded.

A note in the margin of the document appeared to reference credit-default swaps: "How have spreads moved?" And a box was drawn around a chart in the report highlighting CDO issuance for 2001 and 2002. Minor pointed out, "For the record, there are a series of diagonal and straight lines and arrows and to the left is a series of numbers: 10/5/1. What is it?"

"I have no idea," said Berkowitz. "I am sitting here trying to figure it out. It looks like I'm trying to do some compound-interest calculation of some sort, but I really have no idea."

Several pages later there were more drawings, numbers, and arrows. "Do you know what this refers to?" Minor asked.

Then it came back to Berkowitz. "I think it's a brain teaser of some sort," he answered. "One of those things like how do you get five people across the river in a boat that carries only two people? I think that's it."

It clearly wasn't the revelation that Minor was looking for.

"Did you solve it?" Minor asked.

"At the risk of being a little boastful, I generally solve them," Berkowitz replied.

The questioning concluded shortly after. Berkowitz was not called back. The investigation was turning up nothing.

Chapter Eight

Crimes and Cockroaches

MBIA might just be the biggest business generator on Wall Street. No one wants me to be right on MBIA.

—BILL ACKMAN, JUNE 2003, UNDER OATH

WHEN BILL ACKMAN RETURNED to 120 Broadway to give testimony in the New York attorney general's investigation of Gotham Partners in June 2003, the focus shifted from MBIA to the Federal Agricultural Mortgage Corporation (Farmer Mac). Ackman had written critical research reports on both MBIA and Farmer Mac after purchasing credit-default-swap (CDS) protection that would gain in value if perceptions about the companies' credit worsened. The attorney general wanted to know if Gotham had intended to send a troubling signal to the market by pushing up the price of default protection on these confidence-sensitive firms.

There were similarities in Ackman's criticism of the two companies as well. Farmer Mac and MBIA both provided financial guarantees. Both were perceived as being of the highest credit quality. Both appeared to serve a public policy function. Yet behind the scenes, MBIA and Farmer Mac were both highly leveraged and had ventured over time into riskier lines of business. In the companies' financial statements and other

81

disclosures, Ackman noted a tendency for management to gloss over potentially troublesome topics.

Lydie Pierre-Louis took the lead on this round of questions, and Ackman was no less eager to talk. Just as Roger Waldman did with MBIA, Pierre-Louis started a running tally of Ackman's reasons for shorting Farmer Mac.

Ackman cited Farmer Mac's low reserves and rising delinquencies as the first red flag he spotted. The company also was highly leveraged, largely with short-term debt, Ackman explained. Another red flag: Farmer Mac's top executives were the beneficiaries of an excessive compensation plan, with 35 percent of the outstanding shares set aside for management. Meanwhile, Farmer Mac's board of directors was crowded with representatives from affiliated companies, clients, and political appointees with no one representing public shareholders. "I can speak for hours on the subject," Ackman told the attorneys, "but those are some of the general things I've thought about."

Pierre-Louis tallied 12 reasons Ackman had stated for shorting the stock. "Were there others?"

"Yes. There are more. I don't mean that to be an exhaustive list." The company's disclosure is misleading, Ackman said. "I read every one of their financial statements from the beginning of time until today, and when you compare them in terms of disclosure and how it changes year by year, you begin to get a sense that management is trying to create an impression that is, in my opinion, very often not the truth."

"You're saying their disclosure statements, which I believe are filed publicly, are inaccurate?" Pierre-Louis asked.

"They are often inaccurate and clearly misleading," Ackman said, adding, "They have gotten materially better since [Gotham] published its report."

Marcu called for a recess at that point, taking Ackman out into the hall. If Marcu's hope was that Ackman would stop volunteering so many opinions, he was soon to be disappointed. When they returned, Ackman picked up where he left off: "Just to be clear, when I say their disclosure is inaccurate, I am referring not just to their public filings but also to conference calls, statements made by management, the things we address in our report."

The attorneys decided to back up and start from the beginning, asking how Ackman first became interested in Farmer Mac. Ackman explained that a friend and hedge fund manager, Whitney Tilson, mentioned the company to him. Farmer Mac's stock had been recommended to Tilson by Guy Spier, another investor with whom Tilson attended regular breakfast meetings at which money managers shared ideas. Tilson called Ackman and suggested he take a look at Farmer Mac. That evening Ackman stayed up until 4 a.m. going through the company's Securities and Exchange Commission (SEC) filings.

"If you go to the company's cash flow statement, it's a fairly extraordinary thing, which I had never seen before. Looking down the line items, you see that they borrowed $150 billion or so" over the course of one quarter, Ackman said. "It's a huge number relative to their balance sheet. What they're really doing is just recycling approximately every seven days their commercial paper." This constant reliance on rolling over short-term debt meant Farmer Mac had to be able to remarket half a trillion dollars of debt over the course of a year. This requires the market's absolute trust, Ackman explained, yet the company didn't even have a credit rating.

There was also the matter of management's disclosure about delinquent loans. The definition of a delinquent loan kept changing over time so that it became narrower, and consequently there were fewer to report, Ackman said. For instance, loans that were "in the process of collection" were at one point no longer considered delinquent. "I thought that was, candidly, an absurd concept," Ackman told the investigators.

After reading the financial statements, Ackman felt that the company was trying to create an impression for the reader that things were better than they really were. "This was the first stock I shorted in a very long time, but it was glaring, I thought," Ackman said.

"This is the most incredible opportunity I've ever seen," Tilson remembers Ackman saying, when they spoke again about Farmer Mac. Tilson told him he worried the stock might be trading at a steep multiple to earnings, but Ackman cut him off, clarifying the kind of bet he had in mind: "Not as a long, as a short!"

Ackman, Tilson, and Guy Spier decided to dig deeper. They took the train to Washington to meet with Farmer Mac executives, including chief executive officer Henry Edelman.

Pierre-Louis asked Ackman to describe his meeting. "What questions did you ask the chief executive officer and the chief financial officer during the meeting?"

Ackman recalled asking why the company hadn't sold any securities backed by farm mortgages. One of Farmer Mac's mandates was to create a secondary market for farm mortgages, the way Fannie Mae and Freddie Mac created a market for home mortgages by financing them through the bond market. "I asked, 'Is it because you have not been able to sell [the securities] in the market? Is it because you can no longer sell them at a profit?'"

"What was their answer?" Pierre-Louis asked.

"'Absolutely not!'" Ackman remembered both executives saying. "I remember it so well because they stood up in unison as they said it," he told her.

———

LATER THAT SUMMER, Whitney Tilson also was summoned to 120 Broadway to give his version of events. The *Wall Street Journal* had detailed Tilson's activities prominently in its January article about hedge funds ganging up on MBIA and Farmer Mac. It described how he attended the meeting at Farmer Mac, participated along with Ackman in a Farmer Mac conference call, and posted negative commentary on MBIA on a Web site.

Tilson began his July 29, 2003, testimony by describing his career history, which included Harvard Business School and stints working for nonprofits, including the Initiative for a Competitive Inner City and Teach for America.

Lead attorneys Marc Minor and Charles Caliendo then turned to Tilson's interest in Farmer Mac.

The tone of the questions soon became hostile.

"Is this group of friends that you referred to also known as 'the posse'?"

"That is my wife's name for us, yes."

"It has obviously caught on if it is your wife's name."

"She referred to it that way, and I thought it was cute, and I called it 'the posse.' Some other guys said 'Don't call it the posse.' There was quite a dispute over the name, the proper name or the appropriate name."

"Do you know or do you recall if MBIA was presented at a posse meeting as well?"

"I don't think it ever was."

"Do you know if Allied was presented at a posse meeting?"

"I don't believe so."

"Is David Einhorn a member of this group?"

"No."

"Mr. Berkowitz is not a member?"

"No. And Bill Ackman rarely came."

Attorney Marc Minor wanted to know if Tilson had ever worked for Bill Ackman or in any organization that Ackman ran or owned.

"The only time I have worked with him was when I first met him," Tilson said, referring to their time as undergraduates at Harvard. "We were hired for the summer to sell advertising in the *Let's Go* travel guides."

"And when exactly did you decide to take a short position in Farmer Mac?" Minor asked.

"Immediately after the meeting, the two of us said, 'Oh, my God, this is the biggest fraud we have ever seen in our lives.' Both of us had the identical reaction," Tilson said.

Later, when the questions turned to some handwritten notes on Farmer Mac that Tilson had provided to comply with a subpoena, Minor asked him to read a line from the notes.

"Constantly, debt comes due every week," Tilson read.

"What was it about that issue, do you recall, that was remarkable? What caused you to write it down?" The questions were delivered rapid-fire.

"Well, any financial institution that has to refinance its balance sheet every week is subject to imploding if [it] can't access the capital markets for that week. That is one of the risk factors I am identifying here for Farmer Mac."

"You stated that the debt coming due every week would be an issue for any company."

"Yes."

"Does it matter whether or not all the debt comes due each week?"

"Yes, very much."

"And if it were a portion of the debt that came due each week, how would you calibrate your concerns?"

"Well, if it is 1 percent of their debt, I wouldn't worry about it too much. If it is—you know—north of 50 percent, which, as I recall, is the case with Farmer Mac, it is a grave concern."

"You mentioned that these notes may have been taken in a subsequent conversation with someone else other than a meeting with the company," said Minor. "Who could those people have been?"

"Well, the most obvious candidate is Bill Ackman."

After a few hours, the tone of the questions was less aggressive. The attorneys seemed to be running through a checklist of issues. When

Tilson got up to leave, one of the attorneys asked him, "Are you really friends with Bill Ackman?"

"The idea seemed to create incredible cognitive dissonance for him," Tilson recalls.

———•———

WHEN ACKMAN RETURNED to the attorney general's office to talk about Farmer Mac, the tension rose again. The lawyers turned their attention to Ackman's comments in his research report on Farmer Mac, which suggested the company was funding long-term assets with high levels of short-term debt.

"Where are you getting your numbers to show what percent of the company's debt is short term?" Pierre-Louis wanted to know. "And how are you so sure the company's loans are, in fact, long term and illiquid? What would happen to your assumption if, in fact, these various assets— the investment securities, the Farmer Mac–guaranteed securities, and the loans—which you referred to, by definition, as illiquid and long term, were not, in fact . . . "

"If they were liquid and short term? Then I would be wrong," said Ackman.

"Then you would be wrong?"

"But they are not liquid and short term; they are illiquid and long term. Look at the filings, the company's public statements," Ackman said. "Look at the terms of the farm loans it carries on its books. They're not one-week loans."

Ackman's frustration was boiling over, leading Aaron Marcu to ask to take a break, but Pierre-Louis said no to that. "I am not done asking my questions."

"We are going to take a break," Marcu insisted.

Pierre-Louis was not happy. "Despite the fact we are in the middle . . . "

"I don't want to take a break," Ackman interjected.

"We are going to take a break," Marcu said.

"I don't want to," said Ackman.

"All right, fine," Marcu told him. "This is your life."

"What else can I tell you?" Ackman asked Pierre-Louis, sounding more composed.

They returned to the business of the 10-Qs and 10-Ks, trying to piece together how Ackman determined that Farmer Mac had a large percentage of long-term assets being financed with short-term debt.

Pierre-Louis wanted to know exactly how Ackman arrived at his number. Ackman said he'd need a copy of the Farmer Mac filing he'd used when putting together his report. Someone called for a calculator.

When Marcu jumped in with a suggestion, Pierre-Louis snapped at him, reminding Marcu not to make statements that could be seen as leading his client. Marcu couldn't let that one pass. "Perhaps you have noticed that Mr. Ackman does not follow my instructions much of the time," Marcu said. "It's below 1 percent; it's perhaps below zero percent."

"If my lawyer would be quiet, I would give my answer," Ackman said.

Pierre-Louis wanted to know about a type of financial guarantee Farmer Mac offered called a "long-term stand-by purchase commitment." Ackman had criticized the guarantee, saying it carried "the greatest risk with the least adequate compensation" of all of Farmer Mac's lines of business. Under the program, Farmer Mac promised to buy individual farm loans out of a pool of loans designated by a bank. The arrangement allowed the bank to hold loans on its balance sheet while transferring the future risk of default to Farmer Mac.

These obligations have a risk similar to CDOs, Ackman said. Midwestern farm banks have the same incentive as Wall Street firms to transfer their worst assets to someone else. The loans Farmer Mac is obligated to buy aren't newly issued loans, Ackman explained, but ones that have been around long enough for banks to figure out whether they're at risk of going bad. Banks then make the questionable loans subject to the Farmer Mac stand-by purchase commitment and can "put" or sell their loans to Farmer Mac at any time, not just if the loans default.

If the banks get nervous about Farmer Mac's financial position, Ackman said, they might exercise their put options en masse rather than risk losing the protection if Farmer Mac fails. That would leave Farmer Mac with the obligation to fund the purchase of a huge portfolio of loans in a short period of time. Without the resources to buy and hold the loans, Farmer Mac might be forced to sell the loans in a short period of time, leading to likely losses. "It wouldn't take much of a discount to wipe out Farmer Mac's equity," Ackman said. "That's how risk turns into catastrophe."

Also disturbing and worth noting, Ackman said, was that the program transferred risk from the Farm Credit Banks to Farmer Mac, even though the banks carry 10 times more capital than Farmer Mac. It isn't even clear that regulators approved Farmer Mac's expansion into this type of guarantee, Ackman said.

In one particularly prickly encounter, Waldman asked about Ackman's statement that Farmer Mac was not able to sell mortgage-backed securities. "If you're so sure that Farmer Mac has not sold securities to investors, then what about the prospectuses filed with the SEC?"

"I would love to see them," Ackman said.

"You did not see them when you did your research for your report?"

"Absolutely not. Where are they filed with the SEC? I would love to see them."

"Mr. Ackman . . . " Waldman interrupted.

"I know. You guys ask the questions."

"We ask . . . "

"I'm sorry," said Ackman. "I apologize."

"They were, in fact, filed with the SEC, Mr. Ackman, and those three prospectuses are available to the public, and the fact that you did not find them . . . "

Ackman cut Waldman off, finishing his sentence for him. "Is a crime?"

"Let's take a break," Waldman suggested. When they returned, Ackman broached the issue again, with less emotion. "With respect to the comments I just made, my question is if, in fact, there were three such sales and if, in fact, the prospectuses were filed and I didn't see them, is it a crime? I know you don't necessarily have to answer me, but I am just curious," Ackman said.

"Your curiosity is noted," Waldman said. They moved on to other matters.

ALTHOUGH REGULATORS didn't appear to be finding the criminal acts they were looking for, it was a stressful time. Ackman's wife, Karen, remembers the low point as the day Marcu passed along a message to Ackman from one of Spitzer's attorneys: "Tell him to pack his toothbrush because we're going to find something."

Ackman's plight drew sympathy. When a college friend, having read coverage of Gotham's problems in the newspaper, wrote to offer support, Ackman responded: "While it is a time-consuming process and I am not used to being perceived by anyone as having done something wrong, I have a clean conscience and am not afraid of any of the facts. Believe it or not, I actually enjoy testifying."

He had no shortage of opportunities to do so. In June 2003, Ackman headed to Washington for two days of testimony at the Securities and Exchange Commission, accompanied by Mark Stein, an attorney with Fried, Frank, Harris, Shriver & Jacobson.

The SEC sent Gotham Partners an informal inquiry that it later upgraded to a subpoena shortly after news broke that the hedge fund was being investigated by the New York attorney general's office. Eliot Spitzer had been setting the agenda for holding Wall Street accountable, and clearly the SEC didn't want to be left behind on this one.

"This is an investigation by the United States Securities and Exchange Commission entitled 'In The Matter of Gotham Partners Management Company, LLC,' to determine whether there have been violations of certain provisions of the Federal securities laws," the lead attorney told Ackman as questioning got under way in a windowless basement room at the SEC. Two attorneys and an accountant from the SEC were present.

Many of the questions were similar to those Ackman had been asked at 120 Broadway: Did he try to undermine confidence in Farmer Mac and MBIA? Did he exaggerate the possibility of losses? Did he try to create a liquidity crisis by saying the companies were vulnerable to one?

The SEC attorneys also were interested in Ackman's use of the still relatively obscure credit-default-swap market to place his bets against the companies.

"What was the notional amount of credit-default-swap contracts Gotham bought on Farmer Mac?" one attorney asked.

"Two hundred twenty-five million dollars," said Ackman.

"At what level did the fund start buying?"

"Fifty-five basis points," Ackman said. That meant Ackman could buy protection against default on $10 million of Farmer Mac default for $55,000 a year.

"At what level did you start selling?"

"Three hundred basis points," Ackman replied. That price indicated that the cost of buying protection on $10 million of debt had risen to $300,000 per year.

"And what caused you to take these profits?"

"I got a call from the head of the Merrill Lynch credit-default-swap desk begging me to take him out of the trade," Ackman said. "And I thought it was particularly ironic that they wanted to unwind, because

Merrill was one of [Farmer Mac's] underwriters and the biggest seller of their bonds."

"When did you buy the swaps?"

"Starting shortly after I stayed up until 4 a.m. reading the financial reports."

"Why was your report issued? What was your intent?"

"I wanted to shine sunlight on the problem," Ackman said. "My view was that if people were aware of the facts I knew about Farmer Mac, the stock would go down. We'd make money on our short position." At the same time, the report had the added benefit of "being good for America," Ackman explained. "I thought it was abusive that a government-sponsored enterprise was doing the things [it was] doing."

Already, his efforts had roused some action, Ackman pointed out. The Government Accountability Office (GAO) launched a review of Farmer Mac as a result of the reports and the *New York Times*'s coverage of the company. Officials from the GAO attended a five-hour meeting with employees from Gotham to discuss points raised in their research reports, Ackman said. The lead investigator phoned the next day and "effusively thanked me not only for coming down and presenting but also for all of the work that we did on Farmer Mac." Ackman told the SEC lawyers.

Officials at the GAO had initially suggested Gotham would be given an opportunity to comment on the government agency's report. "We are no longer being given that opportunity," Ackman added.

"Why is that?"

"I don't' know," said Ackman. "Because we're being investigated?"

"You're speculating?"

"Speculating, yes."

The SEC lawyers asked why Gotham sent its reports directly to the GAO.

"Frankly, we wanted the SEC to take a look at Farmer Mac, and we didn't have much success there," Ackman said. "So we broadened the mailing to send to anyone we thought would be relevant or interested."

Ackman said he believed the pressure he exerted on the company actually caused it to provide better disclosure. "Look at a side-by-side comparison of the company's recent quarterly filing with one filed two years ago and you can see the improvement," Ackman said. "Frankly, I think I should get an award from the SEC for improved disclosure at Farmer Mac."

The SEC attorneys did not comment on the suggestion.

"After this improvement in disclosure," the attorney asked, "would you change your investment strategy on Farmer Mac?"

"If I were still in business, I would short more. I have more conviction on the basis of the new disclosure."

"Who else did you talk to about the company?"

"The auditors," said Ackman. Farmer Mac had just changed its auditing firm to Deloitte & Touche, so Ackman took the opportunity to call them. The accountants told him they could only listen; they could not give feedback, Ackman explained. So he spent a few hours in a one-way conversation.

David Klafter, Gotham's general counsel, later dubbed the ensuing monologue with the auditing firm "the wind tunnel," an example of Ackman's ability to bombard someone with "torrents of ideas and explanations." The image it always conjures for Klafter is of the old Times Square billboard advertising Maxell cassette tapes, which showed a young man sitting in a large upholstered chair, bracing his arms against the arms of the chair while the sound flooded over him, blowing back his tie and hair. The auditors at Deloitte & Touche were hardly the only ones subjected to it. "He's incredibly passionate about his views, and he always has a mountain of evidence to back them up, so when he wants to explain something, you can feel like you're in a wind tunnel," Klafter says.

The SEC attorneys' questions moved on to a new topic: "Have you heard of a company called MBIA? How did you get interested in the company? What kind of research did you do?"

Ackman explained how he was drawn to look at other companies that were perceived to be low risk after his success with Farmer Mac. He got a trial subscription to Moody's Investors Service and printed out about 15,000 pages on structured finance and the bond-insurance business. He searched for articles and everything he could find on LexisNexis that mentioned the company, and he looked at regulatory filings. "This was one of those cases where the more work I did, the more confident I got," Ackman said. "The more people I spoke to, the more I learned, and the more conviction I had with respect to the investment."

The attorneys reviewed Ackman's trading records with him. "How many swap contracts did Gotham purchase on MBIA?"

"All told, $1.955 billion," Ackman said.

"That was 'billion'?"

"That is correct."

As the morning wore on, the room became increasingly hot. Several weeks earlier, David Einhorn had suffered in silence over the uncomfortable heat, assuming it was the SEC's way of sending him a not-too-subtle message. Ackman had no qualms about complaining. "It's getting a little warm in here," Ackman said, shortly after 10 a.m. "It started out cool. Is there any way to keep it cool?" The proceedings were halted for 15 minutes. When they resumed, Ackman had obtained a fan and water.

"Excuse me. I don't mean to be a pain about this," the court reporter said, "but when that fan's on, it's a little difficult to hear you." There was a short recess while the attorneys rearranged the fan and the chairs.

The SEC lawyers had just raised a question about a conversation between Ackman and one of his investors when Ackman interjected: "I apologize. I drank a little too much water. Can I just run to the men's room?"

"You want to take *another* break?" one of the SEC attorneys asked.

"It will take me literally two minutes," Ackman replied.

After lunch, the SEC attorneys turned on the air conditioning before questioning continued. Ackman described his frustration in trying to get answers about whether MBIA's guarantees of credit-default-swap contracts were legal, and how Fried Frank attorney Bonnie Steingart canceled her appearance at the New York State Insurance Department because partners in the firm's structured finance group didn't want to be in an adverse position with MBIA. He explained that Gotham tried numerous firms but had no luck finding an attorney willing to take on the issue. "We called around and we got the same answer pretty much everywhere," Ackman recalled.

During the second day of questioning, the SEC attorneys became less confrontational. They even sought Ackman's opinion on a few topics, including the credit-default-swap market.

"The problem with the credit-default-swap market," Ackman said, "is that banks often have more information than their counterparties. That means they're shifting risk to someone who knows less about the risk than they do." But when Gotham made an investment—including one in the credit-default-swap market—"we want to know more than anyone in the world can know based on the public information," Ackman explained. "And usually, by the way, most people don't read the stuff anyway," Ackman added. "So you've got a huge edge just by reading, right? And then if you really dig into something, you can really know more than the market."

Ackman had even surprised himself with the extent of his MBIA research. It wasn't until the law firm Covington & Burling sent him a photocopying bill to comply with the attorney general's subpoena that Ackman realized he'd read and marked up 140,000 pages of documents on MBIA, including financial statements, notes, and securitization reports.

He was determined not to let all that research to go waste. At any opening, Ackman tried to hammer at the importance of the issues he'd raised in the MBIA report.

The SEC might find it interesting, Ackman offered, that when he had talked to Alice Schroeder at Morgan Stanley she had told him that a rating-company downgrade of MBIA would have a significant impact on the capital markets.

"What does that mean?" one of the SEC attorneys asked. "A significant impact on the capital markets? What are you referring to?"

"Well, imagine a highly levered institution that for regulatory-capital purposes needs to hold only a small amount of capital against its triple-A exposures. What if people wake up one day and find out that MBIA is not really a triple-A-rated company and, in fact, it is insolvent," Ackman said. "That institution might have to put up more capital to meet its regulatory requirements, which could cause problems for them."

It was not a topic regulators were interested in pursuing on a June afternoon in 2003. But five years later, downgrades of bond insurers would create gaping holes in the balance sheets of financial institutions around the world.

During his testimony, Ackman kept returning to the issues he'd raised in the MBIA report. MBIA was an important topic for the SEC, he argued.

"In my experience looking at companies, where there is one cockroach, there are more. And I found plenty of cockroaches," Ackman insisted.

"I didn't find anything that was fraud . . . you know, where I found some fraudulent . . ." Ackman stammered for the first time in hours of testimony. "It was all aggressive accounting, disclosure."

He continued haltingly: "I just wanted . . . I don't want it to come out later. I just want you to know everything I know . . . about everything."

Ackman tried to engage the investigators in a discussion about the credit-rating companies. Given that the SEC was already looking at rating-company conflicts of interest, it ought to consider the glaring conflicts of interest created by bond insurer ratings, Ackman argued.

"Companies like Moody's make huge fees every time they rate a security backed by MBIA," Ackman said. "It's a fairly easy analysis given that the securities simply acquire MBIA's rating. For CDOs, the rating fees run about half a million dollars. This is a big, interesting topic."

"Yes. We might want to talk about that on another day," one of the attorneys said.

The investigation found nothing, yet it touched on just about every issue that would come back to haunt the financial system: too much leverage, too much trust in the triple-A rating, too little skepticism about credit-rating companies, and an unreasonable amount of complexity. Ackman revealed in his testimony that a company prohibited from writing CDS contracts was nonetheless writing billions of dollars of them. Regulators seemed to simply ignore the information. Hours spent debating the vagaries of MBIA's asset-backed commercial paper program failed to stir questions about the standards of a market deemed one of the safest places in the world to invest. The asset-backed commercial paper market collapsed in the summer of 2007, marking the beginning of the financial crisis.

Regulators never appeared to resolve why Ackman and MBIA could be so far apart on their estimates of the company's CDO losses. The next time serious questions were raised about super-senior CDO values, it was too late. By late 2007, confidence in one financial institution after another cratered on fears they weren't admitting the full extent of their losses, including those on massive portfolios of super-senior CDOs.

"Anything else before we end for the day?" the other attorney asked.

Ackman seized his chance. "It is worth remembering," Ackman said, "that every Wall Street firm does a huge amount of business with the bond insurers, including MBIA, Ambac, and FSA. Frankly, the fixed-income markets are what have saved investment-banking profits, because the IPO [initial public offering] market is basically gone. That means MBIA might just be the biggest business generator on Wall Street," Ackman added. "No one wants me to be right on MBIA."

The SEC attorneys told Ackman they'd be happy to hear his concerns about MBIA if he wanted to come back at a later date.

Of course, he wanted to come back, Ackman told his attorney, Stein. Ackman wanted the opportunity to make his case to the SEC that he was right and that MBIA would fail.

Stein didn't see it that way. "Drop it and go home," he told Ackman.

Chapter Nine

Turning the Tables

There is a saying from the Lakota Indians which goes: "You will be known forever by the tracks you leave behind."

—DAVID ELLIOTT, FORMER CHIEF EXECUTIVE OFFICER OF MBIA

B Y LATE SUMMER 2003, the New York attorney general's investigation of Gotham Partners went silent. Aaron Marcu, Gotham's outside counsel, had rejected the offer of a civil settlement with the attorney general's office earlier in the summer. "You just don't have it right. He's done nothing wrong," Marcu told Roger Waldman in Eliot Spitzer's office. Marcu offered to come in and review the report line by line with Waldman to show that Gotham had sources to support every assertion. Waldman never responded to Marcu's offer.

The attorney general's office typically doesn't announce when it is ending an investigation, leaving a lingering uncertainty in the minds of those investigated. "The classic advice you get from attorneys is to stay out of regulators' sight," says an individual who was involved in the Gotham investigation. The idea is to let some time pass and hope the regulators forget about you. "Going back into the den had to have been against any sane attorney's advice."

In fact, Marcu did advise Bill Ackman to let it be. "Twenty-five, maybe thirty times," Marcu remembers.

But Ackman was determined to get back in front of both the Securities and Exchange Commission (SEC) and the attorneys in Spitzer's office. To bolster his case, he set out to find a well-regarded accountant to support his arguments and lessen the skepticism he had encountered as a short seller. His first choice was Lynn Turner, the former SEC chief accountant who had recently joined the forensic accounting firm Kroll, Zolfo, Cooper as a senior adviser. Turner, who couldn't take on the assignment because it involved appearing before the SEC too soon after leaving the agency, recommended Roger Siefert, another accountant with the firm.

Ackman decided Siefert was the right choice after he read a report Siefert worked on as part of a team of court-appointed examiners in the bankruptcy of Spiegel, a Chicago-based mail-order company. Ackman found it to be a brilliant piece of forensic accounting and research that described how a 100-year-old company collapsed under the weight of subprime lending.

Under the heading of "accounting irregularities," the examiner's report described how Spiegel covered up its surging delinquency rates on its credit cards. A borrower who was six months delinquent on a $1,000 credit-card bill could be considered current again just by making one minimum payment. The company initially disclosed this unusual accounting treatment but later stopped mentioning it in its filings. The omission had a material impact on how investors viewed the performance of the loans, according to the examiner's report. Eventually the company stopped filing financial statements with the SEC altogether, and later it collapsed.

That MBIA had insured $840 million of bonds backed by Spiegel credit-card receivables piqued Ackman's interest all the more in the report.

Siefert clearly understood the complex world of securitization and how companies could use it to play games and hide underlying weaknesses. But he was reluctant to take the assignment with Ackman. He'd never done work for a short seller before. Besides, there wasn't much upside to taking on MBIA.

"MBIA is a powerful company, a scary company," Siefert remembers. "I wasn't sure I wanted to be in an adversarial position with [it]."

But Ackman persisted. "Spend 40 hours looking through the information [about MBIA]," Ackman told Siefert. "If at the end of the week you don't want to go forward, I'll pay you and we'll part friends."

Siefert agreed. He and another accountant with the firm, David Brain, arrived at Gotham's offices for the one-week review. Ackman had set up four folding tables piled with MBIA documents. In short order, Siefert was hooked.

The first issue that caught Siefert's attention was the company's reserving. Siefert had audited small-town savings-and-loan (S&L) associations early in his career. These institutions mostly made local mortgage loans, often with mortgage insurance attached. As a result, the S&Ls had a history of almost zero losses, and they reserved as if they expected the future to look much like the past. Then the industry was deregulated, and the S&Ls moved into riskier commercial finance. When Siefert said they needed to start reserving more, management would invariably insist, "But we've never taken losses." MBIA's situation was reminiscent of that of the S&Ls. The company was moving into a fundamentally different type of business by guaranteeing structured finance, yet it insisted on seeing its future as an extension of its past.

Something else caught his eye: MBIA's accounting treatment of its largest loss—the result of the 1998 bankruptcy filing by the Allegheny Health, Education, and Research Foundation (AHERF). MBIA did not take a loss in the third quarter of 1998 to reflect the expected claim; instead it bought reinsurance *after* the bankruptcy filing to offset the loss. The reinsurance contracts magically erased the loss. "My first reaction was, 'This really smells,'" Siefert remembers. "They're willing to do anything to protect the triple-A rating."

I HAD TRIED TO FOLLOW up on some of the issues in the Gotham report earlier in the year but had no luck. MBIA declined to comment. Ackman didn't return my calls. After reading about Gotham in the newspapers, I assumed charges were pending against Ackman.

Then I was assigned to do a story on MBIA in the fall of 2003. Jim Lebenthal, an MBIA director and the chairman of the municipal bond investment firm Lebenthal & Company, told me there is only one thing I really needed to know about bond insurance. "They don't insure anything that needs insuring," he explained. "That's the whole story of MBIA. Period."

That's not to say that there wasn't a benefit to bond insurance, MBIA's supporters insisted. By insuring a bond and stamping the triple-A credit rating on it, companies such as MBIA and Ambac turned the security into a kind of commodity that could be easily traded. No one needed to understand the credit fundamentals of a water-and-sewer authority in rural Ohio if the debt was insured. Hy Grossman, the legendary Standard & Poor's municipal bond analyst who made the fateful decision to suspend New York City's rating in 1975, once told a colleague, "The minute a bond is insured, it loses its identity."

What MBIA provided was not so much insurance, the argument went, but it was in the business of marketing triple-A ratings. To talk about the company experiencing material losses was to be naive about the real nature of the business.

When I asked an insurance analyst whether he thought the credit-rating companies would ever rethink MBIA's top rating, he was skeptical. "For Moody's or [Standard & Poor's] to put a bond insurer on negative watch (indicating a rating cut was being considered) could have extremely negative ramifications" for the entire bond-insurance business, said David Merkel with Hovde Capital Advisors in Washington, DC. "It's a bit of a confidence game."

The last time I had tried calling Ackman, back in January 2003, he wasn't talking to the press. When I called him again in the fall of 2003, he appeared to be on the offensive again. We met at his office, and he reviewed his arguments on the company. He told me he believed the Gotham investigation had concluded without finding that he had done anything wrong, but he couldn't be sure. For that reason, he didn't want to be quoted on MBIA, but he was happy to talk about it.

I asked him if he'd read about Student Finance Corporation, a company that securitized student loans made by truck-driving schools. Not surprisingly, he had.

MBIA insured hundreds of millions of dollars of the company's bonds. The program was successful for a while, then suddenly the loans were defaulting at a 70 percent rate. Student Finance Corporation filed for bankruptcy, leaving MBIA and another insurance company called Royal Indemnity Corporation to battle over who would pay off the bondholders.

How could the company expect to maintain zero losses while insuring bonds backed by loans on which 7 out of 10 borrowers defaulted? MBIA insisted that even though the deal had gone wrong, its insurance unit ultimately wouldn't suffer a loss. This was part of a broader view in the credit markets that bad lending could somehow be free from negative consequences. The deal was one of many that made reporting on MBIA such a fascinating intellectual challenge.

Ackman and I had found some common ground, and we began a conversation that continued for more than five years.

Years later, Ackman would court the press again. But for a long while he kept a low profile. This was not surprising. The general perception on Wall Street and among financial reporters was that he had tried to destabilize confidence in MBIA and that charges were pending against him.

The company encouraged that view. Whenever I called MBIA, press director Michael Ballinger immediately labeled my questions "short sellers' questions."

"That was in the Gotham report, no?" Ballinger would say. Then he'd remind me that the report and its author were under investigation. Because Ackman had covered just about every aspect of MBIA's business in the report, there wasn't much one could ask MBIA that the company considered fair game.

This line of defense only increased my interest in scrutinizing MBIA further. It was a version of the company's mantra that there was never "new news." "A marked enjoyment can be found in identifying self-serving belief and contrived nonsense," economist John Kenneth Galbraith once wrote. Listening to MBIA deflect criticism and discuss its carefully guarded "no loss" underwriting was actually quite fun.

If you knew where to look, new things were happening all the time. Ackman kept constant tabs on MBIA's Web site, particularly on a section where MBIA addressed frequently asked questions. Quarter by quarter and even day by day, the disclosure changed. Yet MBIA always sought to give the impression that nothing new ever happened in its business. MBIA was immune to surprises.

After every MBIA earnings call or press release, my phone would inevitably ring. "It's Bill!" Ackman would announce, with a slightly accusatory tone that seemed to say "There's something going on and you're missing it! But, rest assured, I've called to fill you in."

Aaron Marcu remembers the phone ringing one August evening in 2003. It was Ackman—on vacation in Italy—wanting to chat with Marcu about an article he'd come across in a bankruptcy law journal that he thought might relate to MBIA's involvement in the credit-default-swap market.

"Bill, it's 9 p.m. here," Marcu told him. "It must be 3 o'clock in the morning where you are."

"This is incredible stuff," Ackman said. "I can't put it down."

Here's a person, Marcu says, who seems to have gotten quite a few things in life right. "He's tall, good looking, rich. He has a great family, lives in an incredible apartment," Marcu says. "So what is he doing reading a bankruptcy treatise at 3 a.m. in the morning when he's on vacation in Tuscany?"

If MBIA executives had hoped that the investigation would cause Ackman to focus less on their company, they were wrong. With Gotham's main funds being wound down, Ackman was left with one active investment on which to concentrate his full attention—the short position in MBIA.

By the fall of 2003, Ackman was finalizing plans to launch a new investment firm with a $50 million commitment from Leucadia National Corporation. After Ackman's surprise encounter with the company's chairman Ian Cumming at the swimming pool in Las Ventanas in February 2003, the pair had lunch and discussed the idea of Leucadia staking Ackman's next venture. Under the deal they struck, Leucadia and Ackman would be partners in a newly created fund called Pershing Square, LP. Leucadia put up $50 million, and Ackman agreed not to take on new investors for two years.

Ackman began looking for analysts to build the fund's investment team. Scott Ferguson, a recent Harvard Business School graduate, began working out of Ackman's office on a trial run that fall. His assignments included analyzing Eastman Kodak Company and trying to get into MBIA's investor-day meeting up in Armonk.

Ferguson drove to MBIA headquarters, hoping to gain admittance to the meeting. "I didn't know what the hell the company did," Ferguson remembers. He figured sitting through a day of presentations would be a good way to find out. He made the drive up to Westchester on an October morning.

"I told them I was a Harvard Business School student doing some work on the company," Ferguson recalls. A woman sitting at a table outside the auditorium at MBIA's office building in Armonk asked Ferguson if his name was on the list. He said no, and after disappearing inside for a few minutes, she returned and told him he couldn't come in.

"I was just an innocuous-looking guy in a suit," shrugs Ferguson.

Though he was turned away, he got the job with Ackman anyway. It wasn't the last time Ferguson would be frustrated by Ackman's interest in MBIA. Shorting an arcane financial institution wasn't the sort of investment one learned about in business school, Ferguson says. And the position created hostility. But Ackman had no intention of dropping this one.

The fall of 2003 also brought vindication for Ackman. In September, a unanimous five-judge panel of the Appellate Division of the Supreme Court of New York overturned Judge Ramos's decision to halt First Union's merger with Gotham Golf, calling Ramos's decision in the case "disingenuous."

The ruling came too late to save the Gotham funds, Ackman wrote in a broadcast e-mail to Gotham's investors and other friends and associates. It provided a lesson about risk, however, which is that one should never risk a business on a situation with a large downside even if it appears that the chance of winning is nearly 100 percent. "Every once in a while, the roulette wheel comes up green," Ackman wrote. "The unthinkable and unimaginable happen more often than one expects."

Ackman also took satisfaction in reading the report by the Government Accountability Office (GAO) on Farmer Mac. The government watchdog's report shared the concerns Ackman raised in his three research reports on Farmer Mac. Many of the questions that had led to hours of tense debate at the attorney general's office were settled in a simple statement in the GAO report's conclusion: If Farmer Mac "were to undergo stressful economic conditions, it could face substantial funding liquidity risk," the report concluded.

There was no such feeling of closure with the MBIA position. "The more I look, the more I find," Ackman wrote in an e-mail to Cumming. MBIA was increasing its exposure by billions of dollars every week, Ackman told him. It couldn't be easy to find that many good risks, ones in which MBIA could price the risk below market and still make money. "All they need to do is to keep signing their name with the blessing of the rating agencies and they can refinance any broken credit and the cash just keeps pouring in," he wrote. "It will be years before anyone knows how the deals will perform."

"Keep going," Cumming wrote back. "You will eventually be seen as a prophet, but hopefully not as a prophet in rags railing against the wind!"

Ackman had explored every path to get the word out about MBIA. In the process, he'd given days of testimony about it. He'd talked to colleagues, investors, friends, Wall Street analysts, insurance regulators, attorneys, and reporters. He'd attempted to engage the heads of all three credit-rating companies. He'd cornered the chief executive officer (CEO) of MBIA's audit firm. Ackman's wife and other family members also were frequently subjected to his latest thoughts on the company.

Of all the responses he'd gotten to his arguments and presentations, his 5-year-old daughter's pleased him the most. "What is MBIA?" she finally asked him one night as he was reading her a bedtime story. Ackman launched into an explanation, describing MBIA as a company that wasn't what it appeared to be and explaining how no one would stand up to it and point out the obvious. The story seemed familiar to her. "It sounds like *The Emperor's New Clothes*," she concluded.

WITH THE HELP of Roger Siefert, Ackman drafted a letter to the Securities and Exchange Commission seeking a meeting to discuss MBIA. "The potential impact of the overstated credit quality of MBIA on market participants is substantial since MBIA guarantees a total of over $800 billion of such obligations," Ackman wrote. The exposure, he noted, is "growing by approximately $100 billion per year." The day after he sent the letter, Ackman got a call from Walton Kinsey, an attorney at the SEC. "When can you come down?" Kinsey asked.

On February 3, 2004, Ackman and Siefert traveled to Washington. Their appearance at the SEC drew a crowd: lawyers, accountants, an insurance expert, officials from the enforcement and corporate finance divisions. They distributed their presentation, which opened with the question, "How can this AAA-rated, S&P 500, governance-award-winning company have material and undiscovered false and misleading accounting, liquidity, and solvency risks?"

Ackman explained that the credit-rating companies were MBIA's de facto regulators, which created a serious conflict of interest. The company guaranteed 31,000 securities, almost all of which would have to be downgraded if MBIA lost its top rating. It would be a serious embarrassment for Moody's and S&P. "We jokingly refer to MBIA as the mañana company," Ackman had told the SEC when he'd testified, and now he had the chance to lay it all out. "Anything they can do to defer expenses or problems into the future, they do. Anything they can do to accelerate revenues into the present, they do. All this stuff is cumulative."

Ackman and Siefert took turns presenting their argument.

"There were audible gasps," Siefert remembers, when he told the group that he estimated that MBIA was under-reserved by more than $6 billion. How can that be right? the SEC lawyers demanded. The company had taken only $300 million of losses in 30 years of business. The idea that it needed to shore up reserves against losses by $6 billion was absurd.

Yet it easily could have been more than that. The $6 billion estimate was just a sliver—1.1 percent—of the company's outstanding guarantees, Siefert pointed out. The model was dangerous. The track record was deceptive, he told them.

Incentives, however, pushed management to take more risk. Despite the long-term nature of MBIA's guarantees—which meant it would be years before investors knew whether MBIA was reserving enough— the company had structured its executive compensation in a way that encouraged management to push the stock price higher in the short term. Jay Brown's compensation agreement called for stock options and restricted stock to vest if MBIA's stock price traded above $60 for 10 consecutive days. Just a few days before Ackman and Siefert's presentation to the SEC, the target was hit, an event worth more than $30 million to Brown.

Ackman and Siefert described for regulators the 1998 reinsurance transaction that allowed MBIA to avoid reporting a loss after AHERF filed for bankruptcy. It was deceptive, they argued. The accounting was wrong.

"How can you guys sit here and tell us that it was audited wrong?" one of the SEC lawyers asked Ackman and Siefert.

Either the auditors overlooked something or MBIA hadn't disclosed everything about the deal, Ackman responded.

"Who was the company's auditor?" another official wanted to know.

"PriceWaterhouseCoopers."

"Let's move on," someone else suggested.

The presentation lasted about five hours, running through lunch and well into the afternoon. Ackman left the SEC feeling optimistic.

———

ONCE BACK IN NEW YORK, Ackman continued to sell off the assets in Gotham's main funds. Ackman also worked out a deal with David

Berkowitz to assume nearly full ownership of Gotham Partners Management Company, the entity overseeing the liquidation. It was not a particularly valuable asset, bringing in a fee of just 1 percent of the fund's steadily dwindling assets, which was not enough to cover the wind-down costs.

The former partners struck a deal. Berkowitz agreed to accept a Gibson acoustic guitar, which originally cost about $1,000, in exchange for his stake in the management company. "He got a bargain," Ackman remembers.

And he didn't have to deal with Carl Icahn.

On April 16, 2004, Hallwood Realty Partners announced that it would be merging with another company and that the shareholders would be bought out for $137.91 a share, a substantial premium to the $80 per share Carl Icahn had paid Ackman. It looked to Ackman like the "schmuck insurance" was going to pay off.

Ackman called Icahn to congratulate him on the deal and to find out when Icahn would wire him $5 million, the amount Ackman believed his investors were entitled to under the schmuck insurance contract. Icahn told Ackman he was not getting anything because, in Icahn's opinion, the transaction didn't qualify as a sale.

Then the issue of MBIA came up. After Ackman had pitched Icahn on the idea of shorting the bond insurer, MBIA's shares had risen to around $62 from $36. Icahn later disclosed that he lost $70 million shorting companies, including MBIA, when he released marketing materials in early 2005 for a hedge fund called Icahn Partners.

According to Ackman, Icahn said that not only was he not going to pay him on Hallwood but also he was going to sue him over his losses on MBIA.

Icahn denies the assertion. "I pulled his ass out of the fire with Hallwood," Icahn says. "Instead of saying thank you, he sues me," Icahn remembers. "And then there's that goddamn MBIA." Icahn doesn't recall threatening Ackman with a lawsuit, though he remembers ending his conversation with Ackman by announcing, "I wish I'd never met you!"

In the end, Icahn says he made $40 million to $50 million by sticking with the MBIA short position, but it took a long time. "Look, I read the report. I found it interesting. I spent the whole evening reading the report, as I remember," Icahn says.

But the schmuck insurance has yet to be resolved. Ackman sued Icahn over the Hallwood deal in 2004, and it was still being litigated five years later. In June 2009, the judge in the Hallwood case ordered Icahn to post a $7.6 million bond following a judgment in Ackman's favor while Icahn appealed the ruling.

"He's a bit of a cry baby," Icahn says. "The irony is we could have been friends."

———

ACKMAN CONTINUED TO BUILD his investment team in the spring of 2004, when, ever on the lookout for talent, he met Jonathan Bernstein. Bernstein, a recent college graduate, was getting into a taxi on Park Avenue on a rainy evening, when he realized he'd jumped the queue in front of Ackman. "Sorry. This is your cab," Bernstein said. Ackman suggested they share it.

"I don't think I'd ever shared a taxi with someone I didn't know before," Bernstein remembers.

They got stuck in traffic, and Ackman asked Bernstein what he did for a living. Bernstein explained that he was about to accept a position working at Merrill Lynch analyzing financial institutions. They talked about banks and about Roger Lowenstein's biography of Warren Buffett, which both had recently read. Then Ackman asked Bernstein if he was single.

"I was a little taken aback," Bernstein says. "Here I am, trapped in the back of this taxi with this gray-haired man asking me if I'm single." It turned out that Bernstein was about to get invited to a party that Ackman and his wife throw every year for their single friends and relatives.

Bernstein accepted the invitation. Although he didn't find a romantic interest, he did land a job with Pershing Square, becoming the third member of its investment team.

Over at MBIA, changes were under way. Gary Dunton was made the company's chief executive officer while Jay Brown remained chairman of the board. Dunton, who graduated from Harvard Business School in the 1980s, had worked at Aetna Life & Casualty Company and USF&G Insurance before joining MBIA in 1998.

Business at MBIA was booming. In February 2004, MBIA reported a profit of $182 million for the fourth quarter of 2003, a 50 percent jump. The banner results were driven in part by a rise in demand for insurance on collateralized-debt obligations (CDOs).

———

BY THE SUMMER OF 2004, Ackman was losing patience with the SEC. Months had gone by since his meeting with the SEC staffers, and he hadn't heard back from them. Marty Peretz, the *New Republic* editor-in-chief and Ackman's longtime friend and investor, offered to write to SEC Chairman William Donaldson, with whom he was friendly.

"Dear Bill, I am writing to bring to your attention a company that is deserving of substantial SEC scrutiny that to date has appeared to escape the SEC's normally careful review process," Peretz wrote in a July 2004 letter to Donaldson. Peretz described Ackman's two-year effort to publicize problems at MBIA, including the initial report, the hiring of forensic accounting experts, Ackman and Siefert's 33-page letter to the SEC, and the five-hour presentation to a group of SEC officials in February 2004.

"It is Mr. Ackman's counsel's view that the SEC has not pursued Mr. Ackman's and [accounting firm] Kroll's allegations seriously, and may have dropped the matter entirely," Peretz wrote.

He continued: Ackman's research on Farmer Mac led to a GAO report recommending various changes to improve the company's liquidity, reduce its off-balance-sheet risk, and protect U.S. taxpayers from loss.

Whistleblowers should be taken seriously, even if they have something to gain from drawing attention to problems at a company, he wrote. "If Ackman's research on MBIA proves correct, the collapse of Enron will look like a corner grocery business by comparison."

Peretz's appeal stirred a response at the SEC, which asked Ackman to return to Washington on September 8, 2004. Ackman, Siefert, and Brain flew down to present their concerns again. As the day ended, Ackman remembers Kinsey asking, "If you had to give us one thing, one thing that's black and white, one thing that you could take before a judge and that he would understand, what would that be?"

"AHERF," Ackman said without hesitating. "It's buying insurance after your house burns down."

The day after their return appearance at the SEC, Siefert got a call from the SEC. They wanted to meet with the two accountants again, this time without Ackman. "They might have thought we were suffering from Patty Hearst syndrome," Siefert jokes, referring to the kidnapped newspaper heiress's apparent loyalty to her captors and willingness to break the law for them. Essentially, the SEC wanted to know whether the forensic accountants would tell the same story without Ackman present. They did.

ON NOVEMBER 18, 2004, MBIA announced that it had received subpoenas from the SEC and the New York attorney general's office. Within a few days, MBIA clarified that regulators wanted to know more about the AHERF reinsurance deal. In all the hours of testimony Ackman gave at the attorney general's office and at the SEC, he was asked almost nothing about his statement in the Gotham report that the AHERF transaction "was a loss-deferral, earnings-smoothing device." It appeared to Ackman that the regulators' questions largely came from MBIA. Ackman took the absence of questions about AHERF to mean that the subject was not something the company wanted the attorney general's office or the SEC delving into. Rereading the 1998 annual report, Ackman noticed MBIA's carefully worded discussion of the AHERF transaction, which gave the impression that MBIA was prepared for AHERF's bankruptcy filing.

"Though we had not experienced a major loss in nearly a quarter century of operation, our years of testing worst-case scenarios paid off," David Elliott, MBIA's CEO and chairman at the time of the AHERF loss, wrote in his letter to shareholders. "When a large issuer whose debt we insured filed for bankruptcy protection, reinsurance mitigated any impact on our earnings." Elliott was rewriting the company's history to make sure it didn't undermine the no-loss business model.

At the end of the 1998 letter, Elliott told shareholders that he was retiring, handing off the company to Jay Brown, a longtime board member, with the satisfaction and peace of mind of knowing MBIA was in good health. Ackman had underlined the next sentence: "There is a saying from the Lakota Indians which goes: 'You will be known forever by the tracks you leave behind.'"

Those tracks showed that MBIA had veered from the business of zero-loss underwriting and then strayed even further in trying to cover it up.

Chapter **10** *Ten*

Scrutiny

MBIA projects an image of financial health and rectitude. Woe to executives—and investors—if regulators prove it's a facade.

—JONATHAN LAING, *BARRON'S*, APRIL 2005

TWO YEARS AFTER BILL ACKMAN wrote to his investors that he would wind down Gotham Partners, he was signing up many of those same investors in a new fund. Leucadia National Corporation had agreed to let Ackman take on outside investors a year ahead of schedule. The Leucadia-only fund had returned 29 percent over the first three quarters of 2004. Many of Ackman's previous investors were eager to sign on again.

When the newly opened fund began operations on January 1, 2005, Ackman was far from Wall Street, angling for giant sea trout at a fishing lodge in Tierra del Fuego, at the southernmost tip of South America. He had bid for the stay at the Kau Tapen Lodge along the Rio Grande at a charity auction. The trip was a chance to celebrate the successful launch of his fund and to kick back—except that Ackman isn't very good at kicking back.

"He's so technical and inquisitive that he drove everyone crazy," remembers Oliver White, the fishing guide assigned to work with

Ackman. "It wasn't enough to know how something was done. He always wanted to know why—why is it done that way," White says.

For six days, Ackman and White, a philosophy graduate from the University of North Carolina at Chapel Hill, talked and fished. White explained technical details to Ackman about fly selection, casting the line, and luring the fish. Meanwhile, Ackman spotted the next member of Pershing Square's investment team.

"At the end of his stay, he asked me—no, he told me—I should come to New York and work for him," White says. It wasn't uncommon for guides to be offered jobs by visiting executives and entrepreneurs. Camaraderie was easily kindled while fishing. "But usually you could just tell it wasn't sincere," White recalls. This time it was. Several months later, White returned home to North Carolina and found a box had arrived from New York in his absence. It was from Ackman and filled with books: Graham and Dodd's *Security Analysis,* Peter Lynch's *One Up on Wall Street*, Benjamin Graham's *Intelligent Investor*, Lawrence Cunningham's *The Essays of Warren Buffett,* and Thornton O'glove's *Quality of Earnings*.

These were Ackman's favorite books on investing, and he wanted White to read them all. Ackman made his reputation on Wall Street as an activist investor, a high-profile role that requires a knack for showmanship. But those who know Ackman well say he is an analyst at heart.

"He is the smartest analyst I've ever met," says Rafael Mayer, managing director of Khronos LLC, a family office and fund of funds investor, and a friend of Ackman's. "He looks at something and he just decomposes it."

That process began with questions, lots of questions, including the one Ackman had badgered White with so many times while they were fishing: "Why?" It was also the question Ackman had tried to answer when he looked at the MBIA reinsurance transaction now being investigated by regulators. "Most investors have no clear conception of how companies can report earnings that are partially illusory; to them, numbers are numbers," O'glove wrote in his 1987 book. Meaningful analysis requires one to understand the quality of earnings numbers, he stressed. And the reason so few investors do this kind of work, he added, is that "such research is usually negative. Most investors would rather kill the messenger than think about the message."

SEVERAL WEEKS AFTER he returned from South America, Ackman, along with Marty Peretz, and Eliot Spitzer were huddled around a small table in the attorney general's office, eating pressed turkey sandwiches. Peretz had arranged the lunch meeting. Ackman wanted to point Spitzer toward the important issues at MBIA, including its use of bogus reinsurance in 1998.

This was an important transaction. It showed how MBIA could not tolerate the perception that it sometimes made mistakes. In fact, Ackman insisted, the bankruptcy filing of the Allegheny Health, Education, and Research Foundation (AHERF) threatened MBIA's zero-loss business model. As the hospital cracked under the weight of too much debt, its management raided charitable endowments it controlled for cash and propped up earnings by understating the amount of uncollectible hospital bills it carried on its books. In July 1998, when the city or any other government entity failed to come to its rescue, AHERF's Philadelphia subsidiaries filed for bankruptcy protection.

"We did not understand that while most hospitals are essential, not all hospitals are essential," Jay Brown had explained to Ackman in August 2002. MBIA's guarantee of hundreds of millions of dollars of hospital bonds had been a miscalculation, and it came back to bite the bond insurer at the worst possible time.

Russia had recently defaulted on more than $30 billion of debt and severed the ruble's link to the U.S. dollar. Asia's year-old currency crisis was morphing into political and social chaos in Indonesia and Malaysia. Long Term Capital Management, a hedge fund run by a team of Nobel Prize–winning mathematicians, was unraveling and threatening to take the financial system with it.

Almost immediately after the AHERF bankruptcy filing, MBIA sought to reassure investors by stating that it had $75 million of reserves that would be adequate to absorb the loss. Yet confidence in the bond insurer continued to falter that summer on a combination of AHERF concerns and the Asian financial crisis. For the first time, investors were asking whether MBIA's triple-A rating was at risk. MBIA's shares had been sinking all summer, dropping from a high of around $53 in April to $43 by late summer and then tumbling precipitously in early September.

On September 11, 1998, the company held a conference call to set the record straight. "I understand that we have exhausted the phone line capacity of the provider, and I think we have something like over

250 participants on this conference call," MBIA's then chairman and chief executive officer (CEO) David Elliott said.

Elliott told listeners that MBIA was in the process of making arrangements in the reinsurance market, which—at very little cost—would double its reserves, ensuring that even if the loss was larger than $75 million, the company could cover the loss and eliminate an impact on its earnings.

"We have an excellent track record," Elliott said. "And we intend to keep that track record." The stock ended the day more than 13 percent higher at $35.63.

The only problem, Ackman told Spitzer seven years later, was that MBIA didn't really use reinsurance. It borrowed the money to pay for the loss and accounted for it improperly as insurance.

Spitzer called in the head of his investor-protection unit, David Brown, to join them. A former Goldman Sachs attorney who attended Harvard Law School with Spitzer, Brown had coordinated his boss's assault on corrupt Wall Street research, improper trading by mutual funds, and kickbacks by insurance brokers. Brown seemed a bit stressed, Peretz recalls. "I had a dim foreboding that the attorney general's office couldn't confront another big scandal." But Brown heard Ackman out, starting with the AHERF deal.

Ackman took the attorneys through the particulars of the deal: Three reinsurers—AXA Re Finance S.A., Converium Reinsurance (North America) Incorporated, and Muenchener Rueckversicherung-Gesellschaft (Munich Re)—agreed to make a payment to MBIA of $170 million in the fall of 1998. In exchange, MBIA agreed to reinsure $45 billion of bonds with the three reinsurers in the future. Converium reimbursed MBIA $70 million and was promised reinsurance business for which MBIA would pay it $102 million in premiums. Munich Re and AXA Re reimbursed MBIA $50 million each under the same type of policy. AXA was promised $98 million in future premiums; Munich Re would receive $97 million.

The transactions allowed MBIA to net the gains on its reinsurance contracts against its future AHERF claims payments, erasing the loss from its earnings statement. The reinsurance allowed MBIA to meet analysts' expectations that it would earn $433 million in 1998 rather than report the first quarterly loss in its history.

"One simple question will enable you to determine whether reinsurance accounting is appropriate," Ackman wrote in a follow-up e-mail to the attorney general's office. "Ask the reinsurers whether they would have agreed to cover the $170 million in cash to MBIA to absorb the

AHERF loss without some kind of offsetting arrangement—verbal, written, or otherwise."

The answer would, of course, be no, Ackman wrote. The reinsurers took a $170 million cash loss the day they signed the AHERF reinsurance contract. "If you interview executives at Munich Re and they say that they would have agreed to cover the $170 million loss without a commitment of future premiums or some other form of reimbursement from MBIA, they are lying. The same, of course, holds true for the executives at the other reinsurers.

"Reinsurance of a known loss without some kind of payback is better known as a gift," Ackman wrote. "As you know, there is no free lunch on Wall Street."

The transaction, announced on September 29, 1998, solved all of the company's problems in one fell swoop—$170 million of reinsurance would cover the AHERF claim, allowing MBIA to avoid taking a loss and leaving its entire unallocated reserve intact for possible future claims.

Yet Ackman believed that the deal had created conflict behind the scenes. The company's chief financial officer, Julliette Tehrani, left her post 10 days after the September 11, 1998, conference call to become an adviser to Elliott. Then both executives left the company a few months later and Brown stepped into the role of chairman and chief executive. Ackman found the explanation for these changes unconvincing. "I would like a little time to do various pursuits that are crazy, I realize, to most people," Elliott told a reporter. "But I like to work outdoors—raking the leaves and mowing lawns—which I have had very little time to do."

Now, six years later, Ackman hoped regulators would get to the bottom of the story.

"I always suspect management is trying to hide something," O'glove wrote in the introduction to *Quality of Earnings*, one of the books Ackman sent Oliver White. "What is it they are trying to do cosmetically? I ask. And I start out by assuming the worst."

ON MARCH 8, 2005, MBIA announced that it would restate its financial results for the last seven years to account for one of the AHERF reinsurance contracts as a loan. MBIA did so because, based on an internal investigation, it appeared there might have been a side agreement made by an executive at MBIA to reassume almost all of the AHERF risk that was transferred to Converium Re. The other two contracts, covering $100 million of losses, were not restated. The next day, MBIA said federal prosecutors had joined the attorney general's office and SEC in seeking information about the reinsurance transactions.

Ackman returned to the attorney general's office several weeks later. He had more to tell about MBIA's disclosure, its accounting, and its derivatives business. He described the investment-management business as an abuse of its New York state–regulated insurance unit. MBIA Inc., the publicly traded holding company, sold securities that received a triple-A rating because they were guaranteed by MBIA's regulated insurance subsidiary. MBIA Inc. then invested the funds in higher-yielding securities, pocketing the difference between its cost of funding and the return on the securities, Ackman explained. The insurance unit would not offer guarantees to other companies to engage in this business because the risk was too high, he argued. In effect, Ackman said, the transaction was a disguised dividend from the insurance company to its parent company.

The story Ackman presented was complex. He was deconstructing MBIA's entire business, and regulators had no idea how to deal with that. Just getting everyone in the group up to speed on bond insurance was hugely time consuming, as one person involved in the MBIA investigation recalls. Insurance is mind-numbingly complicated even before one considers the municipal finance, asset-backed securities, collateralized-debt obligations, and credit-default swaps (CDSs) that made up MBIA's business. "Ackman," he says, "had been marinating in it."

"He comes across as very smart, with an unusually intense affect," explains the person who attended a number of Ackman's presentations. "He's leaning in, staring fixedly, talking for long periods of time. He's bright. And he knows he's bright."

At his best, Ackman had a way of making others in the room feel like they were as smart as he was. At his worst, he came across as the only one smart enough to get it. Then there was the sheer volume of information he presented. "He had a tendency to throw in everything including the kitchen sink," the person says.

———————

ON MARCH 30, 2005, MBIA received a second round of subpoenas from the Securities and Exchange Commission and the attorney general's office. Regulators wanted to know more about many of the issues Ackman had raised during their most recent meeting. They wanted more information on how the bond insurer accounted for advisory fees and determined how much to set aside as reserves against future possible losses. They wanted details about a company called Channel Reinsurance, which MBIA had set up to reinsure billions of its guarantees. The next day the stock tumbled $4.36 to $52.28, its biggest drop in more than two years.

Despite the investigation, the New York State Insurance Department allowed MBIA to take special dividends out of its insurance unit for the first time in its history. The dividends were approved in both the fourth quarter of 2004 and the first quarter of 2005. MBIA used the cash to buy back shares, helping to boost its share price. A few days after the announcement that it had received a second round of subpoenas, MBIA issued a press release saying it had purchased more than 3.4 million shares in the first quarter and planned to continue purchasing shares whenever market conditions permitted.

Although New York State insurance regulators clearly weren't worried about the creditworthiness of the company, the market was growing more skeptical. News of the regulatory investigation had pressured CDS spreads wider on both MBIA Inc. and its insurance unit. On April 26, it cost $55,000 a year to buy protection against a default on $10 million of MBIA debt compared with $33,000 to buy the same amount of protection on its largest competitor, Ambac Financial Group. In a letter during the last week of April, Ackman told Pershing's investors that the fund's short position on MBIA was its second most profitable investment during the first quarter of 2005.

The regulatory attention on MBIA generated lots of press, with articles appearing in the *New York Times* and the *Wall Street Journal*, and this time MBIA was on the defensive. *Fortune* magazine revisited the arguments Ackman made in his original report on MBIA. MBIA's chief executive officer, Gary Dunton, bristled at Ackman's criticism. "Think about what we do. We build infrastructure around the world. We enable countries to build markets. We do good. I don't know why anyone would question the legitimacy of this business," MBIA CEO Gary Dunton told *Fortune*'s Bethany McLean. "My mom says there are evil people out there," Dunton added.

The investment weekly *Barron's* wrote about MBIA after the firm received a second round of subpoenas. "MBIA projects an image of financial health and rectitude," columnist Jonathan Laing wrote. "Woe to executives—and investors—if regulators prove it's a facade."

Success inspired Ackman to try again with Moody's Investors Service. "Mr. Rutherfurd, two years ago we had an e-mail dialogue concerning a research report I wrote on MBIA," his message began. He explained that since his last contact with Rutherfurd, the Gotham investigation had ceased, MBIA had restated six years of earnings, and the bond insurer had received more subpoenas related to issues raised in the Gotham report. "It is clear that you did not take me seriously two years ago, I guess because of all of the negative publicity," Ackman wrote. "I would be willing to meet with you, your chief risk officer, and anyone you would like to attend such a meeting."

He received a one-line response: "Dear Mr. Ackman, I am retiring from Moody's and have forwarded your letter to my successor."

But in the early summer of 2005, Chris Mahoney, Moody's chief credit officer and vice chairman, contacted Ackman about setting up a meeting. Roger Siefert, the Kroll accountant, accompanied Ackman, along with Scott Ferguson and Jonathan Bernstein from Pershing's investment team, to Moody's downtown office.

"It was the first time that a third party had come in and lobbied for a rating downgrade," says a person who attended some of Moody's many subsequent meetings with Ackman. "It was unprecedented." And in many ways, it was unappreciated. "He made so much noise, ran it as high up the org chart as he could. So we said, 'Okay. Let's just humor him,'" the person recalls.

Ackman delivered what was becoming a well-practiced monologue. He talked about MBIA's move into insuring structured finance, what he described as MBIA's misleading track record of losses, and its unique vulnerability to a downgrade because it relied on its triple-A ratings to survive.

One of the Moody's analysts stopped him there. If the bond insurer were threatened with a downgrade, then it could go out and raise more capital, he said. Ackman disagreed. The need for capital would undermine management's and the business model's credibility, Ackman said. No one would want to put money into a company that had just proven its business model was broken, he added.

"Well, there's no way they could survive a downgrade," one of the Moody's analysts said.

"Wait a second. You don't mean that," said Moody's chief credit officer Mahoney.

"How can a company that would go out of business if it lost its triple-A rating be triple-A rated?" Ackman asked Mahoney.

Mahoney agreed that it couldn't. "That would make no sense," he said. "We wouldn't rate a company triple-A that couldn't withstand a downgrade."

"It was a little victory, and there weren't many victories with Moody's," Bernstein says. Siefert remembers the comment, too. It was a moment when he thought someone at Moody's saw the huge paradox of a company being triple-A rated even though the only thing that stood between the company and its collapse was a triple-A rating.

And maintaining that triple-A rating was only going to get harder. Ackman noted that MBIA faced a nearly impossible task of increasing its earnings and guarantees without venturing into riskier lines of business. In fact, the company had already stumbled. That's why MBIA engaged in the AHERF transaction and others that helped it bury losses. "Management integrity has been compromised to uphold the 'no-loss illusion,'" he said.

Chapter Eleven

The Black Hole

We're losing our shirts. That's what's going on.

—CHRISTOPHER TILLEY, MBIA EXECUTIVE, 1998

I N THE SPRING OF 2005, as the Securities and Exchange Commission (SEC) and the New York attorney general's office were investigating MBIA's handling of its largest loss, Bill Ackman had moved on to the company's second-largest loss.

What made this loss particularly intriguing was that the bonds had been issued not by a municipality or a Wall Street firm, but by an MBIA-owned company called Capital Asset Research Management. The firm purchased past-due tax bills from cities and counties at a discount and then tried to collect on the debts. These tax certificates also gave holders the right to collect interest and penalties and, if the debt went unpaid, to foreclose on the property. The plan had been for Capital Asset to purchase tax liens and use them as collateral to back bonds. MBIA would then insure the bonds.

But Capital Asset ran into problems. In late 1998, MBIA bought out the company's founder and part-owner Richard Heitmeyer. MBIA said it saw great prospects for Capital Asset, but less than a year later MBIA took a $102 million charge to write down its stake in the tax lien company and exit the business. Capital Asset sold three bond issues backed by tax liens and guaranteed by MBIA before the business was shuttered. By the spring of 2005, MBIA's insurance unit had set aside $100 million to pay expected claims on those bonds.

Ackman had obtained a copy of a letter Heitmeyer wrote to MBIA's chief executive officer (CEO) Jay Brown in 1999. Ackman suggested I call Heitmeyer. When I did, he was eager to tell his story about Capital Asset and faxed me the letter.

"I thought we should open the lines of communication directly between the two of us," Heitmeyer wrote in the August 1999 letter. "Unfortunately, your president's latest announcements that the losses attributable to Capital Asset are 'one-time' in nature and 'represent management's best estimate of its cost of exiting the business' are at best inaccurate and more than likely could be construed as deliberately misleading.

"The troubling aspect of this situation," the letter continued, "is not the sheer magnitude of risk for MBIA—albeit a significant sum—but the fact that MBIA's management appears to have failed to adhere to its zero-loss underwriting standards.

"Even more troubling is that the company may have made this transition without informing shareholders, regulators, auditors, creditors, or even the rating agencies," Heitmeyer continued. "In fact, it appears that senior management may have gone to great lengths to conceal and disguise its exposure to Capital Asset and the tax lien industry as a whole."

Lehman Brothers had been lending Capital Asset hundreds of millions of dollars so it could purchase tax liens, Heitmeyer explained. The loan, which gave Lehman a claim on Capital Assets' tax-lien portfolio, was called a "warehouse line of credit," and it provided short-term financing for the tax liens until they could be bundled together and financed for the long term through the sale of asset-backed bonds. It appeared to be a relatively low-risk way for Lehman to lend money because the bank could always sell the assets to recover on its loan.

As added protection, Lehman asked MBIA to absorb the first losses on the warehouse line in the event the tax certificates fell in value before they could be securitized. Starting in 1997, Lehman had gradually increased the percentage of losses it expected MBIA to cover. Eventually, Lehman became so concerned about the value of the tax certificates that it demanded to be fully paid back on the warehouse line by the end of 1998.

"Throughout MBIA's required disclosure documents, no mention is made regarding this unique, substantial, and deteriorating relationship with Capital Asset and Lehman," Heitmeyer said in his letter to Brown.

Brown wrote back to Heitmeyer, saying he would look into the matter, but it was the last Heitmeyer heard from MBIA.

When I called MBIA to ask about Heitmeyer's letter, MBIA press director Michael Ballinger told me that the company had looked into Heitmeyer's allegations years earlier and found nothing of substance. Furthermore, Heitmeyer was a disgruntled former business partner whose accusations should be taken in that context. As always, Ballinger insisted "this is not new news."

When I called Heitmeyer back, he dropped a bombshell. "If you don't believe me," Heitmeyer said, "watch the videotape."

The videotape of Capital Asset's September 24, 1998, board meeting arrived in the mail several days later. Gary Dunton, who would later become MBIA's chief executive officer; Chris Tilley, the MBIA executive who oversaw Capital Asset; and Richard Weill, MBIA's vice chairman, had flown in from New York for the meeting at Capital Asset's offices in West Palm Beach, Florida. They took seats around a conference table along with Heitmeyer, several Capital Asset employees, and Matthew Poiset, an independent board member.

It was clear Capital Asset was careening toward a crisis. Lehman Brothers had informed MBIA it was pulling the warehouse line of credit at the end of the year. There was no way the tax liens could be converted into cash in time to repay Lehman. Tempers flared.

During a break in the meeting, Poiset stopped Tilley as he was leaving the room. He wanted to know if Tilley could explain the obvious tension between Heitmeyer and the MBIA executives.

"Is the tape recorder still running?" Tilley asked. They checked the recorder in the center of the table and saw that it was off. What they didn't realize was that everything taking place in the room was being picked up on a closed-circuit camera.

"We're losing our shirts. That's what's going on," Tilley said with exasperation.

Dunton laid it out in more detail: MBIA had lent Capital Asset nearly $100 million in subordinated debt to fund its tax-lien portfolio; it had guaranteed the first 25 percent of losses on Lehman's $400 million line of credit; and it had insured more than $250 million of bonds backed by Capital Asset liens.

"So you've got close to $500 million of exposure to them," Poiset said with astonishment.

"So if you think we don't have the best interests of the company in mind," Dunton snapped, "you are sorely mistaken."

When the meeting resumed and the tape recorder was turned on again, Poiset brought up Dunton's figures, this time for the whole board to hear. "MBIA has gotten incredible exposure," Poiset said. "Close to $500 million."

The statement appeared to rattle Dunton, who pushed his chair back from the table suddenly as if he'd been punched in the stomach.

"I don't know that anyone knows what the level of exposure [is] here," Poiset said.

MBIA's predicament offers a cautionary tale about the risks of securitization. Securitization is all about transferring risk from the original lender to a group of bondholders. But the process is not seamless. Millions of dollars of loans have to be aggregated—typically via warehouse lines of credit—before there are enough loans to create asset-backed securities with a face value of $50 million or more. The size of a loan portfolio can dwarf the balance sheet of the loan originator. If the value of the assets falls far enough, the lender will often require the loan originator to make up the shortfall. This demand can open up a sinkhole in a company's balance sheet as the company is suddenly forced to assume huge liabilities. These sinkholes would swallow scores of mortgage originators beginning in 2007 as the value of subprime mortgages collapsed and banks asked the companies to offset the loss in value.

As the meeting progressed, it was clear that the ground was beginning to give way beneath MBIA.

Dunton responded: "The whole issue is obviously to get as much off-balance-sheet, get as much senior warehouse paid down as possible. It's obviously the key objective."

The way to do that was by securitizing the liens: selling the tax liens to a special-purpose vehicle (SPV) and having the SPV sell debt to fund the purchase. An outside adviser joined the meeting and told the Capital Asset board members that several Wall Street firms had expressed interest in underwriting such a deal. The problem was they were all looking to MBIA to provide a guarantee on the bonds.

The MBIA executives balked. "Just so you understand, our franchise is not to take first losses," Dunton explained. "That's how we keep our triple-A rating. Our franchise is insured against Armageddon."

"Zero losses," Poiset said.

"Right, zero losses," Weill said.

And it looked like this portfolio of tax liens contained some losses. The company had tried to sell some of its New Jersey tax liens, but the results had been disappointing. "I've got an analysis of it, but I understand that the pricing on it is ludicrous," Gary Dunton told the group.

"Two cents on the dollar," Heitmeyer interjected.

"No, I think it was 19 [cents on the dollar]," said Dunton. "I mean, it's just not where it should be."

MBIA needed to decrease its exposure to Capital Asset's tax liens, Weill explained. It had no intention of getting in any deeper.

"We try to be a certain kind of company. And these kinds of situations stress all of that," Weill said. "And the difficulty is that it's very hard to be a triple-A company. Incredibly hard to keep a triple-A. Frankly, you found a way to stress us at levels that really stress us."

The group agreed they would do whatever was necessary to arrange financing for the tax liens. There had to be a way to sell the bonds without MBIA insurance. For now, though, there were more immediate problems. A hurricane was barreling up the coast, and the MBIA executives had to get to the airport. "I love coming to town in a hurricane," Weill joked. "Sometimes these things just blow over," Dunton said, as the executives grabbed their briefcases and disappeared from the videotape.

In the summer of 1999, MBIA announced that it was getting out of the tax-lien business and sold a final bond issue. It was privately placed and never rated. Inside the company, the transaction was known as the "Caulis Negris" deal, and it caused MBIA's Capital Asset problems to vanish from sight.

THE STORY WAS INTRIGUING because it opened another front on MBIA's no-loss business model. It showed that MBIA's problems in 1998 went beyond a bankrupt hospital. The Capital Asset fiasco also offered a revealing look at how the securitization market worked, and how it could break down. Securitization was billed as a highly formulaic process in which securities were carefully manufactured to spec. Who would have thought that desperation was sometimes one of the key inputs to the equation?

I pitched the idea of the story to the *Wall Street Journal*, which sometimes picked up my stories from Dow Jones Newswires, and an editor seemed interested. The first and most obvious question was, what did "Caulis Negris" mean? Professor Frank Mantello, chair of the Greek and Latin Department at the Catholic University of America, responded to my e-mail query: "With 'caulis,' you may have one of the inflected forms of 'caulae.' The Latin adjective 'niger, nigra, nigrum' means 'black,' or 'dark.' In combination, 'caulae nigrae' (black hole) would be the correct nominative case form, and the one that might be used in an English context." Even if technically incorrect, it was close enough.

I also contacted everyone on MBIA's audit committee at the time of the Caulis Negris transaction and asked: "As a member of MBIA's audit committee, perhaps you can shed some light for me on how well informed MBIA's board was kept regarding the company's involvement with Capital Asset?"

Only one responded: James Lebenthal, who headed up the family-owned municipal bond brokerage Lebenthal & Company. "I heard about growing losses," he said, "but I can't speak for the committee."

"But wasn't this a big topic?" I asked. "The company faced a huge liability. Weren't there serious concerns about the solvency of the holding company? About shifting the liability to the insurance company? What about the name Caulis Negris? Didn't that raise concerns?"

"I can understand giving unpleasant subjects unpleasant names, but I don't know if you go to jail for that," he responded.

My final call was to MBIA. The company had dodged my questions on Capital Asset for days. But when Michael Ballinger realized that the story would appear in the *Wall Street Journal* and a *Journal* reporter, Mark Whitehouse, was also working on the story, he arranged a call.

Ballinger put the company's general counsel and chief financial officer on the phone. Whitehouse and I were given only a few minutes to speak with MBIA's chief financial officer Nicholas Ferreri while MBIA's general counsel listened in. Ferreri assured us that the transaction was properly disclosed and that the company couldn't have foreseen that the bonds would create losses for their insurance company. When I made one last attempt to ask a question, Ballinger insisted that the executives were late for another meeting. "Wait, there's something I still don't understand," I said.

But Ferreri cut me off: "We know you don't understand, Christine." The comment hung in the air for a few seconds, and I wondered if it would give Mark Whitehouse pause. The story was complex. It involved events going back seven years. Heitmeyer had been involved in a legal dispute with MBIA. The facts were indisputable, and the story ran.

The article described how a former business partner had come forward with a videotape showing that MBIA, already under investigation for improper accounting in 1998, failed to disclose additional risks it faced that year. Those risks had been transferred to MBIA's insurance company using a transaction called "Black Hole."

Yet MBIA's stock ended the day up nearly $1 at $55.74. It was the type of story one would expect to cause a drop in the share price. Or, if the market dismissed the story as untrue or irrelevant, the stock price should have been unchanged. But a sharp rise?

MBIA later disclosed that it bought 6 million shares during the first half of the year. I do not know if MBIA bought shares the day my story ran, but the shares had a habit of rising almost anytime there was negative news on the company.

The rise in the shares certainly won me no points with my editors. Even Ackman cooled on speaking with me for a while. For financial reporters, the stock market is the instant arbiter of good journalism.

Nevertheless, the article prompted the SEC to call Heitmeyer, who had waited years to tell his story. The first time Heitmeyer considered going public about Capital Asset was a few months after the September 24, 1998, board meeting. He had drafted a press release detailing the problems at Capital Asset and described how MBIA failed to disclose its $500 million exposure to Capital Asset and how management misled investors about that exposure during a conference call.

But Heitmeyer never issued the press release. On a Sunday morning in December 1998, as he sat on the veranda of his house in Admiral's Cove, a gated community in Jupiter, Florida, he was alerted by the security guard that he had visitors. Three lawyers who had been advising him on the sale of his Capital Asset stake to MBIA were waiting at the gate.

"You can't go ahead with the press release," one of the attorneys told him when they'd settled back on the veranda. What if revelations in the press release caused MBIA to get downgraded? The attorney answered his own question: Investors might start liquidating MBIA-insured debt, and pension plans and retirees could lose huge amounts of money on bonds they thought were triple-A rated. The financial markets, only recently recovered from the upheaval caused by the failure of Long Term Capital Management, could be thrown into turmoil again.

They were silent for a few minutes, looking out over the tranquil waterway that winds through Admiral's Cove and to the nature reserve beyond. "You're going to go down in the history books," another of the lawyers suggested. "You'll be as well known as Lee Harvey Oswald. You're going to cause a major collapse."

Then one of the attorneys cautioned that if Heitmeyer did go public, he should have 24-hour security.

"Don't give me that shit," Heitmeyer said, laughing off the suggestion. "Nobody is going to kill me."

But the conversation rattled Heitmeyer more than he realized. Less than a week later, after returning from an evening out, he absent-mindedly tried to put his key into the wrong lock on his front door. His first thought was that something had been jammed into the keyhole. He feared someone had been trying to break into the house. Next thing he knew, he had triggered the burglar alarm and alerted the Admiral's Cove crack security detail. Within minutes, he was surrounded by security guards with snarling German shepherds and guns. He decided to take his lawyers' advice and drop the idea of the press release.

Seven years after that unsettling evening, Heitmeyer arrived at the SEC to discuss MBIA's dealings with Capital Asset. "Gentlemen, do you realize the magnitude here?" Heitmeyer began. "This company has tentacles that go all over the place. You can only imagine what happens if they're downgraded." Regulators needed to look into the Caulis Negris deal, he told them. The final securitization of Capital Asset's tax liens was a fraud, he said. "If they can do this, anyone can."

Heitmeyer's talk with the SEC lasted into the late afternoon. The SEC attorneys called a car to take him back to the airport. While they waited for it, Heitmeyer told them, "Call me anytime. Call me at 3 o'clock in the morning if there's something you don't understand." But they never called.

Heitmeyer did, however, hear from Ackman, who called to request a copy of the Capital Asset board meeting tape and several other documents. Ackman used them to compose a 29-page letter to the New York attorney general, the SEC, the U.S. attorney's office, and the New York State Insurance Department.

In light of the problems at Capital Asset, the losses at the Allegheny Health, Education, and Research Foundation (AHERF) were even more dire, Ackman explained in the letter. "Consider that management's lies [about Capital Asset] were contemporaneous with their public statements and SEC filings that said that the company's unallocated loss reserves, of approximately $78 million, were sufficient to cover all of the losses from AHERF. It was only 18 days later that the company announced the AHERF retroactive reinsurance transaction, which the company recently partially restated when it acknowledged a previously undisclosed verbal side agreement." The company had been dishonest about both problems, Ackman concluded.

"In the September 11, 1998, MBIA investor conference call, which occurred only 13 days before the Capital Asset board meeting, management misleads investors not only about Capital Asset but also about the AHERF transaction," Ackman pointed out.

During that same call—with more than 250 people listening in to get an update on MBIA's financial condition—executives were asked about MBIA's exposure to Capital Asset and several other businesses it had recently acquired, including any insurance guarantees extended as part of the investment.

"I would not characterize what we are doing as being aggressive," David Elliott, MBIA's chairman and CEO, said before handing the question off to Gary Dunton, who became CEO six years later.

Dunton laid out the numbers: MBIA had invested about $40 million in equity in the four companies that made up MuniServices, including Capital Asset. Total financing to all the companies was "something in the order of $100 million or so in financing of one type or another." The number fell far short of the $450 million exposure that Dunton had revealed to Poiset during the board meeting only days earlier.

"On the conference call, both Dunton and then-Chairman and CEO David Elliott obfuscate and outright lie about the facts," Ackman wrote.

If Dunton had answered the question about Capital Asset honestly, the stock would have plunged, and the rating companies likely would have put MBIA on credit watch or downgraded the credit rating, Ackman wrote. Rather than disclose its exposure, MBIA securitized it. "In the third quarter of 1999, MBIA securitized the remaining tax liens using an inflated value," Ackman wrote. The liens "were sold in a securitization issued by an entity called 'Caulis Negris, LLC,' an entity named after a flawed Latin translation for 'black hole,' that is, a place where you might hide something that you hope no one will ever find."

Ackman waited for the boom to fall. It didn't.

He attempted to meet with MBIA's audit committee to discuss Capital Asset. But the committee's counsel rejected the offer, saying the audit committee members did not want to meet with Ackman because it could create the appearance of giving credence to his views.

"I assure you that if the audit committee is willing to meet with Pershing Square and its representatives, the only inference that will be drawn is that the audit committee is truly interested in understanding and evaluating the facts," Stephen Fraidin, a legal adviser to Pershing Square and an investor in the fund, wrote. The audit committee proposed that Ackman meet with their lawyers and lawyers representing MBIA. But they had reached a stalemate. Ackman would not meet with MBIA attorneys, and the audit committee would not meet with a short seller.

Ackman did manage to get another meeting at Moody's Investors Service, and he ran through a lengthy presentation on MBIA and Capital Asset. But the rating company remained silent about the issue.

Ackman grew increasingly frustrated. He sent a steady stream of e-mails to Chris Mahoney at Moody's.

"In the rating agency congressional hearings that took place after Enron, a number of your colleagues testified to Congress about why Moody's missed downgrading Enron," Ackman began one late-night e-mail. "If and when MBIA blows up, and it will—it is simply a matter of time in my opinion—Moody's representatives will again be dragged into a congressional hearing. Moody's will not be able to say that it was unaware of what was going on at MBIA. That it was misled. It is no longer true that you don't have the facts. You have the facts you need and you have the ability to get more than we have been able to dig up."

"I apologize for putting you and Moody's on the spot," Ackman concluded. "I have simply lost patience, and it is 2 in the morning."

Then, on August 11, 2005, the *Wall Street Journal* reported that Spitzer and the SEC were drafting a civil complaint in anticipation of reaching a settlement with MBIA on AHERF. MBIA's stock started the day at $57.71 and shot higher on the news, closing at $60.55. "A resolution appears close," Deutsche Bank analyst Darin Arita wrote in a research report the same day. "Should the civil settlement be limited to the items already discussed, we believe the rating agencies are likely to reaffirm the ratings."

On August 15, 2005, Ackman pounded out a nine-page e-mail to Mahoney, insisting that the rating company was risking its credibility by continuing to assign a triple-A rating to MBIA. "Every day that Moody's holds off on acting, its exposure to this situation grows," Ackman wrote. "I know that you would probably prefer that [the] whole situation just disappear, but I assure you that it will not. I understand the reluctance to react and to wait for a regulator or someone else to go first. I believe that you have all the information you need for MBIA to be downgraded or at a minimum to be on credit watch, yet so far Moody's has failed to act. As far as the world knows, Moody's believes MBIA is squeaky clean and rock solid financially."

On August 19, 2005, MBIA announced that it had received a notice from the SEC that indicated the staff was considering bringing a civil injunction against the company over the AHERF transaction. The following Monday, Moody's weighed in, saying it didn't plan to take any rating action on MBIA. The SEC appeared to be interested only in the AHERF transaction and that had occurred under different management, the rating company asserted. MBIA's stock gained 10 cents to close at $58.55 on the news.

"No big surprise here," wrote Jim Chanos, who runs the hedge fund Kynikos Associates, in an e-mail that was forwarded to Ackman by a mutual friend. Chanos poked fun at Moody's complacency with a headline of his own: "MBIA Execs Found Poisoning Nation's Water Supply— Rating Agencies See No Reason for Downgrade."

It looked as if regulators might just let the issue of Capital Asset drop, even though they'd been provided with a detailed road map and a videotape. "This example of misconduct is clearer than the others," one of Ackman's investors wrote him in an e-mail message after Moody's affirmed MBIA's rating. "Seems hard to understand how they can remain uninterested, but I guess the regulators are more interested in stability than controversy when it comes to the biggest insurer of munis."

Rafael Mayer at Khronos LLC frequently spoke with Ackman about his sleuthing into MBIA. In hindsight, Mayer says, the Capital Asset fiasco was a warning to the capital markets. How could MBIA have assumed responsibility for providing hundreds of millions of dollars of financing without threatening its credit rating? What sense of complete invulnerability allowed a triple-A-rated company to dub an SPV "Black Hole"? How could regulators have shrugged off the potential conflicts behind the deal? Much of the story was actually captured on videotape. But how often did these types of deals go on behind the scenes?

"Many people will say that it was through Bill and MBIA that they started to come face to face with the messes that Wall Street was making," says Mayer.

Chapter Twelve

The Court of Public Opinion

You're asking me to speculate on the divinity of the emperor [MBIA]. The emperor is divine.

—JAMES A. LEBENTHAL, CHAIRMAN EMERITUS OF LEBENTHAL & COMPANY, 2005

I N THE FALL OF 2005, Oliver White arrived at Pershing Square. He had spent the summer working as a fishing guide in Jackson Hole, Wyoming, and reading the investment books Bill Ackman had sent him. White had also searched the Internet for information about Ackman. Most of what he found was from the Gotham Partners era: the investigation, the pump-and-dump allegations, the suggestions of market manipulation. "It was all about how bad Gotham was," White says. "I chose to go anyway. He was different from the person I was reading about."

The first thing Ackman did after White arrived was drop the report *Is MBIA Triple-A?* on White's desk. "Bill never doubted that he could possibly be wrong," White recalls. "It was never that [MBIA's] stock was going to go down and we were going to make money that way. It was that the whole business model was going to come apart."

Not everyone at Pershing Square was so convinced. Other members of the investment team weren't as eager to talk about MBIA as they were about some of the fund's other positions. Often, when White followed up with someone in the office about some MBIA issue Ackman had raised in a meeting, he was told, "Look, it just doesn't matter."

Members of the investment team believed Ackman was right about the company, but the problem was that the market just didn't care. Unless the market reacted, Pershing Square's investment in MBIA credit-default swaps would be a drag on performance.

By all indications, that drag was going to continue. On November 2, 2005, the *Wall Street Journal* reported that an MBIA settlement with regulators was expected by the end of the week. According to unnamed sources, the bond insurer would pay less than $100 million to settle the probe into its handling of losses related to the Allegheny Health, Education, and Research Foundation (AHERF), wrapping up the year-long inquiry as soon as the end of the week.

MBIA stock soared $5, or nearly 9 percent, to close the day at $62.49. It was the biggest gain for the shares in more than three years. "The real concern has been that regulators would find broader issues that would implicate current management or threaten the ratings," Mark Lane, an analyst at William Blair & Company in Chicago, told Bloomberg News. The article "is reducing anxiety about broader issues," he added.

Ackman's friend Paul Hilal sent him the *Wall Street Journal* article in an e-mail headlined: "Ouch."

"I don't believe it," Ackman shot back.

The article was titled "MBIA Nears Civil Settlements—Investors Hope the Pacts Will Silence Bearish Critics." Though the article didn't quote any of these hopeful investors, it did note that an unusually high percentage of MBIA's shares had been sold short.

If the story was leaked to the *Wall Street Journal* to silence further negative articles, the strategy was successful. I'd been pushing my editor to let me write again on the Caulis Negris transaction. I had even proposed taking a short unpaid leave of absence so I could dig into the story without the distractions of day-to-day market reporting.

The response was not positive. The managing editor, who oversees bond coverage at Dow Jones, told me I was obsessing over a story that was too complex and didn't interest our readers. Look at the *Wall Street Journal's* article on MBIA and its pending settlement, he suggested. That story moved the stock. "That's the kind of story you should be breaking." My story on MBIA and its complicated Caulis Negris transaction had been completely ignored, he added.

"If taking a leave of absence to write about bond insurance is what you really want to do," he continued, "you should think about whether Dow Jones is the right place for you." By the end of 2005, I was thinking about a new job.

Meanwhile, the *Wall Street Journal* article predicting a settlement lit a fire under Ackman. He wouldn't let regulators drop the investigation. Several months earlier, Ackman had been contacted by David Farner, an executive at the University of Pittsburgh Medical Center (UPMC). Farner had followed the AHERF situation closely throughout the 1990s because its health-care operations in Pittsburgh, including the group's flagship facility, Allegheny General Hospital, were a direct competitor of UPMC. Long before AHERF filed for bankruptcy, Farner had seen red flags in Allegheny General Hospital's financial statements. In a 14-page report sent to both MBIA and the credit-rating companies, Farner, a former Arthur Anderson accountant, had taken apart the hospital's disclosure. He flagged problems with arrows and notations all through the financial statements: "Investment income included in operating revenue." "Cash transfers to AHERF exceed $14 million." "Statements and footnotes for 1996 financials do not allow comparison with 1995 numbers." But no one responded, and AHERF collapsed into bankruptcy the following year.

Farner had recently drafted another report. This one addressed events that *followed* the AHERF bankruptcy, and it had been inspired in part by a reading of Ackman's report *Is MBIA Triple-A?* "This document describes the actions that we believe MBIA was willing to take to conceal another AHERF-related loss," UPMC's report began. The report wasn't about the reinsurance transactions regulators were investigating but about how MBIA dodged additional losses related to AHERF.

One year after the AHERF properties in Philadelphia filed for bankruptcy in 1998—and MBIA arranged its reinsurance transactions—AHERF's Pittsburgh properties were teetering on the verge of collapse. Those facilities avoided bankruptcy after the Pittsburgh group's creditors agreed to write down some of its debt and refinance the rest. Banks, including JPMorgan and PNC Bank, took a 33 percent writedown. MBIA, however, did not report any losses or writedowns.

Farner believed the bond insurer embedded its losses in the complicated refinancing transaction that took place in 1999. The refinancing of Allegheny General Hospital's debt "represents a particularly egregious example of the claims in the Gotham Report that MBIA's practice is to defer losses by restructuring troubled credits," Farner wrote.

Here's how it worked, according to the report. MBIA charged just $500,000 to insure the hospital's new bonds even though the insurance lowered the hospital's borrowing costs by what Farner estimated was $25 million. Bond insurance was supposed to be priced to reflect credit risk, and the hospital had below-investment-grade ratings. Farner believed that the cheap insurance policy was a disguised writedown. In fact, MBIA effectively took the same 33 percent writedown as some of the hospital's other lenders. MBIA had originally insured $68 million of Allegheny General bonds, so a 33 percent writedown would have amounted to just about $23 million or the approximate savings from the bond insurance that was essentially given away. "We can only conclude that MBIA's management valued the ability not to admit any additional AHERF-related losses," the report concluded.

Ackman wanted regulators to see the document. He called Farner's office, leaving him a voice-mail message at 9:15 a.m.: "I don't know if you saw the *Wall Street Journal* today, but it says that MBIA is close to a settlement with the regulators. It could come as early as next week. We are meeting with the [Securities and Exchange Commission] tomorrow at the SEC's request. It may be the last time that we have an opportunity to present information to the SEC. I am certainly aware of the West Penn situation, but I do not know the details as well as you do. I appreciate the fact that you want to speak with them without your being perceived as being influenced by us. I don't think there will be any harm in having a conversation."

Farner was traveling, so his secretary sent him a message about Ackman's call, but before Farner could respond, Ackman called again, shortly after 10 a.m. "There are real issues out there on what MBIA did. You know better than anyone else. I don't want to have to do this, but I will have the SEC and [the attorney general] send you a subpoena. We are at the 11th hour now, and I do not want to see MBIA get away with a crime. Let me know if you will be going voluntarily on this, or will I have to have the regulators subpoena you."

Ackman hoped that if regulators could piece together what they knew about the AHERF reinsurance deal with Caulis Negris and the refinancing of Allegheny General Hospital's debt, then they would see the truth about MBIA. The company had encountered serious problems in the late 1990s, and the only way it kept investors believing in its zero-loss business model was by using deceptive accounting and disclosure.

When Ackman and Farner finally spoke, Farner said he would be happy to get a subpoena. The requests for information arrived a few weeks later. Farner sent his report to the Securities and Exchange Commission and the New York attorney general's office. Farner expected regulators to have questions about his analysis of the transaction, but he never heard from them again.

———

A SETTLEMENT WAS PROVING elusive, too. When MBIA announced third-quarter earnings on November 8, 2005, there was no news about a resolution. Instead, the company took a $75 million charge to account for its best estimate of what it expected eventually to pay in order to settle the regulatory investigation. MBIA had managed to "beat the numbers," coming in below the $100 million amount leaked to the *Wall Street Journal*.

MBIA slipped in another bit of news. Although it had previously said that only one of the three AHERF reinsurance contracts needed to be restated as a loan, it now acknowledged that all three contracts were loans, not insurance.

"Can you tell us what changed with respect to the other two reinsurers on AHERF that required you to restate earnings?" asked Ken Zerbe, the bond-insurance analyst from Morgan Stanley, during the MBIA's earnings call. "I thought these were—these other two—were true risk arrangements."

"I don't want to be too specific in terms of the regulatory matters," replied Nicholas Ferreri, MBIA's chief financial officer. "But going through the investigative process and going through all of the risk transfer requirements . . . and based on all of the information that has come through, it's appropriate at this time to correct and restate the financials on those contracts." MBIA had managed to turn the settlement into old news without actually coming to an agreement with regulators.

By the end of 2005, it seemed clear that Spitzer's office had lost interest in everything except the AHERF transaction. It fit nicely into Spitzer's high-profile pursuit of insurance giant American International Group (AIG) and his headline-grabbing takedown of the company's CEO, Maurice "Hank" Greenberg. Spitzer showed that AIG used "insurance" contracts to make itself appear financially stronger while also entering into reinsurance arrangements with others, such as Brightpoint and PNC, to help them conceal losses.

Ackman's other issues with MBIA weren't as easy to pin down. "There was a lot of interesting stuff," one person involved in the investigation recalls. "But it was a swamp, a morass." Regulators couldn't rely on Ackman's accusations and analysis, he explains. Everything had to be checked out.

Still, Ackman pushed on. He and Jonathan Bernstein, the Pershing Square analyst assigned to cover MBIA, made frequent trips to Moody's offices. For the most part, the meetings were professional and cordial, but things got a bit emotional on one occasion, Bernstein remembers. Ackman had been telling Moody's analysts that he felt MBIA management had responded disingenuously to some of his criticisms in a posting on the company's Web site.

One of the Moody's analysts jumped in: "Wouldn't any company defend itself if short sellers were making statements like this?"

"These are people who challenged my reputation," Ackman said. "Do you understand what it's like to have a company try to destroy you? To see your children's friends shy away from them because their parents read lies about you in the *Wall Street Journal*?" Ackman was visibly angry.

"Let's take a break," Ackman said and walked out of the room.

Bernstein remembers it as his least favorite moment. It was detrimental when their arguments were seen as personally motivated. And they were up against enough resentment already, Bernstein felt. "They (the Moody's analysts) were there because Bill had complained to their boss's boss's boss," Bernstein says.

One Moody's executive who attended a number of the meetings with Ackman recalls his reaction to the hedge fund manager. "He was persuasive, organized. He came off as a bit crazy." And, yes, he agreed, "it seemed like a personal crusade." Ackman, he felt, "was emotionally vested and obviously financially vested." That was always a big issue: the huge gains that Ackman would make if Moody's downgraded MBIA. "Were we there to make him wealthy or to do the right thing?" the Moody's executive asked.

As far as many in the market were concerned, a downgrade of MBIA remained unthinkable. When the *Wall Street Journal* asked James Lebenthal, chairman emeritus of municipal bond broker Lebenthal & Company and a former MBIA board member, what would happen if MBIA were to lose its top rating, he summed up the view held by many people. "You're asking me to speculate on the divinity of the emperor," Lebenthal said. "The emperor is divine."

Ackman's frustration with Moody's boiled over at the end of 2005 when he wrote to the credit-rating company's board of directors. "I am writing to bring to your attention two inaccurate Moody's ratings that threaten the reputational integrity of Moody's and potentially create personal liability for you as a director of Moody's Inc.," the letter began. Among those receiving the letter were Raymond McDaniel, Moody's chief executive officer and chairman of the board; Robert Glauber, president of the National Association of Securities Dealers in Washington, DC; and Ewaldus Kist, the former chairman of ING Groep NV in Amsterdam.

Ackman explained that he was sending the letter to the board because Moody's had failed to act on MBIA even though Pershing Square and Roger Siefert, one of the top forensic accountants in the country, had met three times with high-level Moody's executives and analysts, providing evidence of aggressive and fraudulent accounting and "poor management character and candor." Despite an ongoing investigation that had led to MBIA's having to restate its results twice, he continued, Moody's had not even placed MBIA's ratings under review. There were many other issues that Moody's was missing, which Ackman wanted to explain to the board.

"Moody's Aaa rating is so powerful and credible that investors don't do any due diligence on the underlying credit," Ackman pointed out. These MBIA-insured obligations were piling up at a rate of about $2 billion a week, he explained. "Every day that Moody's incorrectly maintains an Aaa rating on MBIA, these extremely risk-averse investors unwittingly buy bonds that are not deserving of Moody's Aaa rating."

The board declined Ackman's offer to meet. John Goggins, Moody's general counsel, wrote to Ackman to say that board members were not permitted to engage in discussions about individual credits. The policy was designed to avoid "even the appearance of inappropriate influence," he wrote.

ON FEBRUARY 6, 2006, Ackman wrote to investors with the good news that they had earned 40 percent, after fees, on their investment in Pershing Square in 2005. The return would have been better without the short position on MBIA, which contributed a negative 3.3 percent to the result. "MBIA was our largest loser for the year despite news flow which would make any short seller proud," Ackman wrote.

Wendy's International was the fund's biggest winner in 2005. The fast-food company's shares surged after it agreed to a plan proposed by Ackman to spin off its Tim Hortons coffee and donut unit. Ackman's most recent activist campaign, directed at McDonald's, landed him on the cover of *Barron's* under the headline "Meet Mr. Pressure."

Pershing Square moved its offices from the Bowery Bank building on 42nd Street to 888 Seventh Avenue with views of Central Park, where tenants included hedge fund manager George Soros and private equity investor David Bonderman. At the end of 2005, Ackman bought a $26 million co-op in the Beresford Building overlooking Central Park.

Ackman's success elsewhere made Jonathan Bernstein's job all the more frustrating. As the primary analyst on MBIA, Bernstein read every article and every credit-rating company report that mentioned MBIA. He helped Ackman organize vast amounts of material for presentations to regulators and rating companies.

Despite all of Ackman's efforts, "the court of public opinion just wasn't ruling on MBIA," Bernstein says.

When Bernstein met friends after work for drinks, they asked him what Pershing investments he was working on. He could never tell them that he'd been assigned to work on the profitable ones, the ones that were catapulting Ackman into the news as a successful activist investor. Bernstein recalls a few friends who worked for funds of funds, which invest in hedge funds, sharing their bosses' views on Ackman: "It's the MBIA obsession; that's why our fund isn't investing with Pershing Square," they told Bernstein. The consensus on Ackman and his persistence about MBIA was that he was either "a genius or a lunatic," says Bernstein.

Rafael Mayer, an early investor in Pershing Square, says that Ackman's drive to bring people around to his way of thinking can backfire. His impatience can make people feel a bit used, and his thoroughness can be seen as obsession, Mayer says.

"Look at Markopolos," Mayer says, referring to Harry Markopolos, the fund manager who tried for 10 years to warn the Securities and Exchange Commission in detailed letters and e-mails about Bernie Madoff's Ponzi scheme. "Unfortunately, if you write long letters, people think you are crazy," Mayer says.

Even Ackman's friends poked fun at his relentless pursuit of MBIA. For his 40th birthday, Ackman's wife Karen threw him a party, inviting more than 100 family members and friends to the Blue Hill at Stone

Barns restaurant in upstate New York. Former Gotham colleagues David Berkowitz and David Klafter composed a song in Ackman's honor set to the tune of the 1936 hit "The Way You Look Tonight." The song—hitting as it did on Ackman's well-known self-assurance—elicited laughter and applause from the crowd.

For those of Ackman's investors who heard the song, some of the spoof lyrics would prove prescient. These were good times for investors—the Dow Jones Industrial Average was flirting with 11,000, and the rise in property prices seemed unstoppable. But the good times wouldn't last forever. "Some day, when we're awfully low, when the world is cold," Klafter and Berkowitz sang, "we will get a glow just thinking of you, and the way that you were right."

Chapter Thirteen

The Insurance Charade

If it is true that municipal bond defaults are made improbable by implicit (and explicit) state guarantees, then what we have is a whole industry that serves essentially no function other than to transfer money from the pockets of the public to the pockets of management and shareholders.

—RAFAEL MAYER, INVESTOR, FALL 2006

WHEN HURRICANE KATRINA slammed into the Gulf Coast in the summer of 2005, it raised some uncomfortable questions about bond insurance. For years, bond insurers thrived on the unspoken understanding that municipalities did not file claims. Yet it seemed possible that vast numbers of municipalities could default after Katrina blew through. Eight months after the devastating storm, half the citizens and businesses had yet to return to some ravaged towns and neighborhoods. Municipalities in Louisiana hit by the worst of the hurricane had issued $9.1 billion of debt, and $6.4 billion of that debt was insured, mostly by MBIA and Financial Guaranty Insurance Company, a competing bond insurer.

Yet during MBIA's conference call to discuss first-quarter 2006 earnings, Nick Ferreri, MBIA's chief financial officer, told listeners that the company had not set aside reserves to cover claims related to the hurricane.

One analyst followed up, asking if municipalities had begun to tap reserve funds to meet their bond payments. Doing so would be an early indication that a municipality might have trouble meeting future bond payments.

"There are definitely transactions down there that we have insured, and the reserve funds have been hit," Ferreri said. "Clearly, the area is still under a lot of stress, and we are still looking at those credits with a lot of caution. But we will have to see how that's going to work through. But certainly at this point in time we can't make any calls about what's going to happen down there."

The analyst asked Ferreri to disclose the par value of the bonds issued by municipalities that had tapped reserve accounts.

"I am sorry?" Ferreri said.

"Can you tell us what the par value of the bonds that have had reserve funds hit to date has been?" the analyst repeated.

"Par value of the . . . ?"

"Of the bonds where the reserve funds have been tapped?" the analyst repeated, sounding a little exasperated.

"No," Ferreri said.

The analyst gave up. "Okay. All right."

Despite MBIA's 30-year track record of insuring municipal bonds, its executives seemed reluctant to discuss the most fundamental questions about why or when a county or town might turn to an insurer to cover their bond payments.

A letter written by Louisiana Treasurer John Neely Kennedy to Governor Kathleen Blanco made the situation a bit clearer: "Wholesale defaults on debt of this size, or even a portion of it, would destroy the credit ratings of our local governments, the state of Louisiana, and the bond insurers themselves," Kennedy wrote. No one could afford to stop believing in the no-loss illusion.

———

IN THE SPRING OF 2006, I left Dow Jones for Bloomberg News, taking with me a pile of articles, credit-rating reports, and interview notes. Many of these papers were about municipal debt issuers that appeared to be on the verge of defaulting and filing claims on their bond insurance. When I dug in further, it seemed a number of these issuers had been on the verge of collapse for years. So why didn't they default?

The first place I went was Oklahoma to follow up on a story about the Grady County Jail.

It was built in the late 1990s when Oklahoma's rural counties were told their dilapidated Depression-era jails weren't up to code. Inspectors cited leaky pipes, crumbling walls, and faulty wiring, and they gave the counties an ultimatum: Fix your jails or empty them. Without a jail, Grady County would have to pay someone else $100,000 a year to house its prisoners.

That's when a Missouri architect named Lawrence Goldberg entered the picture. In the "law and order" state of Oklahoma, where incarceration rates are high and sentences long, the business of housing prisoners was both expensive and potentially profitable. Goldberg pitched the Grady County commissioners on the idea of building a new jail that would be big enough to house the county's prisoners and still have space left over to rent cells to other counties or the federal government.

The county put the question of selling bonds to finance the construction of the jail to a vote. It was overwhelmingly rejected, not once but twice. In the state of Oklahoma the sale of long-term bonds requires voter approval. Safeguards against local governments' taking on excessive debt are part of every state constitution.

Grady County proceeded with plans to build the jail despite voter objections. Rather than owning the jail, the county decided to lease it. And instead of selling bonds backed by the full faith and credit of the county, the Grady County Industrial Authority sold certificates of participation (COPs). The securities were backed by the county's annual lease payments on the jail. The stream of payments Grady County expected to make were no different under the lease arrangement than they would have been under the terms of a bond financing. But COPs aren't considered long-term debt and therefore don't require voter approval. So while voters in nearby Mayes County sold $3.2 million of debt with voter approval to build their new jail, the Grady County Industrial Authority sold $12 million of COPs over the objections of its citizens. Due to cost overruns on the project, the Grady County Industrial Authority later sold another $5 million of COPs, bringing the total cost of the jail to $17 million.

Almost immediately, the jail had trouble covering payments on its $17 million of debt. Four years after the builders broke ground for the project, a 15-member grand jury found that "officials built a jail that was too big for the county's jail needs, yet too small to produce enough revenue to sustain the [bond] payments." Charged with investigating the construction, financing, and operation of the Grady County jail, the grand jury placed the blame on "an inaccurate and overly opportunistic feasibility study," including "a fatal assumption that the federal government would lease out a large number of beds at a rate of at least $40/day." One projection submitted by the developer had the federal government paying $60 to $275 a day to house each prisoner. The jail was lucky to get $40 for a federal prisoner.

The report concluded: "These are private bonds and this debt should never be placed on the taxpayers of Grady County without a vote of the people. This debt and financing risk should be shouldered by the private individuals who chose to invest in these revenue bonds." But most of the bondholders had purchased insured bonds, meaning they expected MBIA to shoulder the losses if the issuer couldn't pay off its debts.

To get to Chickasha, I took Highway 81 south out of Oklahoma City. The two-lane highway stopped occasionally at an intersection with a gas station, a feed store, or, more often, a building whose long-ago purpose was concealed by a faded sign, weathered shingles, and boards nailed over the windows. By 10 a.m., the temperature already was creeping toward 100 degrees. "If you think this is hot, it's this hot in Hell for Eternity" read a sign in front of a roadside Baptist church. The first person I spoke with was Keiran McMullen, the Grady County sheriff, who oversaw the jail's complicated financing. A small, unassuming-looking man who wears an oversize cowboy hat, McMullen said there had been a basic disagreement about the ultimate responsibility for the bonds. "MBIA always has wanted to treat the bonds as if they were general obligation bonds," said McMullen, referring to debt backed by the full faith and credit of a local government. The way they saw it back at MBIA headquarters was that the jail provided an essential service, so the county and ultimately the state would back it up, according to McMullen.

It might be an essential service but the county couldn't get the taxpayers to agree to fund it, McMullen said. The only way the bond payments could be made was if the jail took in enough prisoners at a high enough rate. "The whole business is a bit like running a Holiday Inn," the sheriff said with a smile. "You just never know who's going to turn up."

The shortfalls were chronic, but the county always found ways to avoid drawing on its bond insurance. Then in the fall of 2004, it told MBIA that it needed help. MBIA told the Grady County Industrial

Authority that unless it came up with the November bond payment, it would stop insuring any more debt across the state. "From where I was sitting, it looked like they blackmailed the state," said McMullen. Shortly after, the Oklahoma Department of Corrections cut a check to the jail for $645,183 to help meet its November 2004 bond payment.

Chris Angel, the accountant who audits the jail's finances, sat in his office in a small building just outside of town, tallying up all the sources the county had tapped over the last few years to meet the bond payments on the jail: "County General Fund, Grady County Housing Authority, Sheriff-Prisoner Housing Fund. And, of course, the payment from the state for $645,183 after MBIA threatened to stop insuring Oklahoma bonds." The latest plan under discussion, said Angel, was for the U.S. Department of Agriculture to lend the jail more money so it could finish the top floor and hold more prisoners. MBIA was not one of those sources. "They came in their expensive suits and looked at the same numbers we did before they insured it," Angel said.

So I called the Oklahoma Department of Corrections to see why they covered the November 2004 bond payment. Jerry Massie, a spokesman for the department, said he'd have to call me back on that but added, "I believe there was legislative involvement to help protect the state's credit rating."

While I waited to hear back from Massie, I headed down to the Oklahoma state capitol building in search of an explanation. Most of the senators' offices were locked and empty on an August afternoon, but I found longtime senator Cal Hobson in his office. "MBIA appeared on our doorstep" in September 2004, Hobson remembered. The company cautioned that if the state didn't make sure that Grady County came up with the money for the bond payment, the state's credit rating could suffer. MBIA also hired a lobbyist to try to get the state to take over the facility, Hobson said. In the end, the state decided it wasn't worth risking its credit rating, and the department of corrections was told to make the payment.

The senator said he would have liked to see the unused top floor of the Grady County jail converted into a drug-treatment facility. The state could use fewer prisons and more treatment for drug addicts, he said. But rehabilitation didn't pay as well as incarceration, and the Grady County jail needed the money.

When Jerry Massie from the department of corrections called me back, he had an explanation. The $645,183 wasn't given to the jail to cover the bond payment per se. It was an advance payment for housing state prisoners. The Grady County Industrial Authority decided to use the extra cash to pay the bonds.

I might have accepted that answer had I not stumbled on the Central Purchasing Act. It prohibits state agencies from making advance payments for products or services. If the state prepaid to house prisoners at the Grady County jail, then it broke the law. So I called Massie again and asked him whether the department of corrections broke the law when it wrote that check.

A few days later, Massie called me back with an answer. It was true that the state couldn't pay for services in advance. That's why the department tapped into the Canteen Fund to cover the bond payment. The Canteen Fund sells products and services to prisoners. It's not subject to the Central Purchasing Act because it's not funded by taxpayers, Massie explained. Most of the money in the fund comes from a surcharge on incoming phone calls to prisoners.

I might have accepted Massie's answer that there was no problem with using this extra phone money had I not spoken with Lynn Powell. Powell runs a support group for people with family members in Oklahoma prisons, and she knew all about the phone system. Powell sent out e-mail messages to families in her support group, asking them to contact me if they wanted to comment on the phone system. My e-mail inbox filled up with messages, mainly from women with husbands and sons in prison. "I have a son incarcerated in Oklahoma. My monthly phone bill averages a little over $100, but it's been $200," wrote one woman. "The first minute is the one that hurts . . . about $3.25," explained another. "Even though I am retired, I now have a part-time job to be sure I am able to pay the phone bill." That's who made the $645,183 bond payment.

Why spend days in 100-degree heat chasing down the source of funds for a $645,183 check? The only way to understand how bond insurers avoided paying claims was to trace a payment on a troubled deal back to its source. By doing this in Grady County, I realized that the "no-loss illusion" encouraged, if not outright dishonesty, at the very least a lack of accountability in local government. "Zero-loss" underwriting required such extraordinary machinations to stay on the right side of the law that it was hard to believe the concept was not a fraud.

ON AUGUST 23, 2006, Ackman wrote to Pershing Square's investors to deliver what had become a familiar message: "MBIA has proven to be a frustrating short-sale investment simply because no matter what the news or the poor operating performance on the company, the company's stock price and credit spreads remain stubbornly out of line with our assessment of the company's grim business prospects and flawed financial reports."

As the end of summer rolled around, MBIA credit-default-swap spreads narrowed, indicating rising confidence in the company. "MBIA AA 5-year [credit-default swap] continues to march tighter on relatively active trading," a Goldman Sachs broker said in an e-mail message to Erika Kreyssig on Pershing's trading desk. "We would currently call the market 24 to 28 basis points. Do you have any interest down there? We can probably pull out $25 million or so, should you care."

Ackman still cared. Pershing Square continued buying.

During the summer of 2006, Ackman returned to the Securities and Exchange Commission's (SEC's) offices in lower Manhattan to meet with the attorneys involved in the MBIA investigation. Roy Katzovicz, a former Wachtell Lipton attorney who had recently been hired as Pershing Square's chief legal officer, accompanied Ackman. He was in for a surprise.

The group met in a small conference room. Instead of the usual three SEC attorneys, only two were at that meeting. Gerald Russello, the attorney who had been leading the investigation, had taken a job in the general counsel's office at Bear Stearns. The presentation was going according to plan when Katzovicz noticed that Ackman was getting agitated. "I've shown you this fraud. I've shown you that fraud," Ackman said. "What do I have to do? What do I have to prove to you before you take some action?" His face was flushed, his eyes misty.

Katzovicz was dumbfounded. Ackman was giving the SEC attorneys what could only be described as a tongue-lashing. In all his experience as an attorney, he had never seen an SEC lawyer treated with anything but deference. Katzovicz broke out in a cold sweat. He reached out and put his hand on Ackman's shoulder, hoping to send a message that things might be getting a bit too intense.

"Bill, to be clear, we do not work for you," replied Steve Rawlings, one of the SEC attorneys. "We appreciate your passion, but this is not a two-way conversation. Do you think the people on this side of the table aren't sincerely trying to do their best?"

Still, Ackman persisted. "What do I have to do? What does it take?"

Rawlings thought about it for a minute. Then he told Ackman that sometimes the right kind of press coverage had done the trick in the past. "A story on the front page of the *Wall Street Journal* or the *New York Times*, especially the *New York Times*," Rawlings told him.

How would MBIA ever be held accountable if everyone was looking over their shoulder, waiting for someone else to act? The regulators were waiting for the press. Most of the press was content to wait for regulators to make the MBIA story front-page news. Everyone was waiting for the credit-rating companies to blink, but they were taking comfort from the silence of the regulators.

Ackman regained his composure. "Okay. I have something else for you," he said and pulled out a trustee report for a collateralized-debt obligation (CDO) called Sagittarius. A trustee report is a kind of report card that shows how a CDO's assets are performing and how the various layers of protection for each class of CDO investor are holding up. This CDO was running into trouble, and yet MBIA had not taken any reserves against it, Ackman explained. "It's yet another fraud."

He passed around copies of the trustee report and then launched into an explanation that Katzovicz describes as "a blizzard of information." The SEC attorneys flipped back and forth through the pages of the report as they tried to keep up with explanations about defaults, subordination, and super-senior tranches. Soon people all over Wall Street and even in remote corners of the financial world would be doing the same thing.

───────

AFTER OKLAHOMA, I MOVED on to Texas in search of more troubled municipal projects that were somehow maintaining the no-loss illusion. Las Colinas—a Disneyland-inspired business park near the Dallas–Fort Worth International Airport—fit the bill. The development stood incomplete decades after it was first conceived by Ben Carpenter, a wealthy Texan who sought to turn 12,000 acres of ranchland along the Trinity River into a sprawling community of offices, homes, resorts, and golf courses. No expense was spared to fulfill Carpenter's vision, which was funded with insured, tax-exempt municipal bonds. Canals were dug throughout Las Colinas, and canal boats were imported from Venice to ferry office workers around the development. A monorail system was planned and partially built to zip workers between high-rise office buildings. Deep-pile turf and palm trees replaced the scrubby grassland.

When taxes fell short of covering the bond payments, the issuer looked for ways to tap into the coffers of surrounding communities. One plan diverted money from a program that redistributed funding from wealthy Texas school districts to poorer districts in the state. Another proposal called for selling off some of Las Colinas's assets to other communities, including its drainage ditches and a flower clock in the middle of a traffic circle. Residents objected, saying the "assets" were just maintenance burdens. In a planned residential neighborhood, the houses had to be so closely packed together in order to achieve the necessary amount of projected tax revenue that the local fire chief warned that it would be impossible to lean ladders against the houses in the event of a fire. But the debt continued to be paid.

In California, the San Joaquin Hills toll road was threatening to default on MBIA-insured bonds. Local authorities worked out their own unconventional solution. The Foothills toll road, a more successful project run by the same authority, agreed to make a $120 million payment to the San Joaquin Hills toll road even though the two toll roads were expressly prohibited from subsidizing one another. In exchange for the payment, the San Joaquin project promised not to sue the Foothills toll road if it built an extension and drew drivers away from the San Joaquin route. Brittany McKee, an employee of the Sierra Club, which opposed the plan, summed it up this way: "It's a weird concocted financial bailout plan." That seemed to sum up a lot of what I found going on that summer.

"If you think rationally about it, [bond insurance] sounds a lot like extortion," said Professor David Schultz at Hamline University in Saint Paul, Minnesota. "The people who are put on the hook are the taxpayers."

This extortion costs the U.S. taxpayers $2.5 billion a year, Bloomberg News estimated in an article titled "The Insurance Charade" in the fall of 2006. Darrell Preston, a Dallas-based public finance reporter, and I took some ribbing over the article.

"Yes, Virginia, bond insurance does save issuers money," George Friedlander, Citigroup's municipal bond strategist, chided in a research report. The Bloomberg story turned reality on its head, he argued. Bond insurance saved issuers more than $2 billion a year.

Sean McCarthy, chairman of the Association of Financial Guarantee Issuers, the bond-insurance trade group, also disputed the idea. "No issuer is forced to buy insurance," he said. "It is an economic decision based on simple mathematical calculation of whether the borrowing cost is lowered by raising the rating to triple-A."

But there was nothing simple about this. Why did municipalities have to buy triple-A ratings when they were the ones shielding the triple-A-rated bond insurers from having to cover claims? Richard Nixon's disgraced attorney general, John Mitchell, knew that if America wanted ever more debt, it was going to have to stretch rules. The bond insurers played by rules that few understood. But perhaps the article had shed some light on those rules.

Rafael Mayer wrote Ackman a quick e-mail the day he read the *Bloomberg Markets* story: "I had never given this any thought. If it is true that municipal bond defaults are made improbable by implicit (and explicit) state guarantees . . . then what we have is a whole industry that serves essentially no function other than to transfer money from the pockets of the public to the pockets of management and shareholders."

Chapter **14** *Fourteen*

When Crack Houses
Become Collateral

The Caulis Negris venture was a small-scale example of what eventually sank the subprime market.... Securitization can create value from thin air and assumptions.

—DAVID BOBERSKI, EXECUTIVE DIRECTOR AT UBS INVESTMENT BANK,
CDS DELIVERY OPTION (BLOOMBERG PRESS, 2009)

B Y THE FALL OF 2006, there was still no word of an official settlement between regulators and MBIA. Perhaps regulators had
delayed announcing a settlement with MBIA because they were
looking into the Caulis Negris deal after all.

In an e-mail to regulators, Bill Ackman wrote that he believed MBIA's
pattern of writedowns on the Caulis Negris bonds was suspect. "It's illustra-
tive to follow this last sentence into the future," Ackman wrote, including
excerpts from MBIA's 2004 filings. "This transaction (Caulis Negris) matures
in 2008 and has an outstanding balance of $118 million, or $81 million net
of existing loss reserves of approximately *$37 million*," the company
disclosed. The next quarter, reserves jumped by $2 million to $39 million
and the amount due on the bonds fell by $2 million to $79 million. Three
months later, the reserves climbed by another $5 million to $44 million
while the amount due dropped by exactly the same amount to $74 million.

The outstanding amount of Caulis Negris bonds remained unchanged, but each quarter the value of the bonds declined by additions to reserves. MBIA appeared to be making no collections on the tax liens.

"It appears MBIA is simply straight-lining the hit to earnings between now and when the Caulis Negris bonds mature in 2008," Ackman concluded.

I thought it would make an interesting story. But the only way to know whether the company was writing down assets it already knew to be worthless was to look at the properties on which it held tax liens. That seemed like an impossible task because Caulis Negris had purchased thousands of tax liens from municipalities in multiple states.

Then MBIA's chief financial officer gave away a clue that made it possible. During MBIA's first-quarter 2006 earnings conference call in April, Morgan Stanley analyst Ken Zerbe asked about the ongoing tax-lien losses. "You mentioned that you took additional losses related to your tax-lien portfolio," Zerbe said. "Is there any reason why you can't take a one-time large loss as opposed to taking small losses every quarter?"

Nicholas Ferreri, MBIA's CFO, offered an explanation. "The bulk of the liens are in one city. Up until this point, there were other states in that transaction," Ferreri said. He didn't really answer Zerbe's question, but he answered mine. The Caulis Negris properties were in Pittsburgh.

Michael Malakoff led me down a hallway crowded with file cabinets to his office overlooking Grant Street in downtown Pittsburgh. Malakoff, the class-action attorney who sued Capital Asset and later Caulis Negris on behalf of thousands of delinquent taxpayers in the city of Pittsburgh, told me there were legal problems from day one with Capital Asset's purchase of the city's tax liens. The city had never aggressively gone after delinquent taxpayers. It was politically untenable to throw little old ladies out on the street because they couldn't pay their taxes. Yet Capital Asset had spent nearly $50 million to buy the right to collect overdue taxes, and it planned to be aggressive. It also had an agreement with the city allowing it to charge 18 percent interest on overdue balances. A lawsuit, *Pollice v. Capital Asset*, was filed in 1998, charging Capital Asset with unjust enrichment.

Malakoff dug out some filings on the case. He had added Caulis Negris to the lawsuit after MBIA transferred all the Pittsburgh tax liens to a special-purpose vehicle in August 1999. The timing was important because Caulis Negris was created only three weeks after a preliminary opinion that Pittsburgh property owners couldn't be charged more than 10 percent interest on past-due tax bills. The value of the assets would have been very uncertain at that point, Malakoff said. It would take years for the legal issues to be worked out.

As I was leaving, Malakoff said he hoped MBIA hadn't insured many deals like Caulis Negris. He had lots of his own money in insured municipal bonds. "I'd be terrified if I thought MBIA couldn't meet its obligations," Malakoff said.

Aggie Brose, a community activist in Pittsburgh for more than 25 years, told me she was all too familiar with Capital Asset. It was obvious that Capital Asset wouldn't collect much money on the Pittsburgh tax liens. "If they want to find the owners of these properties, they need to go looking down in the Allegheny County cemetery," Brose said. We were talking after one of the regular meetings held at a community center in Pittsburgh's Hill district to discuss the problem of the city's thousands of vacant properties.

As steel mills across the region closed, Pittsburgh's population declined. During the 1980s, the city was losing 50,000 residents a year, according to Allegheny Places, a report by the University Center for Social and Urban Research at the University of Pittsburgh. Between 1970 and 2000, 20 percent of the population vanished.

In Pittsburgh's declining neighborhoods, many of the homes were seized by the city for nonpayment of taxes in the 1970s and 1980s after their once middle-class owners died or moved away. Batches of houses were sold by the city, sometimes for as little as $1 apiece, just to get people living in and looking after the properties. But someone who can afford to pay $1 for a house can't necessarily cover the other costs that come with homeownership, Brose said. The condition of the houses declined, the taxes went unpaid again, and the slide continued.

The daughter of two union stewards, Brose is sentimental about Pittsburgh, particularly about Garfield, the neighborhood where she grew up and raised her own three children. "Aggie was always sweeping her stoop and sweeping all the way to the corner," a former neighbor told the *Pittsburgh Gazette*. Even in her 60s, she exudes an energetic drive to get things cleaned up. The task is a daunting one.

Kendall Pelling, who worked across town at East Liberty Development, explained to me that numerous projects had been held up by Capital Asset refusing to accept less than it was owed on a property. On thousands of properties, the amount due was far higher than the market value of the property that secured the liens. Pelling was not sure why Capital Asset wouldn't negotiate; there was no obvious benefit to letting the property sit. "I've always felt we don't know enough about Caulis Negris's motivations and how it works," said Pelling.

When I told him that the name loosely translated means "black hole," he replied: "It's certainly appropriate."

Pelling gave me a list of all the properties in Pittsburgh with Caulis Negris liens. I started my search several blocks away on Dinwiddie Street, which runs down a steep hill toward the abandoned Fifth Avenue School. The building, which was closed in 1976, was surrounded by a tall chain-link fence on which someone has posted a "For Sale" sign. In the 1960s, there were 80,000 students in the Pittsburgh public school system. By 2006, the number was closer to 25,000.

The Hill district, which rises just beyond downtown Pittsburgh, was cut off physically from the hub of the city by the construction of a civic arena in the late 1960s. Race riots, white flight, and the decline of the steel industry share the blame for the neighborhood's demise. In the 1980s, the district became the inspiration for the television police drama *Hill Street Blues*.

My list showed Caulis Negris–controlled properties scattered up and down the street, though some were impossible to identify. A few houses stood like Roman ruins with roofs gone and vines creeping up the walls. No. 217, a three-story row house with $4,987.27 in back taxes, interest, and penalties owed to Caulis Negris, was still intact, though it looked as if it hadn't been lived in for years. A crude porch, covered in green and black tar paper, created a sinister-looking shelter behind the tall weeds. A chain-link fence kept garbage tossed into the tiny yard from blowing away and had created a kind of wastebasket effect. A sign posted just outside the front porch warned that rat poison had been laid on the property.

"Don't be so certain no one's home," Wilbert Washington said. He had come out of the house to the right of 217 Dinwiddie. "No one lives there," he explained, "but it gets plenty of visitors, and you probably don't want to meet them." When I asked him who owned it, he told me that the last person who lived there, a man who drove a bus for the city, had died, maybe 10 years ago. Washington said he had tried to buy the house himself, to have it knocked down, but couldn't afford to pay the back taxes and demolish it. "I wish the whole house would just fall down," he said.

The place had become a magnet for neighborhood addicts, who huddled on the porch to smoke crack cocaine. Raccoons were also a big problem. They got inside the house and scratched at the walls, keeping Washington awake at night. Sometimes he took a boom box upstairs in his house, turned it toward the wall, and tried to blast them away. It worked for awhile, but they always came back.

I imagined the value of the property must be meaningfully less than zero.

The next afternoon, with the list of Caulis Negris properties in hand, I went out to see more. I explained to a taxi driver that I was taking a look at a portfolio of properties owned by a New York insurance company. We drove up and down through Pittsburgh's steep hillside neighborhoods, tracking down addresses. Almost invariably, we stopped at the worst property on the block, though sometimes that was a hard call. Most seemed vacant. Hardly any appeared habitable. Occasionally, one of the properties would have a weathered "For Sale" sign stuck to the door. As we pulled away from one house, the taxi driver asked me, "What did they do, buy them blind?"

Adriane Aul in Pittsburgh, who headed up the Pittsburgh Community Reinvestment Group's efforts to deal with vacant properties, helped me figure out the full picture: Caulis Negris owned liens on 11,000 properties in Pittsburgh, nearly 10 percent of the entire city. The outlook for those properties was bleak, given that there were 20,000 abandoned houses and vacant lots across the city, almost 20 percent of all residential real estate.

MBIA controlled so much property in the city of Pittsburgh that an unwillingness to recognize losses on the Caulis Negris bonds could hold up the redevelopment of entire neighborhoods. "When they own the liens, it's easy for them to just do nothing," Aul said. That was my story.

During the last week of November, Bloomberg News ran the story— "MBIA Debt Backed by Crack Houses Perpetuates Pittsburgh Blight." I received a flurry of e-mail from readers, much of it critical of MBIA: How could a triple-A-rated company get away with something like this? Why didn't the city seize the properties if MBIA was unwilling to acknowledge that they were overvaluing the tax liens?

And some of it was critical of my article: How could I so irresponsibly sensationalize the situation? Why point a finger at MBIA when it was the people who weren't paying their taxes who were to blame? That one was easy. "I think a lot of those people are dead," I wrote back.

The stock market weighed in with its verdict. MBIA's shares rose nearly $3, closing up $1.77, their fifth-largest gain in 12 months.

"MBIA gets a bad article and the stock goes up," Michael Ovitz e-mailed Ackman after the story ran. "Is everything in your world counterintuitive?" he asked.

The stock market reaction was frustrating. Yet a few days later, MBIA and the city of Pittsburgh reached an agreement. Luke Ravensthal, Pittsburgh's 26-year-old mayor, announced that the city had struck a deal with MBIA to buy back $40 million of Capital Assets liens for just $6.5 million. The next day, MBIA said that it had sold its MuniServices unit, which owned Capital Asset. All traces of Caulis Negris were gone.

And the stock continued to rise. Several days after the lien sale was announced, MBIA's shares broke through $70. On December 28, the stock hit $73.31, a level that would prove to be a pre–credit crisis high-water mark.

Ackman put his thoughts about the rise in the company's share price in an e-mail to the SEC. He explained that not only did MBIA's shares rise on a day when the only news in the public domain was a negative story, but also the shares then fell the next day when Keefe Bruyette & Woods put out a positive research report, raising its price target on MBIA to $81 from $75. Something was not right.

The Keefe Bruyette insurance analyst covering MBIA, Geoffrey Dunn, upgraded MBIA to "outperform" after attending a meeting with Neil Budnick, the president of MBIA's insurance unit. At that meeting Budnick said that the insurance company now had $1.5 billion in excess capital. MBIA was likely to lift its moratorium on share buybacks, given this huge buildup of capital, Dunn concluded.

"Budnick or others at MBIA likely told Mr. Dunn and other investors they met with on their 'marketing trip' that—wink wink—the company has $1.5 billion of excess capital and is about to renew its share repurchase program (despite previous statements to the contrary) and the program will be substantially larger than originally anticipated," Ackman wrote to the SEC.

Dunn's report contained "remarkably specific" estimates about how many shares MBIA might buy back, Ackman pointed out. Dunn had expected MBIA to purchase about 4 million shares in 2007. Now he thought the company would move ahead despite the status of the investigation, buying 10 million shares. That was 3 million to 4 million shares per quarter through 2008, which would return approximately $2 billion to shareholders over the following two years.

Ackman suggested the SEC look into the matter because if what he suspected was true, the company had used inside information to prop up its share price. "It is inappropriate and illegal in my understanding of the law for the company to selectively disclose material information to analysts and certain favored shareholders without simultaneously providing it to all investors," Ackman wrote.

He also pointed out that the positive research couldn't have been more timely for MBIA executives. MBIA chairman Jay Brown and CEO Gary Dunton had compensation arrangements under which millions of dollars of options and restricted stock would vest if MBIA's share price traded above $70 for 10 days. The scenario was worth $24 million to Brown and $10 million to Dunton. Brown would lose restricted shares valued at about $2.5 million if the $70 target was not hit by December 31, 2006. The compensation arrangement, Ackman wrote, "obviously creates an incentive to push the stock price up over the next two weeks." The day my story about MBIA's tax lien exposure in Pittsburgh ran on Bloomberg News, MBIA's share price ended a dollar shy of the $70 target.

I spoke with Dunn after the article ran and asked him why he thought the stock was up. He wouldn't discuss his research or send me a copy of the report, though he told me his theory about why the article failed to stir negative sentiment on the company: "Everyone knows you're in the pocket of short sellers," Dunn told me. "That's why they ignore what you write."

Brown stood to make or lose millions on a small move in the stock price, yet Dunn focused on phantom payouts to reporters. Though I never received any compensation from short sellers, I did win a $250 prize from the National Association of Real Estate Editors for the article.

In late 2009, Ackman continued to stand behind his comments to the SEC. When I called Dunn for this book, he refused to speak with me about this or any topic. Budnick, who left the company several months after the story ran, did not return a call seeking comment on the marketing meeting. By late 2009, the SEC had no public record of any action regarding Dunn or Budnick. The reason the stock price went up that day remains unknown.

Citigroup analyst Heather Hunt summed up the prevailing view when she wrote on MBIA shortly after the Pittsburgh article appeared. "Although unfavorable articles provide a forum for short sellers' debate about the AAA rating, rating agencies continue to defend it."

Over the next several years, the market would find out that MBIA executives weren't the only ones who used securitization to transfer questionable assets. David Boberski, an executive director at UBS Investment Bank, wrote in 2009 that MBIA's dealings in Pittsburgh, brought to light in a "widely ignored" Bloomberg article, had been a warning about what was to come: "The Caulis Negris venture was a small-scale example of what eventually sank the subprime market (and its derivatives) on a national scale. Securitization can create value from thin air and assumptions."

AT THE END OF 2006, however, bond insurers and their supporters were confident in the future. At a conference on the financial guarantors at the Sofitel in Midtown, Moody's Investors Service analyst Jack Dorer took the stage. The first slide of his presentation showed how the bond-insurance business had grown from $450 billion of guarantees outstanding in 1995 to $1.8 trillion in 2006. "That's remarkable," Dorer said before moving on to the next slide.

Despite this phenomenal growth, risk remained well contained, according to Moody's. Dorer flipped to another slide to show that losses were expected to remain extremely rare. "What it's saying," Dorer explained, "is [that] for every 100 dollars of par outstanding, a company would lose 39 cents."

Not everyone was convinced. A week before Christmas 2006, Sanjay Sharma, the chief risk officer of Natixis, a European financial institution that owned bond insurer CIFG, wrote a letter to his boss. He was frightened by what he saw unfolding: "The housing market [has become] systemically susceptible to a significant downturn given the current market weakening in home prices, increasing delinquencies, and the low visibility of mortgage performance in a stressful environment."

Sharma believed that CIFG needed to immediately pull back from the market. "The risks are heightened by the nontraditional risk layering inherent in many current mortgage products," Sharma added, referring to collateralized-debt obligations (CDOs). Sharma's advice to drastically slow the business of guaranteeing CDOs was rejected. He received a quick response: "The U.S. mortgage market is one of the deepest, most studied, most liquid, and most orderly markets in the world," Charles Webster, CIFG's chief risk officer, wrote in reply. "While not immune to volatility, there are too many participants in the mortgage market for it to fall apart. The market is so broad that there are many places of relative safety."

Almost everyone was certain that bond insurers had found one of those safe places. As 2006 drew to a close, Ackman wrote to his investors: "MBIA is, by a large margin, our largest loser for the year."

But the hedge fund's short position on MBIA was more than that. It was Ackman's obsession with an overleveraged company that needed— but did not have—a near-perfect track record. It was also a great hedge, downside protection for the fund in the event that years of ballooning debt, easy money, and investor complacency ended in disaster.

Credit-default-swap contracts on MBIA were priced as if the company was only slightly riskier than the U.S. government. Yet with leverage of 140 to 1, MBIA was vulnerable to the unexpected. "If nothing else, MBIA was virtually zero-cost financial-disaster insurance," says Ali Namvar, one of Pershing Square's analysts. And by late 2006, with the U.S. housing market faltering, disaster was on its way.

"Let's hold off on more [credit-default swap] purchases," Ackman wrote to Erika Kreyssig, the Pershing Square trader, in an e-mail in late 2006. "We are big enough in MBIA so that if it works, we will be happy."

Chapter Fifteen

Storm Warnings

MBIA holds itself out to the investing public as a company that does not risk significant losses on the insurance it writes. In fact, MBIA's winning streak came to an end in 1998.

—NEW YORK ATTORNEY GENERAL'S COMPLAINT AGAINST MBIA, JANUARY 2007

ON THE LAST FRIDAY in January 2007, word began to circulate that MBIA was about to announce a settlement with the New York attorney general's office and the Securities and Exchange Commission (SEC). The settlement had been expected any day for more than a year. Now it appeared that the probe into the Allegheny Health, Education, and Research Foundation (AHERF) reinsurance transactions would end with MBIA paying $75 million, the amount it had taken as a charge more than a year earlier in anticipation of the settlement.

After more than two years, the regulatory cloud was about to lift. The stock surged in heavy volume in the final hour of trading after Bloomberg News reported the upcoming announcement. "We would view settlement as a huge relief," Citigroup analyst Heather Hunt wrote in a research note to clients. "Expect short covering to drive up stock near term."

MBIA was, after all, the third-most-shorted stock in the Standard & Poor's (S&P) 500 Index, she reminded investors.

After reading the news, Bill Ackman walked over to the firm's trading desk to check prices on MBIA shares and credit default swaps (CDSs). For more than two years, Ackman had been waiting for regulators to take sweeping actions on MBIA. He had spent hours at the SEC and attorney general's office describing what he believed were multiple offenses. It was not supposed to end this way, with a slap on the wrist for the AHERF transaction.

Yet Ackman wasn't looking to close out the position. He wanted to short more stock and buy more credit protection on MBIA.

The investment team's offices faced the trading desk, and through the glass partitions members of the team watched in amazement. Phones were put down. Eyebrows were raised. Within a few minutes, the team was standing around the trading desk, trying to figure out what on earth Ackman was thinking. Scott Ferguson, the first analyst to join Pershing, took the lead. He and Ackman had been sparring over the MBIA position for years. It was a loser for Pershing among a field of winners, and it had absorbed huge amounts of Ackman's time and attention.

"Are you sure about this?" Ferguson asked Ackman.

"Yes," Ackman insisted. There was no more upside in the stock, Ackman said. The shares were fully valued even under the flawed models used by Wall Street analysts. The only reason for the stock rise was that everyone believed the short sellers would be forced to cover. He was not going to cover.

As Ackman tried to move closer to the trading desk, Ferguson physically restrained him, as if he were "an alcoholic reaching for a bottle," Ackman remembers.

"We need to think about this," Ferguson insisted. The stock was up nearly $3 on the news of the settlement.

"This is the highest price it will ever trade," Ackman insisted.

He also wanted to buy more CDSs. The premium on 5-year MBIA CDS contracts was 16 basis points, indicating that for $16,000 per annum, Ackman could buy protection against default on $10 million of debt. He had never seen the price that low. There was just no downside. It didn't really matter if regulators had decided to let MBIA off easily. The company was overleveraged, and eventually that would take it down.

Mick McGuire, another Pershing analyst, remembers fearing that the MBIA short position was suffering from "investment analysis creep." "First it was AHERF, Capital Asset, then Katrina. Was the reason for

MBIA's demise going to keep changing to support the idea of being short?" McGuire wondered.

No one doubted that MBIA was vulnerable, remembers Paul Hilal, Ackman's longtime friend who joined Pershing Square's investment team a year earlier. It wasn't a matter of *if* but *when* the stock price would fall, Hilal says. But would MBIA blow up in a reasonable time frame? Did it make sense to keep putting money into a position if there was no catalyst? For years, the investment team had watched Ackman put his faith in the regulatory investigation. The regulators seemed to get it. After every meeting with the SEC, Ackman had been optimistic. Clearly, they didn't get it. So, why add to the position now?

"Is Bill Ahab? Is he in denial?" Hilal recalls wondering, in a comparison of Ackman to the obsessed and doomed captain in *Moby Dick*. "We were operating on faith and out of respect for the guy. No one else had done the work on MBIA."

That was about to change.

"This is why someone else is going to do the work," Ackman announced to the investment team. Someone else at the firm needed to understand MBIA.

All of Pershing Square's other investments were analyzed by Ackman and at least one other analyst. Jonathan Bernstein, who had left the firm in 2006, had spent time on it, but MBIA had always been Ackman's baby. No one had stepped into Bernstein's shoes since he left the firm to go to business school, and no one wanted to. "It was complicated. It was personal," says Ali Namvar, who joined the investment team in early 2006 from Blackstone Group, where he had met Ackman while working on the Wendy's International transaction for Pershing Square.

The MBIA job wouldn't be about analyzing and predicting cash flows, Namvar remembers thinking. In fact, it seemed to be turning into a letter-writing campaign more than anything else as Ackman tried to get others to see the risk he saw in MBIA. "As an analyst, it's just not what you want to do," Namvar says.

Perhaps the biggest drawback to the job was that no MBIA analyst was ever going to know as much about the company as Ackman, Namvar remembers. It just wasn't possible.

"That's why Mick is going to do the work," Ackman said, turning to Mick McGuire. Namvar breathed a sigh of relief.

THE FOLLOWING MONDAY, January 29, 2007, MBIA formally announced the settlement. The company neither admitted nor denied any wrongdoing. The SEC and attorney general's complaints made public the full story of the AHERF reinsurance contracts. MBIA engaged in a "fraudulent scheme" to mask the earnings effect of the default by the Allegheny Health, Education, and Research Foundation, the attorney general's complaint said. The scheme guaranteed that the three reinsurers who covered the AHERF loss got back "every cent of their money plus a profit." To pull off the scheme, MBIA lied to its investors, its auditors, the credit-rating companies, and its reinsurers, according to the complaint.

Without the improper use of reinsurance, MBIA would have reported its first quarterly loss ever in 1998, the complaint stated. Instead, it preserved the appearance of an unbroken track record of strong earnings. "MBIA holds itself out to the investing public as a company that does not risk significant losses on the insurance it writes," the complaint said. "In fact, however, MBIA's winning streak came to an end in 1998."

These details didn't dampen analysts' enthusiasm for the company's prospects. "We reiterate our 'buy' rating," Bank of America analyst Tamara Kravec wrote, increasing her target for the share price to $85 from $78.

"Let the Repurchases Begin," Merrill Lynch analyst Rob Ryan headlined his report. With the investigation behind it, MBIA was clear to restart its stock buyback program, Ryan wrote. He reiterated his "buy" rating.

"Settlement Finally Announced, Shares Benefiting from Short Squeeze," JPMorgan told clients in a research note. "Shares have rallied about $4 since late Friday following the news alerts, which we believe has largely been driven by short covering." The negative overhang had been removed from the stock, the report added.

During a conference call to discuss fourth-quarter earnings, MBIA chief financial adviser Chuck Chaplin explained that MBIA's dealings with Capital Asset would be reviewed by an independent consultant as part of the settlement with regulators. "We don't expect any further enforcement action," Chaplin, who had replaced Nick Ferreri, reassured listeners on the call.

Geoffrey Dunn, the insurance analyst from Keefe Bruyette & Woods, asked the first question on the call. "Good morning and congratulations on getting past all that regulatory stuff," he told Chaplin.

It appeared the coast was clear.

A few days later, MBIA's board approved a $1 billion stock-buyback plan. The timing would depend on receiving approval from the New York State Insurance Department to take further dividends out of the insurance unit, MBIA said.

In early February 2007, Ackman attended the funeral of longtime family friend James Williams. A Michigan attorney, Williams had invested early on with Ackman in Gotham and later served on the board of First Union Real Estate. A reception was held after the funeral at the Bloomfield Hills Country Club. Ackman walked over to say hello to Williams's daughter, who was standing with another woman. When he put out his hand to introduce himself to the other woman, she said: "I know who you are. You're Bill Ackman." She introduced herself as Heather Hunt and said she had reason to know him well because she was the equity analyst who covered the bond insurers for Citigroup.

Ackman had read her reports and considered her to be the most upbeat of the analysts following MBIA. "Any friend of the Williams family is a friend of mine," he said, shaking her hand. Then he added, "This isn't the time or place, but I think you've got it wrong on MBIA." He suggested that they should get together and talk about it back in New York.

Hunt seemed amenable to the idea, even though it looked like the short sellers had been wrong about MBIA. Even where the short sellers had been right in their criticism, it seemed MBIA was going to get the last laugh. On February 13, 2007, a judge ruled against the plaintiffs, a group of shareholders who were seeking to sue MBIA after its share price fell in the wake of the AHERF restatements. The reason for the ruling: The plaintiffs waited too long to begin questioning whether the company had committed fraud. Shareholders had a duty to begin investigating the AHERF transaction after it was described in Gotham's report, the judge said. "When the circumstances would suggest to an investor of ordinary intelligence the probability that she has been defrauded, a duty of inquiry arises," he wrote.

Events that give rise to a duty to inquire are referred to as "storm warnings," and the court believed Ackman's report was one of them.

"The Gotham Partners report, in conjunction with the earlier disclosures regarding the 1998 transactions, effectively put the market, including plaintiffs, on notice of the probability of misrepresentations and deception," the judge wrote. The plaintiffs argued that they were thrown off track by management's immediate denial of allegations raised in the report, but the judge had no sympathy. "Plaintiffs could not have reasonably relied on MBIA's December 9, 2002, vague and general press release to allay the concerns raised by the Gotham Partners report and the series of prior disclosures," the judge decided.

When I spoke to Roy Katzovicz, Pershing's chief legal officer, he couldn't help but admit to a grudging appreciation of the legal strategy.

"Remarkable development," Aaron Marcu, the outside attorney who represented Gotham when it was investigated by the New York attorney general, wrote in an e-mail to Katzovicz and Ackman after a Bloomberg News article ran describing the ruling. "The chutzpah is stunning."

<hr/>

AS MBIA PUT one crisis behind it, storm clouds were forming over the U.S. subprime mortgage market.

The subprime mortgage market had become an increasingly important part of the U.S. mortgage market. In the mid-1990s, only 5 percent of mortgages were considered subprime; in early 2007, that number grew to 20 percent. Outstanding subprime mortgages rose from $35 billion in the mid-1990s to $625 billion in 2005 and $1.7 trillion by 2007.

Most of these mortgages had been used to back trillions of dollars of supposed safe securities. A research report making the rounds in early 2007 reminded investors that it had yet to be seen whether the securitization market was sufficiently regulated, transparent, and stable to entrust with the funding of the U.S. mortgage markets. Josh Rosner, a consultant, and Joe Mason, a finance professor at Louisiana State University, warned that lenders had become far more aggressive in recent years, making it very difficult to predict default rates and losses on mortgages. If those losses exceeded expectations, then the deterioration in mortgage-backed securities could be dramatic.

"When mortgage pools do not perform . . . the outcome is final and dramatic," Rosner and Mason wrote.

To complicate matters, many of these subprime mortgage–backed securities had been purchased by collateralized-debt obligation (CDO), shrouding the risk of the underlying mortgages in one more layer. "Risk that is more difficult to see, by virtue of complexity, is risk just the same," Rosner and Mason warned.

These rumblings did little to dampen spirits as more than 6,000 people descended on the Venetian Hotel in Las Vegas for the annual American Securitization Forum conference in the winter of 2007.

Participants were guardedly optimistic that the concerns about the subprime mortgage market would blow over. Between gambling, golfing outings, and dealmaking, panelists batted around a number of troubling issues.

Mark Adelson, a structured finance analyst with Nomura Securities, took notes during the conference and shared them in a research report. "One panelist feels strongly that BBB subprime ABS [asset-backed securities] are lousy investments because they exhibit cliff risk," Adelson's notes rather ominously read.

Adelson labeled one section of his notes "Scary Topics." It included this idea: "A slowdown in housing can create a feedback loop in the labor market as construction, mortgage lending, and real estate industries contract." And then there was this observation: "Borrowers may start to behave differently than they have in the past in deciding whether or not to default on their loans."

Still, the mood was upbeat. One panelist suggested that the structured finance market was on track to turn out an astounding $1 trillion of CDOs during 2007. Countrywide Financial Corporation, one of the largest providers of credit to the housing market, sponsored a cocktail party networking event. Citigroup executives held court in the Tao bar. *Tonight Show* host Jay Leno headlined the group's annual dinner.

"Looking toward the horizon, one sees the telltale signs of a possible storm," Adelson concluded in his notes. "It could blow over and amount to nothing. Or it could develop into a tornado."

One particularly fateful meeting at the Las Vegas conference was between executives from Financial Guaranty Insurance Company (FGIC), a bond insurer that for years had shunned structured finance in favor of the stodgy, predictable municipal bond business, and IKB Deutsche Industriebank AG, a bank that had lent to middle-sized manufacturing companies in Germany since the 1920s.

In 2001, IKB began to use more of its capital to invest in CDOs. In 2002, it created an off-balance-sheet SPV called Rhineland Funding to purchase these exotic securities. By holding the CDOs in an SPV rather than on its own balance sheet, IKB needed less capital. The CDOs purchased by Rhineland were highly rated: mostly triple A, or super senior, and supposedly better than triple-A risks.

Rhineland obtained funding through the commercial paper market. To attract the risk-averse investors who bought commercial paper, Rhineland needed to reassure those investors that someone stood ready to buy the commercial paper in an emergency. This was known as *liquidity support*. For awhile, IKB provided the liquidity support guarantee, agreeing to buy the paper if the market boycotted it for some reason. But as Rhineland Funding's outstanding commercial paper grew to 12 billion euros, it was clear that the bank wouldn't have the cash if it was called on to buy Rhineland Funding's commercial paper. IKB had come to Las Vegas pitching a structure it called "Havenrock II" to solve that problem.

The German bank had developed a complicated plan. French bank Calyon had agreed to buy $2.5 billion of CDOs from Rhineland Funding if Rhineland couldn't roll over its commercial paper. The proceeds would give IKB the cash or liquidity it needed to pay back some commercial paper investors. Calyon, however, sought to protect itself from any loss on that contract by entering into two credit-default-swap contracts with Havenrock II, a Jersey-registered SPV created by IKB.

Havenrock II was essentially a shell company that lacked the assets to meet its obligations. This is where FGIC came in. IKB executives Winfried Reinke and Michael Braun explained to FGIC executives that they were looking for someone to provide a backstop on Havenrock's obligations. They assured FGIC officials that the bank had never drawn on its liquidity facilities and wouldn't do so in connection with Havenrock II, according to legal documents filed in a later suit over the transaction. Comforted, FGIC agreed to pursue the idea of doing the swap with Havenrock II.

At each step in the chain, an entity agreed to assume the risk that the CDOs could fall in value, but that entity immediately contracted to offload the risk to someone else. FGIC agreed to be the last in the chain only because it believed the ultimate risk resided in the first link of the chain back at IKB.

FGIC officials later met with Stefan Ortseifen, the head of IKB in Dusseldorf. In court documents, they recalled Ortseifen's stressing the importance of Rhineland to IKB. The bank would always stand behind Rhineland and had in the past taken 10 CDOs out of Rhineland when they performed poorly, though the bank had no obligation to so. And although Rhineland had liquidity contracts with banks, it would be unthinkable for IKB to draw on those contracts and to shift distressed assets to third parties, the FGIC employees remember being told. The risk came full circle back to IKB, or so IKB seemed to be saying. On paper, FGIC assumed much of the risk, although the company's business model called for assuming essentially zero risk.

Somewhere in between IKB's assurances that FGIC would never have to cover losses and FGIC's promises to cover any and all losses, the risk vanished.

Bill Gross, manager of PIMCO, one of the world's largest bond funds, might have been poking fun at the goings-on in Las Vegas that year when he wrote about the market's dangerous reliance on the triple-A ratings assigned to securities backed by subprime mortgages:

"AAA? You were wooed, Mr. Moody's and Mr. Poor's, by the makeup, those six-inch hooker heels, and a 'tramp stamp.' Many of these good-looking girls are not high-class assets worth 100 cents on the dollar."

—•—

WHEN ACKMAN WROTE to investors in the early spring of 2007, he had never been more enthusiastic about the fund's MBIA position. "For some time, I have believed that our investment in MBIA credit-default swaps offers the most attractive risk/reward ratio of any investment I have come across in my investment career," Ackman wrote in a March 5, 2007, letter to investors. It cost the fund about $10 million a year to have a bet on MBIA in the credit-default-swap market. The potential payout in the event MBIA filed for bankruptcy was $2.5 billion.

"The price of CDS on MBIA today continues to imply that the market assesses the probability of the company defaulting to be nominal," Ackman wrote. "We believe otherwise."

On the same day, Ackman sent an e-mail to his investment team: "I think we should short some Ambac." He had been reading Ambac Financial Group's 10-K filing, and the second-largest bond insurer had "larger mortgage-backed securities and home-equity exposure than MBIA, at around $60-plus billion, or approximately 10 times shareholders' equity."

The e-mail raised concerns for the team. Now Ackman was looking to short a second bond insurer. Scott Ferguson countered Ackman's suggestion by saying that the shares of both MBIA and Ambac traded at around 10 times earnings per share. "I'm not bullish on multiple contraction from here," said Ferguson, "unless we have a view that the market thinks 'fair' for these guys is eight times earnings."

Someone else noted that virtually every analyst had upgraded MBIA in the last two or three months, "which seems to indicate that the stock price is just going to go right back up to the mid-70s."

"My understanding of the reason for being short MBIA is because we think it is a fraud. If no one is willing to pursue and punish them for it, should we still be shorting it?" Mick McGuire wrote.

But Ackman found their arguments unconvincing. They were in deep trouble, he argued, given "what is going on in the subprime credit world."

The entire investment team was about to get a lesson on just what was going on in the subprime world. In April, Boaz Weinstein, the head of credit trading at Deutsche Bank, called Ackman to set up a meeting. He wanted to bring along Greg Lippman, a trader with the German bank, who helped to create the ABX Index, a benchmark for the performance of various securities backed by subprime mortgages. Among those who helped Lippman create the index, which would become a gauge for the market's fear of subprime, was Rajiv Kamilla, a Goldman Sachs trader with a background in nuclear physics.

The idea behind the ABX Index was to create reference points that could be used as a proxy for the state of the mortgage market. The ABX was actually a series of indexes. Each index averaged prices on a basket of credit-default-swap contracts written on 20 mortgage-backed securities, all originated around the same time and with the same credit rating.

Lippman had come to pitch Pershing Square on betting against the BBB-rated ABX index. Spreads on these mortgage-backed bonds had widened in recent months, but there was more to come, Lippman said. That was because spreads on these bonds had been kept artificially low. The buyers of the securities had been mainly CDO managers—and they'd been overpaying, Lippman said. In some ways, that was not surprising because the same banks that were underwriting the mortgage securities were underwriting the CDOs. There was no real third-party investor involved in the market. As subprime losses worsened, there was potential for "devastation of the sector," according to the presentation.

The trade wasn't the type of investment Pershing typically put on, McGuire remembers. Ackman liked to take positions in large, publicly traded companies that he believed were under- or overvalued by the market. Deutsche Bank's trade, using credit-default swaps to bet on the rising risk premiums on an index of asset-backed securities, was esoteric and seemed initially like "a bunch of witchcraft," McGuire says. "Looking back, it was the playbook for everything that was going to happen [in the subprime crisis]."

It was stunning how vulnerable BBB-rated mortgage bonds—considered safe, investment-grade securities—were to losses. It would take only a minor downturn for the securities to be wiped out. And the housing market was headed for more than a minor downturn. Housing prices had surged for years, mortgage loans had become more aggressive, and borrowers had put down less money. The strong housing market kept default levels in check. But if home prices were to lose their momentum, there would be huge problems, Lippman explained.

In a good housing market, losses on subprime-mortgage pools were typically about 6 percent. Deutsche Bank's models predicted that if home-price appreciation slowed to 4 percent a year, losses on subprime-mortgage pools would jump to nearly 8 percent. That would be enough to wipe out most bonds rated BBB–. If home prices remained flat, then the next level, the BBB-rated bonds, would be wiped out. If home prices actually fell, higher-rated bonds would be in jeopardy.

Pershing didn't put on the trade Lippman pitched, but the presentation affirmed Ackman's view that Pershing should be shorting not just MBIA but also the other bond insurers, including Ambac Financial Group and Security Capital Assurance. On the surface, the bond insurers appeared well insulated. They hadn't guaranteed BBB-rated subprime mortgage–backed bonds. But they had guaranteed something called *mezzanine CDOs*. These securities were backed by mortgage bonds rated A and BBB, levels in between the AAA-rated front row and the B-rated bleacher seats.

If Lippman's projections were right and it took only a small drop in home prices to wipe out BBB-rated securities, then the bond insurers were in deep trouble. MBIA and Ambac may have insured only the AAA-rated parts of the mezzanine CDOs, but if the securities backing those CDOs were worthless, there was no hiding in the highest-rated tranche. By shorting the bond insurers, Ackman could capture rising subprime defaults, the rating-company folly that allowed investment-grade securities to be vulnerable to flat home prices and complex CDOs that failed to structure away risk. Besides, at the time Ackman met with Lippman, it cost $170,000 a year to buy protection on $10 million of the BBB-rated ABX index, whereas the same amount of protection on MBIA cost just $30,000 a year.

The Lippman meeting had started a bit after 5 p.m., but the group was still in the conference room at 8:30 p.m. Several of the attendees canceled dinner plans as the meeting ran late and lights in surrounding office buildings clicked into darkness.

"It was an epiphany moment," says McGuire.

Chapter Sixteen

An Uncertain Spring

As recently as February, there were people saying, "Oh, in the spring buying season, the housing market's going to come back." But right now, on the precipice of July, all of those numbers support a very bearish view.

—KAREN WEAVER, HEAD OF GLOBAL SECURITIZATION, DEUTSCHE BANK, JUNE 2007

G REETINGS FROM ARMONK, where it is springtime," MBIA chief financial officer Chuck Chaplin told listeners on MBIA's first-quarter conference call. It was April 26, 2007, the company had put a more than two-year regulatory investigation behind it, the subprime mortgage crisis wasn't going to touch the company, and the board had authorized a huge share buyback plan.

"We continue to monitor the developments in the subprime mortgage market, but at this time these developments have not caused any significant concern," Chaplin told investors. MBIA's total direct exposure to the subprime market was $5.4 billion, or "less than 1 percent of the outstanding book of business," Chaplin said. The company always explained losses or exposure as a percentage of total exposures, which helped to make the problem appear immaterial. More relevant was looking at MBIA's ability to withstand a loss. MBIA's insurance unit had assets of $11 billion in 2007 and an approximately $1 billion cushion protecting it from a downgrade of its triple-A rating. In that regard, $5.4 billion was an enormous number.

MBIA had backed away from the subprime market over the previous several years, recognizing that the lending had become too risky. Yet MBIA ramped up its business guaranteeing collateralized-debt obligations (CDOs) even though CDOs were backed by securities that were, in turn, backed by subprime mortgages. The important point to remember, however, was that all of these CDOs had "super-senior" underlying ratings, Chaplin reassured listeners.

If ever there was a hint that ratings in the structured-finance market had become inflated, it was the creation of the term "super-senior." Less publicized—but key to understanding the success of the bond insurers— was another revelation about ratings. In the spring of 2007, Moody's Investors Services released a report that showed how municipal bonds would be rated if they were analyzed the same way corporate bonds were. The ratings on city, state, school-district, and sewer-system debt would be much higher if Moody's evaluated the bonds based on the likelihood of default, the report said. In assigning municipal ratings, Moody's ignored the long history of taxpayers and higher levels of government bailing out municipal bond issuers if they came to the brink of default. Instead, they rated these public entities with the assumption they wouldn't be bailed out.

That explained the existence of bond insurance. It explained why the state of California could be insured by a tiny company in Westchester County. Bond insurers weren't less likely to default than the municipalities they insured. They just had a "better" credit rating because they were rated on the corporate scale.

With the help of municipal bond analyst Matt Fabian, I estimated that the double-standard credit-rating system cost municipalities about $3.6 billion on bonds sold in 2006.

"It's the biggest open secret in the market that insurers are insuring municipal bonds that don't need it," JB Hanauer & Company analyst Richard Larkin told me.

It was also the missing piece we did not have when we wrote the "Insurance Charade" article in the fall of 2006. Municipalities were publicly rated as if there was real risk they wouldn't pay their debts. But on a second—largely undisclosed—scale that risk was assessed based on the track record of municipalities finding a way to avert default.

The "moral obligation" that Jay Brown had spoken of in his meeting with Bill Ackman was factored into the second rating scale.

This second scale determined the capital charges applied by the credit-rating companies to the bond insurers when they guaranteed municipal debt.

The article struck a nerve. "Moody's overrates MBIA and massively underrates municipals, thus generating this huge business of bond insurance," one investor wrote me in an e-mail. "It is a racket that the taxpayers are subsidizing private bond-insurance companies. The ultimate irony is that the triple-A-rated bond insurers, who are rated on the corporate scale, are in fact riskier than the A-rated muni issuers, who are rated on the muni scale but are much less likely to default than the insurers. Who is insuring whom?"

ON MAY 23, 2007, Ackman joined the lineup of hedge fund managers making presentations at the Ira Sohn Investment Conference, an annual charity event held at the Time Warner Center in New York. Ackman made a presentation titled "Who's Holding the Bag?" He answered this question by explaining that when the bond insurers were unable to meet their obligations on the billions of dollars of subprime securities and CDOs they had guaranteed, Wall Street banks and brokers would be left without the protection they were counting on.

Bond insurers presented a huge risk to the market, Ackman said. They had virtually no margin for error and yet financial institutions around the world were relying on them to maintain their triple-A rating. Investors trusted them so much, in fact, that bond insurers were one of the few counterparties in the credit-default-swap market that weren't required to post collateral when the value of the CDOs they backed fell. "When losses hit, these guarantees will have no value, and the counterparties will be left holding the bag," Ackman said.

Money had been flowing into the subprime mortgage market because CDO managers had been devouring all the mortgage-backed securities they could lay their hands on, Ackman explained. All that would be needed to halt this flow of money was for investors to get spooked about buying the lowest-rated tranche of a CDO. This piece of a CDO—the smallest, riskiest, and highest-yielding piece—had to be sold or the economics of the transaction didn't work. If the CDO couldn't be sold, then a huge source of demand for mortgage-backed

securities would disappear. If the demand for mortgage-backed securities dried up, then originators wouldn't be able to make as many
mortgages. Every $1 invested in these lower-rated tranches of CDOs
made it possible for the market to originate $111 of subprime mort-
gages, Ackman explained.

The demand for mortgage securities to create CDOs had made
credit too easily available for subprime mortgages. Loan standards
became shoddy. Buyers stretched their finances to get into homes they
couldn't afford. Adjustable-rate mortgages had become common, and
now that loan rates had begun to reset in one giant wave that would
continue for more than a year, borrowers would succumb in droves.
Ackman used scatter graphs, flowcharts, and bar charts to tell a scary
story: If the rating companies were wrong, as Ackman alleged, and the
CDOs weren't as safe as they seemed, then the subprime boom would
turn to bust. Desperate borrowers wouldn't be able to refinance into
lower-rate mortgages. When losses on mortgage pools hit 9 percent, all
mortgage-backed bonds rated triple B and below would become
worthless. Moody's was predicting losses of 6 percent to 8 percent, a
recent upward revision.

Where did MBIA fit into this precarious picture? It had insured
$22 billion worth of CDOs backed by subprime mortgages. Of those,
$5 billion were mezzanine CDOs backed by the securities that would get
wiped out when losses broke through 9 percent, Ackman said.

"How is MBIA preparing for the coming credit storm?" Ackman
asked the audience. It took a $500 million dividend out of its insurance
unit in December, got permission to take another $500 million dividend
out in April, announced a $1 billion stock buyback, and had already
spent at least $300 million of the money raised on buybacks.

The next day, MBIA and Ambac shares fell. It was the beginning of a
long slide. "Wrapper Stocks Down. Why? Pershing Square Is Back,"
wrote Jordan Cahn, a credit-default-swap trader at Morgan Stanley in an
e-mail message to clients.

On Thursday, May 31, Heather Hunt e-mailed Ackman with her
latest report on the bond insurers, which said worries that the bond
insurers would be hit by subprime losses were overstated. "Please don't
take offense," Hunt said. "There are a lot of long investors who are
interested."

The bond insurers might sell off "on bear case suggestions the
companies are exposed to subprime woes, which we believe is out of

context," Hunt wrote. She noted that only 4.5 percent of subprime mortgages were in default at the end of 2006. "Ninety-five percent of the market is still intact."

"No offense taken at all," Ackman wrote back the same day. "Everyone is entitled to their opinion. My only advice is that you should understand what we are saying before you issue a report disagreeing with us." He suggested they set up a meeting.

Ackman was not averse to giving the MBIA presentation for an audience of just one. That spring, Ackman and his wife spent a weekend at Canyon Ranch, a health spa in Lenox, Massachusetts. During an afternoon hike in the Berkshire Mountains, Ackman struck up a conversation with their guide, an older man with the pleasant, incredulous voice of Jimmy Stewart.

The man told Ackman that he had retired from corporate America to do something completely different with his life.

"Where did you work before?" Ackman asked, as they huffed along the steep trail.

"A division of a company you've never heard of," the guide replied. "It's called MBIA."

Now, that's a coincidence, Ackman told him, explaining that he had been trying to warn investors about MBIA for the last five years.

"Oh really," the guide replied. He told Ackman that he still had a significant amount of his retirement funds invested in his former employer's stock.

"You should think very carefully about continuing to own those shares," Ackman said. For the remainder of the hike, as the three wended their way back to Canyon Ranch through pine forests filled with the springtime sound of birds, Ackman told him why.

ON JUNE 5, 2007, Ackman and Roy Katzovicz, Pershing's lawyer, flew to Boston to meet with Congressman Barney Frank (D-Massachusetts), chairman of the House Financial Services Committee. Ackman had opened a new front in his battle with MBIA and hoped that Frank would recommend congressional hearings on the bond insurers. Ackman and Katzovicz wanted to talk to Frank about the coming crisis for the bond insurers and about the dual-scale rating system. They rented a car in Boston and picked up Marty Peretz, who knew Frank from their student days at Harvard. They arrived in Newton early and spent some time running through the presentation at a Starbucks. Ackman and Katzovicz had prepared for the meeting with Frank to last at least 60 minutes.

As soon as the meeting got under way, the group realized that Frank wasn't going to grant them the amount of time it usually took for Ackman to give one of his marathon presentations. Frank is known for his wit and self-deprecating nature. He also has an abrupt way of cutting to the chase. As Ackman began to distribute his PowerPoint representation, Frank slammed his hand down on the document. "No. No. I can see in my head what you tell me with your mouth," Peretz remembers Frank saying.

Katzovicz, who often found himself hauling documents to and from presentations, got a certain satisfaction from Frank's insistence that all this paperwork wasn't necessary. Without missing a beat, Ackman slid the document back to his side of the table and began to tell Frank about the risk the bond insurers posed to the financial system. He talked about how MBIA was underreserving against its guarantees. He also told Frank how Moody's had recently revealed that it rated municipal credits on a scale that made it necessary for many cities and states to buy insurance if they wanted a triple-A rating. He got that argument right away. The conversation was over in 12 minutes. It was the shortest meeting Katzovicz ever remembers attending. It was certainly the shortest presentation Ackman had ever given on MBIA, but it was a success. "We'll hold hearings this fall," Frank said.

On June 13, 2007, word began to circulate about problems at Bear Stearns. The firm had been trying to sell $3 billion of highly rated mortgage-backed securities. Apparently, Merrill Lynch had called in a loan to the Bear Stearns High-Grade Structured Credit Enhanced Leverage Fund, a hedge fund run by the firm's star mortgage trader, which invested in double- and triple-A-rated mortgage-backed securities and CDOs. These sales were testing market demand for the securities, and the results were not encouraging. No one wanted to touch securities tainted by subprime, no matter how high the rating.

On June 20, 2007, J. G. Kosinski of Kore Capital e-mailed Ackman to tell him MBIA credit-default swaps had jumped. "The Street is using it as a proxy hedge for the Bear Stearns CDO-squared fire sale." CDO-squareds are securities largely backed by other CDOs, which are high risk and extraordinarily complex to analyze.

On June 25, Deutsche Bank held a conference call to address investor concerns about the Bear Stearns funds, CDOs, and the subprime market. Investors bought triple-A-rated securities because they didn't want to worry about credit issues; now these securities had become the focus of the market's fears. "You must understand that we're very much in uncharted territory in many ways," Karen Weaver, head of global securitization at Deutsche Bank, said as the conference call in New York got under way.

Weaver explained that the market had been flooded with new types of mortgages that had never been tested in a downturn such as no-income-verification mortgages and loans that let borrowers pay only part of their monthly payments and roll the rest into a larger principal balance. Home-price appreciation had been unprecedented, which might invalidate models that tried to predict the performance of the housing market. "And when you take that and lever it within a structure and then take that structure again and lever it into a CDO obligation," Weaver said, "you've taken that uncertainty and really magnified the impact."

"Is it possible that everyone is thinking 'Oh, Jesus, this is the tip of the iceberg'?" an investor asked the Deutsche Bank analysts. Might the market be realizing that next year after the inevitable downgrades hit "that some of these, let's say double-A, triple-A instruments could go for 50 cents on the dollar? Is that possible?"

"We don't have a crystal ball," replied Anthony Thompson, Deutsche Bank's head of asset-backed and CDO research.

But the crisis was drawing nearer. "We were expecting not to see the first downgrades probably until fall," he said. "It looks like they're going to be coming sooner than that."

Not only was it impossible to predict how deep the loss of value would be on some securities, but also the breadth of those losses was an unknown. The so-called synthetic CDO market added to the uncertainty, Thompson said. These CDOs didn't actually hold mortgage-backed securities. They referenced the securities through a credit-default swap. So although Countrywide Financial might have sold only one $2 billion bond issue backed by subprime mortgages in October 2006, that bond issue might have been referenced 20 times in synthetic CDOs. "This is what has allowed the CDO market to essentially grow much faster than what we'll call the collateral market—this ability to reference the security many times over," Thompson said. If that bond defaulted, the losses would reverberate through securities with 20 times the value of the original bond issue.

It was hard to be optimistic about what lay ahead. "As recently as February, there were people saying, 'Oh, in the spring buying season, the housing market's going to come back,'" Weaver told listeners on the call. "But standing here, right now, on the precipice of July, all of those numbers support a very bearish view."

———

AT AROUND 4:30 p.m. on July 4, 2007, Ackman arrived back in New York on the shuttle from Boston. "Please take a look at MBIA's CDO disclosure. Worse than we expected," Ackman e-mailed Mick McGuire. The previous day, MBIA had posted a document on its Web site detailing its CDO and subprime exposures. It was part of an effort by all of the bond insurers to quiet critics by providing more information on what they had guaranteed.

"I haven't had a chance to access it myself yet, but I saw the release," answered McGuire, who was on his way back from Los Angeles. "By 'worse,' I'm assuming you mean even more exposure, or more risky exposures, than we had estimated?"

"Yes. They give detail on the other collateral in multisector," Ackman responded. "It is mostly subprime and CDOs."

Two days later, Ackman and McGuire met with Heather Hunt from Citigroup. At the end of the meeting, she told them she remained convinced that the bond insurers were insulated from problems in the subprime market. Management's case that the industry was going to dodge this bullet was convincing, she said.

She wasn't alone in her optimism. But several days later, the ground began to shift in the credit markets. On July 10, 2007, Standard & Poor's said it might cut the ratings on $12 billion of subprime mortgage–backed debt, a total of 612 separate bond issues. S&P was also reviewing the "global universe" of CDOs that contained subprime mortgages for possible downgrades. Most of the bonds were in the triple-B range, though some had ratings as high as double A.

News of the sweeping downgrades spooked the market, sending the yield on the 10-year Treasury bond tumbling as investors sought the security of government debt. "I'd like to know. Why now?" Steven Eisman, a portfolio manager at Frontpoint Partners in New York, asked during an S&P conference call later that day to discuss the downgrades. "The news has been out on subprime now for many, many months. The delinquencies have been a disaster for many, many months. The ratings have been called into question for many, many months. I'd like to know why you're making this move today instead of many months ago."

McGuire followed up with Citigroup's Hunt that day in an e-mail. The S&P announcements raised further concerns for MBIA, he insisted.

"Biggest point": S&P said there were indications that losses on securities created in 2006 could hit the 11 percent to 14 percent range, McGuire wrote. "In a world where losses reach this level, all the BBB paper in the (CDO) would be wiped out and much if not all of the A tranche would also be done. This has dire implications for not just mezzanine CDOs but also high-grade CDOs." Mezzanine CDOs are backed by securities rated A and below whereas high-grade CDOs are backed by securities rated A and higher.

McGuire suggested Hunt ask MBIA management the following question: "What levels would cumulative losses in the subprime market have to reach before MBIA would expect to have to pay a claim? I believe that the answer to this question would be well below the 11 percent to 14 percent range that S&P now thinks is possible," McGuire wrote.

Later that day, the dominoes continued to fall. Moody's cut ratings on $5.2 billion of subprime mortgage–backed debt. The downgrades were concentrated on bonds issued by companies including Washington Mutual's Long Beach Mortgage, General Electric's WMC Mortgage, New Century Financial Corporation, and Fremont General Corporation.

The next day, July 11, 2007, Moody's said it might cut ratings on $5 billion of CDOs backed by subprime, a total of 184 debt issues. On July 12, Fitch Ratings said it might downgrade $7.1 billion of subprime-backed debt, including CDOs. Before the day was out, S&P had cut ratings on $6.39 billion of subprime bonds, just two days after putting the debt under review.

By mid-July, the structured finance market was collapsing into crisis. On July 17, investors in one of the two troubled Bear Stearns hedge funds received the bad news: They wouldn't be getting any money back after the fund was forced to sell its assets at distressed prices. On July 18, 5-year credit-default swaps on MBIA's holding company were quoted at more than 100 basis points, indicating that it now cost $100,000 a year to buy protection against a default on $10 million of MBIA debt. The next day, S&P downgraded 75 synthetic CDOs—securities backed by Credit default swap (CDS) referencing bonds. By mid-July, the structured finance market, the multitrillion-dollar experiment that had helped fuel years of debt-propelled spending across the U.S. economy, was shutting down.

Not everyone noticed that the music had stopped. On July 19, the Dow Jones Industrial Average closed above 14,000 for the first time ever.

In Dusseldorf, FGIC and IKB officials were toasting the closing of the Havenrock II transaction. A July 25 dinner followed all-day meetings during which the group discussed its next joint venture, Havenrock III. That transaction was expected to provide another $5 billion in liquidity support for Rhineland Funding and its CDO holdings. Over dinner, Winfried Reinke, the managing director from IKB, brushed off the recent decline in the bank's share price. FGIC executives would later recall that Reinke attributed the drop to activity by short sellers.

Two days after the celebratory dinner, with rumors of IKB's exposure to subprime swirling in the markets, Rhineland Funding was unable to sell new commercial paper. IKB called on Deutsche Bank to provide it with funding under a credit line. Instead of providing the funds, bank officials telephoned German banking and finance regulators and reported that IKB was in financial trouble. Over the weekend, officials began to piece together a rescue. Although it had been deemed an unthinkable scenario, Rhineland called on Calyon to buy $2.5 billion of its CDOs. Calyon, in turn, called on Havenrock II to compensate it for the losses on the CDOs. Havenrock II called in its guarantee from FGIC.

It turned out that Rhineland Funding was supporting an additional 32 special-purpose vehicles known as the Loreley Purchasing Companies, which bought CDOs. The Loreleis are a group of rocks in a particularly beautiful and treacherous stretch of the Rhine River. They are immortalized in German opera and poetry as enchanting female spirits that lured men to their deaths.

That same week, MBIA announced earnings for the second quarter. It posted profits of $1.61 per share, largely in line with expectations. But the market was nervous. MBIA's shares, which had traded above $70 in April, had dropped to just above $57.

MBIA insisted it had anticipated the problems in the subprime market and would evade the losses. "We didn't insure a single residential mortgage-backed securities deal in the quarter," MBIA's chief financial officer Chuck Chaplin told listeners during the July 26 call. But it was hard to be certain it had avoided the danger. MBIA did "insure two multisector CDOs, both high-grade CDOs with approximately 50 percent subprime residential mortgage–backed securities in their collateral pools," Chaplin added. These were "super-senior" guarantees, of course, reflecting a level of protection that would withstand a near end-of-the-world scenario before MBIA took losses.

MBIA also announced it had taken a $10-million charge to write off more than 90 percent of its investment in the Bear Stearns mortgage hedge fund. The amount of the write-off was immaterial to MBIA, yet it was one more disconcerting indication that the very people on Wall Street who were supposed to understand the risk were the ones who had been fooled.

On July 30, 2007, the MBIA investigation was completed. The company released a copy of the report done by the independent consultant who reviewed MBIA's dealings with Capital Asset, the tax-lien company it purchased in the late 1990s. The consultant, John Siffert, a partner with Lankler Siffert & Wohl LLP, said it would have been better practice for MBIA to disclose that it guaranteed the Lehman line of credit. MBIA also should have consolidated Capital Asset on its balance sheet after buying out founder Richard Heitmeyer in late 1998. The bottom line, though, Siffert concluded, was that these shortcomings were immaterial because no one would have cared had they known.

Analysts wouldn't have been bothered about MBIA's Capital Asset exposures because they were focused on other potential problems, including the bankruptcy of the Allegheny Health, Education, and Research Foundation, the report said. The reasoning was oddly circular. Because analysts weren't concerned about Capital Asset, in Siffert's view, it wasn't necessary for MBIA to provide them with more complete information. He didn't address whether they would have focused more on the problems at Capital Asset had they been aware of them.

Siffert's report made particularly interesting reading while the structured finance market was in the process of unraveling. Siffert explained that the $400 million Lehman line of credit would have been deemed an immaterial obligation by analysts and credit-rating companies because "it was collateralized operating debt as opposed to unsecured debt." In other words, the debt was backed by assets, so it didn't present a material risk to MBIA. If need be, MBIA could have sold the assets and repaid the debt.

But what if assets backing a bond are worth far less than the outstanding debt? In the summer of 2007, investors were beginning to question the safety of trillions of dollars of asset-backed debt. Debt might be backed by assets such as subprime mortgages or 10-year-old tax liens in the city of Pittsburgh, but that didn't mean the assets would be enough to repay the debt.

Several issues, including internal e-mails, initially raised suspicions about the Caulis Negris bond issue, Siffert wrote. These included the use of a so-called black-box conduit structure that was provided by Bear Stearns and, of course, the name, an incorrect Latin translation for "black hole." Siffert mentioned but didn't explain how he got comfortable with several breaches of the company's stated underwriting guidelines. These include bypassing the underwriting committee in favor of having several MBIA executives sign off on the transaction and forgoing a review of the bonds by the credit-rating companies.

Siffert didn't address the allegations of numerous community activists and Pittsburgh residents who said MBIA had been slow to acknowledge the true value of the liens (the issue I wrote about in a 2006 Bloomberg article). He also didn't explain why MBIA sold the tax liens back to the city at a fraction of their carrying value. "At no time did MBIA learn that the Capital Asset securitizations contained large, inevitable losses," Siffert stated.

I called Siffert to ask him why he didn't discuss the Pittsburgh lien buyback or the poor quality of the underlying collateral in his report, and he refused to comment. When I pressed him for answers, he told me I was being rude, adding, "I'm not paid to talk to you."

Richard Heitmeyer, who founded Capital Asset and had put himself forward as a whistleblower, told me Siffert never interviewed him as part of his investigation. Not getting his side of the story seemed like a glaring omission by Siffert, Heitmeyer said.

But everyone was eager to put MBIA's problems behind it. "It's another piece of good news for the company—and much-needed good news," Rob Haines, an analyst with the research firm CreditSights, said of the report. Given the concerns in the credit markets about bond insurers and CDOs, a negative finding by the independent consultant "could have been disastrous," he added.

During the last week of July, Gerald Russello, the former lead investigator in the Securities and Exchange Commission (SEC) probe of MBIA, e-mailed Ackman a copy of an article headlined "MBIA Independent Review Finds No Wrongdoing."

"I have lost confidence in the SEC," Ackman replied.

When Ackman met again with the SEC later that summer, he lost his temper and told the government attorneys, "This company will implode, it will take the global capital markets with it, and you could have prevented it."

Chapter **17** *Seventeen*

Apocalypse Now

Super-senior CDOs: "The greatest triumph of illusion in twentieth century finance."

STRUCTURED FINANCE AND COLLATERALIZED DEBT OBLIGATIONS (JOHN WILEY & SONS, 2008)

O UTSIDE PERSHING SQUARE'S offices on Seventh Avenue in Manhattan, Bill Ackman, Pershing analyst Mick McGuire, and Roy Katzovicz, the firm's chief legal officer, piled into a taxi. All three were wearing suits on a hot and sticky first day of August for a 9:30 a.m. meeting with New York State Insurance Superintendent Eric Dinallo.

They were running late after the usual last-minute debate over cutting pages from the presentation. "For every page of one of Bill's presentations, you can be sure there were two or three that were cut," McGuire remembers. "If it was up to Bill, every presentation would be an eight-hour seminar." Katzovicz carried a box filled with copies of their latest presentation: "Bond Insurers: The Next S&L Crisis?"

After a few minutes, the taxi slowed in the crawl of rush hour traffic. "We shouldn't have taken a taxi," Ackman fretted. As they reached Houston Street, Ackman insisted they get out and take the subway: "It will be faster." The subway left them several blocks from the insurance department on Beaver Street in lower Manhattan, and they closed the remaining distance at a high-speed walk in muggy Manhattan heat, Katzovicz struggling with the box of presentations. The pace was nothing unusual for Ackman. "Bill walks faster than anyone I know," McGuire says.

Dinallo had been appointed to the top insurance post by New York Governor Eliot Spitzer in January 2007. A New York University–educated lawyer, Dinallo worked under Spitzer during his crusading days as the state's attorney general. Dinallo masterminded the use of the Martin Act to go after Wall Street fraud and stood on the podium along with his boss at press conferences when Spitzer announced settlements with some of the country's largest financial institutions. Since taking up his post at the insurance department, Dinallo had already pushed through a long-stalled insurance settlement to cover the September 11, 2001, destruction of the World Trade Center. On that hot August morning, new problems were looming.

The group took seats around a conference table and Ackman delivered the "Who's Holding the Bag?" presentation he had given at the Ira Sohn Investment Conference in May. He described how the incentives to securitize and sell mortgages created enormous moral hazard in the mortgage market, how faulty structures allowed billions of dollars of doomed securities to be built out of the riskiest parts of bonds, and how small losses on $100 billion portfolios of collateralized-debt obligations (CDOs) could wipe out a bond insurer's entire capital base.

He also reviewed other issues specific to the insurance department's role in overseeing the bond insurers, such as how bond insurers were engaging in prohibited credit-default swaps (CDSs) and how MBIA's growing fixed-income arbitrage business amounted to a disguised dividend from its regulated insurance subsidiary. Ackman argued that Dinallo couldn't stand by and allow the credit-rating companies to usurp the department's role as the de facto regulator of bond insurers. The ABX index referencing triple-B-rated subprime mortgage bonds indicated investors expected to recover just 65 cents on the dollar for those bonds before the credit-rating companies began to downgrade the debt, he said. Wait for the rating companies to "regulate" the market and it will be too late.

Ackman made the case that the insurance department should stop dividends to the holding companies of bond insurers and halt holding-company share buybacks because those funds would be needed to pay claims at the insurance subsidiaries. Pershing Square's short interest in the holding companies had aligned the hedge fund's interests with those of policyholders, Ackman argued. "There's a huge crisis on the horizon, and it's going to come sooner than you think," he told the assembled group.

When the Pershing Square group got back to the office, others at the fund were eager to hear how things went. "Everybody would pile into Bill's office for a recounting of events," McGuire remembers. It was more than an investment-team event. Everyone was eager to hear about it: the investor-relations group, the traders, the tech guys, the assistants. "People appreciated the position, its significance to the firm and to Bill personally."

"It was an incredible meeting," Ackman told the group. Regulators were going to see that MBIA shouldn't be taking any more money out of its insurance unit because policyholders are in jeopardy. "They're toast," Ackman concluded of MBIA.

From the outside, Ackman was the ultimate skeptic, the guy who didn't believe in the most trusted company on Wall Street. Around the office, however, he could be seen as hopelessly idealistic for believing he would be able to convince the world he was right about the bond insurers. After every meeting it was as if the same regulators and credit-rating company analysts, who hadn't acted yet despite years of presentations, finally got it. Scott Ferguson, with the investment team, was much more the in-house skeptic.

"Really? What did they say?" Ferguson asked.

"They're regulators," Ackman told him, "so, of course, they can't really *say* anything."

Eventually, one of Ackman's phrases for describing the success of his MBIA meetings was adopted around the office as shorthand for Ackman's optimism. "Bill's meeting? Ten out of ten?" "Yep. Ten out of ten."

———

MBIA HAD SCHEDULED a conference call for the next day, August 2, to allay concerns about its CDO and subprime exposure. MBIA management put in place a new protocol for the call. All questions were required to be submitted in advance by e-mail. Mick McGuire, figuring questions from Pershing Square wouldn't make the cut, messaged Jordan Cahn, on the credit-default-swap desk at Morgan Stanley, with some thoughts.

"The company, and much of the analyst community, speaks to the idea that the MBIA guarantees attach at super-senior levels of the capital structure and have a large cushion below them, making it highly unlikely that they suffer a loss," McGuire wrote. "Yet it appears to me that every one of their high-grade CDOs has subprime exposure that exceeds the cushion protecting MBIA. If the subprime collateral is A-rated or lower and losses reach 15 percent, then the collateral is worthless and MBIA will begin to incur losses on its guarantees.

"The Holy Grail question relates to cumulative losses," McGuire continued. "What would the cumulative losses within the 2006 subprime universe need to be for MBIA to incur a loss in its CDO portfolio?"

The company received hundreds of questions in advance of the call, Greg Diamond, the head of investor relations, told listeners as the call got under way. Diamond warned listeners to try to keep up with the slides because the presentation provided some "challenging and detailed information."

"Bottom line, there may be downgrades in this portfolio as a result of the unprecedented housing crunch," said Chuck Chaplin, MBIA's chief financial officer, "but our subprime-mortgage exposure does not appear to pose a threat to the company's balance sheet."

At some point in the long queue of questions, McGuire's got asked: "What would be the cumulative losses within the subprime universe needed for MBIA to incur a loss in its direct and CDO portfolio?"

The question elicited a long response but not an answer. If 100 percent of the collateral rated A and below defaulted with no recovery, "certainly the CDOs of high-grade mezzanine collateral would be materially impacted," said Anthony McKiernan, head of MBIA's structured finance. But he didn't say what level of losses would trigger that scenario. Ten percent? Fifteen percent? Fifty percent?

The scenario—hundreds of A-rated securities all defaulting—sounded far-fetched. But as Deutsche Bank's Greg Lippman had pointed out to the investment team at Pershing Square just a few months earlier, it was not. In a good housing market, with double-digit annual gains in home values in many markets, losses on subprime loans had run about 6 percent. Deutsche Bank figured that if home-price appreciation fell to 4 percent a year, subprime losses would jump to 8 percent. A market in which home prices remained flat would completely wipe out triple-B-rated bonds. A triple-B rating is a low investment-grade-rated security. A decline in home values would cause the damage to move up the rating scale, putting even single-A-rated bonds in jeopardy.

The subprime market contained the hallmark of every Ponzi scheme. It worked only as long as more money was put into the scheme. When home prices were rising, overextended borrowers usually could pay off their first mortgage—and often a home-equity loan and credit-card bills on top of that—by selling their house in a rising market. Once home prices stopped rising, the game was over, and home prices would plummet.

The mortgage market may have become perilous in many places, but MBIA executives said the company remained open for business. There was strong demand for bond insurance, and the premiums that insurers could command in the current market had improved, said Patrick Kelly, head of CDOs and structured products at MBIA. "We want to take advantage of the current situation where we can, even in the ABS CDO market," Kelly said. "We also want to avoid getting stuffed with the risk that people are just looking to get off their own books."

THREE WEEKS LATER, on August 24, 2007, Merrill Lynch's head of fixed income, Osman Semerci, along with three other executives from Merrill, boarded a helicopter for the short flight to MBIA's Armonk headquarters.

Janet Tavakoli, a CDO guru who runs her own structured finance research firm in Chicago, later dubbed Merrill Lynch's last-ditch effort to dump toxic securities on MBIA the *"Apocalypse Now* helicopter ride," a reference to the scene in the Francis Ford Coppola movie in which U.S. helicopters level a Vietcong village while blaring Wagner's highly dramatic "Ride of the Valkyries." These CDOs were so loaded with toxic subprime mortgages that Tavakoli expected the bond insurer to take losses on this so-called "super-senior" exposure.

In her book on CDOs, *Structured Finance and Collateralized Debt Obligations* (2008), Tavakoli calls super-seniors "the greatest triumph of illusion in twentieth century finance." A major motivation of creating super-senior tranches of CDOs, she says, is that this layer of risk is very difficult to price. Investors know what the going rate is for a security rated A or triple-A, but what yield should an investor earn on something that's rated higher than triple-A?

Over the last several years, Merrill Lynch, known as the "Bullish on America" stockbroker to millions of retail investors, had become a huge player in the mortgage business. The firm hired Christopher Ricciardi, a Credit Suisse trader, in 2003 to ramp up its presence in the CDO business. Ricciardi turned Merrill into what the *Wall Street Journal* later dubbed "the Wal-Mart of CDOs." In 2006 and 2007, Merrill underwrote 136 CDOs, raking in $800 million in underwriting fees on the business, according to Thomson Financial. To assure a steady supply of raw material for these CDOs, Merrill in late 2006 bought First Franklin, a subprime-mortgage originator.

When the music stopped in the housing market in late 2006, Merrill Lynch's balance sheet was loaded down with exposure to risky borrowers. "By September 2006, Merrill Lynch carried on its books inventory that included at least $17 billion in RMBS CDO securities, as well as an additional $18 billion in mortgage-backed bonds, and a further $14 billion in subprime loans," according to a complaint MBIA later filed against Merrill Lynch.

By the time Merrill executives left Armonk on that August afternoon, Gary Dunton, MBIA's chief executive officer, agreed to back another $5 billion of CDOs.

Merrill Lynch wasn't the only institution terrorized by collapsing asset values during the summer of 2007. At UBS, the chairman and chief executive officer (CEO) of the Swiss banking giant got a crash course in super-senior CDOs during the first week of August 2007. The lessons were shocking. UBS had ballooned its super-senior CDO exposure to $50 billion by September 2007, up from virtually zero just 19 months earlier.

Later, in the spring of 2008, UBS issued a report to Swiss banking regulators and to its shareholders explaining how the bank lost $18.7 billion on U.S. subprime mortgages. The risk management group "relied on the AAA rating of certain subprime positions, although the CDOs were built from lower-rated tranches of residential mortgage–backed securities," the report said. Banks built models to predict the future performance of mortgages using just five years of data, and data taken from a period of strong economic growth, no less. Meanwhile, no one at the top imposed any limits on how much of this super-senior exposure the bank could hold. "The balance-sheet size was not considered a limiting metric," the report said.

About the only thing UBS could say in its defense was that it believed "its approach to the risk management and valuation of structured-credit products was not unique and that a number of other financial institutions with exposure to the U.S. subprime market used similar approaches."

RATING	CAPITAL REQUIREMENTS PER $100 OF EXPOSURE
AAA	0.56
BBB	4.80
BBB–	8.00
BB+	20.00
BB	34.00
BB–	52.00

As the summer of 2007 wound down, the heads of major financial institutions were coming to grips with a terrifying scenario: Severe credit-rating downgrades of super-senior CDOs were going to wipe out their capital. Banks and brokerages around the world were moving toward implementation of BASEL II guidelines, under which capital charges are minimal at high ratings but escalate dramatically as securities are downgraded (see figure above).

A bank with $50 billion of AAA-rated CDOs on its books would have to hold about $280 million in capital against the position. If those securities were downgraded to triple-B, then the bank would need $4 billion of capital. A further downgrade to double-B would increase the bank's capital need to $26 billion, or nearly 100 times the capital it needed when the securities were rated triple-A. This steep increase in capital requirements turned the collapse in the value of CDOs into a global banking crisis. Financial institutions were relying on credit-rating companies to determine how much capital to hold against trillions of dollars of securities. That meant every time the credit-rating companies stamped a security with a triple-A rating, more capital was sucked out of the financial system. Triple-A-rated securities— considered the safest of safe investments—actually posed enormous risk to the financial system. The risk of a triple-A rating was that it was wrong.

As banks watched CDO ratings collapse, they saw one way to get those ratings back to triple-A: get the securities wrapped by bond insurers. Pressure was building for the credit-rating companies to rethink the triple-A ratings on bond insurers. Credit-default-swap contracts on the bond insurers were trading at levels that suggested the companies were rated far below triple-A.

The time was ripe. Ackman sent a note to Chris Mahoney, the chief credit officer at Moody's Investors Service. "There is still time for Moody's to revisit its analysis and our numerous presentations to you on MBIA and the bond-insurance business," Ackman wrote in an e-mail. "The notion that these companies are triple-A is as much an absurdity as the triple-A ratings Moody's has placed on subprime mezzanine CDOs and other highly rated structured finance vehicles on which investors have incurred large losses."

Mahoney wasn't the only one fielding questions about triple-A-rated securities. American International Group (AIG), the world's biggest insurance company, was also faced with questions about its massive amounts of guarantees on super-senior CDOs during its second-quarter conference call on August 9. Investors and analysts were concerned about a unit called AIG Financial Products (AIGFP), a small operation head-quartered in London, which specialized in guaranteeing CDOs using credit-default swaps. AIG, like the bond insurers, guaranteed these securities at the super-senior level and, also like the bond insurers, it insisted that it did not foresee making any payments on these exposures.

On the call, Goldman Sachs analyst Thomas Cholnoky asked just how bad things would have to get before AIG would take losses on these super-senior exposures. "It is hard for us, without being flippant, to even see a scenario within any kind of realm or reason that would see us losing $1 in any of those transactions," answered Joseph Cassano, who ran AIG Financial Products.

"That's okay," Cholnoky replied.

"Just okay?" AIG's Cassano shot back.

"I agree with you," Cholnoky said. "I tend to think that this market is overreacting."

But was it?

In testimony before Congress a year later, Joseph St. Denis, a former SEC enforcement officer and the vice president of accounting policy at AIG Financial Products, reported that the process of valuing super-senior CDOs turned contentious in the summer of 2007. The problems intensified over an off-balance-sheet entity called Nightingale, St. Denis said. Nightingale was a structured-investment vehicle (SIV) created by AIG Financial Products. SIVs are intended as stand-alone entities, much like asset-backed commercial-paper programs such as Rhineland Funding. They finance themselves by selling short-term debt and using the proceeds to purchase securities with longer maturities such as super-senior CDOs.

St. Denis was vacationing in Puerto Rico in the summer of 2007 when he began receiving e-mails from the credit traders in London wanting to know if AIGFP would have to shift Nightingale onto AIG's balance sheet if AIG Financial Products purchased all of its outstanding debt. That might become necessary, the traders told him, because the market was rejecting the commercial paper. When St. Denis returned from vacation, he discovered that the group had already bought the debt. He immediately scheduled a call with the firm's Office of Accounting Policy (OAP) in London to discuss the problem of the company's massive super-senior exposure. The instant the call was over, Cassano burst into the conference room. "He appeared to be highly agitated," St. Denis later told Congress. His statement was cleaned up to remove objectionable language before being released to the public.

"What the [expletive deleted] is going on here?" Cassano asked.

"We've just finished a call with OAP," St. Denis replied. "They agree with our approach . . . "

Cassano let loose with a string of expletives. Then Cassano said, "I have deliberately excluded you from the valuation of the super-seniors because I was concerned that you would pollute the process."

St. Denis resigned from AIG shortly thereafter.

———————

DURING THE SECOND WEEK of August 2007, three issuers of asset-backed commercial paper (ABCP)—American Home Mortgage Investment Corporation, Luminent Mortgage Capital, and Aladdin Capital Management—opted to extend the maturity of their commercial paper. Under the terms of the debt, the issuer was permitted to do this as an alternative to arranging a bank liquidity line. It was a clever idea, allowing holders of the commercial paper to earn a small additional yield by granting this option to the issuer. Unfortunately, when the option was exercised, it triggered a panic. Investors didn't buy commercial paper to find out that they'd lent their money to an issuer undergoing a crisis of confidence. "The subprime tsunami has come to the beach, as it were, to the safest of the safe," Lee Epstein, CEO of Money Market One, told Bloomberg News.

For years, Wall Street had been expanding this market, using it to finance all types of loans—including high-risk subprime mortgages. The key had been to diversify the risk, to elevate the ratings to the highest-possible level and wipe away any perception of risk. But investors now feared the $1.5 trillion market was contaminated. Subprime and CDOs had turned the ABCP market into a field strewn with land mines. Investors tiptoed toward the fringes, hoping their commercial paper matured without a problem. Once they were out, they stayed out, leaving no one to provide funding for more than a trillion dollars of mortgages, credit card balances, and auto loans.

Some market commentators later pointed to August 9 as the official beginning of the credit crisis, the point at which isolated problems turned into systemic failure. The next day, central banks around the world coordinated a massive intervention for the first time since the September 11, 2001, terrorist attacks. The U.S. Federal Reserve System added $43 billion to the banking system, the European Central Bank flooded the interbank market with $215 billion, and the Bank of Japan added $8.4 billion.

On August 14, 17 Canadian ABCP sellers couldn't roll over their commercial paper. It appeared the banks had an "out" for providing liquidity support in the event of a market disruption. They decided that what was happening qualified as a market disruption. Simon Adamson, an analyst with CreditSights in London, told Bloomberg News that the situation was developing "a frightening momentum."

Ackman wrote to Pershing Square investors the same day: "In 2006, our short position in MBIA's stock and our investment in credit-default swaps were a source of significant mark-to-market losses," Ackman said. "We have more than recouped our previous mark-to-market losses on this investment." Investors seeking to protect $10 million of MBIA debt against default for five years would have agreed to pay $16,000 a year in premiums on the day MBIA announced its settlement with regulators in January. That same insurance now cost $250,000 a year. "We believe that we are still in the early innings," Ackman wrote.

As the summer drew to a close, Ackman attended the U.S. Open as a guest of JPMorgan. He made his way through the crowd at the Arthur Ashe Stadium in Flushing Meadows to the bank's court-side suite. Inside, JPMorgan CEO Jamie Dimon and his wife chatted with guests. Dimon shook Ackman's hand and mentioned that he'd seen the "Who's Holding the Bag?" presentation. "Very interesting," he told Ackman.

Guests milled around the open bar and dug into a buffet of filet mignon and Caesar salad. Several people gathered in front of the plate glass window to watch the action below. The event, a favorite entertainment venue for Wall Street clients, was packed. For all the problems in the credit markets, stocks were still on the way up and wouldn't peak until October 9, 2007, when the Dow Jones Industrial Average would hit an all-time high of 14,164.

By the end of August 2007, the collapse of Wall Street was nevertheless well under way. The financial system was breaking down in places unfamiliar even to those who worked on Wall Street: the asset-backed commercial paper market and the world of off-balance-sheet entities like SIVs. It deteriorated as investors struggled with how to price billions of dollars of super-senior CDOs and as investors came to realize that sometimes it isn't good enough to be 99.99 percent certain about the future.

"Make sure you don't have any bond-insurer exposure," Ackman told Dimon as the matches played on.

Chapter 18 *Eighteen*

Parting the Curtain

As the credit market continues to weaken, our confidence that guarantors will survive the credit meltdown is waning.

—KEN ZERBE, MORGAN STANLEY ANALYST, NOVEMBER 2007

IF ONE WERE to pinpoint the day when faith in the bond insurers was irreparably undermined, it would probably be October 25, 2007. That was the day MBIA reported the second quarterly loss in its history. It had taken years, a short-seller crusade, and a two-year regulatory investigation to get MBIA to acknowledge its first quarterly loss.

This time, there was no disguising the fact. MBIA reported mark-to-market losses of $342 million to reflect the decline in the value of collateralized-debt obligations (CDOs) it had insured. Still, not everyone was convinced that the company was coming clean. "I'm trying to understand how the guarantors can take such low levels of mark-to-market losses relative to what the rest of the Street is taking on these securities," Ken Zerbe, an analyst with Morgan Stanley, said during the company's conference call.

The day before, Merrill Lynch had reported the largest loss in its 93-year history, taking $7.9 billion of writedowns mainly on

197

super-senior CDOs backed by subprime mortgages. The writedowns reflected a discount of 19 percent to 57 percent of the face value of various types of securities Merrill held. "Bottom line is we got it wrong by being overexposed to subprime," Merrill's chief executive officer (CEO) Stan O'Neal told listeners on the firm's October 24, 2007, conference call.

Then O'Neal did something extraordinary. He apologized for having been too slow to lay off the firm's exposure to other firms and investors. As the subprime mortgage market collapsed during the first quarter, Merrill Lynch faced a desperate scramble to get mortgages, mortgage-backed securities, and CDOs off its balance sheet, O'Neal explained.

Unfortunately for MBIA shareholders, Merrill Lynch had succeeded in getting MBIA to assume more than $5 billion of its CDO risk. MBIA and Merrill had exposure to very similar securities. Yet if MBIA had taken writedowns of the same magnitude on securities it guaranteed as Merrill took on securities it held, then MBIA would have reported $3 billion, rather than $342 million, of losses, the equivalent of more than 45 percent of its insurance company capital.

MBIA chief financial officer Chuck Chaplin gave Zerbe an answer as to why Merrill and MBIA were taking such different markdowns on super-senior CDOs, but it was not easy to follow: "The vast majority [of CDOs] are marked using market quotes for the collateral in the deals and then the subordination of the deal as inputs into an analytical mode that then incorporates assumptions about correlation and the relationship between collateral spreads and financial guarantee premiums to calculate an implied premium for the deal," Chaplin said. "And then the present value of the difference between the implied premium and the premium that we receive is the balance sheet value at period end," he added.

The explanation left many peplexed and unsatisfied. MBIA's shares, already under pressure, began to drop.

Zerbe wasn't the only equity analyst raising questions. Heather Hunt, who covered the bond insurers for Citigroup, asked why all of these super-senior CDOs were getting insured in the first place. Was it because the market is just at a standstill and having insurance is the only way of getting the deal done? Hunt asked.

"Heather, these are assets that are sitting on the balance sheets of the banks," Chaplin explained.

"These are assets the banks already held?" Hunt asked.

"Those assets could be there for a variety of reasons," Chaplin offered.

So the insurance was put on after they bought the CDOs? asked Hunt.

"Right," Chaplin replied. "So as the banks and investment banks faced growing notional balance-sheet size, this was an opportunity to hedge some of that."

"Got it. Okay," said Hunt.

Equity analysts had cheered MBIA's move into the CDO business, yet it seemed they had a poor understanding of what was driving that business. This wasn't the bond insurance business anymore. MBIA was providing a service that allowed banks to make huge amounts of securities disappear from their balance sheets. This disappearing act was known as a "negative basis trade." It allowed financial institutions to book all their profits on vast CDO holdings up front while assuming away the risk of default. As the risk seemingly disappeared, so did the need to hold capital. All the banks had to do was buy protection on the CDOs from a bond insurer, and then hope the bond insurer didn't go bust.

This was the trade Ackman had asked Warren Buffett about at the 2003 Berkshire Hathaway annual meeting, the transaction that Buffett had warned would bring out the brokers "with their fins showing."

Then Chaplin touched on a topic that equity analysts watched very closely. MBIA had halted its buyback plan. "Going into a period of uncertainty, we think it's critical for our balance-sheet strength to be unquestioned," Chaplin explained. Within minutes, the stock swooned.

As the call drew to a close, the questions became more accusatory. "Are you saying that the mark-to-markets here are irrelevant because the markets are wrong?" one caller asked. "Because so far this year, the markets have been more than right, and the rating agencies have been totally wrong on virtually everything."

The logic of the entire bond-insurance business was under fire. "Why would someone have wrapped these portions of the portfolios? The point of insurance is to protect yourself from losses. It seems that there is no instance that you could have a loss. That's what MBIA seems to be telling us. So why do people buy your product?" a caller asked.

"What we are providing is protection against remote losses," Chaplin replied. "That's an important part of our business model, and there has been ongoing demand for protection against those remote losses at least going back over the 34-year history of our company."

"Okay, if it's based on remote losses and your model goes back 34 years, have you ever seen a housing market like this in the last 34 years?" the caller asked. "And what is your definition of remote? I mean, at which level is this a problem? At what point do you start to worry?"

If Chaplin knew where that level was, he didn't appear eager to share it. "It is possible that as we see the housing market deteriorate that there will be pressure on transactions in our portfolio, and I think I said that pressure could be manifested as losses in the future," Chaplin said. "We have not seen any to date. That doesn't mean, given the potential for an unprecedented experience in the housing sector, that there will never be any losses, so it would be unfair to say that we expect that there never will be any loss no matter what happens."

By the time the call ended, MBIA's shares had dropped 21 percent. It was the single biggest drop in its share price since the stock market crash in 1987.

During the Gotham investigation four years earlier, the question of MBIA's CDO losses had generated intense debate. Bill Ackman was asked to justify the dealer estimates he used in his report. To regulators, the gulf between Ackman's and MBIA's estimates for the bond insurer's CDO losses suggested wild exaggeration on Ackman's part.

"Why is their number $35.5 million and yours comes out to somewhere between $5 [billion] to $7 billion?" an attorney for the Securities and Exchange Commission (SEC) asked Ackman. "That is a big number."

"Someone is wrong," Ackman said. "That is the answer."

Someone was clearly wrong in the fall of 2007. This time, however, it wasn't so easy to say that MBIA's critics—or those skeptical of Merrill Lynch's or Citigroup's numbers—were the ones exaggerating.

By October 30, credit-default-swap (CDS) premiums on MBIA Inc. were bid at 250 basis points, meaning it cost $250,000 to buy protection against default on $10 million of MBIA Inc. debt. The next day it cost $295,000; by November 1, it jumped to $345,000. "The problem now is that investors fear the relationship between the rating agencies and the guarantors is so incestuous that the rating agencies cannot issue downgrades without implicitly conceding that their proprietary capital models are flawed," wrote Kathy Shanley, an analyst with the research firm Gimme Credit.

By November 2, CDS rates jumped to $470,000; one day later, the cost stood at $510,000. "As the credit market continues to weaken, our confidence that guarantors will survive the credit meltdown is waning," Zerbe, the Morgan Stanley analyst, wrote in a November 2 report ominously titled *Financial Guarantors on the Knife's Edge.* Zerbe was forecasting that MBIA and Ambac each would take losses of $2.3 billion to $11.7 billion. For years, MBIA had guided analysts so that their forecasts came within a few cents of the company's earnings-per-share results. Ideally, MBIA would beat the forecasts by just enough to show that any surprises were positive ones. That steady, predictable, pleasing world was gone.

Then on November 5, Fitch Ratings, the smallest of the three rating companies, said it planned to spend the next six weeks reviewing the capital of all the bond insurers. Fitch stopped short of putting the companies under formal review for downgrade. The credit-rating company warned, however, that recent downgrades of mortgage securities had been "broader and deeper" than Fitch had anticipated. Any bond insurer that failed the test would have a month to raise capital or have its rating cut. The companies were being given a running start.

On November 8, 2007, Moody's Investors Service followed up with a similar warning. By the end of the month, Standard & Poor's (S&P) began its unofficial review.

What would it mean if the bond insurers lost their triple-A ratings? Bloomberg News collected some data and came up with an estimate that it would cost investors roughly $200 billion. It was almost certainly a conservative guess. Greg Peters, head of credit strategy at Morgan Stanley, summed it up. "We shudder to think of the ramifications," he told me. It would be "a huge destabilizing force."

For several weeks, the financial world waited for the credit-rating companies to rule. "We're all rooting for the bond insurers," a banker on the asset-backed securities desk of a bank in London told me. Without bond insurance, underwriters were going to find it next to impossible to sell asset-backed securities. Everyone's job depended on the market picking up again. "Believe me," he added, before leaving me with an indelible image of Wall Street's support for MBIA and its competitors, "we come into work every morning with our pom-poms."

ON NOVEMBER 8, the day ACA Capital, the smallest bond insurer, announced results, it became clear just how devastating a credit-rating downgrade could be. ACA Capital was the only A-rated bond insurer among a field of companies with triple-A ratings. The New York–based company was founded by Russ Fraser, a longtime ratings-company executive, who had been forced out by the board of directors in 2001 over his refusal to insure CDOs.

Fraser didn't understand or trust CDOs that required analysts to abandon traditional credit analysis and rely instead on complex financial models. "Every PhD in the world is saying this is noncorrelated risk," Fraser recalled of the CDOs brought before ACA's credit committee. "But every CDO we looked at had the same 60 to 100 names. And they were never Exxon, Mobil, and Shell. The names were WorldCom and Enron and Tyco."

By the fall of 2007, ACA Capital backed $65 billion of CDOs. Now, instead of exposure to Enron, the insurer had exposure to subprime. As a result, it announced a $1.7 billion writedown on its portfolio. Alan Roseman, ACA's CEO, came out swinging on the conference call to discuss the quarter's results. "We do not have a capital-adequacy issue according to S&P's commentary and analysis," he said. "Any public speculation or rumor to the contrary is at best misguided or at worst an intentional effort to negatively influence our stock price."

The bond insurer's clients were being "fed fiction" about the company, Roseman told listeners. The company faced no liquidity issues, at least not at its current rating level. And there was no reason to believe its rating would be cut.

"ACA is principally paid to absorb market price volatility," he explained. "We assume the positive and the negative over the life of the transaction, thereby providing a market hedge for our counterparties." The company was "absorbing" losses of $1.7 billion for its counterparties. But that was only from an accounting standpoint. ACA Capital didn't expect to actually pay any claims on the CDOs. In fact, the company had only $425 million in capital.

If ACA Capital was downgraded to triple B, however, it would be required not only to "absorb" those losses on its income statement but also to terminate the contracts and pay its counterparties in cash for the decline in the market value of the CDOs.

An analyst on the call asked Roseman to run through the downgrade scenario just to be sure he understood the implications: "So right now, you'd have to meet about $1.7 billion, or whatever the number would be," the analyst said. "Something is wrong here."

"One point seven billion dollars was our negative mark at the end of the third quarter," Roseman explained.

"So that's the amount you'd have had to meet at *that* point," the analyst said.

"Approximately," Roseman replied. "I mean I can't tell you exactly."

The analyst nearly apologized for the question: "Just hypothetical, and we understand you're nowhere near breaking through that."

"That's correct," Roseman said.

But at 4:25 p.m. that afternoon, S&P placed ACA Capital's A rating under review for a possible downgrade. There was no way the bond insurer could meet termination payments if it was downgraded, JPMorgan Chase & Company analyst Andrew Wessel told Bloomberg TV. "ACA is a likely candidate to get thrown to the wolves first," Wessel said.

It was a hint of what was to come in the credit-default-swap market.

<hr>

JUST WHEN IT SEEMED that no sensible person could believe in the bond-insurance business anymore, Warren Buffett tossed his hat into the ring. The *Wall Street Journal* reported that Berkshire Hathaway might provide capital to the bond-insurance industry. On November 13, 2007, the day the story ran, MBIA shares surged on the prospect of a capital infusion, though there was no indication Buffett was considering investing in the company. Investors hoped that Buffett—who coined the adage "Be fearful when others are greedy and be greedy when others are fearful"—believed the worst was over for the bond insurers.

The industry remained on the defensive. At a Bank of America conference in New York on November 27, 2007, executives from the bond-insurance companies sought to assure investors. "We're going to defend the triple-A credit rating," Ambac's chief financial officer Sean Leonard told the assembled group.

"Job No. 1 is to show that we have the stability around our triple-A ratings that investors expect," said Edward Hubbard, president of XL Capital Assurance, the bond-insurance unit of a company called Security Capital Assurance.

Chuck Chaplin, MBIA's chief financial officer, reminded the group that all the bond insurers, also referred to as *monolines* because they insured only debt, were in this together. "If any major monoline were to have a rating change, it would have a real impact on all the business of the monolines," Chaplin said.

That's what made Domenic Frederico's comments so shocking. Frederico, the CEO of Assured Guaranty, explained why his company had not followed its competitors into the business of guaranteeing CDOs backed by subprime mortgages.

"When we ran the correlations, the model [for such underwriting] blew up," Frederico told the group.

CDOs backed by subprime mortgages were much more vulnerable to a complete wipeout than bonds backed by mortgages.

As homeowners default on their mortgages and the underlying properties are sold for less than the amount of the mortgage, losses begin to build up in the pools of loans backing bonds. If a bond insurer guaranteed a security with a 30 percent subordination cushion beneath it, then the insurer would start to pay claims once losses on the pool hit 30 percent. Every percentage point increase of loss beyond 30 percent would translate into a dollar-for-dollar loss for the bond insurer. For a bond insurer to lose 100 percent on a guarantee, every mortgage would have to default and every foreclosed house would have to be sold at a complete loss. That scenario was unimaginable.

CDOs can create a more devastating outcome once bond insurers begin to pay claims. The insurer might start paying claims on a CDO guarantee once losses in underlying mortgage pools hit 30 percent, just as it would on the straight mortgage-backed bonds. But the insurer may find itself paying off 100 percent of the value of the entire CDO it has insured by the time underlying pool losses reach just 35 percent.

The slicing, dicing, and repackaging of securities can concentrate risk. Mortgage-backed bonds are supported by payments on thousands of mortgages; everyone has to default before there's a complete loss. CDOs, however, rely on the cash flow from hundreds of mortgage-backed securities. Recall that mortgage-backed securities have different ratings depending on where they reside in the payment waterfall. Lower-rated securities are completely shut off from the cash flow as losses increase. If all the securities backing a CDO are rated triple-B, they may be completely starved of cash as losses on underlying mortgage pools move from 30 percent to 35 percent. That means the entire CDO is cut off from cash even though most people whose mortgages are in the pool continue to make their payments.

The speed with which losses can burn through a mortgage-backed bond versus a CDO is akin to the difference between a fireplace log burning over the course of an evening and a newspaper incinerating within seconds. "We told Moody's that ABS CDOs don't meet our credit criteria," Sabra Purtill, head of investor relations at Assured Guaranty, once related to me. "We told them ABS CDOs are dangerous. They never asked why. It was like we were talking to a tree."

———

ON NOVEMBER 28, 2007, Ackman took the stage at the Value Investors Conference in Manhattan.

For the first time, Ackman had hired security guards to accompany him to a presentation. Many people believed Ackman was fanning a dangerous fire with his criticism of the bond insurers. During a Barclay's Capital conference call on the financial guarantors earlier in the month, one caller prefaced his question by stating that he believed those writing and speaking negatively about the bond insurers were "financial terrorists."

For years Ackman had asked regulators, reporters, and just about everyone he spoke to about MBIA to see no contradiction in shorting a company and being a decent person. It is an idea that many people simply can't accept.

When Ackman had testified at the Securities and Exchange Commission in 2003, this issue of doing good by short selling had come up. Ackman had said it was one reason he decided to short Farmer Mac. "I prefer investments where I'm not fighting against the country. You know, where there's public policy on my side instead of against me," Ackman had told the investigators.

But the SEC attorneys had been skeptical. Wasn't he really interested in Farmer Mac because he was seeking to profit from the company's collapse?

"I'm a bit idealistic so it isn't only a profit motive, but there was a profit motive, absolutely," Ackman had responded.

Now Ackman asked the packed auditorium of investors to believe that he had devised a plan that would both hasten the collapse of a company he was betting against and do some public good in the process. Not many people would try to pull that off, but Ackman had his unrepentant idealism.

Ackman's 146-page presentation was titled "How to Save the Bond Insurers," and it laid out his plan for conserving capital within the insurance subsidiaries of MBIA and Ambac. Holders of insured bonds and the Wall Street firms that had sold credit-default swaps to MBIA would benefit from the additional capital, Ackman said. "The holding companies are the problem," he told the audience. The holding companies wanted to take as much capital as possible out of the regulated insurance subsidiaries, but the policyholders were going to need that capital. Take back improper dividends, said Ackman. Void the intercompany guarantees that allow MBIA to run what is effectively a fixed-income hedge fund. Void the transactions done using credit-default swaps. Possibly even void all the deals backed by home-equity loans since bond insurers weren't permitted to guarantee mortgages. The plan was fatal to the holding companies.

Ackman also announced that—at least as far as his personal profits were concerned—he was now shorting the bond insurers for charity. "We are going to make hundreds of millions of dollars on the failure of the holding companies," Ackman concluded. "So I'm pledging to give my share of the profits to the Pershing Square Foundation." Ackman had set up the foundation to provide funding for education and other charitable causes.

"He may be aggressive, he may be over the top, he may not be able to speak in short sentences," *New York Times* columnist Joe Nocera concluded following the presentation. "But he's doing the hard work, and thinking the hard thoughts that they refused to do for so long."

Ackman seized the moment to remind some people of that.

On Sunday evening, just after 11 p.m., Roy Katzovicz got an e-mail from Ackman. He'd been copied on a long message that Ackman sent to the Securities and Exchange Commission. Katzovicz read the subject line—"The SEC's Enforcement Failures with the Bond Insurers and Other Issues"—and scanned the addressees in the "To:" column: SEC Chairman Christopher Cox; SEC Commissioners Annette Nazareth, Paul Atkins, and Kathleen Casey; the SEC's director of enforcement, Linda Thomsen; Brian Cartwright, the SEC's general counsel; John Nester, the SEC's director of communications; and Mark Schonfeld, director of the SEC's New York regional office.

Without reading any further, Katzovicz told his wife, "I may have to quit my job tomorrow." His boss's habit of writing long, emotional, late-night missives without having him vet them was one of the aggravations of Katzovicz's job. But this one was the worst yet. There was no point now in reading the message and spending the entire night tossing and turning over all the points that might have been made with less fractious wording or—better yet—deleted altogether before the message was sent. He let it wait till morning.

When he got up at 5 a.m., Katzovicz opened the message. "The SEC has completely fallen on its face in stepping in to prevent the upcoming mushroom cloud that will envelop the bond insurers," the letter began. Ackman added that he had pointed out the problems with the bond insurers years ago in the Gotham report. "I addressed CDO and derivative mark-to-market issues, the illegality of bond insurers entering into derivative transactions, their inadequate reserves, their aggressive and fraudulent accounting, and a whole host of other issues," Ackman wrote. "The SEC, as you well know, first spent time investigating me and my then firm, Gotham Partners, for writing the original report on MBIA, rather than focusing on the issues I raised in the report."

Even though the SEC exonerated Ackman of all wrongdoing and invited him to make multiple presentations to regulators on the industry, "the SEC still has not had the courtesy to give me a letter for my files about the termination of the Gotham investigation without any finding of wrongdoing, despite repeated requests from my counsel for the same," Ackman wrote.

The letter was also addressed to the three New York SEC staff attorneys with whom Ackman had met over the years: Alan Kahn, Steve Rawlings, and Chris Mele. But the real barbs were directed to those higher up at the SEC. "My sense is that it's more likely that the responsibility for the lack of pursuit of these issues lies at the highest levels of the SEC including Chairman Cox," Ackman wrote.

He concluded by offering to meet with the SEC again to further explain how losses might yet be prevented for policyholders. "It is an incredible embarrassment to the SEC and to the quality of our country's regulatory oversight for you to have dropped the ball here," Ackman concluded.

When he got into the office that morning, Katzovicz walked into Ackman's office to confront him about the e-mail. "Why shouldn't I just quit?" Katzovicz demanded. "This is the kind of thing you send off to our principal regulator without running it by me?"

Ackman told him it would have been a mistake to show him the e-mail. Katzovicz would have stopped him from sending it, and every thing in the e-mail needed to be said, Ackman insisted.

Katzovicz said he would not have stopped him, but he might have suggested some changes, some omissions. Perhaps the letter wouldn't have been such a personal attack on Cox. Sometimes Ackman needed to be protected from himself, and that had to be a part of Katzovicz's job. If Katzovicz was going to stay with the firm, they needed a new rule. Katzovicz spelled it out: "You cannot kick our chief regulator in the nuts without consulting with me first." Ackman agreed, and Katzovicz stayed.

Within a week, a junior staff attorney at the SEC called Pershing's outside counsel to find out where to send a notice of discontinuance. The letter arrived on Ackman's desk a few weeks later. It stated, "This investigation has been completed as to Gotham Partners Management Co., LLC and William A. Ackman, against whom we do not intend to recommend any enforcement action by the Commission."

It was the closure Ackman had been waiting to receive for nearly five years.

Chapter Nineteen

Ratings Revisited

To keep the music playing required increasingly egregious excesses—ever greater quantities of increasingly risky loans, structures and leveraging

—Doug Noland, David Tice & Associates, December 2007

I N December 2007, Bill Ackman went door to door with his presentation on the bond insurers, launching perhaps the most aggressive "short" campaign in the history of Wall Street.

Activist investors typically buy a stake in a company and then pressure management to make changes that will drive up the stock price. Short selling and activism are a much more complex pairing. An activist can't exactly advocate for changes that will cause the company's share price to collapse or cause it to file for bankruptcy. At least not very often.

Ackman, however, saw his short position in MBIA as a cause. He believed his interests were aligned with those of MBIA's policyholders because both would benefit if MBIA's publicly traded holding company had less cash. He also argued that the taxpayer was being cheated by bond insurance, or at least by the crooked municipal bond ratings system that made bond insurance necessary.

MBIA summed it up this way at Congressional hearings on the bond insurers in early 2008: "Ultimately, the [short sellers'] goal would be to see MBIA become insolvent, which would maximize their profits by driving the stock to near zero and triggering payments on the credit-default swaps they executed."

In December 2007, Ackman and Roy Katzovicz flew to Boise to meet with Idaho's attorney general, who was also the head of the National Association of Attorneys General. Ackman hoped to interest Attorney General Lawrence Wasden in launching a national investigation into municipal bond ratings.

By this time, Katzovicz's assistant had purchased a luggage trolley to haul around the documents that accompanied Ackman's presentations. It tipped over. It collapsed. It was a constant source of frustration. But the presentations weren't getting any shorter because the bond-insurance story was not getting any less complicated.

The bond insurers were both more and less risky than they appeared, Ackman argued. The subprime crisis threatened the bond insurers' ratings and their solvency, despite assurances by management that the companies were largely insulated from losses. That's why Ackman had developed a plan to save MBIA's insurance company by cutting off dividends to its publicly traded holding company, MBIA Inc. (If regulators believe an insurance company needs to preserve its capital, then they can prohibit the insurance company from sending dividends up to its holding company.) Then there was the issue of the municipal-bond rating system, which allowed bond insurers to sell their triple-A ratings to municipalities even though many already had triple-A ratings under an unpublished scale.

When I first reported on how this system was costing taxpayers billions of dollars a year, it generated little interest. Then one evening, after a presentation at UBS, I rode the elevator down with Katzovicz. He mentioned the article in passing and wondered if there was a way to see just how much higher rated a municipality would be if it were judged on the same default risk criteria as MBIA. I explained that Moody's had included a "map" in its research report, showing, for example, that water and sewer authorities could be ranked more than five levels higher under the undisclosed scale. "There's a map!" Katzovicz announced with enthusiasm in the crowded elevator, causing a few people to turn and look at us. Now Ackman and Katzovicz were making sure everyone knew about it.

As Ackman and Katzovicz packed up after the presentation in Idaho, Katzovicz remembers one of Wasden's deputies telling them that people who bring issues to the attorney general's attention often end up incriminating themselves. That didn't happen to Ackman, but the hedge fund manager didn't hear back from Wasden either.

Ackman and Katzovicz had better luck in Connecticut. During the first week of December, they drove up to Stamford to meet with Richard Blumenthal, the state's attorney general. Blumenthal already was investigating the credit-rating companies and their failure to alert investors to the risks of subprime mortgage–backed securities. He took an immediate interest in the idea that the rating companies had two sets of books that they used to rate municipal bonds.

"The first thing [Ackman] told us is that he stood to benefit," Blumenthal remembers. "He was outraged. It was almost a personal crusade with him." Blumenthal had learned early in his career as a prosecutor working on drug cases for the U.S. attorney's office that "a lot of times people are going to have self-interest in what they're alleging is fact. Your information doesn't usually come from choir boys," Blumenthal says. That's why it had to be checked out, and, according to Blumenthal, in Ackman's case the provided information proved very useful and accurate.

Ackman was far from the only investor to make money on the collapse of the financial system, Blumenthal says. Many people made money betting against financial firms, but they did it without ever going public, he says, describing the conventional wisdom: "'Why should I be the bearer of bad news? Why should I have everyone at the country club or the commuter train or the downtown eating club upset with me? It's the old boys' network, and they won't let me in on deals. I know this is going to come crashing down. Why warn the world?'" Ackman adopted a different tactic, Blumenthal says.

Ackman and Katzovicz were getting some traction in Washington as well. Ackman had written to Massachusetts congressman Barney Frank, reminding him that the bond insurers' situation had continued to deteriorate since Ackman and Frank met in June. Based on estimates of the values of collateralized-debt obligations (CDOs), "the capital of nearly all of the bond insurers has been materially impaired or eliminated," Ackman wrote in an October 2007 letter to Frank. "As a result, the risk of insolvency is a real and present danger." Frank had written back several weeks later to say he expected to hold hearings on the bond-insurance industry in 2008.

The meetings continued at a frenetic pace throughout December 2007. Ackman and Mick McGuire met with Moody's Investors Service analysts, including Stan Rouyer and Jack Dorer. This time, hedge fund manager David Einhorn, who had been shorting MBIA and comparing notes with Ackman on the company for several years, came along.

Ackman did most of the talking, telling the analysts that while they dithered over MBIA's rating, the market had already decided MBIA's and Ambac's insurance units were no longer triple-A rated. Reassurances from the management of the bond-insurance companies that CDO losses were only mark-to-market losses just didn't make sense, Ackman told Moody's. "Either they're lying to you or they don't understand what they're doing."

The conversation turned to the risk Moody's itself faced by keeping the bond insurers triple-A rated. Einhorn told the analysts that leaving the triple-A rating on bond insurers was destroying the company's credibility and its franchise. "Full disclosure: I am short Moody's," he told the group.

The meeting, not exactly warm up to that point, became even more tense. "There was a tangible change in people's physical posture and facial expressions. Answers became terse, one-word answers," McGuire says. The meeting wrapped up quickly.

"Investors who bought triple-rated structured products thought they were buying safety but instead bought disaster," Einhorn would tell the audience at an investment conference in May 2009 when he made his short position public. "If your product is a stamp of approval and your highest rating is a curse to those that receive it and shunned by those who are supposed to use it, you have problems."

After the December 2007 meeting, Ackman, Einhorn, and McGuire headed for the nearby Roc Restaurant in Tribeca. "That was a great meeting," Ackman said as they took their seats.

Einhorn wasn't so sure. "I need to figure out how Bill does meetings," Einhorn joked, adding, "I always feel like those kinds of meetings are a waste of time."

Not Ackman. "Bill was optimistic every time," McGuire remembers.

MBIA HAD SOME REASON to be optimistic as well. On December 10, 2007, private-equity firm Warburg Pincus announced it would invest as much as $1 billion in the bond insurer. The firm would buy $500 million of common stock at $31 a share and support an additional public offering of shares by spending as much as $500 million to support the offering if interest was weak. The stock jumped 13 percent on the news, closing at $33.95. Credit-default-swap (CDS) rates narrowed almost 100 basis points, cutting the annual cost of insurance on $10 million of debt by $100,000 a year. It was a resounding victory for MBIA.

Ackman didn't share Warburg's confidence, telling the *Wall Street Journal*, "I generally think that Warburg Pincus is a very smart private-equity firm, but I don't think they understand what they just bought. It's likely that they'll lose their entire investment."

Ackman's efforts to explain this comment further to David Coulter and Kewsong Lee, who were spearheading the Warburg investment in MBIA, were rebuffed. One Pershing Square investor who had contacts within Warburg came back to Ackman with this message from Coulter and Lee: "We have made a firmwide decision not to speak with the shorts."

One of MBIA's largest investors had another message for Ackman. During an interview on CNBC in late December 2007, Marty Whitman, the 83-year-old chairman of Third Avenue Management LLC, was asked whether Ackman's criticism of MBIA had caused him to rethink his 10 percent stake in the company. "Mr. Ackman," Whitman replied with a smirk, "is a slick salesman who doesn't know much about insurance."

Ackman had tried to talk to Whitman several years earlier when he attended a presentation Whitman gave at Columbia University. After the talk, students pressed around the famous value investor to shake his hand. Ackman squeezed through the crowd and introduced himself, saying he was hoping to speak with Whitman about one of his largest holdings, MBIA Inc. Ackman explained that he had a very different view of the company. "Give me a call, and we'll talk about it," Whitman told him, as the students looked on.

But Ackman's follow-up call was met with an icy reception. He started off by mentioning that his father had had a brokerage account with Whitman for years.

"Yes. I know your father," Whitman said.

Ackman moved on to the topic of MBIA but wasn't given time to say much. "It would be a waste of my time to talk to you," Whitman replied and slammed down the phone.

THREE DAYS AFTER the Warburg Pincus announcement, Pershing Square held an advisory board meeting. Marty Peretz, editor-in-chief of the *New Republic* and a member of Pershing Square's advisory board, recalls that the Warburg Pincus investment in MBIA was a big topic of discussion. What did Warburg know about MBIA that allowed it to feel comfortable committing $1 billion to the company?

Without Ackman present, Mick McGuire and Scott Ferguson, analysts on Pershing's investment team, answered questions from the board. There was no doubt Pershing's current investment thesis on MBIA was working, and no one at the firm saw the Warburg investment as an indication that Ackman's analysis was wrong. Still, unexpected things had begun to happen, and that worried the group. "It didn't make sense that smart investors would do the work of analyzing MBIA and then invest," said McGuire. "If one smart investor could make a mistake, others might, too."

The MBIA position had taken Ackman years to build, buying $10 million blocks of protection day after day. The lowest price he agreed to pay in premiums was 13 basis points, or $13,000 a year, and the highest was 700 basis points, or $700,000 a year. Most of the position was bought for less than 60 basis points. With MBIA 5-year credit-default swaps trading at around 450 basis points, there was a strong argument for taking profits.

In very round numbers, an investor buying protection on $4 billion of MBIA debt on the day the company announced its regulatory investigation in January 2007 would have agreed to pay $6.4 million a year for the protection. By the middle of December 2007, the same protection would cost $180 million a year. The value of the investment had increased by nearly 30 times. Of course, if MBIA filed for bankruptcy, the holder of those contracts stood to receive as much as $4 billion, or 600 times the annual cost of the insurance.

Might MBIA still blow up? Sure. But that was only part of the picture. "There is a real risk in using an outcome to validate a decision process," McGuire said. For Ackman to insist on staying with the position, satisfied with nothing less than seeing the company file for bankruptcy, would be a mistake.

"The staff was impatient with Bill. They wanted him to get out of the position even when it seemed he was winning," Peretz remembers. It wasn't said directly, but you could sense their thinking: "You've proved your point; get out while you can."

Of course, Ackman hadn't yet proved his point because MBIA was still in business.

Pershing's position—largely in credit-default swaps—created its own issues. The CDS market can be very illiquid and tends to get one-sided very easily, McGuire explained. On a day when there's bad news about a company, everyone wants to buy protection, and when the news is good, everyone's looking to sell. The market gaps hugely at such times and creates a real psychological barrier to closing out a position, McGuire said. It forces one to sell the position into bad news, even though that's when the investment thesis is proving itself out.

When prices were swinging that wildly, it was hard not to have regrets. The investment team would steel itself at those moments when the market moved dramatically against it. The frustration boiled over if someone mentioned it.

"We should have sold there."

"No shit."

"It was better just not to talk about it," says McGuire, remembering the tension.

Peretz sensed the investment team's frustration. "You could see their exhaustion with it, almost a visceral discontent." He suspected what they were thinking: "This is Bill's *mishigas*," the Yiddish word for craziness.

When Ackman met with the advisory board to give his views on the MBIA position, he repeated what he'd been telling investors for years. Despite the 30-fold rise in the value of MBIA CDS contracts, he remained convinced that Pershing Square should continue to hold its short position: "I have never seen such a good risk-reward opportunity in my entire career."

MEANWHILE, DOWNGRADES of subprime-mortgage securities continued to cascade through the structured finance market. By the middle of December, Standard & Poor's (S&P) had downgraded or placed under review $57 billion of CDOs. Moody's had cut the ratings on CDOs originally valued at $50.9 billion and still had another $174 billion of CDOs under review. Fitch put its CDO downgrade tally at $67 billion by the end of November.

Moody's was the first to act on its warning that the downgrades of mortgage securities might undermine the triple-A ratings of some bond insurers. On December 14, 2007, it put two bond insurers—FGIC and

XL Capital Assurance—formally under review. MBIA and CIFG were assigned negative outlooks, although their AAA ratings were affirmed. The ratings of Ambac, Assured, and FSA were affirmed and assigned stable outlooks. Over the next few days, Fitch put nearly every bond insurer under review. S&P assigned negative outlooks on the ratings of several bond insurers, including MBIA and Ambac. In any other industry, these rating changes would be trivial tinkering. But for the handful of companies whose businesses were built on their mainly AAA ratings, this rethinking of the ratings was a shot fired across the bow.

One company, however, took a direct and apparently fatal hit. S&P cut ACA Capital's rating 12 levels from A to CCC. The slide was so precipitous because once S&P determined that ACA should be rated in the triple-B category, just two notches below its existing rating, the downgrade itself effectively bankrupted the company. At a triple-B rating, ACA's counterparties had the right to terminate their contracts.

That changed the nature of ACA's exposure dramatically. Instead of requiring ACA to cover any defaults on the CDOs as they occurred, the termination required an immediate payment to cover the decline in the market value of the CDOs. There was no way that ACA, with less than $500 million of capital, could cover the $1.7 billion decline in the market value of the CDOs it had guaranteed.

Shortly after the announcement, Canadian Imperial Bank of Commerce said it might have $2 billion of writedowns on $3.5 billion of subprime-mortgage securities guaranteed by ACA. Thirty other counterparties also were going to have to admit losses.

But not just yet.

ACA announced that their counterparties had agreed to forbear on their contracts. They would not demand that any collateral be posted or any contracts terminated. ACA had not defaulted on its obligations. It just had no way to pay them. Wall Street was going to pretend for a while longer that the credit-default-swap market—with $62 trillion in outstanding contracts—had not just suffered its first catastrophic failure.

CREDIT-DEFAULT SWAPS were causing embarrassment all over Wall Street. On December 19, 2007, Morgan Stanley revealed a $7.8 billion loss due to subprime exposure. "I know everyone has been dancing around it, but my question would be . . . how could this happen?" an analyst asked Morgan Stanley's chief financial officer during a call to discuss earnings.

His explanation: A single trading desk at Morgan Stanley had sought to profit from the subprime collapse by purchasing protection through the CDS market on $2 billion of low-rated mortgage-backed bonds. The trade would have been a home run, except the traders came up with the cash to put on the trade by selling protection on $14 billion of top-rated subprime mortgage securities. What they thought was free money quickly turned into a massive loss as the value of the top-rated securities collapsed. Morgan Stanley's CFO called it "a very expensive, and by the way, humbling lesson."

A few minutes before 11 p.m. on December 19, Jim Chanos, the fund manager famous for shorting Enron, was reading through his e-mail when he spotted a research report on MBIA sent out that evening by Ken Zerbe, the insurance analyst at Morgan Stanley.

"What's New: MBIA published an updated list of its CDO exposures. It disclosed that it has a massive $8.1 billion of exposure to CDO-squared transactions," Zerbe wrote. "We are shocked that management withheld this information for as long as it did." A CDO-squared is a CDO backed by tranches of other CDOs. The market distrusted these securities and their added layer of complexity and risk even more than CDOs. It was becoming obvious that any extra layer of risk transfer created more risk for investors. "Gee, only $8.1 billion. Wow!" Chanos wrote in an e-mail to Ackman, attaching the report.

Zerbe's recommendation was to avoid the bond insurers as a sector until it was possible to get a better understanding of the losses they would take on CDOs and other mortgage securities.

David Einhorn at Greenlight Capital spotted Zerbe's report around midnight and passed it along to Ackman and others. The subject line read, "What is that under the rug?"

"We had originally questioned how Moody's and S&P could have taken a more negative view of MBIA than Ambac, given our analysis suggested Ambac had a more risky portfolio," the Morgan Stanley report continued. "Now we know. MBIA simply did not disclose arguably the riskiest parts of its CDO portfolio to investors: $8.1 billion of CDO squareds."

Whitney Tilson, at T2 Partners, had received the report as well and messaged Ackman a little after 7 a.m. "Stop the presses! An analyst with a spine, holding a management team's feet to the fire! I think this is a first!"

At 8:11 a.m., Erika Kreyssig on Pershing Square's trading desk messaged Ackman to tell him that CDS contracts on MBIA Inc. had widened 105 basis points as word of the report got around. The contracts were now bid at 580 basis points, indicating that it cost $580,000 a year to protect $10 million of debt against default. "We bought $25 million at 570 basis points," she wrote. "Really tough to get offers. Got lucky with that one."

MBIA's shares plunged. More than 50 million shares traded that day, by far the highest-volume day in the company's history. After the market closed, MBIA released a statement saying that it hadn't broken out the numbers before because these complex CDOs had less than 25 percent of their collateral in subprime mortgages.

Investors and analysts took little comfort in the statement. "Happy Holidays," GimmeCredit analyst Kathy Shanley wrote later that day. MBIA "found one more present for investors tucked away in the back of its closet. Just what you always wanted and just your size too—$8.1 billion of CDO squareds."

Wall Street's clever packaging and repackaging of debt was now seen as a scam. "To keep the music playing required increasingly egregious excesses—ever greater quantities of increasingly risky loans, structures, and leveraging," Doug Noland, a credit analyst with David W. Tice & Associates, wrote the day after MBIA disclosed its CDO-squared exposure. The bond insurers had both abetted the process and been duped by it. "The credit insurers destroyed themselves," Noland concluded.

Chapter Twenty

The Panic Begins

When this story hits the newspaper, the headline is going to be "How Wall Street Ate Main Street."

—ERIC DINALLO,
NEW YORK STATE INSURANCE SUPERINTENDENT, JANUARY 2008

B Y JANUARY 2008, the bond insurers were up against a tight deadline. They had less than a month to raise billions of dollars of capital to preserve their triple-A ratings. Yet the entire business model was being questioned. The companies' share prices had collapsed. Credit-default-swap (CDS) contracts on MBIA and Ambac, the industry leaders, were priced at levels that suggested investors believed the companies faced a good chance of filing for bankruptcy. "The clock is ticking for all these companies," Robert Haines, an analyst with CreditSights Incorporated, a bond-research firm in New York, said.

During the first week of January, Bill Ackman got an e-mail from a Harvard Business School classmate. Fiachra O'Driscoll, then the managing director of Synthetic CDO Trading at Credit Suisse. He had been watching the situation with the bond insurers with interest. "Was wondering if you would have 15 minutes for a chat about potential outcomes," O'Driscoll wrote.

A few days later, O'Driscoll arrived at Pershing Square's offices with a stack of printouts. The Credit Suisse group had come up with a model for predicting for how much MBIA and Ambac would lose on mortgage-backed securities and collateralized-debt obligations (CDOs) backed by these securities.

The traders had looked at how a sample of 1,200 securities backed by the bond insurers would perform under various housing market scenarios. Then they used the performance of various types of securities to predict how thousands of other, similar securities that the bond insurers had exposure to would perform.

When Credit Suisse forecast a 10 percent decline in home prices in year one, a 10 percent drop in year two, and no change in prices in year three, the results for the bond insurers were devastating. And the problems weren't just with subprime mortgage-backed securities or CDOs. Securities backed by adjustable-rate, Alt-A mortgages originated in the first half of 2007 were projected to be nearly wiped out. The lowest-rated double-B tranches were a 100 percent loss, and the triple-Bs were a 99.75 percent loss. Even the triple-As were expected to lose more than 40 percent.

The presentation gave Ackman an idea. If he could make the Credit Suisse model available to the public, investors could input their own forecasts and make their own decisions about the fate of bond insurers. O'Driscoll agreed to the idea.

———————

ON JANUARY 9, 2008, MBIA said it would cut its dividend and sell $1 billion in so-called surplus notes through its insurance company, to raise capital and secure its triple-A rating. The company had to move quickly. Conditions had worsened. MBIA preannounced some of its numbers for the fourth quarter, setting aside nearly $800 million to pay claims on home-equity-loan–backed securities just one month after saying it didn't expect to take any losses on home-loan–backed securities. The company also expected to pay about $200 million on CDOs. The mark-to-market losses on CDOs for the fourth quarter increased by another $3.3 billion.

As MBIA's underwriters marketed the notes, it was clear investors were nervous. Early price talk on the bonds suggested investors wanted a yield of 12 percent to 15 percent, the type of return demanded from a distressed borrower.

Ackman wasn't helping matters. On January 10, he appeared on Bloomberg Television to talk about MBIA and the surplus note offering. He warned that investors should think very carefully about buying MBIA's surplus notes. The New York state insurance superintendent must approve every payment on the notes. Given the mounting losses at MBIA, Ackman didn't believe a single payment should be allowed. "The superintendent will take the money in, but he's not going to let money go out of the system," Ackman said. Even with the Warburg Pincus investment in MBIA and the proceeds from the surplus note offering, "the amount of capital required here is vastly in excess of the capital MBIA is trying to raise," Ackman said.

MBIA's future was bleak, Ackman insisted: Neither MBIA nor Ambac would write another municipal bond policy in the future, he predicted. Furthermore, unless it raised additional cash, MBIA Inc., the holding company of the insurer, would be out of cash by the end of the year. "We have a bigger short position than we did two weeks ago," he told viewers. "Almost every week, we've increased our position here."

MBIA sold the notes the next day, January 11, with a 14 percent yield. A month later, Warren Buffett commented on the transaction: "When a company issues a 14 percent bond when U.S. Treasuries are below 4 percent and it's rated triple-A, we've now seen the cow jumping over the moon." Among those snapping up the high-yielding securities was Marty Whitman of Third Avenue Management LLC, who had recently disclosed that his fund owned 10 percent of MBIA's common stock.

Nearly everyone—with the exception of the short sellers—was happy to see MBIA pull off the deal. "It's good news for the company, good news for the bond-insurance sector, and good news for the credit markets," Kevin Murphy, a fixed-income portfolio manager at Putnam Investments in Boston, told Bloomberg News.

———

LESS THAN A WEEK LATER, on January 16, Ambac announced its plans to fend off a credit-rating downgrade. It also preannounced disastrous fourth-quarter results. Driven by mark-to-market losses on its CDO portfolio, Ambac reported a loss of more than $32 a share.

Its plan was to raise $1 billion through the sale of equity and to cut the dividend. With Ambac's shares down 80 percent over the previous year, however, the offering would massively dilute existing shareholders. The decision had been a contentious one. Ambac's chief executive officer

(CEO), Robert Genader, had resigned. Michael Callen, an Ambac board member and former Citigroup executive, had replaced him.

"More shoes dropping at Ambac," Kathy Shanley at Gimme Credit wrote. The company said it would take $5.4 billion in pretax mark-to-market losses on CDOs and that $1.1 billion of those markdowns reflected actual claims the company expected to pay. "In laymen's terms, Ambac is conceding that mark-to-market losses are likely to turn into real cash losses on at least some of its exposure," Shanley wrote.

Jim Cramer, the manic host of CNBC's program *Mad Money*, launched into a tirade about Ambac earnings that afternoon, and then concluded about the bond insurers generally: "There's only one triple-A—the guys who come and change your tire when you break down on I-95. Those guys are reliable."

After the market closed, Moody's dropped the hammer on Ambac, saying—just one month after it had affirmed its rating—that it was considering stripping the company of its triple-A rating.

Early the next morning, January 17, Ramy Saad, Pershing Square's head trader, messaged the investment team with an update on the bond insurers' CDS prices. "Brace yourself," read the subject line. CDS contracts on MBIA Inc., the publicly traded holding company, and Ambac Financial Group were being quoted at a midprice of more than 1,200 basis points, a jump of 220 basis points since the previous afternoon. It now cost $1.2 million a year to buy protection on $10 million of MBIA debt.

There was giddiness as the Pershing Square team picked up the message.

"Woo hoo!" Erika Kreyssig, on the trading desk, e-mailed in response to the prices.

"Yooooo hoooooo!!!" Ali Namvar responded a few minutes later.

"Isn't that the chocolate soda CBRY makes," Scott Ferguson e-mailed, using the stock ticker for Cadbury PLC, a stock Pershing Square owned.

Timothy Barefield, the fund's chief operating officer, jumped into the conversation, writing: "Yooo Hooo! I had it for breakfast."

"There was elation," Namvar remembers. "Your boss had been telling the world for years this was going to happen. Now he's being proven right and world is wrong."

"My God," Paul Hilal responded when he picked up the message.

The cost of buying protection for five years on MBIA Inc. had risen nearly one hundred times over the last year. In late January 2007, when

MBIA announced that it was settling the regulatory probe the cost of protection was quoted as low as 13 basis points. Now it was approaching 1,300 basis points.

The magnitude of change in MBIA CDS prices between January 2007 and January 2008 was equivalent to a $13 stock rising to $1,300.

To some members of the investment team, it seemed like insanity not to take some profits after that kind of move. But Ackman showed no indication that he planned to do that. Namvar remembers Ackman telling the investment team on a number of occasions, "We're going to ride this into bankruptcy." Then he'd smile and walk away. The rest of the investment team would stand there, looking at each other. Once Ackman was out of earshot someone would inevitably ask, "Is he serious?"

At one point in early 2008, when the volatility of the MBIA position was fraying everyone's nerves, Namvar walked into Ackman's office to have a talk with him. Namvar, who had played guitar in a rock band for five years before going to business school and landing at Blackstone Group, wasn't involved in the day-to-day analysis of the bond insurers. He also was viewed by others on the investment team as a good intermediary, someone who could hear both sides.

"Let's take some exposure off the table," Namvar said, confronting the issue with Ackman directly. "Look, it's not about the thesis. It's about the size of the exposure," he reasoned.

MBIA and Ambac credit-default swaps were moving 50 to 100 basis points in a day. It was one thing when the position was a small fraction of the fund's assets, but it had become a substantial part of the portfolio as the price of the contracts had surged. Too much hinged on it.

Ackman heard him out, and then he told Namvar simply, "Don't be weak." There was nothing more to say.

"When the investment was successful, that's when it was hard to sleep," Namvar remembers.

At 3 p.m. on January 17, the day after Moody's warned about downgrading Ambac, Ramy Saad updated the investment team again: MBIA Inc. was being quoted at 1,500 basis points and MBIA Insurance Corporation at 1,400 basis points. By the end of the day, shares of both companies had suffered their biggest drop on record. MBIA fell 38 percent, and Ambac plunged 65 percent.

Later that afternoon, Evercore Asset Management, a large Ambac shareholder, released a letter to Ambac's board over the newswires, saying that the best approach for shareholders was to put the company into runoff: It would assume no new business and pay claims as they came due on existing policies until all the business had expired. Shareholders would fare better under a runoff scenario rather than having their holdings massively diluted through a share sale. "The company gambled its AAA rating and has now lost that bet," chief investment officer Andrew Moloff wrote. "Attempting to buy back the AAA rating by giving away most of the company makes no sense."

Just after 4:30 p.m. on January 17, Moody's said it was considering a downgrade of MBIA as well as Ambac. "Today's rating action reflects Moody's growing concern about the potential volatility in ultimate performance of mortgage and mortgage-related CDO risks, and the corresponding implications for MBIA's risk-adjusted capital adequacy." MBIA shares fell another 11 percent in after-hours trading.

Even for MBIA's staunchest supporters, this was too much.

In a report headlined: "Throwing in the Towel," Heather Hunt, the Citigroup analyst, downgraded the shares to "hold" from "buy" and wrote, "After a stunning ride down, we are capitulating."

The companies' inability to understand the risk they were taking was shocking, Hunt explained. "This kind of systemic failure to assess risk has been difficult for us to believe," Hunt confessed.

At 8:33 a.m. on January 18, Ambac announced its own capitulation. It released a short statement: Management "has determined that as a result of market conditions and other factors, including the recent actions of certain ratings agencies, raising equity capital is not an attractive option at this time."

The announcement immediately cost Ambac its triple-A rating. At 2:25 p.m., Fitch Ratings downgraded Ambac, citing the warning it issued in December that Ambac was short of capital by $1 billion. Fitch also cut the ratings on 137,500 bonds Ambac guaranteed, including bonds of thousands of cities and states across the United States.

"This makes Ambac toxic," Rob Haines, the CreditSights analyst, said. "The market has no tolerance for a ratings-deprived insurer." Indeed, the Dow Jones Industrial Average closed down 700 points for the week.

The problem was going to be bigger than Ambac. "Today, the models behind so many strategies that have come to permeate contemporary finance have completely broken down," wrote Doug Noland, the credit analyst at David W. Tice & Associates.

The Friday before the Martin Luther King holiday weekend, Ackman drafted an e-mail to the heads of the three credit-rating companies:

Raymond McDaniel at Moody's, Deven Sharma at Standard & Poor's, and Stephen Joynt at Fitch, chiding them for not stripping the bond insurers of their top ratings.

He ended the letter with a very long rhetorical question about MBIA: "Does a company deserve your highest triple-A rating when its stock price has declined 90 percent; when it has cut its dividend; is scrambling to raise capital; completed a partial financing at 14-percent interest (and trading at a 20-percent yield one week later); has incurred losses massively in excess of its promised zero-loss expectations, wiping out more than half of book value; has Berkshire Hathaway as a new competitor, having lost access to its only liquidity facility; and has concealed material information from the marketplace? How can this possibly make sense?"

THE NEXT MORNING, New York State Insurance Superintendent Eric Dinallo was skiing in the Berkshires with his family for the Martin Luther King weekend when the incoming phone calls began. He heard from Vikram Pandit, CEO of Citigroup; David Coulter at Warburg Pincus; Michael Callen, the new chief executive officer at Ambac; and Timothy Geithner, the president of the Federal Reserve Bank in New York.

Fitch had already stripped one insurer of its triple-A rating. Something needed to be done before the downgrades went any further. The people Dinallo talked to clearly had been making many other calls—to the Securities and Exchange Commission, the Treasury, the Fed. "Who's on top of this problem?" they demanded to know. "Is anyone managing this?"

Initially, Dinallo tried to juggle the calls without leaving the ski slopes, but the cell-phone reception was bad. With the wind blowing, it was impossible to hear everything the callers were saying. He took a second room at the Patriot Suites Hotel in Pittsfield, Massachusetts, which became his office for the next two days.

As he learned more, he realized that the only way to solve the bond-insurance problem was to get Wall Street involved. On Monday—Martin Luther King Day—he headed back to the office.

It was a cold, quiet morning in lower Manhattan with the markets closed for the holiday. Dinallo made his way downtown to the New York State Insurance Department's offices on Beaver Street. It was going to take several days to set up a meeting with executives at the major banks.

But Dinallo had arranged to meet with someone else that day—Ajit Jain, the head of reinsurance for Berkshire Hathaway. Dinallo had called Jain back in November to see if he could talk Berkshire into getting into the bond-insurance business in New York state. The plans were expedited, and Berkshire Hathaway was already writing policies.

Now Dinallo had another proposal for Jain. Would Buffett be willing to take over the municipal books of the three biggest bond insurers? It might not be possible to stave off downgrades of the bond insurers' triple-A ratings. Dinallo needed an alternative plan to prevent hundreds of billions of dollars of bonds from losing their top ratings.

Shortly after the meeting, Jain drafted a letter to advisers of the three bond-insurance companies, offering to take over all of their municipal bond guarantees in exchange for premiums equal to one and a half times the original premiums. The transaction "will help stabilize the currently unstable marketplace conditions for the municipal business," Jain wrote in a letter to MBIA's advisers, Lazard Frères & Company, dated February 7, 2008. "In that sense, this approach also has the appeal of serving the greater public good, not an unimportant consideration for us, both as a matter of principle and as a company with a vested interest in national economic conditions."

When markets reopened after the long holiday weekend, the mood was grim. At 8:50 a.m., Pershing Square trader Ramy Saad passed along CDS prices to Ackman. Financial Guaranty Insurance Company (FGIC) spreads had risen by 140 basis points. XL Capital CDS spreads were wider by 120 basis points. Ambac was up 100 basis points over Friday's levels. Saad also passed along a note on the MBIA surplus notes: "Seeing buyers of the surplus note today . . . $74/bid now." The quote indicated that traders would buy the notes at 74 cents on the dollar, a 26 percent discount off the original price.

Dinallo spent the morning on the phone with the credit-rating companies to get an idea of what had to be done. How much capital did he need to extract from the banks to satisfy the credit-rating companies that the bond insurers would remain triple-A rated. The answer: $15 billion to $20 billion, analysts at the credit-rating companies told him. Dinallo also spoke with officials at the Treasury department, who sounded concerned.

There was plenty to be concerned about. The stock market was lurching lower every day. Experts were talking about recession. Home sales, manufacturing, and employment were all weakening.

Then the Federal Reserve stepped in, slashing its benchmark rate by 75 basis points to 3.5 percent from 4.25 percent. It was the biggest cut in 23 years and the first time since the days after the September 11, 2001, terrorist attacks that the Fed had acted between meetings. Despite the move, stocks ended the day down.

———

IN THE WINTER OF 2008, the New York State Insurance Department became an unlikely hub for Wall Street power brokers. The department, with its narrow hallways, fluorescent lights, and suspended ceilings—from which cockroaches occasionally dropped onto the heads of employees—is a far cry from the plush offices of the investors and Wall Street executives who came regularly to meet with Dinallo about the bond insurers. On January 23, 2008, the CEOs and chief financial officers of the largest banks on Wall Street arrived en masse.

By the time the meeting got under way at 11 a.m., nearly 20 bankers were assembled from virtually every firm on Wall Street including Citigroup, Lehman Brothers, Merrill Lynch & Company, and Morgan Stanley. Some crowded around the conference table in the main meeting room. Others took up seats along the wall, and more called in and listened on the speaker phone.

Framed photos of more than 100 years of New York state insurance superintendents stared down at the assembled group. They had debated some difficult problems over the years—floods and fires, war and terrorism—but the issue on the agenda that day was unlike any other: a Wall Street–made catastrophe that threatened to bankrupt an entire class of insurance companies. The bankers were there to figure out what to do about more than $100 billion of contracts they had entered into with bond insurers to protect the value of CDOs backed by mortgages.

The question on everyone's mind was whether a downgrade of the major bond insurers would cause the markets to seize up. If what had been happening in the market in recent days was any indication, there was good reason to be concerned.

Banks were counting on the bond insurers to keep their triple-A ratings so that the value of their hedges could remain intact.

Downgrades of bond insurers would create a growing hole in banks' balance sheets, according to a Barclay's Capital research report. Banks that already had raised $72 billion of capital could need another $143 billion if the bond insurers' ratings were cut to low investment grade, the report warned. Even a downgrade of just one letter grade—to double-A from triple-A—would leave the banks $22 billion short of capital.

Because the bond insurers were rated triple-A, they weren't required to post collateral against their credit-default-swap contracts. In the case of ACA, the company got a free pass on posting collateral as long as it stayed above triple-B. The arrangement set up a catastrophe, however, because ACA was not required to post collateral until its portfolio was so devastated by mark-to-market losses that a downgrade was unavoidable. Once that happened, collateral-posting requirements went from zero to billions of dollars in an instant, and ACA did not have the money.

MBIA, Ambac, and FGIC had more leeway on posting collateral than ACA Capital. They had to be considered insolvent before that became an issue. But how close were they to insolvency? The decline in the market value of the CDOs suggested that the bond insurers were going to have to make billions of dollars of payments. Surely, the banks had the upper hand as counterparties on contracts that, from the banks' perspective, were worth billions of dollars.

"It's a different world we're in," Dinallo recalls telling the group. "This is insurance." The insurance department sets the rules. If the bond-insurance companies were deemed to be insolvent, then the department could halt all payments until the very last insured municipal bond matured. That could take as long as 40 years, during which time the banks would have none of their claims paid. Or the insurance department could simply cancel everyone's policies and return the premiums. Municipalities would be happy. They paid up front and would get all their money back. The value of the insurance in the market had already largely been wiped out.

But for the banks, canceling the policies would be a disaster. Some hadn't made the first premium payment, yet they were counting on the insurance to shield them from massive mark-to-market losses.

If the banks could figure out a way to raise $15 billion for the bond insurers, then the companies might be able to hold on to their triple-A credit ratings, Dinallo told them. That would shield the banks from having to raise more capital, and a trillion dollars of municipal bonds would retain their triple-A ratings.

Dinallo had another card to play with the banks. Was it possible that these bankers had bought insurance after they knew the extent of the coming damage? If so, how was that different from the fraud committed by a man who buys life insurance after the doctor tells him he has only months to live? There was a question of culpability, Dinallo explains. If banks saw the crisis coming and constructed and insured securities to offload the damage, then that would be insurance fraud.

As early as late 2006, it was clear to many people that the housing market was set up for a huge fall. At the same time, financial firms such as Citigroup and Merrill Lynch went on a CDO-creating spree.

Hedge fund manager John Paulson, who made billions of dollars for his investors by shorting the ABX Index, a measure of the performance of mortgage securities, told investors in his Paulson Credit Opportunities Fund in early 2008 that as soon as home prices stopped rising, many securities were doomed. "The value of the CDO securities is simply nothing more than the value of the underlying collateral. If the BBB collateral is worthless then the CDO is worthless," Paulson wrote his investors.

To those knowledgeable about the structured finance market, it would have been clear in early 2007 that BBB-rated securities were in trouble. "The hypocrisy of the CDOs was that mezzanine CDOs, consisting exclusively of BBB collateral, somehow had 70 percent of their capital structure rated AAA," Paulson wrote. "It is the AAA CDO securities that are causing so much turmoil in the markets as their holders (Merrill Lynch, Morgan Stanley, Citibank, UBS, Wachovia) or their guarantors (Ambac, MBIA, ACA) are forced to write down."

Now the banks were threatening to consume decades of municipal bond premiums to offset their losses on toxic securities that they had created in a rush to remove subprime mortgages and other risky assets from their balance sheets. "You people created this mess," Dinallo told the executives. They had to be part of the solution. "When this story hits the newspaper," he said, "the headline is going to be 'How Wall Street Ate Main Street.'"

———————

AT PERSHING SQUARE, Shane Dinneen, the most recent hire on the investment team, was assigned the task of spot-checking the Credit Suisse model, which Ackman had dubbed "the Open Source Model," and put it on the Internet where it would be open to input from users. When Dinneen opened the Excel program which ran the model, the first thing he noticed was that instead of seeing the standard three tabs— one for each linkable spreadsheet—this file had 600.

Dinneen had joined Pershing Square several months earlier after completing a two-year training program with Blackstone Group. He had been "a number cruncher" with the private-equity firm, building

spreadsheets to predict postleveraged buyout profit-and-loss statements, balance sheets, and cash flow statements.

Ackman described Dinneen, a graduate of Harvard College, in a letter
to investors as "our tall, red-headed Shane," who "shares a remarkable
likeness to Conan O'Brien as well as membership in the Harvard
Lampoon." Ackman noted that Dinneen "shows early promise in being an
important contributor to Pershing. At a minimum, he should keep us in
good humor."

In early 2008, Dinneen's job was more tedious than entertaining.
He was assigned to go through the model, cell by cell, making sure that
the logic flowed and that the right cells connected. The process was
tedious, partly because it took more than 40 minutes to rerun the model
after making changes.

Dinneen would push the F9 button, walk away from the computer,
return half an hour later, and find the model was still running. It required
a leap of faith not to assume that the model had crashed his computer or
become stuck in some infinite loop. "Excel thinks top down," Dinneen
says. "When it has to double back, when the connections are so circular,
it takes a long time."

The model ran through three iterations. The first time around, it
peered into all of the CDOs and figured out what the losses on each one
would be based on the projected losses on the approximately 100 securities referenced by a typical CDO. The program cycled through a second
time, checking to see if any of the CDOs had exposure to other CDOs.
When it found such CDOs, it docked the "outer" CDO for its share of any
losses on the "inner" CDO. The final time through, the model reached
down into the "inner" CDOs to see if they held exposure to CDOs. The
"inner-inner" CDOs' losses were passed up to the "inner" CDOs, and
those losses were added to the total losses for the "outer" CDO. The three
iterations gave a total forecast for losses on each directly guaranteed CDO.
These losses were added to the direct guarantees on subprime mortgage–
backed bonds, home-equity-loan deals, and Alt-A securities for a final
tally.

The process gave Pershing Square amazing insight into the bond
insurers' portfolio, but it had to be accelerated. Paul Hilal, Ackman's
college friend who had joined the Pershing Square investment team in
2006, called his brother, Phil, who had recently bought a $16,000 custom-
ized personal computer for Christmas. Phil Hilal agreed to dash back to
his apartment to run the Open Source Model on his computer.

CDOs such as Ridgeway Court Funding II Ltd, which was directly insured by Ambac, demonstrated the tangled web of exposures the model analyzed. Ridgeway Court had direct exposure to one of the worst-performing CDOs in the market, Carina CDO Limited. Ridgeway Court also had indirect interest in Carina through another CDO holding called 888 Tactical Fund Limited that was directly exposed to Carina. But it didn't end there. Ridgeway Court also had exposure to two CDOs called Pinnacle Peak CDO Limited and Octonion CDO Limited that held interests in 888 Tactical Fund, which—if you are keeping track—had an interest in Carina.

While MBIA and Ambac claimed to have been highly selective in picking only the good CDOs to guarantee, there was so much overlap that they couldn't escape the bad ones. There were 534 CDO deals backed by subprime mortgages originated between the beginning of 2005 and the end of 2007. MBIA backed just 25, and Ambac guaranteed 28. But the Open Source Model showed that MBIA was directly or indirectly exposed to 420 of the 534 CDOs, or 80 percent of the market, while Ambac had exposure to 389, or 73 percent of the market. When Phil Hilal pulled up the model and pressed the F9 button, it took just 30 seconds for his computer to run the program. The result was going to shock the market.

Backing securities on which there was supposedly no risk of default had appeared to be the perfect business for the bond insurers, Robert Fuller, who runs Capital Markets Management LLC, a Hopewell, New Jersey–based advisory firm, told me in December 2007. Now the business had "morphed into this monster that is devouring them."

Chapter Twenty-One

Catastrophe and Revenge

It's quite simple. The count is telling us horrible stories with the intention of making us all die of fear.

ALEXANDRE DUMAS, *THE COUNT OF MONTE CRISTO*

W HEN NEWS OF the meeting between New York State Insurance Superintendent Eric Dinallo and representatives from the Wall Street firms was leaked later in the afternoon of January 23, 2008, the stock market soared. The Dow Jones Industrial Average rose more than 600 points, erasing an earlier drop of 300 points, as financial shares rallied. Ambac ended the day 72 percent higher, and MBIA gained 33 percent.

The rally continued in Asia. "Whether investors can sustain their confidence in the U.S. economy's stability is the key," Juichi Wako, a strategist at Nomura Securities Company, told Bloomberg Television News. It seemed a big part of that confidence rested with the triple-A ratings of the bond insurers.

It seemed that Dinallo had become more important to the market than the Federal Reserve. "The prospect of a rescue caused a far bigger stock market rally than the Fed's biggest rate cut in a quarter of a century the day before," the *Economist* magazine later noted. "There may be no better example of how a dull province of finance, when snared by complex risks it barely understands, can become terrifyingly unboring."

Despite the upbeat tone of the market, the bad news kept coming. After the market closed, Security Capital Assurance Limited said it wouldn't raise new capital. The "unprecedented uncertainty and instability affecting our industry make it impractical to consider raising new capital at the present time," the company said in a statement. Fitch Ratings, which had warned that the company needed an additional $2 billion in capital to justify a triple-A rating, took the company's insurance rating down five levels to single-A and left it under review for further downgrade.

THE NEXT DAY, January 24, Bill Ackman and Fiachra O'Driscoll, the head of synthetic CDO trading at Credit Suisse, met with Wilbur Ross. The billionaire investor was rumored to be considering a stake in Ambac. Unlike Marty Whitman and the principals at Warburg Pincus, Ross was willing to hear what Ackman had to say.

Ackman and O'Driscoll described how the companies were going to be destroyed by their exposure to collateralized-debt obligations (CDOs) and other securities backed by home loans.

"If you decide to invest, I'd steer clear of MBIA and Ambac," Ackman said. "We haven't analyzed Assured Guaranty, but the company is coming through this the best so far."

The reason Assured Guaranty never took a single CDO backed by mortgages to committee was because it couldn't review the underlying risk, Sabra Purtill, head of investor relations at Assured Guaranty, once explained to me. What were the FICO (Fair Isaac Corporation) scores on the underlying loans? How much was being borrowed compared with the value of the house? What was the borrower's income?

One of the ironies of the bond insurers' demise is that they were aware by 2005 that subprime loans had become riskier, yet the risk premiums on subprime mortgage–backed bonds were continuing to shrink. The bond insurers stepped back from the subprime market only to stumble into a magnified version of that risk in the CDO market.

When insuring CDOs, the bond insurers became reliant on someone else to do the work on the underlying securities, and it turns out that work didn't get done. The CDO managers who had become major buyers of subprime mortgage–backed securities were interested only in credit ratings and yield. They didn't pull the files on mortgages. Besides, Purtill says, reviewing the underlying loans simply wasn't possible.

Purtill estimated that it took a single employee about one month to spot-check the files on the approximately 1,000 loans behind a mortgage-backed bond. Consider the amount of work necessary to complete the due diligence on a CDO backed by subprime-mortgage bonds—that's assuming it was even possible to get access to information on all the underlying loans. If the CDO referenced 100 mortgage-backed bonds, then it would take one person 100 months, or a little more than eight years, to complete loan-level due diligence.

And what if the deal was a CDO-squared and was backed by 50 CDOs, each backed by 100 mortgage-backed bonds? Now, it would take someone 400 years to review the underlying loans in each of the 50 CDOs (8 years per CDO × 50 CDOs). Nevertheless, the deals were signed off on in a matter of months.

Others were spotting flaws in CDOs, too. A report by a group of Harvard Business School researchers released in June 2007 concluded that investors buying the highest-rated pieces of CDOs had been "grossly undercompensated" for this risk.

The top layer of a CDO was, in fact, an economic-catastrophe bond, similar to catastrophe bonds sold by insurance companies to protect themselves against a highly unlikely event such as a series of category five hurricanes hitting the Florida coast in a single season. The investor in catastrophe bonds sold by a property and casualty company receives a relatively high return on the bonds—compared with other investment grade–rated securities—but if the extreme event occurs, the bond investor will be completely wiped out.

Investors in CDOs, or economic catastrophe bonds, settled for an exceptionally low return even though they faced a similar risk of a total loss.

"The manufacturing of securities resembling economic catastrophe bonds emerges as the optimal mechanism for exploiting investors who rely on ratings for pricing," Harvard researchers Joshua Coval, Jakub Jurek, and Erik Stafford wrote. "We argue that this discrepancy has much to do with the fact that credit-rating agencies are willing to certify senior CDO tranches as 'safe' when, from an asset-pricing perspective, they are quite the opposite," the report concluded.

THAT THE CATASTROPHE was well under way was obvious as O'Driscoll at Credit Suisse tinkered with the final results of the Open Source Model. Ackman planned to send the loss forecasts for MBIA and Ambac to the Securities and Exchange Commission and the New York State Insurance Department. He also planned to make the model available on the Internet so that those with an interest and enough computing power could use their own assumptions to project the bond insurers' losses.

Just after midnight on January 29, 2008, O'Driscoll messaged Ackman: "Should be done in the next few hours." They met at Pershing Square's offices the next afternoon to go through the final results. The model was predicting losses many multiples of what MBIA and Ambac had told investors they expected. Ambac would lose a minimum of $11.61 billion, and MBIA would pay claims of $11.63 billion, the model forecasted.

Those viewing the model would be able to see the names of all of MBIA's CDOs of asset-backed securities (ABS) and CDOs from 2005 to 2007. The collateral underlying the CDOs was identified by CUSIP (the unique number from the Committee for Uniform Security Identification Procedures that identifies every bond), as well as by collateral type, par outstanding, and its original and current ratings.

The losses projected on some of the individual securities were staggering. An Ambac-insured CDO-squared called Class V Funding IV, one in a series of Citigroup deals, was expected to cost the bond insurer $1.3 billion on a guarantee of $1.4 billion. An MBIA-insured CDO called Broderick 3 was expected to result in $758 million of losses on a $1.2 billion guarantee. Both of those guarantees had been taken on at the super-senior level, an indication that they were supposed to be even safer than triple-A-rated bonds.

The Open Source Model produced performance projections for all 524 ABS CDOs created between 2005 and 2007, indicating they would result in probable losses for the entire market of $231 billion, with super-senior tranches alone losing $92 billion.

This disastrous outcome was the result of a basic flaw in the assumptions used to securitize mortgages. Credit-rating companies insisted on diversification: a range of loan originators and servicers, wide geographical distribution, and various loan sizes. Ideally, the diversity protected investors from being exposed to loans that would all come under pressure for the same reason. What the credit-rating companies had overlooked was the time frame, or the so-called vintage, in which the loans were made. Vintage turned out to be the single most important factor in the performance of many loans. Loans made in 2006 and 2007 were made to people who borrowed as much as they could to purchase houses they couldn't afford when prices were peaking.

The credit-rating companies and bond insurers mistakenly assumed that even more diversification was created when mortgage-backed securities were pooled into CDOs. Yet the CDOs were backed by securities all created around the same time, containing mortgages that all originated around the same time. The CDOs perfectly captured the risk that had spread across the housing market of inflated home values and borrowers lying to get into mortgages they couldn't afford. The risk only *appeared* to have been shattered by the securitization process. In fact, it was lethally concentrated.

AT 4:02 A.M. ON JANUARY 30, 2008, Ackman e-mailed more questions to O'Driscoll and his team at Credit Suisse who had been working all night to make sure the data were complete. Before the market opened that day, Ackman gave the model's predictions to Charlie Gasparino, a reporter at CNBC, who announced them on air. Shortly after, Ackman issued a press release describing the model. "Up until this point in time, the market and the regulators have had to rely on the bond insurers and the rating agencies to calculate their own losses in what we deem a self-graded exam," Ackman said in a statement. "Now the market will have the opportunity to do its own analysis."

Ackman's letter, also released to regulators, included a description of how to find the model on the Internet. "By focusing the discussion on a fundamental, data-driven approach, we expect that the dissemination of the Open Source Model will enable market participants and regulators to accurately estimate probable losses by relying on rigorous fundamental analysis of specific credit exposures, a departure from relying on the opaque, faith-based pronouncements that the bond-insurance industry has promulgated to the marketplace," Ackman wrote.

Pershing Square's description of the bond insurers' CDO business made it sound like a veritable Russian doll of risk, with CDOs nested inside CDOs nested inside CDOs. "Users of the model can drill down multiple layers to identify and analyze individual credits of not just the outer CDOs but also those exposures of the CDOs owned by outer CDOs (that is, 'inner CDOs') and further to identify the specific exposures of the 'inner-inner CDOs' owned by those inner CDOs that are, in turn, owned by the outer CDOs that have been guaranteed by MBIA and Ambac."

As traders, analysts, hedge fund managers, and reporters pulled up the model, it began crashing computers across Wall Street. "This model is quite large, approximately 110Mb. Each recalculation of this model on a typical workstation—3.4GHz Dual Core Pentium D with 3Gb of 800 MHz FSB DDR2 RAM—benchmarks at 25–30 minutes," the Pershing Square letter warned in a footnote.

Ackman argued that regulators should stop the bond insurers from paying further dividends to their holding companies because management was underestimating expected claims and thus overstating statutory capital levels. "One would expect management to estimate losses at a level which allows the insurance subsidiary to pay holding-company dividends," Ackman continued. "Rarely is a man willing to sign his own death warrant."

———

DAN LOEB, THE FOUNDER of hedge fund Third Point LLC, who had watched the MBIA saga for years, logged on to Amazon.com and ordered a book for Ackman. Loeb is well known for penning his own sharply worded letters to the management of companies in which he has an investment interest. He is also an avid reader, particularly of stories about heroes, villains, and adventure—books such as *Don Quixote* and Alexandre Dumas's *The Count of Monte Cristo,* the book he bought for Ackman.

The nineteenth-century French novel tells the story of a man known as Dantès, who is horribly wronged and later methodically seeks revenge. Hauled off to the Château d'If, a notorious prison off the coast of Marseille, Dantès is dumped into the dungeon, where Dantès meets a priest with a plan for escape and a map to a buried treasure. The priest does not make it out, but Dantès does. He finds the treasure, uses it to reestablish himself as the Count of Monte Cristo, and goes about creating havoc in the lives of those who have wronged him.

There had always been that personal element in Ackman's criticism of MBIA. Ackman had never doubted that MBIA executives wanted to put him in jail over his report questioning the company's credit rating. In 2009, an individual involved in the 2003 investigation of Gotham agreed that MBIA's response to Ackman had been unusually aggressive. "This was serious stuff," the individual said. "They referred him to Spitzer who not only could have put him out of business but could have locked him up and taken him away from his kids."

Loeb had talked to Ackman for several years about MBIA. He'd also held short positions on the bond insurers. Just now, with Ackman's campaign against MBIA in overdrive, and confidence in the company crumbling by the day, Loeb couldn't resist sending Ackman the Dumas novel. "He is not a vengeful person, but he has a keen sense of justice," Loeb says of Ackman. "It's an important nuance." Loeb explains that the book is not just about revenge but also about perseverance. "It's relevant to Bill because he was so dogged and persistent," says Loeb. And in the spring of 2008, as in the final chapters of *The Count of Monte Cristo*, "everything seemed to be falling into place," Loeb recalls.

———

AT 2:15 P.M. ON JANUARY 30—the day Gasparino at CNBC broadcast Ackman's loss estimates—the Federal Open Market Committee announced another rate cut, taking its benchmark rate to 3 percent from 3.5 percent. The magic worked but only briefly. Fears about bond insurance were weighing on stocks and on corporate bonds. Ackman's startling high loss numbers were not helping matters.

Some people thought Ackman had gone too far. Critics of short selling coined a phrase to describe the very public and unsettling analysis issued by some money managers during the credit crisis: "Short and distort." The charge was leveled at Ackman and later at David Einhorn, who had begun to point to problems at Lehman Brothers.

As Madame de Villefort, one of the nobles caught up in the Count of Monte Cristo's acts of revenge, tells her friends, "It's quite simple. The count is telling us horrible stories with the intention of making us all die of fear."

"Is your terror real, madame?" Monte Cristo asks the half-fainting Madame Danglars.

"No," replies Madame Danglars, "but you have a way of supposing things which gives them an illusion of reality."

Illusion and reality were definitely becoming a bit blurred. Gasparino went back on the air later in the afternoon: "My gut is telling me that the big bond-rating houses are going to downgrade either one or both of the major bond-insurance companies—Ambac and MBIA—and the downgrades will probably come today." There was speculation in the market, the stock prices were down, and Ackman was saying these companies were going to lose $12 billion, said Gasparino. How could it not happen?

MBIA and Ambac made it through the day with their ratings intact, but shortly before the market closed on January 30, time ran out for Financial Guaranty Insurance Company (FGIC). The company, which hadn't come up with a plan to raise capital, became the third bond insurer to lose its triple-A rating at Fitch. MBIA's shares closed down $2.02, or 13 percent, at $13.96. Ambac's dropped $2.08, or 16 percent, to $10.85. Both companies had lost more than 80 percent of their market value in a year.

After the market closed, Standard & Poor's (S&P) announced that it was reviewing the ratings on $534 billion of residential-mortgage securities and collateralized-debt obligations, more than 8,000 classes of securities in all, that had been issued between January 2006 and June 2007.

———

EARLY ON THE MORNING of January 31, 2008, Pershing Square's investment team met for breakfast at a restaurant a few blocks from the office to review the questions it planned to submit to MBIA in advance of its conference call to discuss fourth-quarter results later that day.

In the Open Source letter to regulators, Ackman had chided MBIA for announcing it would only take questions in writing. Pershing Square planned to release its questions publicly, ahead of the call, Ackman explained in the letter. "If the company chooses not to answer these questions, its silence will speak for itself."

In the taxi on his way to the restaurant, Mick McGuire read through the company's earnings release and pulled out a quote to send to the others: "MBIA's below-investment-grade net par exposure includes $10.6 billion of home-equity lines of credit and closed-end second [residential mortgage-backed securities] and multisector CDOs of high grade CDOs." The safety of the securities MBIA had insured was deteriorating rapidly.

When Pershing Square published its questions in a press release shortly before the 11 a.m. call, the Yahoo Finance message board came to life: "Company is going to respond to Ackman's presentation. They will put this snake oil salesman to shame." "Ackman's questions should be ignored!" "Ackman and party should be booked under homeland security for financial terrorism, trying to bring the country down."

The company's executives came out swinging as soon as the call began at 11 a.m.

"We clearly acknowledge that we are taking the microphone, as it were, out of the hands of those inclined to ask questions of us," Greg Diamond, MBIA's head of investor relations, said. "Many of these people have effectively become adversaries of our company, our employees, our clients, and our business relationships. Many of them have demonstrated no problems finding media outlets to proselytize their messages against our company. We see no reason to provide them with another forum to do so."

That said, they were going to answer lots of questions. They had received 282 of them via e-mail, including Ackman's. "The first question was submitted by the likes of Bill Ackman at Pershing Square: How much cash is at the holding company?" Diamond began. "Ackman at Pershing Square: Can MBIA be forced into bankruptcy?"

Asked about the Open Source Model, Mitch Sonkin, who oversaw the firm's insured portfolio, called it "a black box." "The extreme assumptions in the model produced the desired effect of a sensational headline loss number for the firms evaluated. All of the analytical work was done by an anonymous so-called global bank that doesn't wish to be identified with the work and which is disclaimed by the author, who says that he can't vouch for the accuracy or the completeness of the analysis," Chaplin added.

MBIA's chief executive officer Gary Dunton told the callers that the company had raised $2 billion in five weeks, and although MBIA expected to pay significant claims, "no serious analyst expects that we will have $7 billion of economic losses on our portfolio." The only conclusion that could be drawn about the 80 percent drop in the company's share price, he said, was that "the market has overreacted" and that "fear mongering and intentional distortions of facts about our business have been pumped into the market by self-interested parties."

Dunton pointed out that MBIA had achieved a significant milestone during the quarter; MBIA's outstanding guarantees on debt and debt-service payments had breached the $1 trillion mark.

Dunton offered a mea culpa, saying bad underwriting decisions "have tested the Richter scale in the formerly unshakable world of the financial-guarantee industry." He was also reflective: MBIA needed to be "more assertive in countering misinformation about our business," and it needed to be "more open and transparent to the market." He was personal: "It's very difficult seeing the reputation of the company that you love come under fire." And oddly sentimental: "The very first deal that we insured back in 1974 was an $8 million water and sewer bond for Carbondale, Illinois. That was a massive deal back in those days, and we were so proud." And perhaps even a bit sarcastic: "Well, a lot of effluvia have passed through the pipes since then," he told listeners.

Four hours into the call, and with just a few questions left unanswered, Diamond wrapped it up. "I will let you know that none of the remaining questions are Bill Ackman's questions. We have responded to all of those that he has provided."

Later in the afternoon, despite MBIA's spirited defense, which boosted not only the company's stock price but also the entire stock market, S&P announced that it was stripping FGIC of its triple-A rating and considering downgrading MBIA. "Although MBIA has succeeded in accessing $1.5 billion of additional capital, the magnitude of projected losses underscores our view that time is of the essence in the completion of capital-raising efforts," S&P said.

ACKMAN'S WASN'T THE only letter making the rounds that week. Another, this one circulating on the Internet, was a humorous jab at Ackman's campaign against the bond insurers. The letter, from the Robert E. Lee Short Fund, was addressed to the president of the United States, Pope Benedict XVI, Oprah Winfrey, and Bono. It was signed Bruce Wayne, "Most Omnipotent Managing Founder" of the fund: "You don't know me and it is unlikely you would ever seek to, but I am a rich and handsome man and I have made a huge investment whose profit depends on the decline of a stock whose issuing firm is central to the stability of global financial markets," Wayne began.

"You may have no knowledge of or concern about said company, but the mere inclusion of your illustrious names will add to the credibility that is literally money in my pocket," the letter continued. "In fact, it is quite possible you have never heard of the subject company and it would require a graduate level course in financial accounting to even begin to understand the complexity of its business."

Of course, Wayne didn't expect readers to just accept his conclusions that the company was "doomed," so he attached a computer model. "This model is very complicated and looks like something a really smart kid at an investment bank would construct on a computer, *so it must be right.*" It had "a lot of buttons and tabs and lists the names of many evil *subprime*-related securities." "We both know you have no intention of or ability regarding the *model*; just attaching a *model* means my analysis must be right.

"Anyway, thanks for everything," Wayne said in closing. "Thanks for just being you. Thanks for being part of a system where I can seek to systematically destroy a decades-old company that is a lynchpin of the entire financing system solely to enrich myself and further my franchise as a 'shareholder activist.'"

Attempts at ridicule, no matter how cleverly worded, could not deter Ackman. In early February, less than a week after MBIA's earnings call, he wrote another of his trademark letters, this one to Federal Reserve Chairman Ben Bernanke and U.S. Treasury Secretary Hank Paulson, advising against a bank-led rescue of the bond insurers. Such a rescue would only prolong the credit contraction, limit transparency, and increase the risk in the banking system, Ackman argued. "The bond-insurer industry bailout should fail if legitimate banks come out against the practice of propping up insolvent and falsely rated entities or when you and your international counterparts act to stop it."

Although it's not clear what they thought of Ackman over at the Fed, officials there had been pondering the predicament of the bond insurers. Notes from the Federal Reserve's January 29 and 30 meeting, held in Washington, said that policy makers "perceived a possibility that additional downgrades in these firms' credit ratings could put increased strains on financial markets." Though the notes were couched in typical, dulled-down Fed-speak, officials were clearly concerned.

French novelist Dumas would surely have added color to the Fed's story: "You look disturbed and that frightens me," the Count of Monte Cristo tells a financier friend who pays him an unexpected visit. "A worried capitalist is like a comet: He always presages some disaster for the world."

Chapter Twenty-Two

Time Runs Out

We are seeing real harm not only to investors and governments but to the capital markets, and therefore it is time for people to act.

—New York Governor Eliot Spitzer, February 2008

I N A CORNER OF the bond market where municipalities and other issuers sell so-called auction-rate securities—a $400 billion market—another crisis had been brewing for months. By late January 2008, it was about to boil over.

Auction-rate securities (ARS) were purchased by wealthy individuals and corporate treasurers as a safe, short-term investment for cash. The securities were rated triple-A, thanks to bond-insurance policies, so there was no apparent credit risk. ARS had long-term maturities, but the interest rates were reset at regular auctions, giving investors the opportunity to trade out of the securities every few weeks. There was no guarantee that anyone would buy the securities at the next auction, but they always had in the past. On occasion, banks underwriting the securities had quietly stepped in to support the market when bids at auctions were thin.

If no one bid for an ARS when it was reauctioned, then the dealer would increase the yield on the security until it reached a specified cap. In some cases, these caps were set as high as 20 percent. If no one bought at the maximum yield the auction would be deemed a failure, the existing holder would be stuck with the securities, and the issuer would be stuck paying an astronomically high interest rate. Banks made sure this never happened.

That was, until July 2007, when the credit-rating companies began to downgrade subprime securities and collateralized-debt obligations (CDOs) and things began to go drastically wrong.

At just about this time, two brothers from New Jersey sold their family's shipping business, Maher Terminals, for $1 billion. They turned over $600 million of the proceeds to Lehman Brothers to invest while they contemplated a future as entrepreneurs and philanthropists. Lehman parked their money in auction-rate securities, including securities issued by the bond insurers.

These securities—called *contingent preferred stock put facilities*— were created to provide the bond insurers with additional capital if their claims-paying resources ran low. The proceeds of the bond issue were held in a trust that invested in safe securities such as Treasuries. If the bond insurer needed capital, it was permitted to sell the safe securities, replacing them with newly issued preferred shares. Of course, if a bond insurer were in the position of needing to raise capital, those preferred shares probably weren't going to be worth much.

In theory, the securities made perfect sense. The Maher brothers got a slightly higher yield on their funds for taking what seemed like a very remote risk—a capital crisis at a triple-A-rated bond-insurance company. In practice, these securities were a ticking time bomb for the capital markets.

If investors started to worry about the bond insurers, these securities would become impossible to auction. Once investors balked at buying the securities, there was a danger they would rethink the entire ARS market. After all, the only reason most of these securities carried triple-A ratings was that they were insured by bond insurers. If a failed auction began with a bond insurer's own securities, there would be no telling how far it could spread. "Failed auctions are typically self-perpetuating," the Maher brothers' attorneys stated in a complaint filed with the Financial Industry Regulatory Authority in early 2008 against Lehman. "That is, once an auction fails it is unlikely that it will subsequently succeed at a later auction in the absence of intervention."

On August 6, 2007, the auction of contingent preferreds for a small bond-reinsurance company called Ram Re failed. Even though the securities drew no bidders, Lehman reinvested $168 million of the Mahers' money in these same securities, according to the complaint. On August 14, 2007, the first auction for securities held by the Mahers failed. "Over the next four days, [Lehman] invested a further $57 million even as three more auctions failed," according to the complaint.

Problems began to appear in other parts of the auction-rate market. Frances Constable, the head of Merrill Lynch's auction-rate desk, wrote to colleagues in an e-mail on August 9: "Markets are shutting down bit by bit. We have [five] failed auctions so far, with three more likely today."

Three days later, another Merrill employee sent around an e-mail saying he'd been in contact with "John and Fred" at MBIA. "They are obviously concerned about a failed auction and the ramifications thereof." The employee added, "They see a program failure as having potential franchise ramifications."

On August 16, a colleague sent Constable on the auction-rate desk a copy of a Fitch Ratings report discussing the implications of failed auctions for bond insurers' securities. Constable did not need to be reminded of what was happening in the ARS market: "Come on down and visit us in the vomitorium!! We will be sure to provide it to all those holders who, according to the article, are likely to get caught up in this latest round of likely fails."

Over at Lehman Brothers, things weren't any better. On August 21, an adviser to the Maher brothers e-mailed Lehman to say he was concerned about the allocation of their money. After receiving the e-mail, Lehman attempted to liquidate all the securities but failed.

Ominously, the banks did not step in to show support for the bond insurers. "The auction product does not work, and we need to use our leverage to force the issuers to confront this problem," Ross Jackman, who oversaw the short-term securities trading desk, e-mailed David Shulman, global head of municipal securities group at UBS, on December 12.

Three days later, Shulman e-mailed Joseph Scoby, UBS Securities' chief risk officer, asking for guidance on whether the firm could continue to support auctions. The problem with pulling out of the market, Shulman noted, was that retail investors had been told these securities would "be redeemed at par on demand. Although there is no formal liquidity provision in place."

Merrill Lynch was fielding a steady stream of questions from investors and issuers worried about the auction-rate market. On November 30, Constable e-mailed colleagues telling them that any negative news about the bond insurers was leading to a further collapse in confidence.

Two days earlier, on November 28, Bill Ackman had taken the stage at the Value Investing Congress, telling the audience he expected to make hundreds of millions of dollars on the collapse of the companies that were holding together the auction-rate market.

The banks were fighting a losing battle. "The recurring conversation here on the auction-rate desk is a line out of *Marathon Man*," Constable continued in her e-mail. That line was the one made famous by Laurence Olivier as he subjected Dustin Hoffman to torture dentistry while calmly asking a question for which Hoffman had no answer: "Is it safe?"

Wall Street firms continued to insist publicly that it was, but privately the concerns were mounting. "If you find yourself experiencing a horrible auction—that is, you need to support more than 25 percent ... call risk control *before* you support it," Scoby over at UBS cautioned in an e-mail to Shulman a few days before Christmas. "If you see signs that other dealers are walking away from auctions, let us know."

Two days later, Christopher Long, who managed UBS's short-term securities desk, sent an e-mail to Shulman and others laying out his worst fear: "Monoline insurance providers are downgraded multiple notches and the demand for [auction-rate securities] retracts exponentially." He had good reason to be concerned. UBS's inventory of auction-rate securities was ballooning as the firm continued to support the market. Auction-rate securities holdings were limited to $2.5 billion under the firm's risk-management guidelines. Yet, by the end of 2007, the bank had $5 billion of the securities on its book. This accumulation of unmarketable securities came on top of a collapse in the value of $50 billion of super-senior CDOs, against which the bank would now have to hold enormous amounts of capital.

The new year brought no relief to the auction-rate market. During the first week of January 2008, Jackman received an e-mail from Shulman that detailed the firm's options for managing through the crisis. One option was to simply let auctions fail. The firm had no obligation to take on the securities. But Shulman listed one consideration if the bank didn't prop up auctions of securities it had underwritten: "Severe reputational issue."

There might be one way to lessen the blow to the firm if UBS did decide to walk away from the market, Shulman added. Other banks were faced with the same problem. It would be less of a blow if others walked away from the market, too. "If we do fail, be the second to fail," Shulman wrote.

On January 9, a senior trader on the auction-rate desk at Merrill Lynch sent around an e-mail warning that bond insurers XL Capital Assurance and the Financial Guaranty Insurance Company (FGIC) were likely to lose their top ratings. "We anticipate that if that happens, there will be a wave of selling in these issues that we will be unable to support, causing the auction to fail."

Several weeks later, on January 23, the same day that Eric Dinallo was holding a meeting with all the major banks about how to prevent a downgrade of the bond insurers, a Merrill trader sent this ominous message to colleagues: "Lehman failed five auctions yesterday. This is unprecedented."

———

WHEN ELIOT SPITZER arrived at the Rigor Hill Diner in Chatham, New York, he pulled up in a black SUV, with an additional security detail following in a second black SUV. It was a Sunday in early February 2008, and the governor was on his way back from Albany. Ackman had been waiting for him in the parking lot of the restaurant, which was not far from his house in upstate New York. Both he and Spitzer were scheduled to testify at congressional hearings on the bond-insurance industry set for later in the month.

Spitzer had been struggling in the polls. Saving the bond insurers— several of which were headquartered in New York state and all of which had insured debt for the state—might win him some points with voters. Ackman had a plan for saving the bond insurers.

Spitzer's appearance in the diner, with its blue vinyl booths, white formica-top tables, and wagon-wheel ceiling lamps, caused a brief stir. After posing for a photo with one of the diner's patrons, Spitzer slid into a booth across from Ackman. Outside in the parking lot, Spitzer's security guards smoked cigarettes and kept watch.

Over omelets, Ackman described how he would restructure MBIA, sketching out the structure on a piece of paper. First, the insurance company would be split in two, separating the municipal bond business from the tarred structured finance business. The municipal bond insurer would be owned by the structured finance insurer and would pass dividends to its parent company only if it was sure those payments wouldn't jeopardize its own triple-A credit rating. The structured finance insurer would make the same assessment when deciding whether to send dividends up to its parent company, the publicly traded holding company.

Each of the two insurance companies would have an independent board of directors, made up in part of policyholders. The decision to transfer money out of the insurance companies would rest with the boards of directors. Policyholders would have an interest in keeping the money at the insurance units not just to cover claims but also to maintain the highest possible rating on their bonds, Ackman explained.

Money would be transferred only with board approval, and the board would represent the interests of the policyholders. Currently, the MBIA Insurance Corporation board of directors was made up of MBIA Inc. employees, many of whom were compensated with stock options which meant they were more concerned with moving cash to the holding company than protecting policyholders, said Ackman. His plan would result in more capital being retained to protect policyholders. It also could cut off dividends to the holding company for years and increase the chance that MBIA Inc. would be forced to file for bankruptcy. If Spitzer found Ackman's plan self-serving, he didn't say so.

ON FEBRUARY 5, Fitch Ratings put MBIA's triple-A rating under review, less than a month after affirming the rating with a stable outlook. Paul Hilal, a senior member of the Pershing Square investment team, sent Ackman an e-mail about it. "This strikes me as the first time a rating agency has made the important intellectual leap that the inherent fragility of the bond insurer business model disqualifies [it] from a triple-A rating," Hilal wrote. He attached a quote from the release: "A material increase in claim payments would be inconsistent with triple-A-ratings standards for financial guarantors and could potentially call into question the appropriateness of triple-A ratings for those affected companies, regardless of their ultimate capital levels."

On February 6, UBS's Jackman, clearly alarmed, e-mailed Shulman: The firm's holdings of auction-rate securities now totaled $11 billion. The program was no longer sustainable. "We need solutions or we are going to be left buried with below-market securities and no options," Jackman told him. "D-Day will come soon."

MBIA was doing everything it could to keep that day from arriving. On February 8, the company sold $1 billion of stock to shore up its triple-A rating. Warburg Pincus bought $300 million of the shares, further increasing its stake in the company. MBIA had now raised $2.5 billion of capital since November when the rating companies first said they were reviewing the capital levels of the bond insurers. "MBIA bought itself some time," Peter Plaut, an analyst at hedge fund Sanno Point Capital Management in New York, told Bloomberg News.

Wall Street may have been convinced the company was entitled to more time, but Warren Buffett wasn't. On February 12, 2008, Buffett made an early morning appearance on CNBC to broadcast Berkshire Hathaway's proposal to reinsure MBIA, Ambac, and FGIC's municipal bond businesses. Berkshire Hathaway would take over the guarantees, but Buffett wanted to be paid one and a half times what the companies had originally charged for the insurance. Buffett would walk away with virtually the entire municipal bond-insurance business.

Buffett had no intention of bidding for the bond insurers' structured finance business, the guarantees on CDOs and other bonds backed by mortgages and credit-card receivables. "How deep that problem is with the CDOs and the other things they've done," Buffett said, "we can't figure out."

If a bond insurer accepted his offer, it would be given 30 days to back out. If the firm could find a better option, Buffett would release it from the contract for a breakup fee of 1.5 percent of the premium. Either way, "the world would know that the municipal bond-insurance problem was behind it," said Buffett.

"It would be a great deal for Berkshire Hathaway," said CreditSights' Rob Haines. "It would be a terrible deal for the bond insurers. If one of them were to accept this deal, it would be like raising a white flag." Yet the stocks rallied—even the dollar rallied—on word of Buffett's offer. But no one took him up on it.

Buffett made his offer on a Tuesday morning. By Wednesday afternoon, the entire auction-rate market was collapsing. "On February 13, without advance notice to its customers, UBS ceased supporting its auction-rate program, leaving hundreds of customers stuck with securities they couldn't sell. The bankers at UBS could take comfort from the fact that at least they were not alone. Eighty percent of all auctions failed that day.

Banks such as Goldman Sachs Group and Citigroup let more than 100 of their auctions fail during the second week of February. The collapse of the auction-rate market threatened to drain the coffers of thousands of highly creditworthy institutions and municipalities by forcing them to pay the same interest rates as a nearly bankrupt company. The cost of funding on $15 million of Harrisburg International Airport bonds in Pennsylvania jumped to 14 percent. The Port Authority of New York and New Jersey was forced to pay 20 percent on its debt compared with just 4.3 percent a week earlier.

FOR DECADES, BOND INSURANCE had eased the sale of municipal bonds. Now it had turned toxic.

In the early 1990s, James Angel, a finance professor at Georgetown University, had set out to determine exactly what it was that bond insurers provided to the municipal bond market. On the surface, the business didn't make any sense, Angel posited in his paper titled "The Municipal Bond Insurance Riddle."

Angel determined that insurers weren't being paid for enhancing the credit quality of the bond, which was strong to begin with. Instead, investors were paying for what banker Mark Northcross termed the "Good Housekeeping Seal of Approval." That seal turned bonds issued by large cities and small towns into a commodity. Investors didn't need to look beyond the rating and try to decipher the credit quality of a Mississippi sewer authority or a Michigan school district. The bond was simply a triple-A-rated municipal bond, an anonymous security for which a broker could instantaneously find a buyer.

Yet bond insurers never promised to provide liquidity. They were protecting investors against default and that's something very different. The liquidity support provided by bond insurers turned out to be a house of mirrors. As long as the securities were rated triple-A and insured, investors would buy them. As long as investors bought the securities, the banks could claim they stood ready to back the market. But when confidence in the triple-A ratings of the bond insurers crumbled, demand for the securities disappeared. The banks could have supported individual issues, but they couldn't make up for a loss of demand across the entire market.

"Reports of five more failed auctions at Piper Jaffray," a trader at UBS e-mailed colleagues during the first week of February. Later, someone else at UBS passed along this piece of news: "Just heard . . . Goldman Sachs let a Sallie Mae deal fail." On February 13, the day before Congress took up the question of what to do with bond insurers, the auction-rate market collapsed.

CONGRESS COULD NOT HAVE selected a more ironic date—Valentine's Day—to bring together Bill Ackman, the top executives of MBIA and Ambac, and the credit-rating analyst. MBIA executives were furious about Ackman's inclusion in the hearings as an "industry expert."

"Mr. Ackman is in fact not involved in the industry in any capacity except that of a short-seller, and accordingly, MBIA questions the characterization of Mr. Ackman's expertise," MBIA's chief financial officer Chuck Chaplin said in his prepared testimony.

The hearings fueled additional controversy. Shortly after midnight, as Valentine's Day began, Eliot Spitzer left room 871 at the Mayflower Hotel. He had come to Washington to testify about the crisis in the bond-insurance business and about how the state of New York planned to intervene. But the trip would be remembered instead for the disgraceful episode that would end his public career. The arrangements for his rendezvous with a high-priced call girl had been captured by an FBI wiretap.

A thin layer of snow swirled through the streets of Washington, DC, as the start of the 11 a.m. hearing approached. Auctions continued to fail across the market, including a $74 million offering for the District of Columbia's water and sewer authority, which was insured by Ambac.

Spitzer was first to testify and made clear that the banks had little time to act. "The clock is ticking, and as we move forward, we are seeing real harm not only to investors and governments but to the capital markets, and therefore it is time for people to act," Spitzer said.

If banks couldn't come up with a solution, then the state of New York might force a split of the bond insurers, a so-called good bank–bad bank solution that would protect the municipal bond holders. "Time is short," Spitzer stressed. Pressed by committee members about his own time frame for taking action to protect bondholders, he answered, "Three to five days."

A Republican congressman reminded Spitzer of his decision to investigate Ackman over his criticism of MBIA. Spitzer acknowledged that Ackman had accurately predicted the problems with the insurers, but as attorney general he had moved on from investigating Ackman to looking into the company's practices. "What we found, after an exhaustive inquiry, was that there was risk that was within the tolerable balance of business behavior," Spitzer said.

After Spitzer's testimony, the committee recessed to take a vote on the house floor. Members were gone for hours.

Ackman paced the hall, speaking briefly with Michael Callen, the interim chief executive officer (CEO) of Ambac, who joked about suing him. He also spoke with Laura Unger, a former commissioner with the Securities and Exchange Commission (SEC) and an Ambac board member, who appeared unaware of who Ackman was, telling him she believed the industry was the "victim of a huge overreaction." Just a few feet away, Chuck Chaplin, MBIA's chief financial officer, stood waiting to testify on behalf of MBIA, but he and Ackman did not speak.

At one point, Ackman found himself sitting with New York State Insurance Superintendent Eric Dinallo in one of the anterooms along the corridor, exchanging pleasantries. A few minutes later, Dinallo was interviewed on CNBC.

"Mr. Ackman does have to worry about speaking accurately in the marketplace where he holds a tremendous amount of short positions," Dinallo said. "There is an insurance law called 2604 that says you cannot without a factual basis disparage insurance companies because you can cause a run on the solvency. Mr. Ackman performs an important function, but he should be sure that whatever he says is based in fact."

When the hearings reconvened, most members of the committee failed to return. As Ackman took his seat, he got a message from Marco Kheirallah, the Pershing investor at Pactual in Rio de Janeiro: "I am watching the testimony. Has anyone there realized that FGIC has just been downgraded, 6 notches on the insurance sub, 8 notches (to junk!!!!) for the holding company and that they are in charge of 18 percent of the municipal market?" The stock market dropped 175 points.

Congressman Paul Kanjorski (D-Pennsylvania), who chairs the Capital Markets subcommittee, called Eric Dinallo to speak next.

"I think we're in a very volatile situation, and things that we should do and can do should be done as quickly as possible and as cleanly as possible," Kanjorski told him, citing the FGIC downgrade. "I've been trying, Congressman," Dinallo said explaining how the New York State

Insurance Department had been working to help bond insurers raise capital. "I'll take the brass cup anywhere."

The bond insurers' comments at the hearing contrasted with the sense of urgency shown by the insurance department. Chaplin reminded the committee that MBIA continued to be rated triple-A by all three credit-rating companies. The company also had drawn an $800 million investment from Warburg Pincus after an in-depth review.

"Self-interested parties have gone to substantial efforts to undermine the market confidence that is critical to MBIA's business," Chaplin said. "Their efforts have included raising questions about MBIA's capitalization, the losses it will likely sustain, its liquidity position, the legality of its operations, and the viability of its business model." Short sellers had "used the media to create noise around MBIA's solvency and ratings; written letters to regulators and rating agencies, seeking action against MBIA; and held meetings with investors with the intent, the company believes, to dissuade them from purchasing MBIA's debt or equity," Chaplin explained. "They may also have extensively lobbied this committee."

As Ackman testified, Roy Katzovicz, Pershing Square's chief legal officer, sat immediately behind him. Katzovicz had noticed this "adviser" position made for a prominent camera shot on C-SPAN. He was doing his best to present an appropriately calm and composed appearance as Ackman hit on all the points they had discussed in their preparation: the futility of a bank bailout of the bond insurers and the need to reform the municipal bond rating scale's triple-A ratings.

Then Kanjorski posed what Katzovicz saw as clearly rhetorical questions: "How the hell did we get here? How did things get this screwed up?" Ackman's hand went up. *This is not school,* Katzovicz thought. He reached over discreetly and tugged at the back of Ackman's jacket, hoping to apply enough pressure to get him to lower his arm. Ackman resisted and Katzovicz tugged again, meeting with even more resistance. Worried he might detach Ackman's sleeve live on cable television, he gave up.

"Investors clearly don't trust the triple-A rating," Ackman said. "What would create trust would be the transparency of the bond insurers coming clean." The banks needed to be honest about their exposures, including how much they were relying on the bond insurers to shield them from losses. The bond insurers needed to disclose exactly what they had guaranteed.

So why hadn't they come clean on all their exposures? asked Kanjorski. Michael Callen, Ambac's chief executive officer, explained the reaction at Ambac when he suggested listing the names of all the CDO-squareds on the company's Web site. "People that know this [area] much better than I do came and surrounded me with knives," Callen explained.

It was a startling statement even when the knives were viewed as an obvious metaphor. Why the urgent need for secrecy?

Katzovicz looked over to see if someone sitting in the adviser seat behind Callen was trying to silence him, but Ambac's CEO appeared to have free rein.

"They said, 'Are you crazy?' If that information was put out there, it could be used very successfully against you." Such information would "give the short sellers the opportunity to go out and take advantage," Callen said.

It was well after 6 p.m. when Kanjorski asked if anyone had any final comments. Up went Ackman's hand again. "With all due respect to Mr. Callen, I think if providing transparency gives a short seller more information to make his argument, then maybe the information isn't so bullish for the company. And maybe that's why investors are concerned."

"I love short sellers," Callen fired back. "You wouldn't ask Microsoft to publish all its code. That would be a little silly."

The problem with Ambac's portfolio was simple, Callen said. "We made a big mistake, a mistake called correlation," he told Kanjorski. "We thought if we had mortgages in California and mortgages in Maine, they wouldn't both go down together. We were wrong."

By the time the hearings ended, it was nearly 7 p.m. and Kanjorski was the only committee member who hadn't slipped away. It was, after all, Valentine's Day. The other side of the room remained packed until the very end with people from the bond insurance companies, the credit-rating companies, the investment banks, and Pershing Square, along with all of their PR representatives and lobbyists. Wall Street knew the stakes were high. Congress seemed less aware, even though 89 percent of all auctions of municipal securities had failed that day.

———

CAUGHT IN A TRAFFIC JAM on the way to the airport, Ackman and Katzovicz missed their flight. Undeterred, Ackman asked the driver if he would take them back to New York. "It's going to be expensive," the driver told them, "but okay."

They drove in the pouring rain until around 9 p.m., when Ackman suggested they stop to eat. He called Pershing Square's evening receptionist and asked her to search the Internet for the best restaurant in the next town off the highway. They got lost a few times in the heavy rain and the dark streets—despite the driver's GPS system—but eventually found the place they were looking for.

"Gentlemen, Please No Tank Tops or Muscle Shirts," read a sign in the window at the nearly deserted G&S Restaurant in Linthicum Heights, Maryland. Ackman and Katzovicz asked the driver to join them, but he stayed in the car, probably already a bit anxious about how long it would take to get all the way up to New York in the pouring rain, Katzovicz suspected. Or perhaps he dreaded the prospect of having to listen to any more talk about bond insurance.

The specialties of the house were crab cakes and fried seafood, not ideal choices for Katzovicz, who keeps kosher, or for Ackman, who consults weekly with a nutritionist and had convinced Katzovicz he needed to do the same. Still, the dinner felt like a celebration. After five frustrating years, the world had come to see the hidden risks of bond insurance. The truth had exploded into the market. Ackman had been able to report to his investors in his year-end letter that the MBIA position—after years of costing the fund—was by far its biggest winner for 2007. He had been formally exonerated by the SEC. And today Ackman had been called as an expert to testify about the bond-insurance business before a congressional committee. Even Eliot Spitzer had been forced to admit that Ackman had predicted the problems.

"Still," Katzovicz remembers, "it was a pathetic Valentine's Day dinner."

Chapter Twenty-Three

Bailout

It is as if Barney Fife, television's [deputy] Sheriff of Mayberry in the Andy Griffith Show, promised to bring law and order to the entire country.

—Bill Gross, chief investment officer of PIMCO, February 2008

I
N THE DAYS AFTER the congressional hearings, Eliot Spitzer's ultimatum hung over the credit markets. He'd given the bond insurers five days to come up with billions of dollars of capital.

Many shared Spitzer's sense of urgency. Congress wanted the auction-rate crisis solved before half of all the hospitals, school districts, museums, and sewer authorities in the country were bankrupted by rising debt costs.

Then, just five days after the hearings, MBIA announced it was making big changes. The company reenlisted Jay Brown as its chief executive officer (CEO) and chairman of the board. Brown, who had taken the reins at MBIA after the bankruptcy of the Allegheny Health, Education, and Research Foundation (AHERF) and managed the company's strategy for exiting the tax-lien business, returned to address another crisis.

Brown announced that MBIA might split itself into two insurance companies—one that backed municipal bonds and one that backed structured finance securities. To preserve cash, it would cut its dividend; to build up capital, it would stop insuring any structured finance deals for six months. Brown assured shareholders that there was hope for the company's triple-A rating. Although other bond insurers had failed to raise capital, MBIA had obtained $2.6 billion. If the rating companies wanted more capital, then MBIA would raise it, Brown said.

Brown's compensation was tied to the company share price, as it was during his previous tenure. He owned 618,456 shares when he rejoined the company. Under his new incentive plan Brown was eligible to receive an additional 1,634,000 shares. Brown sold part of his extensive car collection, which included Ferraris, Porsches, and BMWs, to buy 359,000 more shares with his own funds. If Brown could get the stock price back up to $70, his stake in the company would be worth more than $180 million. An executive-compensation expert put the value of Dunton's estimated severance package at $11 million, according to an article in the *New York Times*.

Brown also wasted no time before confronting Bill Ackman. "Many of you have asked me in the past few days whether there is something personal between us," Brown wrote in a public letter to shareholders. In fact, Brown wrote, he and Ackman were similar: both were "passionate in our beliefs" and "persistent in overcoming all obstacles." But, Brown told investors, he led a regulated financial institution that provided "security, jobs, and peace of mind to tens of thousands of institutions and millions of individual investors." Ackman, on the other hand, had a single-minded objective. "He will stop at nothing to increase his already enormous personal profits as he systemati- cally tries to destroy our franchise and our industry." Be advised, Brown concluded: "His intent to force a collapse has no chance to succeed."

Even as Brown described for investors his plan to save MBIA's triple-A rating, Ackman was shopping around another idea. The plan he had sketched out for Spitzer at the diner was now a 14-page PowerPoint presentation, which Ackman presented to Eric Dinallo, the New York state insurance superintendent, and Robert Steel, undersecretary for domestic finance at the Treasury department. He also discussed it with officials at the White House Council of Economic Advisors and the Federal Deposit Insurance Corporation.

The day after Brown returned to the helm at MBIA, Ackman made his plan public. He proposed that the insurance company be split in two, with the municipal insurance company becoming a direct subsidiary of the structured finance insurer, which in turn would be a direct subsidiary of the holding company. Dividends would pass up the chain, starting with the municipal insurer. Those dividends would be paid only if each company's board of directors was sure the company could maintain its triple-A rating.

MBIA responded quickly, releasing a statement that called the plan "a continuation of Mr. Ackman's campaign to profit from his short positions and credit-default swaps in the bond-insurance industry." The structure was no more than "an attempt to find some way to make true his predictions that the holding companies are or will soon become insolvent," Brown said. "Mr. Ackman should let the officials charged with regulating the industry do their jobs, instead of continuing a relentless media-driven campaign fueled only by personal financial gain."

Dinallo's office did not express enthusiasm. "Our concern with the Ackman plan is that it would split the company, and the structured side could be substantially downgraded, which would be bad for the banks," said David Neustadt, a spokesman for the New York State Insurance Department. "Our preference is a plan that keeps an AAA rating."

For that the New York State Insurance Department was going to need some help from Wall Street.

—•—

BEFORE THE BOND insurance crisis, New York State Insurance Superintendent Eric Dinallo had been a regular at the Marshall Club. The attorney enjoyed dropping in to the hundred-year-old chess club for impromptu matches and organized tournaments. After graduating from the New York University School of Law, Dinallo chose his apartment for its proximity to the club, which is located in a townhouse on a quiet, tree-lined street in the West Village. Now, in the wake of the Valentine's Day congressional hearings, he was preoccupied with a much bigger game.

The banks, which had billions to lose if the bond insurers were downgraded, were the only hope for getting more capital into the ailing companies. But their relationships with the bond insurers were complex. Many of the banks were relying on bond insurers' triple-A guarantees to support the value of billions of dollars of CDOs they held on their balance sheets. Yet a number of banks had purchased credit-default swaps on the bond insurers themselves, in effect hedging their hedges. "Some were more short than long" the bond insurers, Dinallo explains. In other words, they might come out ahead if the bond insurers failed.

Trying to come to an agreement between the banks and the bond insurers "was the most complicated 3-D chess game you can imagine," Dinallo says. While the game dragged on, confidence in financial markets was faltering.

The most immediate problem was Ambac, the second biggest bond insurer.

On Friday, February 22, with New York disappearing under a blanket of snow and the stock market sinking toward a close, details of the game began to emerge. Charlie Gasparino, the CNBC on-air editor, told viewers that, according to unnamed sources, an Ambac bailout was imminent. The plan involved splitting Ambac in two and having the banks provide enough capital to assure that both its structured-finance and public-finance subsidiaries maintained triple-A ratings. Banks might provide as much as $3 billion in capital, and the deal could be completed by early next week, said Gasparino. Ambac's stock soared. Indeed, the entire market rallied on the report.

Citigroup was rumored to be leading the bailout. That wasn't too surprising given that of Ambac's $22 billion of CDOs backed by sub-prime mortgages, nearly $7 billion of the worst-performing securities had been underwritten by Citigroup.

—◆—

ACKMAN HAD BEEN trying to speak with someone at Citigroup all week. On Sunday, February 24, he drafted an e-mail to Vikram Pandit, the CEO of Citigroup; Brian Leach, the chief risk officer; and Robert Rubin, the former secretary of the Treasury and now an adviser to the bank. "Last week I attempted to reach Vikram," the e-mail began. "Vikram's secretary called and said that Brian would return my call. Having not heard from Brian, I attempted to reach Brian by phone and e-mail. Neither my call nor my e-mail was returned. I have therefore concluded," he wrote, "that Citi may be making the same mistake that Warburg did with MBIA, namely making an investment without adequate due diligence."

Since no one was picking up the phone at Citigroup, Ackman would summarize his views in the e-mail. "While $3 billion may be sufficient to stop some of the rating agencies from downgrading Ambac Assurance today, continued downgrades and losses on the underlying exposures will likely require substantial additional capital," Ackman continued. The figure was inconsequential when compared with Ambac's more than half a trillion dollars of outstanding exposures, Ackman added.

He advised the three men to think carefully about the type of investment they were rumored to be considering in Ambac. A backstop— or an agreement to buy up newly issued shares if there was insufficient market demand—would likely induce other equity investors, including a large number of retail investors, to invest alongside Citigroup. "If the investment works out poorly, as we anticipate that it will, there are significant reputational consequences for Citi that should be considered," Ackman wrote.

It wasn't the first time that week that Rubin had heard from Ackman. Several days earlier, Rubin had given an informal talk for parents and faculty at a school on the Upper East Side. When Rubin offered to take questions from the audience, Ackman—seated in the front row—put his hand up immediately. Before Ackman had a chance to ask his question, Rubin responded, "Bill Ackman! Let me guess. It must be about the bond insurers."

"No, actually it's not," Ackman said. What he wanted to know was whether Rubin, "as a member of the board, a smart guy, and the former head of Goldman Sachs," was able to understand the kind of risks Citigroup was taking.

No, Rubin told him, he was not. He didn't elaborate. Nor did he provide any insights on the Ambac bailout.

The great game of risk transfer had gone on for years on Wall Street, enabling ever more lending, reducing bank capital requirements, and generating big fees. The whole business had always been a bit too good to be true. Now, the gamesmanship in one company bailing out another so it could bail out the first was stunningly obvious.

———————

ON MONDAY, FEBRUARY 25, the market got a reprieve. Standard & Poor's announced that both MBIA and Ambac had passed the credit-rating company's updated stress test. Their triple-A ratings were affirmed.

"This dose of optimism for a narrowly averted wave of monoline downgrades could go a long way to restoring capital market confidence in the near term," Lehman Brothers Holdings analysts led by Jack Malvey in New York said in a report issued to clients.

"It's all in Moody's court now," Jim Bianco, who runs a bond consulting firm in Chicago, told Bloomberg Television News.

It didn't stay there long.

On Tuesday afternoon, Moody's lobbed the ball back into Wall Street's court. The credit-rating company issued a statement saying it was going to give Ambac more time to raise capital. "Ambac is actively pursuing capital-strengthening activities that, if successful, are expected to result in the company's meeting Moody's current estimate of the triple-A target level," Moody's analyst Jack Dorer wrote.

The rating company also affirmed MBIA's triple-A rating, though it assigned a negative outlook.

At 1:09 p.m., Jim Chanos attached the Moody's release to an e-mail message he sent around, expressing his take on the announcement: "Delusional, but concerned."

"MBIA AAs continue to rally," Erika Kreyssig, one of Pershing Square's traders, messaged Ackman, referencing the narrowing of the premiums on MBIA credit-default swaps (CDSs). Shortly after the Moody's announcement, the rates were quoted at about 600 basis points, a drop of 115 basis points. By 7:15 p.m., when Kreyssig sent the next update, the spreads had fallen another 50 basis points to 550 basis points. It now cost $550,000 a year to protect $10 million of MBIA debt.

Peter Plaut, an analyst at hedge fund Sanno Point Capital Management in New York, put it this way: "We've avoided the brink."

———

As CONCERN OVER the bond insurers and their triple-A ratings built to a frenzy, Ackman, for the first time in a long time, was not part of the show. He'd gone back to Tierra del Fuego for more fly fishing, accompanied by his father, Larry Ackman; Paul Hilal; and several others, including Oliver White, the former fly-fishing instructor who had become a member of Pershing Square's investment team. They were back at the Kau Tapen Lodge, along the Rio Grande, where giant sea trout were running from the frigid Atlantic upstream to the Andes Mountains. While New York shivered through the worst of the winter, it was summer at Kau Tapen. Ackman's only contact with the markets and his office was through a satellite phone, and it was not reliable.

"Many men fish all their lives without realizing it's not the fish they are after," Thoreau wrote. There was a connection with nature, a camaraderie, a spirit of competition. At Kau Tapen, the anglers included "an attorney, a structured-finance banker, and a hedge fund manager—a type-A competitive group," Hilal says.

The trout averaged around 12 pounds, but some were nearly 30. On the first day, Ackman caught the biggest fish and held the title for the next several days. Then Al Rankin, deputy chairman of the Federal Reserve Bank of Cleveland, caught "a monster," says Hilal. For a while Ackman's only concern was whether he could regain the title for catching the biggest fish.

Back in New York, Jay Brown wrote to shareholders again. He had Ackman on his mind. "If someone had purchased protection, say, in January of last year, when spreads on our five-year CDS were relatively benign, they would have paid about 40 basis points per year," Brown explained. That meant someone could have bought protection on $7.5 billion of MBIA debt for about $30 million in annual fees. Huge swings in the price of that protection over the last year meant that this hypothetical person would have gained and lost massive fortunes.

"On paper, the value of the trade peaked north of $2.6 billion" and had lost about half its value since, Brown wrote. "The reality is that for the guys who play in this $45-trillion zero-sum game, $30 million is chump change. It's also why, given the amount of money that can be made here, people will go to no ends insisting the company will be broke in mere weeks."

———

FOR NOW, ALL EYES WERE ON Ambac and whether Wall Street could organize a bailout. To Bill Gross, who runs one of the world's biggest bond funds at Pacific Investment Management Company, the premise was absurd. "Rescuing the monolines is not a long-term solution," Gross wrote in the *Financial Times*. Bond insurance was a flawed idea that had helped to get the U.S. economy into the current mess. "Overly generous triple-A ratings" on securities and on bond insurers created "a bubble of immeasurable but clearly significant proportions," Gross explained.

"How could Ambac, through the magic of its triple-A rating, with equity capital of less than $5 billion, insure the debt of the state of California, the world's sixth-largest economy?" Gross wrote. "That the monolines could shoulder this modern-day burden like a classical Greek Atlas was dubious from the start," he added. The whole concept was foolish. "It is as if Barney Fife, television's [deputy] Sheriff of Mayberry in the *Andy Griffith Show*, promised to bring law and order to the entire country," Gross wrote.

Even Jay Brown marveled at the perceived role the bond insurers had come to play in the markets. In his letter to shareholders, he said, "The sheer folly of suggesting that MBIA, the largest financial guarantor, could be the linchpin holding up the market value of the global financial system has lit a bonfire under the financial press that has led to the daily speculation—or real-time, if you follow the TV networks—about our fate."

Folly or not, that's what everyone was counting on when, on February 29, the Ambac plan hit a snag. Before the market opened that day, Gasparino reported that the credit-rating companies had nixed Citigroup's plan to save Ambac. The rating companies wanted more capital and had sent the bank consortium back to the drawing board. Ambac shares fell, and another abysmal day followed for the stock market, with the Dow sliding more than 300 points.

Dinallo and Spitzer continued to work the phones to drum up support for Ambac. They divided the list, with Spitzer calling Citigroup, UBS, Bank of America, and Credit Suisse. The banks could either come up with the capital now to save Ambac's triple-A rating or come up with more capital later to offset the decline in the value of the securities they had hedged with the insurer. Ambac needed $1.5 billion, a fraction of the writedowns banks would face if the bond insurer's rating spiraled downward.

On Tuesday, March 4, Gasparino reported that a bailout of Ambac was progressing. The news made the stock the second-biggest winner in the Standard & Poor's (S&P) 500 Index that day. On Wednesday, Gasparino reported that Ambac might agree to a bank rescue that day. Talks with Citigroup and Barclays had continued past 10 p.m. the previous evening, a tidbit that the market found encouraging. Trading on the stock was halted by the exchange, pending an announcement expected around noon.

In a press release, Ambac said it would sell $1.5 billion of common stock and equity units to bolster its capital. The offering would be led by Credit Suisse. Others in the syndicate group included Citigroup, Bank of America Corporation, and UBS AG.

Traders on the fixed-income desk at Credit Suisse, who had helped to create the Open Source Model, which was predicting that Ambac would need much more than $1.5 billion to survive, were stunned. "We're underwriting this?"

They were not the only ones who were skeptical. "Based on our estimate that Ambac will eventually absorb about $11 billion of losses from insured CDOs and exposures related to mortgage-backed securities, $1.5 billion of new capital at first blush does not seem like enough to fix the capital-adequacy problem," Andrew Wessel, an analyst at JPMorgan Securities in New York, said in a research report on Thursday, March 6.

When Gasparino went on the air later that day, he said there was a backstop in the Ambac deal and private-equity investors might get involved. And it was just possible that the deal might be increased to $2 billion. He sounded out of breath. "If it blows up, if investors walk away, banks have agreed to buy it." So it was a bailout?

Late Thursday evening, March 6, the Ambac deal was completed. The company, which started the day with a market capitalization of less than $1 billion, raised $1.5 billion. Both Moody's and S&P affirmed Ambac's triple-A rating.

"THE SITUATION IN the market probably couldn't have been worse. It's worse than I've seen in 40 years," Michael Callen, Ambac's chief executive officer, told Bloomberg Television News the next morning from his office. "Everybody is very, very pleased that the triple-A is now solid."

But was it enough? The Open Source Model said it wasn't. JPMorgan was also calling for Ambac to take losses of around $11 billion.

Callen, looking exhausted after what had been a sleepless night, wanted to talk about Ackman, not JPMorgan. "There is a gentleman out there who has been given a big microphone a number of times," Callen said. "I won't mention his name; he's known around here as the ax man." Ambac, Callen said, had "drilled down" and found the underlying assumptions in Ackman's model to be "outlandish."

Conditions were not going to "deteriorate to the point where our civilization changes forever. I personally don't believe that. There are people paid to believe that," Callen said.

If you believed Ackman was right, Callen added, "you should short Microsoft. You should short everybody. Short Hank Paulson down in Washington."

LATER THAT DAY, Governor Spitzer appeared on CNBC to assure viewers that Ambac would be able to maintain its triple-A credit rating for the foreseeable future: "A lot of parties helped make this happen, and it was important for the capital markets."

Although Moody's and S&P were willing to say—at least for the time being—that the two biggest bond insurers had triple-A ratings, not everyone was on board. Fitch Ratings, the smallest of the three rating companies, had downgraded Ambac several weeks earlier and was actively reviewing MBIA.

On the afternoon of March 7, MBIA issued a press release saying it had asked Fitch to stop rating its insurance company. Brown said he disagreed with the company's methodology, which required more capital to be held against guarantees on structured finance versus municipal bonds.

Fitch's model also had proven erratic, he said: "We have very little idea why Fitch's capital model produces the charges it does, and why it can change so rapidly at any point in time when there is no obvious change in our circumstances or in the credit market at large," Brown had written in a recent letter to shareholders.

After affirming MBIA's top rating with a stable outlook in January, Fitch had put MBIA back under review for a possible downgrade, Brown noted. "Did the world really change that much in two weeks?" Brown asked. "The only event of note that I can think of is the fact that the other two agencies put us on review for possible downgrade in the intervening time period."

Fitch's chief executive officer, Stephen Joynt, wasn't so certain about Brown's motivations. "Is it because you are aware we are continuing our analytical review and may conclude that MBIA's insurer financial strength is no longer AAA?" Joynt said in an angry letter that Fitch made public. "It would appear that rather than work with Fitch, your intention could be to emasculate our opinion by withholding information and subsequently discrediting our opinion as being uninformed," Joynt concluded.

MBIA had become very aggressive about discrediting people who were skeptical about it. Shortly after Brown returned to MBIA, the company hired a public relations consultant named Jim McCarthy. After a few weeks on the job, McCarthy e-mailed my editor, telling her that he had compiled a list of people who felt I had harassed them in the course of my reporting or misrepresented their views in articles. I had never received any complaints. "This is egregious conduct," McCarthy wrote, adding that he would reveal the names of those who had complained, but only if my editor agreed not to share the names with me.

It seemed that the bond insurers tried to wring the skepticism out of the market in any way possible. Over at Ambac, all eyes had been on the share price following the equity sale. But the gains were meager, with the shares up just 4 cents from where the new issue was priced. Then the closing trades came scrolling across broker screens—$7.38, $7.38, $7.39, $7.37—and then the price and the volume surged. At 4:05 p.m., several last-minute trades were reported at $9.50 on huge volume. These last-minute trades pushed the stock's gain for the day to $2.08, giving those who bought the newly issued Ambac shares a one-day return of 28 percent.

"People think something's going on because the print went up so high," Joseph Saluzzi, co-head of equity trading at Themis Trading LLC in Chatham, New Jersey, told Bloomberg News. "It doesn't look like it's a keypunch error since it was such a large block."

The stock was up. That's what mattered. On March 7, 2008, Ambac executives, insurance regulators, and investment bankers breathed a collective sigh of relief over the salvation of Ambac's triple-A rating.

But events were already conspiring to unwind that bit of confidence. That afternoon, a *New York Times* reporter contacted Spitzer about an outfit called the Emperor's Club.

That weekend, Spitzer huddled with aides and warned them about what to expect. The following Monday, at around 2 p.m., the story hit the *New York Times*'s Web site: Spitzer had been linked to a New York–based prostitution ring.

The story was picked up immediately by CNN and CNBC, which broadcast the sketchy details into trading rooms around the world. The man who had hectored and prosecuted Wall Street for its moral failings had been caught in the tawdriest of scandals. It was shocking, though not exactly market-moving, information.

Then traders began to put the pieces together. The New York governor had played an unprecedented role in corralling the banks into backing an equity issue for Ambac. It seemed almost certain that without Spitzer's prompting, Ambac would have lost its triple-A rating. What if the bond insurers required more help in the future? There was at least one way to trade the news of Spitzer's downfall, and that was to sell the bond insurers. By the end of the day, Ambac shares erased all of Friday's late trading gains and ended the day down 23 percent. MBIA shares lost 10 percent.

Relief had been short lived.

Chapter Twenty-Four

Judgment Day

Irrespective of Moody's debatable incompetence, we believe the downgrades of Ambac and MBIA would officially mark the end of Ambac's and MBIA's more than 30-year franchises without any hope for revival.

—Mark Lane, William Blair, June 2008

JUST TWO DAYS after the scandalous news about New York Governor Eliot Spitzer hit, New York State Insurance Department Superintendent Eric Dinallo was back in Washington. Barney Frank, the chairman of the House Finance Committee, was holding hearings on the municipal credit-rating scale. Richard Blumenthal, the Connecticut attorney general who had launched an investigation into the dual scale after meeting with Ackman, also was scheduled to appear.

Municipal bond insurance was in for scathing criticism. Frank opened the hearings by explaining why municipalities almost never defaulted on their debt. "Here is the point: No state—no state legislators, no governor—can allow any one of its municipalities to default, because then every other municipality would pay through the nose."

When a municipality came under financial stress, workers were laid off, services were cut, and snow didn't get shoveled, but debts got paid.

"If any one municipality falters, every municipality in that state would pay," Frank said. "And there isn't a state governor or legislator in the country who doesn't understand that, and that's why the state guarantee is such a good one."

So why, Frank asked, isn't that implied guarantee reflected in the municipal rating? The question cast doubt on the business practices of both the bond insurers and the rating companies. "To me," said Michael Capuano, a Democrat from Massachusetts, "this is nothing more than legalized extortion."

Richard Blumenthal told the committee that the dual-rating scale benefited the bond insurers, who sold their top ratings to municipalities. Bond-insurance fees were in fact "a secret tax" imposed by Wall Street. "Our findings so far are very, very deeply troubling," Blumenthal said. The investigation had turned up "a concerted effort among supposed competitors to maintain the dual-rating systems and kill attempts at reform."

Blumenthal said he discovered a 10-year record of the rating companies failing to reveal flaws in the municipal rating scale. The first evidence of those flaws had appeared almost a decade earlier when Fitch Ratings published a study showing that public bonds defaulted far less frequently than corporate bonds with the same ratings. In 2001, Standard & Poor's (S&P) published a similar report. Moody's Investors Service followed in 2002 with a report showing that between 1970 and 2000 municipal bonds were 130 times less likely to default than corporate bonds.

Another report published later that year by Moody's stated, "If municipalities were rated on the corporate scale, Moody's would likely assign Aaa ratings to the vast majority of general-obligation debt issued by fiscally sound, large municipal issuers." The report also said top ratings would likely be given to most senior obligations of entities that provided essential services such as water and sewer authorities.

Blumenthal continued to lay out the history of municipal ratings. In 2005, Moody's produced a draft copy of a second public bond–default study, this one focusing on public "enterprise" bonds used to fund projects such as airports, hospitals, and housing projects. The study found that these bonds were as much as four times less likely to default than Moody's highest-rated Aaa corporate bonds. The study was never made public.

Some employees within Moody's raised objections, Blumenthal told the committee. In September 2005, a top Moody's public-bond analyst said in an internal memo that Moody's should clearly identify that municipal ratings weren't comparable to corporate ratings. "Without a 'flag,' users of our ratings may not know what scale a rating is on, and this could understate credit risk if the user thought the rating was on the municipal scale when it was based on the corporate scale." No flags were ever used.

In early 2006, Moody's decided to seek advice from those in the market about what to do. The credit-rating company drafted a request for comment about creating a "corporate-equivalent rating for U.S. municipal obligations." Among those who submitted comments was a bond-insurance executive who wrote, "At first blush this looks pretty serious to me. . . . This is cutting at the heart of our industry, given that investors buy on rating. While we in the industry might agree with the default/loss conclusion (this is in part the basis of our success and ability to leverage as high as we are), to lay it out there like this could be very detrimental."

The conclusion Blumenthal drew was troubling. "We have found no legitimate business reason for this dual standard," he told the committee.

Next to testify was Laura Levenstein, a senior managing director from Moody's, who had the unenviable job of defending the dual-rating scale to the committee. "We've been rating based on this scale since 1920," she told them.

"But the fact that you've been doing it doesn't mean that there is an investor demand that you keep doing it," said Frank.

"We have queried the market many, many times. And the feedback—"

"How did you query?" Frank interrupted. "In what sense? You've done a survey?"

"We've reached out and had one-on-one meetings. We've had briefings. We've done publications. We've—"

"And they've told you that they insist on a separate rating system even though they know that there's no default risk?" said Frank.

"Yes."

"All right," Frank told her. "I'm skeptical sometimes," he said. "You're saying that when people buy municipal bonds, they're not interested in the likelihood of default. They're interested in financial stress on the entity, even though your own evidence shows that financial stress on the entity appears to be unrelated in any statistically significant way to default. Is that a rational basis for the market to do this?"

Levenstein explained that a municipal bond rating provides a measure of default risk relative to other municipalities. The head of Warren Buffett's insurance operations weighed in on the dual-rating scale. Berkshire Hathaway's bond-insurance company, National Indemnity, already had licenses to sell bond insurance in 40 states. Yet Ajit Jain told the committee, "If the ratings agencies level the playing field in terms of how they rate municipal versus corporate obligations," there will be little need for a financial guaranty insurance marketplace."

Before Dinallo could complete his testimony—a description of how New York officials had been working to help the industry raise capital—Representative Paul Kanjorski (D-Pennsylvania) interrupted him with some news: "The governor of New York announced his resignation." If Dinallo was going to bully the banks into helping to fix the bond-insurer problem, he was going to have to do it alone.

———

THE BANKS, HOWEVER, HAD big problems of their own. On Sunday, March 16, JPMorgan announced it would buy Bear Stearns for $236 million, or $2 a share, saving the firm from collapse. JPMorgan's purchase of Bear Stearns was conditioned on the Federal Reserve System assuming losses on $30 billion of Bear's assets after JPMorgan absorbed the first $1 billion of losses.

Although the collapse of Bear Stearns took the attention off the bond insurers, it also turned up the attention on short sellers, particularly those who placed their bets using credit-default swaps (CDSs). Shortly after the collapse, the Securities and Exchange Commission was reported to be looking into the possibility that rumor mongering might have driven Bear Stearns to the brink.

Purchasing CDS contracts on a company was "the ultimate bear bet, and the incentive of CDS holders to accentuate the negative, particularly to the financial press, is almost irresistible," wrote *Barron's* columnist Jonathan Laing. Laing, who had written negative articles on MBIA in the past, now described how Ackman's "poison-pen campaign against MBIA and Ambac" was driving the collapse in confidence in the companies.

Ackman wasn't the only one with concerns. On April 4, 2008, Fitch became the first credit-rating company to strip MBIA of its top rating, cutting the company to double-A. The move had been widely expected following MBIA's request that Fitch no longer rate it.

And the bad news just kept coming. When Ambac announced earn-ings on April 23, 2008, the company said its problems had expanded beyond collateralized-debt obligations, and it would take $1 billion of losses on home-equity loans. James Fotheringham at Goldman Sachs wrote in a research note headlined "Slippery Slope": "We forecast $11.8 billion in total pretax losses for Ambac and $12.6 billion for MBIA." Goldman was now predicting a worse outcome than the Open Source Model.

Credit-default-swap spreads on MBIA's and Ambac's holding companies increased on the news, jumping back above 1,000 basis points, or $1 million per annum, to buy protection on $10 million of the companies' debt.

———

THE BATTLE BETWEEN Ackman and MBIA had become less of a public spectacle during the spring of 2008, but it continued behind the scenes. During the hearings in Washington, MBIA's Chief Financial Officer Chuck Chaplin testified that the $1 billion that the company raised in its February stock sale was part of the insurance unit's total claims-paying resources.

Meanwhile, Jay Brown had described the $1 billion as part of the holding company's liquidity war chest in a March 10 letter he wrote to shareholders explaining why CDS contracts on MBIA reflected an irrational fear of default. "Someone buying one-year credit protection on MBIA Inc. is betting that the $1.6 billion in cash and short-term investments currently held by MBIA Inc. will not be sufficient to cover its $80 million of interest expense," Brown wrote.

The statements prompted Ackman to write to the Securities and Exchange Commission: "MBIA has made false statements to Congress and the public about its claims-paying resources." The company should be required to correct its disclosure, Ackman added. It just wasn't possible for the money to be in both places.

"S&P and Moody's are being a bit disingenuous by affirming the AAA on the insurance company based on its ability to raise capital, even though the capital isn't there," Joshua Rosner, managing director at New York–based research firm Graham Fisher & Company, told me when I wrote an article about the issue in early May.

The next day, Dinallo told Bloomberg Television News, "We thought we had an understanding that the money would be used for the rating and the solvency."

On May 12, MBIA said it would contribute the money to its insurer in 10 to 30 days "after consultation with the New York state insurance department."

"We are pleased that these funds will go to benefit policyholders," Michael Moriarty, deputy superintendent for property and capital markets at the New York State Insurance Department, said in an e-mailed statement. "As MBIA was aware throughout our discussions, the Insurance Department expected this capital to be used to support the insurance entities and we are gratified that MBIA has taken the necessary steps to implement this."

It seemed increasingly likely that MBIA's insurance unit was going to need that money.

Problems in the credit markets, and for bond insurers, were moving beyond CDOs to securities backed by home-equity loans. During the housing boom, these loans allowed Americans to turn their homes into virtual ATM machines, extracting cash for everything from vacations to college educations and remodeling projects. When home prices stopped rising, these boom-time loans quickly soured. On May 1, Standard & Poor's made the ominous announcement that it would no longer rate bonds backed by U.S. second mortgages, calling the deterioration of those loans "unprecedented."

Moody's also was taking a gloomier view. It increased its projections for losses on home-equity loans to borrowers with low credit scores and said that the bond insurers' ratings could be affected by the forecast. Moody's now forecast losses of 45 percent on pools of these loans originated in 2007.

Rob Haines at CreditSights warned that both MBIA, which had backed nearly $19 billion of these securities, and Ambac, which insured $16 billion, would need to raise more capital to keep their triple-A ratings. Ambac responded with a 23-page slide presentation on its Web site disputing Haines's report.

IN EARLY JUNE, Ackman got a call from Andy Kimball, Moody's new chief credit officer. It was the first time in the three years he'd been making trips to Moody's downtown offices that someone from Moody's initiated a meeting. During the meeting, Ackman told the analysts that Moody's was violating its own principles by not flagging the fact that MBIA was under formal review.

A formal review would alert all investors that MBIA-insured bonds faced the real possibility of a downgrade. The retirees who held MBIA-insured municipal bonds were entitled to know that the ratings on their investments might fall, Ackman said. Any other company receiving this much scrutiny would have been put under formal review long ago.

"Well, *you* know it's being reviewed," said Andy Kimball, Moody's chief credit officer.

"I know it is," Ackman replied, "but I've done more work on this company than anyone in America."

<hr />

ON JUNE 4, 2008, ACKMAN was on his way out the door when news crossed the wire that Moody's was reviewing MBIA's and Ambac's triple-A ratings for a possible downgrade. He was already running late for an important lunch at the Plaza Hotel—and for this one, he needed to be on time.

Ackman ran back to his office, printed the Moody's press release, and skimmed through it on the way down in the elevator. "Today's rating action reflects Moody's growing concern that MBIA's credit profile may no longer be consistent with current ratings given the company's diminished new business prospects and financial flexibility, coupled with the potential for higher expected losses and stress case losses within the insurance portfolio," the release said. Ambac's rating would likely be cut to double-A, while MBIA's might go as low as single-A, Moody's warned.

Single-A! A downgrade that deep would trigger huge problems for the company on top of the obvious problem that it would lose the rating essential to its business. Ackman had warned Moody's for years about the potential liquidity risk created by MBIA's asset-management business. Through that business, MBIA offered investors guaranteed-investment contracts (GICs). These contracts were used mainly by municipalities as a place to park the proceeds of bond issues until the money was needed to pay construction and other expenses. Municipalities purchased the contracts because they were insured by MBIA Insurance Corporation and carried a top rating. Many of the contracts allowed investors to terminate their GICs or to require MBIA to post collateral against the contracts if its insurance unit was downgraded as far as single-A.

Moody's had dismissed Ackman's concerns in a 2006 report, saying it saw little liquidity risk involved in offering GIC contracts because the proceeds were invested in highly rated securities. Even if MBIA were downgraded and had to post collateral, it could easily sell these high-quality securities.

But over the last year it had become startlingly clear that "high-quality" securities sometimes sold at far below their face value. A downgrade to single-A could require MBIA to sell billions of dollars of securities in a distressed market. That could leave a cash shortfall at the asset-management company. The holding company, which owned the GIC business, could very well end up filing for bankruptcy. In which case, Ackman would make billions of dollars for his investors.

Ackman predicted at his "Saving the Bond Insurers" presentation in November 2007 that MBIA Inc. would be out of cash by the second half of 2008. His prediction was on the verge of playing out. He was also late for lunch.

By the time Ackman reached the Plaza Hotel, he had broken out in a sweat. The rest of his family had already arrived for his grandmother's 90th birthday party at the hotel's Palm Court restaurant. As they entered the restaurant, soft chamber music played in the background. The restaurant, with its palm trees and stately columns, has "an ambience that is suspended in time," according to one history of the hotel. Ackman's thoughts, however, were racing.

He had been there only a few minutes when Ramy Saad, Pershing Square's trader, messaged him with prices on MBIA CDS spreads: They had surged 275 basis points on the Moody's news. Ambac's jumped by 245 basis points.

Although Ackman believed a Moody's downgrade sharply heightened the chances for a default, his MBIA position had to be pared back. As spreads on MBIA and Ambac debt had increased over the last 15 months, so had the percentage of Pershing Square's assets in the investment. It was time to lock in some profits. The fund's position in both bond insurers' CDS contracts, particularly MBIA's, was huge.

The spreadsheet detailing Pershing Square's short position on MBIA was pages and pages long, listing hundreds of individual trades. It was a patchwork of bets—for $10 million, $50 million, and $100 million—with numerous counterparties and expiration dates ranging from just a few months to five years and more into the future.

"Keep selling," Ackman messaged Saad back. The transactions that day marked the first time Ackman had sold any significant amount of MBIA exposure since he began buying protection on MBIA in 2002.

Under the Palm Court's famous stained-glass ceiling, the birthday group had settled into enormous high-backed upholstered chairs. Ackman's grandmother was dwarfed by the chair, and even Ackman at 6 feet 3 inches looked a bit like a kid at the grown-ups' table. Back at Pershing Square, the investment team was intensely focused on the news. Somebody needed to go through MBIA's financial statements and see at what level the collateral calls on the GIC contracts kicked in, Ackman messaged Mick McGuire.

Not long after the downgrade, more headlines scrolled by on Ackman's BlackBerry, which he checked surreptitiously under the table. MBIA had responded to Moody's, and Brown was clearly angry. The company disagreed with the decision. It had expected Moody's to wait at least 6 to 12 months before reviewing MBIA again after affirming the rating in February.

Then came this bombshell: Brown announced MBIA was going to keep the $900 million at the holding company rather than pass it along to the insurance company. On May 12, MBIA had said it would move the money within 10 to 30 days. Had Moody's waited another week, MBIA surely would have downstreamed the cash. Its ability to meet the collateral calls and terminations would have been further reduced. The company almost certainly would have filed for bankruptcy.

"So, how is your business going?" Ackman's grandmother asked as the party surveyed menus. Ackman was trying not to jump out of his chair.

———

ACROSS TOWN, Keefe Bruyette & Woods was holding an insurance conference. Douglas Renfield-Miller, an Ambac executive vice president, took the podium as scheduled, despite the Moody's warning. "In the last two hours, I've probably had more stress than in the previous 27 years," he told the audience. Since it was clear that Moody's was going to cut the company's top rating, there was no point in raising more capital. Capital was not the problem. Ambac had $2 billion more in capital than it needed to remain triple-A, Renfield-Miller said.

What many people didn't understand, he told the crowd, was that Ambac was confronting the very stress scenario that it had been designed to weather. The company would have to pay some large claims, but it wasn't going out of business. "The current crisis validates the business model, validates it in the way that it has never been validated before," Renfield-Miller said. Investors with uninsured mortgage securities were going to lose hundreds of millions of dollars. Those with Ambac-insured paper would never miss a payment, he told the crowd.

Some in the audience were skeptical. In November, Ambac said it would pay no claims; now, just a few months later, it anticipated more than a billion dollars in claims? What if the company misjudged again? Wasn't it possible Ambac could file for bankruptcy?

Sure, there was a stress case that wiped out Ambac's capital, but it occurred, Renfield-Miller told the audience, in a "Mad Max scenario," a point at which "you've got people running around on trucks with guns."

—◆—

BACK AT THE Palm Court, the plates were cleared. Then the waiters appeared with a cake. Everyone sang "Happy Birthday," and Ackman's grandmother blew out the candles. He was on his way back to the office.

Back on Wall Street, the recriminations continued to fly. "Irrespective of Moody's debatable incompetence, we believe the downgrades of Ambac and MBIA would officially mark the end of Ambac's and MBIA's more than 30-year franchises without any hope for revival," Mark Lane, an insurance analyst with William Blair, wrote in a research report published after the Moody's announcement. "The impairment of the franchises and the public mockery of the business model and the integrity of the rating agencies have been so severe it is difficult for us to see Moody's ever reinstating a triple-A rating for either company once this seal has been broken."

The next day, June 5, 2008, Standard & Poor's beat Moody's to the punch and downgraded both MBIA and Ambac to double-A. In one fell swoop, a trillion dollars of debt lost its triple-A rating.

Chapter Twenty-Five

The Nuclear Threat

There's not likely to be a man left standing in the bond-insurance industry. This thing is over already; the market just doesn't know it yet.

— BILL ACKMAN, JUNE 2008

WHEN STANDARD & POOR'S (S&P) downgraded MBIA and Ambac to double-A on June 5, 2008, the world didn't end, the stock market didn't crash, the dollar didn't collapse. In fact, MBIA's share price rose a few cents. After all, confidence had been unraveling for more than a year. There had been plenty of warning. Still, it was the end of an era in the bond market. Rob Haines, the bond insurance analyst at CreditSights, summed it up this way: "For those of us who follow the monoline industry, last week was akin to the fall of Rome."

The downgrades also left a slightly unsettling feeling of "What's next?" Bond insurers had been pillars of predictability. Not any longer. When Moody's Investors Service downgraded CIFG in May, it took the rating down seven notches. Moody's said CIFG—a company rated triple-A just a few months earlier—was close to breaching its minimum regulatory capital levels, which could cause regulators to take it over. That, in turn, could trigger termination payments like those ACA Capital faced and couldn't meet.

Credit-default-swap (CDS) contracts had changed the rules of the game for bond insurers. Bond-insurance policies obligate a company to cover interest and principal when due on a bond if the issuer defaults. CDS contracts subjected bond insurers to a number of conditions that were poorly understood but potentially lethal.

"Depending on the language in the credit-default swap [contracts], [a termination event] can set off a chain of events that creates a complete unwind of the company," Thomas Priore, chief executive officer of hedge fund Institutional Credit Partners LLC in New York, told me.

The bond insurers guaranteed hundreds of billions of dollars of CDS contracts, including $127 billion on CDOs backed by subprime mortgages. The riskiest hedge fund that sold protection through the CDS market was required to put up cash if the cost of protecting the underlying security rose. Because the bond insurers were triple-A rated when they entered into these contracts, they were deemed so creditworthy that they didn't need to post collateral. Now the companies faced an immediate and overwhelming call on all of their capital in the event they were taken over by regulators.

On June 11, 2008, several days after the S&P downgrade, Jay Brown wrote to MBIA shareholders telling them not to be distracted by the inevitable "articles and reports" that would opine on everything from the company's decision to keep the $900 million at the holding company to the mark-to-market value of its CDS contracts. "Please stay focused on this as the current difference between our estimates of ultimate economic losses (approximately $2 billion) versus the current market estimates reflected in our stock price ($10 [billion to] $14 billion) is really what this story is all about."

Bill Ackman thought there was more to the story than that.

—————

ON JUNE 18, ACKMAN MADE a presentation to a group of attorneys and hedge fund managers at the law firm Jones Day. That presentation, called "Saving the Policyholders," was his last on the bond insurers.

He told the audience that most of the bond insurers, including MBIA, were already insolvent. Insolvency in New York state was measured in two ways: The first trigger is hit when a company has reported so many expected claims that it has essentially flagged for regulators that it won't be able to meet all its obligations.

There is a second test of solvency, however, that asks an insurer to show it has sufficient assets to reinsure all its liabilities. In other words, could the firm pay another insurance company to take on its existing obligations? The answer to that question for MBIA was absolutely not.

The mark-to-market losses—which the companies insisted were no more than a reflection of an irrational market and should be ignored—were critical. In fact, the complicated formulas used to determine mark-to-market losses on CDS contracts sought to answer this very important question: How much more would an insurance company want to be paid—above the premiums already collected—to take on another insurer's obligations?

If the bond insurers couldn't reinsure their obligations with their existing assets, then the New York state insurance department should take them over, Ackman argued. If that happened, the CDS counterparties had the right to terminate their contracts and be compensated for the loss in the market value of their CDOs. It was a fatal sequence of events that began with the mark-to-market losses bond insurers were insisting everyone should ignore.

Investors were unaware of the risk of these termination payments because the bond insurers had not properly disclosed the risk, Ackman said. He read MBIA's disclosure regarding the contracts: "There is no requirement for mark-to-market termination payments, under most monoline standard termination provisions, upon the early termination of the insured credit-default swap. However, some contracts have mark-to-market termination payments for termination events within MBIA Corp.'s control."

Both the bond insurers and the credit-rating companies had "misled the investing public by ignoring and not disclosing CDS mark-to-market termination risk in determining the ratings for bond insurers," Ackman said.

Ackman had a second bombshell to drop that evening. Financial Security Assurance (FSA) and Assured Guaranty still had triple-A ratings with a stable outlook. The fact that two of seven bond insurers still had credibility gave the industry a glimmer of hope. Bonds—even structured finance bonds—could be insured if a company was careful enough. As municipalities shunned the other bond insurers, FSA and Assured had seen business surge in recent months.

"The market has not woken up to FSA," cautioned Ackman. "FSA is AAA stable, but don't look too closely." FSA had steered clear of guaranteeing CDOs backed by mortgages, but it insured billions of securities backed by home-equity and Alt-A loans. It was under-reserving against those losses, Ackman said. The insurer also had a problem with its investment-management business. Like MBIA, FSA issued billions of dollars of guaranteed-interest contracts (GICs) for municipalities. The proceeds were invested in subprime securities, which had tumbled in value, leaving FSA's asset-management business with assets valued at $16.2 billion and liabilities of $20.4 billion. Ackman predicted that Dexia, FSA's European parent company, wouldn't support FSA. The capital hole was too deep.

Summing up his view of the bond-insurance business, Ackman told the audience, "There's not likely to be a man left standing" in the industry. "This thing is over already; the market just doesn't know it yet."

The next morning, risk premiums on FSA credit-default-swap contracts surged. That same day, Dexia announced it was providing a $5 billion credit line to help FSA. The commitment "is a reaction to the attack of Pershing," chief financial officer Xavier de Walque told Bloomberg News. The move was intended "to avoid any doubt and to stop any speculation."

On June 19, the day after Ackman's presentation, Moody's followed through on its threat to strip MBIA and Ambac of their triple-A ratings. MBIA was cut further than Ambac, all the way down to single-A, a rating at which MBIA was obliged to post collateral and terminate guaranteed-investment contracts.

Ackman was certain MBIA's holding company would have to file for bankruptcy. Its asset-management unit had left it with a gaping hole in its balance sheet that probably couldn't be filled even with the $900 million Brown had decided to keep at the holding company.

Meanwhile, the insurance unit was insolvent under one of two New York state tests of solvency, in which case the company's CDS counterparties could force it to terminate contracts and absorb billions more in losses.

On June 27, Ackman wrote to MBIA's board of directors, including Kewsong Lee and David Coulter from Warburg Pincus, telling them that they should seek advice about the solvency of MBIA Inc. and MBIA Insurance Corporation. He followed up a few days later with an e-mail, which he made public: "You don't, of course, have to rely on our analysis in determining MBIA's solvency, but we caution you in relying solely on management's statements or financial statements prepared by management," Ackman wrote. Even if the companies were not insolvent but were approaching insolvency, directors had expanded fiduciary duties. They had to assure that shareholders were not favored over creditors and that one class of creditor wasn't favored over another.

"Don't take our word, but do yourself a favor," Ackman wrote. "I encourage you to hire investment banks of the highest caliber to complete a solvency analysis. If you are unable to engage one or more investment banks to provide an appropriate solvency opinion, you already have your answer as to the company's solvency."

MBIA lashed back at Ackman, saying "the e-mail and its public release were yet another irresponsible attempt to undermine confidence in MBIA."

Copies of the letter sent to Warburg Pincus were returned to Ackman unopened.

ON JULY 15, 2008, Roy Katzovicz sat in his apartment, waiting for Ackman to appear on CNBC's *Squawk Box*. The show's producers had been badgering Ackman for several months to come on the show to talk about the bond insurers. Katzovicz had repeatedly expressed his views on how TV and complicated financial ideas don't mix. In his most recent e-mail to Ackman on the topic, Katzovicz said simply: "TV = Bad."

But Ackman couldn't be dissuaded from making the appearance. He had a plan for recapitalizing Fannie Mae and Freddie Mac, the giant government-chartered mortgage companies, which many investors feared were now insolvent. Ackman also had a short position in Fannie Mae's stock and in both government-sponsored enterprises' subordinated debt, which would rise in value if Ackman's plan was implemented.

Ackman told the anchors on CNBC that it would be a mistake for the government to put equity into Fannie Mae and Freddie Mac. The companies needed to be recapitalized, and taxpayers shouldn't be the ones to do it, he argued.

The two companies had all the capital they needed, Ackman said. It was just in the wrong form. They had too much debt and not enough equity. The company could be recapitalized by wiping out the equity holders, giving the junior debt holders warrants and giving the senior debt holders equity in the company.

Anchor Becky Quick asked Ackman when he had come up with this idea and when he had taken his short positions on the securities.

"I woke up on Thursday morning with an idea," Ackman said. "The more I thought about it, the more logical I thought it was and that it would be implemented."

Ackman made no apologies for his view that the company's equity holders should be wiped out and that he should be able to profit from it. "Investors made a bet and allowed the institution to become too levered over time," Ackman said.

Later that day, the Securities and Exchange Commission (SEC) announced a plan to clamp down on those shorting the shares of Fannie Mae, Freddie Mac, and a number of other financial firms. Short sellers had become—in the eyes of many people, including government officials—the enemies in a battle to stabilize the financial system.

That stability remained elusive, however. A week later, on July 22, 2008, Moody's warned it might cut FSA's and Assured Guaranty's triple-A ratings. Shares of FSA's parent, Dexia SA, plummeted 16 percent to 8.06 euros in early trading. Assured shares plunged 40 percent, or $7.43, to $11.32.

Shortly after the announcement, Moody's held a conference call to discuss the state of bond-insurance ratings. Investors were furious. There was not a single triple-A-rated bond insurer that hadn't lost its top rating or been threatened with a loss of the rating. When the call was opened to questions, the first caller wondered just how devastating the meltdown of bond insurers' credit ratings had been to Moody's credibility. The caller jumped in with his own answer: "The metaphor of Frankenstein's monster comes to mind, with the guarantor in the title role—escaped from the lab and running loose in the rating-agency village!"

———

MEANWHILE, IT WAS NOT just Katzovicz who wished Ackman would stay off CNBC. "I've been reflecting on your high-profile strategy concerning Fannie Mae and Freddie Mac," one of Ackman's investors wrote to him shortly after his appearance on CNBC. While Ackman's "exposé" on MBIA had benefited all Pershing Square's investors, he was now creating a "perception that a self-interested short seller is attempting to meddle in public affairs," the investor wrote.

To make his point, he quoted James de Rothschild of the famous banking family, circa 1816: "As soon as a merchant takes too much part in public affairs, it is difficult for him to carry on with his banker's business." The investor concluded, "I thought I'd share with you this quote, which reflects our general philosophy on the focus desired for investment managers."

Others echoed the criticism of Ackman's high profile role. Marty Whitman, MBIA's second-largest shareholder and a holder of nearly $200 million of the surplus notes sold earlier that year to save the triple-A rating, dedicated a long section of his letter to investors in the summer of 2008 to discussing Ackman. "William Ackman appears to be disingenuous when he writes and talks about saving MBIA's policyholders," Whitman said. "Why does he care about policyholders? Ackman's objective is to drive down the market price of MBIA securities."

Whitman continued: "Bear raiders seem to tend very much to engage in nefarious activities, whether legal or not." Until the SEC began to investigate some of this activity, short sellers were free to say or write whatever they liked, Whitman said. "There is no apparent downside for being a loose cannon."

———

WHILE ACKMAN WAS DETERMINED to show that the bond insurers were insolvent, Eric Dinallo at the New York State Insurance Department was doing everything in his power to prevent a regulatory takeover of the companies.

On July 31, he wrote to the *Financial Times*: "Rumors that can destroy the stock price of banks and investment banks have been the focus of the media and have now attracted the attention of regulators." Insurance companies are also vulnerable, he wrote.

New York state law provides for "civil and criminal sanctions for spreading false rumors or making statements 'untrue in fact' about an insurance company's solvency," he warned. "Recently, some individuals have asserted that some of the bond insurers are insolvent—a far more serious, far-reaching, and risky allegation than claims that the insurer's holding company stock is overvalued," he added, without naming names. "Rumor mongering and inaccurately disparaging insurance-company solvency cross a line," Dinallo concluded.

Several months earlier, Dinallo had worked the phones with Eliot Spitzer to convince the banks to participate in Ambac's equity offering and save its triple-A rating. Now, as confidence in both the bond insurers and the banks continued to collapse, raising more capital wasn't possible.

If the bond insurers couldn't find outside investors willing to put up more capital, then the only alternative was for them to reduce their expected claims. That meant convincing the banks to tear up CDS contracts on the worst of the CDOs. Under these agreements, known as *commutations,* the banks accept a fraction of the payment they expected to receive had they waited for the CDOs to default. The agreements allowed banks to trade a potentially larger but uncertain payment in the future (after all, the bond insurer might run through all its capital) for a smaller but certain payment today.

Among the first deals announced was one between Ambac and Citigroup over an unnamed CDO. Ambac paid Citigroup $850 million in exchange for tearing up a CDS contract on a $1.4 billion CDO. During a conference call shortly after the deal was announced, a caller asked David Wallis, Ambac's chief risk officer, what the projected payout on the CDO would have been without the commutation. "Pretty damn close to $1.4 billion," Wallis replied.

Dinallo says he chose not to play the role of inflexible regulator. "We could have slammed down the gate, not allowed any money to leave the insurance companies," Dinallo tells me as we sit in his office in early 2009. The result would have been an immediate collapse of the company's shares on the expectation that the holding companies would file for bankruptcy. That may have been what Ackman wanted, but there were important people who believed it was absolutely necessary to do more. Among them were officials at the Federal Reserve who told Dinallo that they were getting calls from foreign banks. The world's bankers wanted to know if U.S. financial institutions were going to stand behind their contracts. "This was becoming a geopolitical issue," Dinallo remembers.

Dinallo, the son of a Hollywood script writer who penned episodes of *The Six Million Dollar Man*, kept a collection of superhero action figures and comic books on a shelf in corner of the conference room. And in the summer of 2008, every day seemed to bring another opportunity to save the world.

At the end of July, Dinallo had just managed to pull XL Capital Assurance back from the brink. The threatened collapse of the company was reverberating across the insurance sector. The bond insurer had been spun off from XL Capital Ltd., a catastrophe reinsurer based in

Bermuda, which protected other insurance companies against losses in the event of hurricanes and other natural disasters. XL Capital Ltd. was on the hook to cover some of its former unit's CDO and subprime losses. The stock market was punishing the catastrophe reinsurer over the uncertainty created by this obligation. Other insurance companies were worried about the coverage they had purchased from XL Capital Ltd.

Negotiations took place over several tension-filled weeks at the offices of Fried, Frank, Harris, Shriver & Jacobson, where lawyers from more than two dozen banks, two insurance companies, and the insurance department hashed out a plan to disentangle the bond insurer, its former owner, and scores of bank counterparties. The meetings, held simultaneously in a series of conference rooms, lasted late into the evening. Hampton Finer, the deputy superintendent of the insurance department, recalls weeks of raised voices and boxes of cold pizza. The lawyers were up against a tight deadline; XL Capital Assurance needed to file its first-half regulatory statements before the end of July to show that it was solvent.

Finally, on July 28, Dinallo announced an agreement. XL Capital Ltd. would pay $1.78 billion to its former bond-insurance unit, and Merrill Lynch would tear up $3.7 billion of contracts on CDOs in exchange for a $500 million payment, saving the company from insolvency. "This agreement gives a light at the end of the tunnel," Dinallo said during a conference call with reporters. "Even a distressed bond insurer can be brought out of a dire situation."

Late that afternoon, Dinallo was back on the phone. This time it was a conference call with 40 of bond insurer CIFG's counterparties.

—⊷—

JUST AFTER 11 P.M. ON AUGUST 7, 2008, Mick McGuire was finishing a review of MBIA's second-quarter earnings statement. Pershing Square had issued press releases with questions for MBIA management ahead of MBIA's last two earnings conference calls. McGuire assumed they would do the same this time and was in the process of drawing up a list. There were questions on the fairness of bond insurers canceling CDS contracts. Questions about MBIA's off-balance-sheet debt and when it came due. Questions about the effect on MBIA of its reinsurers being downgraded. "I believe those are probably the issues worth calling out," McGuire e-mailed to Ackman. "I can think of others, but I would guess that other investors might also already be focusing on them."

At 11:50 p.m., Ackman wrote back: "Perhaps we do nothing."

The most obvious question in Ackman's mind was whether MBIA was insolvent. This time, Ackman was going to leave it up to investors and equity analysts to ask the questions.

The next morning, the stock was rallying as the conference call got under way. The news for investors was mixed: New business had completely dried up, but unlike other financial firms, including Ambac and Fannie Mae, MBIA didn't increase its projections for losses during the quarter.

Ackman listened in on the call from his house in upstate New York, where he was setting up for Pershing Square's annual staff party. The office was closed for the day, and all the employees—the investment team, the traders, the accountants, and the administrative assistants— were on their way upstate to spend the day sitting by the pool, barbequing, and playing tennis.

"Having lost our AAA ratings, it will be several quarters before we have a true sense of what exactly our company will look like in the future," Brown told listeners. "The good news is the business models are functioning exactly as we designed them to under this type of stress."

Part way through the question-and-answer session, Greg Diamond, the head of investor relations, read an anonymously submitted question. It was about the company's views on Dinallo's letter to the *Financial Times*: "Given your very vocal opponent who has put out several presentations and press releases containing precisely the type of allegations that Dinallo suggests are illegal under the law, does MBIA intend to file a lawsuit against Pershing Square for disparagement and for losses that Mr. Ackman created for the company's shareholders?"

Brown took that question. "MBIA agrees that statements made by certain short sellers may have, in fact, violated New York insurance law, and we plan on cooperating with any investigation or action brought by the New York state insurance department or any other regulator who may wish to investigate these activities."

He noted further, "MBIA is assessing all of its options and will take such actions as it determines are in the best interest of its shareholders, including any litigation that may be necessary if we believe that's in the best interest of our shareholders."

As the headlines hit the newswires, Pershing Square began receiving phone calls and e-mails from investors. A member of the investor-relations team e-mailed Ackman, asking if he was concerned about the threat of a lawsuit. "I think a lawsuit is very unlikely, but if so, it would be helpful to us because we get access to their books and records. As a result, the probability of their doing so is very low."

The Pershing party continued. As the group gathered around the Ackmans' pool, the mood was upbeat. Ackman manned the barbeque. His children played in the pool. The humidity had been building all day, and now flickers of lightning appeared on the horizon. Suddenly, thunder rumbled surprisingly close by, and the group retreated into the house.

LATE THAT AFTERNOON, ACA Financial Guaranty announced after months of negotiations that it had finally reached a deal with its bank counterparties. The bond insurer would tear up credit-default-swap contracts protecting $65 billion of CDOs and other structured finance securities against default. In exchange, ACA would pay the banks just 3 cents for every dollar of the $9 billion they owed.

David LeMay, a partner at Chadbourne & Parke, which represented ACA's 29 bank counterparties, explained that no one bank could demand to be paid without triggering the same demand from the entire group. "There were 29 nuclear powers, any one of whom pushes the button and the game is over," said LeMay.

Wall Street had trumpeted the CDS market as the ultimate hedge. What could be better than a contract that allowed a bank to lend money with the certainty of being paid back? But now the system's fatal flaw had been exposed. All this risk transfer depended on extraordinarily credit-worthy sellers of protection. ACA Capital, a bond insurer whose main business was to provide protection against default, had just been presented with a $9 billion bill and had only $698 million in the bank.

On that sleepy August afternoon, the event passed little noticed. The Dow Jones Industrial Average was hovering well above 11,000. Investors still believed that those in power could control the outcome: lower interest rates, raise capital, silence critics, restore confidence. Somehow, if everyone just kept hoping and pretending, the crisis could be kept at bay.

On Merrill Lynch's final conference call held earlier that summer, chief executive officer John Thain was asked about the firm's exposure to the bond insurers. Merrill had $20 billion of super-senior CDOs on its books, the majority hedged with counterparties, including bond insurers. Was it possible, a caller asked, that the bond insurers could survive to make good on those guarantees?

"In the case of MBIA, I think it is very unlikely that they will actually default because it's not in their interest to do that," Thain replied. "I think they will simply go into a runoff mode, and they will simply keep collecting their payments and making their payments and they'll live for years and years and years and years."

That would be the best outcome—if they could outrun the reality and wait for the economy to turn and for people to start making their mortgage payments again. But the crisis was coming anyway—for MBIA, for Merrill Lynch and John Thain, and for everyone else.

Epilogue

The bond-insurance industry was destroyed from within.

—JACK BUTLER, MBIA FOUNDER, 2009

IN THE WEEKS AFTER ACA Capital tore up billions of credit-default-swap (CDS) contracts, the stock market traded sideways and analysts were quoted saying "the worst is behind us," as disaster approached.

On September 7, Fannie Mae and Freddie Mac were placed into government conservatorship. Then during the second weekend in September, some of the largest financial institutions in the United States toppled like dominoes. On September 15, Bank of America bought Merrill Lynch & Company as confidence in the broker evaporated. Lehman Brothers, after a failed search for a white knight, filed for bankruptcy protection. The following day, the Federal Reserve Bank of New York announced it would lend $85 billion to American International Group (AIG).

AIG had been downgraded, triggering a requirement for its AIG Financial Products unit to post billions of dollars of collateral on credit-default swaps written on collateralized-debt obligations (CDOs). AIG Financial Products, like the bond insurers, was a business built on the belief that the company would always have a high rating.

The events ignited another backlash against short sellers. The Securities and Exchange Commission temporarily banned short sales of some 800 financial companies' shares.

On January 22, 2009, Pershing Square held its annual dinner at the New York Public Library. Investors ascended the floodlit steps past the stone lions with a dusting of snow on their heads. Bill Ackman's fund had been in business for five years, and 2008 had been its first down year. But the crowd was cheerful. Pershing's main fund fell 11 percent, not bad given that the stock market was down 40 percent.

Losses in the main funds on retailers such as Target Corporation and Borders Group Incorporated were offset by gains on short positions in MBIA and FSA, Ackman explained. MBIA had been "the gift that keeps on giving," but not any longer. Ackman told the group that he had closed out the MBIA position at the end of 2008 after nearly seven years. "It's the end of an era," Ackman said and moved on to the next slide.

Ackman's short position on MBIA had been his highest-returning investment to date. Pershing Square investors made about $1.1 billion as faith in the bond insurer collapsed. As the managing partner with the largest stake in the fund, Ackman received the largest share of those gains, around $140 million. He didn't actually pocket any of it, though. The gains offset losses elsewhere in the fund during 2008. Yet Ackman figures he owes the Pershing Square Foundation the full $140 million. He has given the foundation $50 million and expects over time to pay the $90 million balance as future profits cover 2008's losses.

Gotham Credit Partners, the small fund set up exclusively to short MBIA in the credit-default-swap market back in 2002, was wound down at the end of 2008. Those who didn't add to their investment over time lost most of their money as MBIA CDS contracts expired with no worth. Those who continued to bet with Ackman and kept putting more money into the fund made multiples of their investment.

As the dinner ended, guests dispersed into the evening. Lights from the party illuminated the facade of the library's east wing and the words carved into it: "But Above All Things, Truth Beareth Away the Victory." With the stock market falling, Wall Street in tatters, and millions of people facing foreclosure, job losses, and depleted retirement accounts, the truth seemed to have spirited away more than just the victory; it had taken the country's optimism.

———

ONE OF THE QUESTIONS being asked in the wake of the financial collapse is whether credit-default swaps should be done away with altogether. Should people be able to make vast profits on the collapse of a company?

Charlie Munger, Warren Buffett's business partner, thinks there is something wrong in that: "Do you think it would be desirable if everybody in America could buy life insurance on any person they wanted to buy life insurance on?" Munger told Bloomberg News during an interview at the 2009 Berkshire Hathaway meeting. "That would be pretty dangerous for the person who was insured. Some of that danger exists once you get people who have a vested interest in the destruction of some business."

There's no doubt that these instruments were at the center of the collapse of the financial system—but not because skeptics used these instruments to destroy good companies. Credit-default swaps allowed banks to become very cynical in their lending practices. Firms such as Citigroup and Merrill Lynch were able to create complex securities backed by recklessly underwritten mortgages, knowing that they could pass the risk along to someone else who had less information about the underlying loans. In the end, the $62 trillion CDS market allowed Wall Street to lend without having confidence in the men and women it lent to. Wall Street hedged away the risk of lending and in the process undermined the entire system.

"Where is the conspiracy?" Jim Chanos, the investor who made his name shorting Enron before it collapsed, asks me as we sit in his office on an April afternoon in 2009. We are discussing the allegations that short sellers brought down financial firms in the summer of 2008. "To trade or to induce others to trade on information you know to be false. That's market manipulation and securities fraud. That's what puts you in jail," Chanos says. Otherwise, "if you are a public company, if you trade in the public markets, expect scrutiny."

Certainly, we all would have benefited had more investors scrutinized the reckless way in which many financial firms were piling up debt. Meanwhile, there was no shortage of lawyers, auditors, and credit-rating analysts who earned a living helping to construct rickety financial structures. On a shelf behind Chanos's desk is a model of a house of cards under construction; at second glance, I notice that it is surrounded by a miniature scaffolding.

Some people did benefit from Ackman's very vocal scrutiny, and not all were wealthy hedge fund investors: "You may remember that about a year ago you, Karen and I went trekking up and down the lovely spring-fresh hills of the Berkshires," a letter Ackman received in May 2009 began. It was from the former MBIA employee turned hiking guide at Canyon Ranch.

"Though I may have sounded a bit skeptical of your views at the time, I took it all in and within a week of our discussion I had eliminated my personal position in the company," he wrote. "For the record, my average transaction price was between $59 and $60 per share." The day the letter was written, MBIA shares closed at $8.12. The letter arrived with two bottles of wine and a $250 check for Pershing Square Foundation.

THE BOND INSURERS' credit ratings that once seemed to be made of pure gold continue to tarnish. This response from Ambac to an April 13, 2009, downgrade by Moody's Investors Service summed up the state of play: "While Ambac believes that Moody's is entitled to its opinion of Ambac's financial strength, it notes that this is the 10th such opinion change since January 2008."

By early 2010, none of the bond insurers had been taken over by regulators. Instead, they were being what can only be described as defused. If regulators were to take over a bond insurer, they essentially would create another AIG scenario. The takeover would trigger termination payments based on the decline in market value of the underlying CDOs. These payments would overwhelm the bond insurers' capital. Gradually, Wall Street has agreed to negotiate tear-ups of CDS contracts. It's impossible to know whether this is just delaying the inevitable or will prove a long-term solution.

In early 2009, Jay Brown separated MBIA Insurance Corporation into two businesses with the permission of New York State Insurance Department Superintendent Eric Dinallo. The plan was for MBIA Insurance Corporation to keep the structured finance guarantees, including those on toxic subprime CDOs. Its rating was subsequently downgraded by Moody's deep into junk. MBIA moved its U.S. municipal finance business to a new company called the National Public Finance Guarantee Corporation, which obtained an investment-grade rating.

Brown said that the company will survive its mistakes. In his letter to shareholders in the 2008 annual report, Brown cited something he called "the ninth wave," a sailor's term for a single, freakishly large wave. "Every so often, a giant wave comes long that either sweeps you under and annihilates you, or through skill and vision you successfully ride the wave farther than you've ever gone before," Brown wrote. "I believe that time will prove that we have what it takes to endure for the long ride ahead."

Not everyone is so sanguine about MBIA's future, including some of its former allies. Brown's decision to split the company in two caused Marty

Whitman to file suit against MBIA in April 2009, and refer to MBIA management as "toxic." Whitman owned surplus notes with a face value of $400 million as of September 2008. The notes, sold to help salvage MBIA's triple-A rating, remain the obligations of MBIA Insurance Corporation, which has been left with the contracts on the CDOs and other subprime securities. The notes, which Ackman warned the public against buying, were quoted at 20 cents on the dollar in late 2009, implying that holders expected to lose 80 percent of their investment.

"MBIA sold us these surplus notes and then, to our surprise and distress, stripped away the principal assets as well as the only going concern operations within MBIA Insurance Corporation," Whitman said. "That's wrong, and a big disappointment to us, especially after we went to bat for them with our pocketbooks and more."

In May 2009, 18 financial institutions, including Merrill Lynch, Citibank, JPMorgan Chase Bank, Morgan Stanley, and UBS, sued MBIA, accusing it of siphoning off assets that would be needed to cover claims on securities backed by mortgages in order to set up a new municipal bond insurance company. "As various commentators have observed, the credit markets expect that MBIA Insurance will 'wither and die,' thereby saddling policyholders . . . with billions in losses," according to the suit. The banks also sued Eric Dinallo for approving the split. MBIA said in a statement that the suit lacked merit.

MBIA and the other bond insurers lashed back. MBIA filed a lawsuit against Merrill, saying the firm "resorted to a scheme of repackaging" mortgage securities and CDOs, which it knew would result in losses. The suit alleged that Merrill Lynch was aware that MBIA "stood to earn premiums of less than one-thousandth its nominal exposure." Meanwhile, because MBIA "did not and could not perform a cost-effective loan-level valuation analysis of the ML-series CDOs, it relied on and trusted Merrill Lynch's statements about the quality of the underlying loans." MBIA also sued several mortgage originators, including Countrywide Financial, claiming it had been fraudulently induced to guarantee risky securities backed by home-equity loans and other types of home loans.

Courts will spend years untangling the billions and likely trillions of dollars of risk transfer now under dispute. FGIC's lawsuit against IKB over its Rhineland Funding guarantee was dismissed in January 2009. The judge ruled that New York wasn't the appropriate forum to hear a dispute between the U.K. subsidiary of a New York–based insurance company and a German bank (now owned by a Texas hedge fund) over a transaction in which a Channel Islands company promised to protect a French bank against losses on CDOs held by a Delaware-registered special-purpose vehicle. When the judge asked the attorneys involved in the case to approach the bench, the crowd numbered nearly a dozen.

The city of Los Angeles filed suit against the bond insurers, claiming they conspired to maintain a credit-rating system that required munici-palities to buy insurance if they wanted a triple-A rating. "Bond insurers' cynical use of this discriminatory credit-rating system and inexcusable failure to disclose their high-risk investments in the subprime market also violates California's antitrust laws and common law," city attorney Rocky Delgadillo charged.

Shane Dinneen, the Pershing Square analyst, lists three reasons why one could have known it would all end this way: "MBIA's extreme leverage" was an obvious problem.

Then there was the way MBIA management dealt with problems—shunting them out of sight. MBIA's handling of the Philadelphia hospital group's bankruptcy and the collapsing value of a portfolio of tax liens were warnings that mistakes had to be covered up.

The third reason is not one you would expect from a self-described former Blackstone number cruncher. Somehow the whole thing seemed predestined, he tells me: Ackman's real-world interactions with people read like the plotline of a novel—the tense encounter with Brown, the chance meeting with the Citigroup analyst at a funeral in Michigan, "the way the whole thing became a cornerstone of Bill's life."

It was as if Ackman's bluntness—that boldness that people have called everything from constructive and informed to self-interested, insulting, and even criminal—had a purpose. "He didn't ask other people in the room what they thought about the emperor's clothes or if they ever wondered whether the emperor might be a bit cold," Dinneen says. "He just pointed his finger and said 'Naked!' Bill was just meant to call this industry out."

———

BY ASKING "Is MBIA triple-A rated?" Ackman put the focus on what turned out to be the Achilles' heel of the financial system—the triple-A credit rating. Those three letters became the most profitable brand in the world. That Wall Street eventually would debase it is obvious in hindsight. "Analysts and managing directors are continually pitched by bankers, issuers, investors with reasonable arguments whose use can color credit judgment, sometimes improving it, other times degrading it," Moody's chief executive officer Raymond McDaniel told a congressional hearing in October 2008. "We drink the Kool-Aid."

When McDaniel finished speaking, Representative Dennis Kucinich (D-Ohio) duly noted, "I would like to submit for the record from the *Oxford Dictionary of American Political Slang:* 'To drink the Kool-Aid: To commit to or agree with a person, a course of action, etc.'"

The collapse in the credibility of the triple-A ratings has been astonishing. In 2007, $1.5 trillion worth of triple-A-rated structured finance securities were issued. During the 10-year period between 1999 and 2007, just 2.6 percent of structured finance securities were downgraded; that figure jumped to 35 percent during 2008 for a total of 37,213 credit-rating downgrades.

Nearly 40 percent of the downgrades were of securities that were originally rated triple-A. More than $100 billion of securities originally rated triple-A were cut during 2008 to Ca/C, the lowest rating.

Moody's moved out of its 99 Church Street building in late 2007 and into a glass skyscraper two blocks away. The old building was razed to make way for an 80-story Four Seasons Hotel. The giant bronze frieze with its warning for Wall Street is gone. The full text of the Daniel Webster quote is as follows:

Credit: Man's Confidence in Man

Commercial credit is the creation of modern times and belongs in its highest perfection only to the most enlightened and best-governed nations. Credit is the vital air of the system of modern commerce. It has done more, a thousand-times more, to enrich nations than all the mines of the world.

In early 2008, according to Silverstein Properties, which purchased the site, the frieze was "recycled," though no one there could tell me what that meant. I tried Tishman Speyer, the company building the hotel. The project manager told me that he had no idea what became of the frieze. He did tell me that "Man's Confidence in Man" was not as massive as it appeared. The frieze was, in fact, a very thin piece of metal that had been formed over poured concrete. He suggested I try Waldorf Demolition, the company that took down the old building. At Waldorf, a man named Richard said it might have ended up in the hands of a collector of historical artifacts. Someone like that had come through the building before it was torn down. But Waldorf wasn't in the business of sorting through what had value and what didn't, Richard explained. "We just make things disappear," he added.

"THE BOND-INSURANCE industry was destroyed from within," says Jack Butler, who helped to found MBIA all those years ago. It was a good business, he insists. There was a role for bond insurance in the financial markets. "Common sense went out the window. This bubble was forecast and known," he says. "The U.S. went on a credit binge. There was an unsustainable increase in property values as a result of the binge. We pursued a policy to make sure everybody who could scrape together two cents could buy a home."

Butler has no sympathy for bond insurers who failed to see these glaring risks. The companies who sold triple-A ratings were themselves fooled by triple-A ratings and by something even more absurd—super-senior ratings—on securities that contained stunning amounts of risk. "Here's the insanity," says Butler, "the idea that there is no risk so therefore there is no capital requirement, [that] virtually any premium I charge will produce a nearly infinite rate of return."

Maybe bond insurance was always too good to be true. It would certainly help to explain why the credit-default-swap market—an extension of the bond-insurance business—reached $62 trillion in outstanding contracts in just a little more than a decade. Before the advent of all this risk transfer, there was only one way to bet that a company was creditworthy: Lend it money. CDS contracts allowed investors to bet on the creditworthiness of a company by selling insurance on the company and earning premiums without actually having to put any money down. It was the ultimate leverage. That it ended badly should not be much of a surprise.

"Let's not have any histrionics," Monsieur Danglars, one of the Count of Monte Cristo's foes, tells his wife after their bond-market scheme collapses in angry recriminations. Danglars marvels at the delusional thinking of his wife's lover, who involved them in this scheme that for a while made them all rich: Imagine, Danglars says to his wife, sneeringly, "telling himself that at last he's found something the most skillful gamblers have never been able to discover: a game in which you win without putting up any money and lose nothing when you lose." That game might have been called the "no-loss illusion."

Notes

PREFACE

"America's Total Debt Report" (http://mwhodges.home.att.net/nat-debt/debt-nat-a.htm).

ACKNOWLEDGMENTS

Glenda Busick, *Brevard Good Ole Boys: A Taxpayer Searches for Truth in the Good Ole Boy Network of County Government*, self-published, 1991. Available by request through info@aidomes.com.

CHAPTER 1
THE MEETING

MBIA Inc. 2001 Annual Report, Q&A with MBIA President Gary Dunton, p. 11.

William Ackman and David Berkowitz, letter to Gotham Partners, Oct. 18, 2002.

Continued Examination of William A. Ackman, Gotham Partners Investigation, New York Attorney General's Office, 120 Broadway, New York City, June 4, 2003.

Gillian Tett, *Fool's Gold: How the Bold Dream of a Small Tribe at J.P. Morgan Was Corrupted by Wall Street Greed and Unleashed a Catastrophe* (New York: Free Press, 2009), p. 46.

ISDA Market Survey, http://www.isda.org/statistics/pdf/ISDA-Market-Survey-historical-data.pdf.

Deposition of David Klafter, Gotham Partners Investigation, New York Attorney General's Office, 120 Broadway, New York City, July 10, 2003.

Examination of Gregory Lyss, Gotham Partners Investigation, New York Attorney General's Office, 120 Broadway, New York City, July 11, 2003.

Continued Examination of William A. Ackman, Gotham Partners Investigation, New York Attorney General's Office, 120 Broadway, New York City, March 4, 2003.

Karen Richardson and Aaron Lucchetti, "Bond Insurer's Woes Add to Credit-Market Stress: MBIA Posts Huge Loss on Bad Subprime Bets, Investors See Rebound," *Wall Street Journal,* Feb. 1, 2008, p. A1.

Fax to William Ackman from MBIA's General Counsel Ram Wertheim, Nov. 22, 2002.

CHAPTER 2
THE SHORT SELLER

Gotham Partners Management Co. LLC, "Buying the Farm: A Detailed Examination of Accounting, Investment, and Reserving Practices at the Federal Agricultural Mortgage Corporation," May 23, 2002.

Examination of Whitney Tilson, Gotham Partners Investigation, New York Attorney General's Office, 120 Broadway, New York City, July 29, 2003.

Jay Brown, letter to MBIA Inc. shareholders, MBIA 2001 Annual Report.

Vikas Bajaj and Julie Creswell, "Bond Insurer in Turmoil Turns to Familiar Leader," *New York Times,* Feb. 20, 2008, section C, p. 2.

William Ackman, notes from meeting with Jay Brown, Neil Budnick, and Mark Gold at MBIA's Armonk, New York, headquarters, Aug. 14, 2002.

Gillian Tett, *Fool's Gold: How the Bold Dream of a Small Tribe at J.P. Morgan Was Corrupted by Wall Street Greed and Unleashed a Catastrophe* (New York: Free Press, 2009), p. 63.

Michael Neumann, deposition, Gotham Partners Investigation, New York Attorney General's Office, New York City, July 10, 2003.

Henny Sender, "Backing Corporate Bonds Can Be Risky Business," *Wall Street Journal,* Nov. 5, 2002, p. C1.

Testimony of William Ackman, "In the Matter of Gotham Partners Management Co.," Securities and Exchange Commission, Washington, DC, June 18, 2003.

William Ackman, e-mail to Gotham Partners, Nov. 10, 2002.

Robert D. Hershey, "Omaha Oracle Taps a Medium of Wall Street," *New York Times,* Jan. 31, 1999, section 3, p. 10.

David Klafter, deposition, Gotham Partners Investigation, New York Attorney General's Office, New York City, July 10, 2003.

Greg Lyss, examination, Gotham Partners Investigation, New York Attorney General's Office, New York City, July 11, 2003.

Vinay Saqi and Alice Schroeder, "Headline Risk Remains," Morgan Stanley Equity Research, Nov. 14, 2002.

William Ackman, e-mail to Gotham Partners, Nov. 14, 2002.

Susan Alexander, "They Think Flashing $s Makes Cs, But it Causes !s and Even @&)s," *Wall Street Journal,* May 9, 1991, p. B1.

Seth Klarman, *Margin of Safety: Risk-Averse Value Investing Strategies for the Thoughtful Investor* (New York: HarperCollins, 1991), p. 88.

Christine Richard and Katherine Burton, "Ackman Devoured 140,000 Pages Challenging MBIA Rating," Bloomberg News, Jan. 31, 2008.

Mark Walsh, "Forty Under 40—William A. Ackman, 32," *Crain's New York Business,* Jan. 25, 1999.

Jesse Eisinger, "The Optimist," *Portfolio,* May 2009.

CHAPTER 3
THE QUESTION

Jay Brown, MBIA Chief Executive Officer, presentation at Keefe Bruyette & Woods investment conference, New York City, Dec. 10, 2002. (Transcript included in submission by Gotham Partners to New York Attorney General's Office on Feb. 27, 2003.)

Form of Restricted Stock Award, cited in MBIA Inc. Form 8-K, Exhibit 10.68, May 6, 2004, p. 6.

George Kimeldorf v. *First Union Real Estate Equity*, New York Supreme Court, New York County, April 8, 2002. Docket No. 107176/2002.

George Kimeldorf v. *First Union Real Estate Equity and Mortgage Investment,* George Kimeldorf deposition, Feb. 26, 2003.

Gotham Partners Management Co. LLC, *Is MBIA Triple-A? A Detailed Analysis of SPVs, CDOs, and Accounting and Reserving Policies at MBIA, Inc.,* Dec. 9, 2002.

Joshua Shanker, "MBIA: Price Under Fire from Short Positions," Blaylock & Partners LP, Dec. 10, 2002.

Christine Richard, "MBIA Denies Accuracy of Report by Gotham—Study Asserts Credit Rating of Triple-A Is Undeserved, Warns of 'Liquidity Issues,'" *Wall Street Journal,* Dec. 10, 2002, p. C3.

Jay Brown presentation, Dec. 10, 2002.

William Ackman, e-mail to John Rutherfurd, chairman and chief executive officer of Moody's Investors Service, Dec. 11, 2002.

Charlie Munger lecture, "The Psychology of Human Misjudgment," Harvard University, Cambridge, Massachusetts, June 1995. Transcription by Whitney Tilson, Tilson Funds, New York.

Vinay Saqi and Alice Schroeder, "Gotham's Concerns—Warranted or Not?" Morgan Stanley, Dec. 16, 2002.

MBIA Inc. White Paper, "MBIA's Insured CDO Portfolio," December 2002.

Gretchen Morgenson, "It Still Pays to See Who Did the Research," *New York Times,* Dec. 22, 2002.

Examination of Whitney Tilson, Gotham Partners Investigation, New York Attorney General's Office, 120 Broadway, New York City, July 29, 2003.

William Ackman and David Berkowitz, letter to Gotham Partners, Dec. 27, 2002.

Alice Schroeder, e-mail to Whitney Tilson, Dec. 27, 2002. (Included in Gotham Partners' submission to the New York Attorney General's Office, Feb. 27, 2003.)

Michael Neumann, deposition, Gotham Partners Investigation, New York Attorney General's Office, New York City, July 10, 2003.

CHAPTER 4
BACKLASH

Alice Schroeder e-mail to William Ackman, Jan. 8, 2003.

William Ackman, e-mail to Gotham Credit Partners, Dec. 30, 2002. 10:12 p.m.

Christine Richard, "Egan-Jones Cuts MBIA to A+, Insurer Unit 'Not AAA,'" Dow Jones Newswires, Dec. 20, 2002.

Continued Examination of William A. Ackman, New York Attorney General's Office, 120 Broadway, New York City. March 4, 2003.

David Klafter, e-mail to William Ackman, David Berkowitz, and Aaron Marcu, "Subject: Disclaimer," Jan. 2, 2003.

Henny Sender and Gregory Zuckerman, "Gotham Is Snared by Sand Trap: Problems Rise for Maverick Fund as Major Golf Investment Sours and Spooked Investors Decamp," *Wall Street Journal*, Jan. 8, 2003.

Alice Schroeder e-mail to William Ackman, Jan. 8, 2003.

Svea Herbst-Bayliss, "New York Regulator Eyes Gotham Partners' Activity," Reuters, Jan. 8, 2003.

Whitney Tilson, e-mail to William Ackman, "Subject: Go Public," Jan. 9, 2003.

Aaron Marcu, e-mail to William Ackman, "Subject: Go Public," Jan. 9, 2003.

Examination of David Berkowitz, Gotham Partners Investigation, New York Attorney General's Office, 120 Broadway, New York City, June 26, 2003.

Gretchen Morgenson and Geraldine Fabrikant, "A Rescue Ploy Now Haunts a Hedge Fund That Had It All," *New York Times*, Jan. 18, 2003, Money and Business section, p. 1.

David Einhorn, *Fooling Some of the People All of the Time* (Hoboken, New Jersey: John Wiley & Sons, 2008), pp. 147–148.

Randall Smith and Henny Sender, "Regulators Review Complaints About Hedge Funds' Research; Companies with Beaten Stocks Say That Funds' Negativity Is to Blame," *Wall Street Journal*, Jan. 22, 2003.

Henny Sender, "Hedge Funds: Reward & Risk; Behind an Attack on Farmer Mac," *Wall Street Journal*, Apr. 11, 2003, p. C1.

Andy Brimmer (Joele Frank Wilkinson Brimmer), e-mail to William Ackman, Feb. 21, 2003.

CHAPTER 5
THE WORST THAT COULD HAPPEN

MBIA Inc. 2000 Annual Report, Q&A with MBIA President Gary Dunton.

Moody's Aaa rating definition. http://moodys.com.

Matthew Hanson, "Rating Agencies: 'Matrix' Fitch's New Way to Gauge Insurers' Capital Clearance," *The Bond Buyer,* Jan. 11, 2007, p. 7.

Frank L. Raiter, testimony before House Committee on Oversight and Government Reform, "Credit Rating Agencies and the Financial Crisis," Oct. 22, 2008.

MBIA investor meeting, Fair Disclosure transcript, Mar. 13, 2003.

MBIA Inc. White Paper. "MBIA's Insured CDO Portfolio," December 2002.

Joshua Shanker, Blaylock & Partners LP, "Insurance: Financial Guaranty: Seeing Through the CDOs," Jan. 7, 2003.

Examination of Boaz Weinstein, Gotham Partners Investigation, New York Attorney General's Office, 120 Broadway, New York City, June 6, 2003.

Scott Patterson and Serena Ng, "Deutsche Bank Fallen Trader Left Behind $1.8 Billion Hole," *Wall Street Journal,* Feb. 6, 2009, p. A1.

Weinstein examination, June 6, 2003.

MBIA fourth quarter 2002 earnings conference call, Bloomberg transcript, Feb. 4, 2003.

William Ackman, e-mail to John Rutherfurd, Jan. 25, 2003.

John Rutherfurd, e-mail to William Ackman, Jan. 25, 2003.

William Ackman, letter to Stephen Joynt, Chief Executive Officer, Fitch Ratings, Mar. 8, 2003.

Warren Buffett, letter to shareholders, Berkshire Hathaway Inc., 2002 annual report.

William Ackman, e-mail to Samuel DiPiazza, Feb. 19, 2003.

Jay Brown, letter to shareholders, MBIA Inc. 2002 Annual Report.

Eliot Spitzer, presentation at the Wall Street Hedge Fund Forum, New York City, Covington & Burling transcript, Mar. 3, 2003.

CHAPTER 6
THE TROUBLE WITH TRIPLE-A

William Gross, "The Shadow Knows," *Fortune,* Dec. 10, 2007.

Examination of William A. Ackman, Gotham Partners Investigation, New York Attorney General's Office, 120 Broadway, New York City, Mar. 4, 2003.

Continued Examination of William A. Ackman, Gotham Partners Investigation, New York Attorney General's Office, 120 Broadway, New York City, May 13, 2003.

James Rosen, *The Strong Man: John Mitchell and the Secrets of Watergate* (New York: Doubleday, 2008), p. 11.

"A Conversation with John Mitchell: Moral Obligation Bonds, the Industry's Old Days, and More." *The Bond Buyer Centennial Edition 1991*, p. 62.

Bill Ackman's notes from Aug. 14, 2002, meeting with Jay Brown.

Examination of William Ackman by the New York Attorney General's Office, Mar. 13, 2003.

Examination of Gregory Lyss, Gotham Partners Investigation, New York Attorney General's Office, 120 Broadway, New York City, July 11, 2003.

Nathan Flanders, Thomas Abruzzo, and Ralph Aurora, "Credit Analysis: MBIA Insurance Corp.," Fitch Ratings, September 22, 2004.

Warren Buffett, excerpts from 2003 Berkshire Hathaway annual meeting, Gotham Partners transcript.

Jay Brown, letter to shareholders, MBIA 2002 Annual Report, p. 6.

CHAPTER 7
UNANSWERED QUESTIONS

Continued Examination of William A. Ackman, Gotham Partners Investigation, New York Attorney General's Office, 120 Broadway, New York City, May 28, 2003.

William Ackman, e-mail to Gotham Credit Partners, May 7, 2003.

William Ackman, e-mail to Neil Budnick, May 7, 2003.

Ram Wertheim, e-mail to William Ackman, May 13, 2003.

William Ackman, e-mail to Gotham Credit Partners, May 7, 2003.

Examination of William A. Ackman, Gotham Partners Investigation, New York Attorney General's Office, 120 Broadway, New York City, June 24, 2003.

Rick Schmitt, "Prophet and Loss: Brooksley Born Warned that Unchecked Trading in the Credit Derivative Market Could Lead to Disaster," *Stanford Magazine*, March/April 2009 (www.stanfordalumni.org).

Continued Examination of William A. Ackman, Gotham Partners Investigation, New York Attorney General's Office, 120 Broadway, New York City, May 28, 2003.

Einhorn, *Fooling Some of the People All of the Time*, pp. 157–159.

Examination of David Berkowitz, Gotham Partners Investigation, New York Attorney General's Office, 120 Broadway, New York City, June 26, 2003.

CHAPTER 8
CRIMES AND COCKROACHES

Continued Examination of William A. Ackman, Gotham Partners Investigation, New York Attorney General's Office, 120 Broadway, New York City, June 24, 2003.

Examination of Whitney Tilson, Gotham Partners Investigation, New York Attorney General's Office, 120 Broadway, New York City, July 29, 2003.

Continued Examination of William A. Ackman by the New York Attorney General's Office, June 24, 2003.

Testimony of William Ackman, "In the Matter of Gotham Partners Management Co.," Securities and Exchange Commission, Washington, DC, June 5 and June 18, 2003.

CHAPTER 9
TURNING THE TABLES

David Elliott, letter to shareholders, MBIA 2001 Annual Report.

Stephen Crimmins, Piper Hamilton LP, Independent Examiner's Report Concerning Spiegel Inc., *United States Securities Commission* v. *Spiegel Inc.* (forensic accountants: Kroll Zolfo Cooper LLC), Sept. 5, 2003.

Christine Richard and David Feldheim, "Truck School Loan Defaults Catch Insurers in Headlights," Dow Jones Capital Markets Report, Nov. 7, 2002.

John Kenneth Galbraith, *The Economics of Innocent Fraud: Truth for Our Time* (New York: Houghton Mifflin Harcourt, 2004), p. xi.

Decision and order of the Supreme Court, Appellate Division, First Department, *George Kimeldorf* v. *First Union Real Estate Equity and Mortgage Investment*, Sept. 4, 2003.

William Ackman, broadcast e-mail, "A Lesson in Probability," Sept. 25, 2003.

U.S. Government Accountability Office, "Farmer Mac: Some Progress Made, but Greater Attention to Risk Management, Mission, and Corporate Governance Is Needed" (GAO-04-116), Oct. 16, 2003.

Christine Richard, "Reinsurance Probe Reaches Out to MBIA—Government Subpoenas Focus on 1998 Transaction Linked with a Bankruptcy," *Wall Street Journal*, Dec. 24, 2004, p. C3.

William Ackman, letter to Steven Walker and Walton Kinsey at the Securities and Exchange Commission, Jan. 9, 2004.

"Presentation to the Securities and Exchange Commission Regarding MBIA," Gotham Partners Management Co. LLC and Kroll Zolfo Cooper LLC, Feb. 3, 2004.

Martin Peretz, letter to William Donaldson, July 12, 2004.

"MBIA Receives Document Subpoenas Regarding 'Non-Traditional Products,'" MBIA press release via Business Wire, Nov. 18, 2004.

"MBIA Provides Additional Information Regarding Subpoenas," MBIA press release via Business Wire, Nov. 23, 2004.

Gotham Partners, *Is MBIA Triple-A?*

Elliott, letter to shareholders.

CHAPTER 10
SCRUTINY

Jonathan Laing, "Truth and Consequences," *Barron's*, Apr. 4, 2005.

Thornton L. O'glove, *The Quality of Earnings: The Investor's Guide to How Much Money a Company Is Really Making* (New York: Free Press, 1987), p. xii.

Lawton Burns, John Cacciamani, James Clement, and Welman Aquino, "The Fall of the House of AHERF: The Allegheny Bankruptcy," *Health Affairs*, vol. 19, January/February 2000 no. 1.

William Ackman, notes from Aug. 14, 2002, meeting with Jay Brown.

MBIA Inc. conference call, Sept. 11, 1998, Gotham Partners transcript.

"MBIA Does Not Expect Philadelphia Hospital Group Bankruptcy to Affect Earnings," MBIA press release via Business Wire, July 21, 1998.

E-mail from former senior executive at MBIA to William Ackman, "A Very Good Research Piece," Dec. 15, 2002.

Gotham Partners Management Co. LLC presentation to Attorney General Eliot Spitzer, "MBIA Inc./MBIA Insurance Corp.: Insurance Law and Martin Act Issues," Jan. 27, 2005.

William Ackman, e-mail to New York Attorney General's Office, "Continued False Statements and Misleading Disclosure by MBIA," Feb. 7, 2005.

William Ackman, e-mail to the New York Attorney General and the Securities and Exchange Commission, Apr. 10, 2005.

Ted Hampton, "MBIA's Elliott Sees Steady Course Under Successor," Bloomberg News, Jan. 8, 1999.

O'glove, *The Quality of Earnings*, p. xiii.

MBIA Inc. 8-K filing with the Securities and Exchange Commission, Jan. 12, 2005.

"MBIA to Restate Financial Statements for 1998 and Subsequent Years," MBIA press release via Business Wire, Mar. 8, 2005.

"MBIA Document Subpoenas Supplemented," MBIA press release via Business Wire, Mar. 30, 2005.

"MBIA Purchases Shares as Part of Its Buyback Program," MBIA press release via Business Wire, Apr. 4, 2005.

William Ackman, letter to Pershing Square investors, "Re: First Quarter 2005 Performance," Apr. 25, 2005.

Bethany McLean, "The Mystery of the $890 Billion Insurer," *Fortune*, May 2, 2005.

William Ackman, e-mail to John Rutherfurd, Apr. 20, 2005.

John Ruherfurd, e-mail to William Ackman, Apr. 22, 2005.

CHAPTER 11

THE BLACK HOLE

Video of Capital Asset Board Meeting, Capital Asset headquarter, West Palm Beach, Florida, Sept. 24, 1998.

Richard Heitmeyer, letter to Jay Brown, Aug. 27, 1999.

Jay Brown, MBIA Chairman and Chief Executive Officer, letter to Richard A. Heitmeyer, Sept. 7, 1999.

Professor Frank Mantello, Chair, Department of Greek and Latin, Catholic University of America, e-mail to author, May 20, 2005.

Christine Richard and Mark Whitehouse, "MBIA Didn't Tell Full Exposure to Capital Asset, Ex-Partner Says," *Wall Street Journal,* May 26, 2005, p. C3.

Letter from William Ackman to the New York Attorney General, Securities and Exchange Commission, U.S. Attorney's Office, and New York State Insurance Department, "Re: MBIA Inc. and MBIA Insurance Corp.," Aug. 18, 2005.

Transcript of MBIA conference call, Sept. 11, 1998.

William Ackman, e-mail to Christopher Mahoney, Chief Credit Officer, Moody's Investors Service, June 19, 2005.

William Ackman, e-mail to Christopher Mahoney, July 29, 2005.

Letter from Ira Lee Sorkin at Carter Ledyard & Milburn LLP in New York to Stephen Fraidin at Kirkland & Ellis LLP in New York, July 27, 2005.

Ian MacDonald, "Moving the Market: Regulators Are Close to Bringing Civil Suit Against MBIA," *Wall Street Journal,* Aug. 11, 2005, p. C3.

Darin Arita, "MBIA Inc.: Bringing Regulatory Matters to a Close," Deutsche Bank Securities, Aug. 11, 2005.

William Ackman, e-mail to Christopher Mahoney, Aug. 15, 2005.

"MBIA Receives Wells Notice from SEC Relating to AHERF," MBIA press release via Business Wire, Aug. 19, 2005.

Jack Dorer and Margaret Kessler, "Moody's Comments on MBIA's Ratings in Light of the Wells Notice," Moody's Investors Service, Aug. 22, 2005.

Jim Chanos, e-mail to undisclosed recipients, Aug. 22, 2005.

William Ackman, e-mail to Christopher Mahoney, Sept. 28, 2005.

Jonathan Laing, "Meet Mr. Pressure," *Barron's,* Dec. 5, 2005, p. B25.

R. Scott Frost, "Barron's Watch: MBIA," HSBC Global Research, Oct. 3, 2005.

CHAPTER 12

THE COURT OF PUBLIC OPINION

Ian McDonald and Theo Francis, "MBIA Nears Civil Settlements—Investors Hope the Pacts Will Silence Bearish Critics," *Wall Street Journal,* Nov. 2, 2005, p. C4.

Internal Report by University of Pittsburgh Medical Center, "MBIA, Citigroup and West Penn Allegheny Health System," Oct. 17, 2005.

University of Pittsburgh Medical Center, transcript of voice mail messages left by Bill Ackman for David Farner, Nov. 2, 2005, 9:17 a.m. and 10:16 a.m.

Martin Peretz, e-mail to William Ackman, draft of letter to Eliot Spitzer, Nov. 3, 2005.

MBIA third quarter 2005 earnings conference call, Bloomberg transcript, Nov. 8, 2005.

Mark Whitehouse and Theo Francis, "Unsettling Claim: Old Deal Bedevils Key Player in World of Municipal Bonds," *Wall Street Journal,* May 2, 2005, A1.

William Ackman, letter to Moody's Corp. board of directors, Dec. 21, 2005.

John J. Goggins, Senior Vice President and General Counsel, Moody's Investors Service, letter to William Ackman, Jan. 18, 2006.

William Ackman, letter to Pershing Square investors, "Re: Fourth Quarter and Annual Performance for 2005," Feb. 6, 2006.

William Neuman, "Completing a Comeback," *New York Times,* Aug. 13, 2006, section 11, p. 2.

CHAPTER 13

THE INSURANCE CHARADE

MBIA first quarter 2006 earnings conference call, Bloomberg transcript, Apr. 27, 2006.

Christine Richard and Darrell Preston, "The Insurance Charade," Bloomberg Markets, November 2006.

William Ackman, letter to Pershing Square investors, "Re: Second Quarter 2006 Performance," Aug. 23, 2006.

Charles Pollock, Goldman Sachs, e-mail to Erika Kreyssig, Pershing Square, Aug. 29, 2006.

George Friedlander, "Calendar Continues to Languish," Citigroup Smith Barney, Oct. 6, 2006.

CHAPTER 14

WHEN CRACK HOUSES BECOME COLLATERAL

David Boberski, *CDS Delivery Option: Better Pricing of Credit Default Swaps* (New York: Bloomberg Press, 2009), p. 27.

MBIA first quarter 2006 earnings conference call, Bloomberg transcript, Apr. 27, 2006.

Letter from William Ackman to the New York Attorney General, Securities and Exchange Commission, U.S. Attorney's Office, and New York State Insurance Department, "Re: MBIA Inc. and MBIA Insurance Corp.," Aug. 18, 2005.

Heather Hunt, "MBI: Shifting to Hold from Buy on Valuation," Citigroup Global Markets, Dec. 3, 2006.

Diana Nelson Jones, "Garfield's Aggie Brose Sees the Payoff of More Than 25 Years of Activism," *Pittsburgh Post-Gazette*, July 29, 2001.

William Ackman, e-mail to Steven Rawlings, Allan Kahn, and Christopher Mele at the Securities and Exchange Commission, Nov. 30, 2006.

Boberski, *CDS Delivery Option*, p. 27.

Jack Dorer, Stan Rouyer, and James Eck, Moody's Financial Guaranty Industry Outlook Briefing, The Sofitel, New York, Nov. 17, 2006.

AIG second quarter 2007 earnings call, Bloomberg transcript, Aug. 9, 2007.

Sanjay Sharma and Louis Aricson, letter to Jacques Rolfo and Charles Webster, "IXIS Risk Position Regarding the Residential Mortgage Market," Dec. 18, 2006.

Chuck Webster, letter to CIFG Risk Committee, Dec. 19, 2006.

William Ackman, letter to Pershing Square investors, "Re: Third Quarter 2006 Performance," Nov. 21, 2006.

CHAPTER 15
STORM WARNINGS

"The People of the State of New York, by Eliot Spitzer, Attorney General of the State of New York against MBIA, Inc., MBIA Insurance Corporation," Assurance of Discontinuance, Jan. 25, 2007.

Heather Hunt, "MBI: Settlement Likely on Monday; Great News, But Still a Hold," Citigroup, Jan. 28, 2007.

Securities and Exchange Commission v. *MBIA, Inc.* Complaint. United States District Court, Southern District of New York, Jan. 29, 2007.

Tamara Kravec, "MBIA Inc.: Settlement Overhang Removed; Room for More Multiple Expansion," Bank of America, Jan. 29, 2007.

Robert Ryan, "MBIA: Let the Repurchases Begin," Merrill Lynch, Jan. 29, 2007.

Andrew Wessell, "MBIA Inc.: Settlement Finally Announced, Shares Benefiting from Short Squeeze," JPMorgan, North American Equity Research, Jan. 29, 2007.

MBIA fourth quarter 2006 earnings conference call, Bloomberg transcript, Jan. 30, 2007.

"MBIA Announces $1 Billion Share Repurchase Authorization," MBIA press release via Business Wire, Feb. 1, 2007.

Christine Richard, "MBIA Used Short Seller's Report to Help Get Lawsuit Dismissed," Bloomberg News, Feb. 22, 2007.

Josh Rosner, "How Resilient Are Mortgage Backed Securities to Collateralized Debt Obligation Market Disruptions?" Feb. 15, 2007.

Mark Adelson, Nomura Fixed Income Research, "Report from Las Vegas 2007," Feb. 5, 2007.

Financial Guaranty Insurance Company and FGIC UK Limited v. *IKB Deutsche Industriebank AG, IKB Credit Asset Management GMBH, Havenrock II Limited, and Calyon Credit Agricole CIB.* Complaint filed Mar. 10, 2008, New York Supreme Court, New York County. Docket No. 08600704.

William Gross, "Looking for Contagion in All the Wrong Places," *PIMCO Investment Outlook,* July 2007.

William Ackman, letter to Pershing Square investors, "Re: Fourth Quarter and Annual Performance for 2006," Mar. 5, 2007.

Mark Pittman, "Subprime Securities Market Began as 'Group of 5' Over Chinese," Bloomberg News, Dec. 17, 2007.

Hamish Risk, "Asset Backed Derivatives Index Get $5 Billion of Trade," Bloomberg News, Jan. 20, 2005.

Deutsche Bank Securities presentation, "Shorting Home Equity Mezzanine Tranches: A Strategy to Cash In on a Slowing Housing Market," April 2007.

CHAPTER 16
AN UNCERTAIN SPRING

Deutsche Bank, "Conference Call on Bear Stearns Hedge Fund Ramifications," Global Markets Research, June 25, 2007.

MBIA first quarter 2007 earnings conference call, Bloomberg transcript, Apr. 26, 2007.

Moody's Investors Service, "Special Comment: Mapping of Moody's Municipal Ratings to the Global Scale," June 2007.

William Ackman, presentation at the Ira Sohn Conference, "Who's Holding the Bag," New York City, May 23, 2007.

Heather Hunt, "Maintain Comfort with MBS? Woes; Near-term Volatility a Buying Opportunity," Citigroup Investment Research, May 31, 2007.

William Ackman, e-mail to Heather Hunt, May 31, 2007.

Deutsche Bank, "Conference Call on Bear Stearns Hedge Fund Ramifications."

Mark Pittman, "S&P May Cut $12 Billion of Subprime Mortgage Bonds," Bloomberg News, July 10, 2007.

Financial Guaranty Insurance Company and FGIC UK Limited v. *IKB Deutsche Industriebank AG, et al.*

Günther Bräunig, "On the Way to Realigning the Business," IKB Deutsche Industriebank, Oct. 16, 2007.

MBIA second quarter 2007 earnings conference call, Bloomberg transcript, July 26, 2007.

Christine Richard, "MBIA Consultant Ends Probe Into 'Black Hole' Deal," Bloomberg News, July 25, 2007.

Lankler Siffert & Wohl LLP, Report of the Independent Consultant to MBIA Inc., July 24, 2007.

CHAPTER 17
APOCALYPSE NOW

Janet Tavakoli, *Structured Finance and Collateralized Debt Obligations: New Developments in Cash and Synthetic Securitization,* 2nd ed. (Hoboken, New Jersey: John Wiley & Sons, 2008), p. 334.

William Ackman, presentation to the New York State Insurance Department, "Bond Insurers: The Next S&L Crisis?" Aug. 1, 2007.

Mick McGuire, e-mail to Jordan Cahn at Morgan Stanley, "MBIA Subprime Call," Aug. 1, 2007.

MBIA presentation, "MBIA's Disciplined and Selective Approach to Subprime RMBS and Multi-Sector CDOs," Bloomberg transcript, Aug. 2, 2007.

Deutsche Bank Securities presentation, "Shorting Home Equity Mezzanine Tranches: A Strategy to Cash In on a Slowing Housing Market," April 2007.

Lisa Kassenaar and Yalman Onaran, "Thain Makes Like Komansky in Pledge on Subprime Orgy," Bloomberg News, Jan. 3, 2008.

MBIA Insurance Corporation and LaCrosse Financial Products, LLC v. Merrill Lynch, Pierce, Fenner and Smith Inc., and Merrill Lynch International, First Amended Complaint, New York Supreme Court, New York County, May 15, 2009, Index No. 09-601324.

Janet Tavakoli, "MBIA and Ambac: Structured Finance Underwriting Standards," Tavakoli Structured Finance, Feb. 18, 2008.

Shareholder report on UBS's writedowns, Apr. 18, 2008 (www.ubs.com).

Fitch Ratings, "Basel II and Securitization: A Guided Tour through a New Landscape," Oct. 14, 2009.

William Ackman, e-mail to Christopher Mahoney, Aug. 3, 2007.

AIG second quarter 2007 earnings conference call, Bloomberg transcript, Aug. 9, 2007.

Joseph S. St. Denis, letter to Henry A. Waxman, Chairman of House Committee on Oversight and Governmental Reform, Oct. 4, 2008.

Henry Tabe and Martin Rast, "SIVs Represent an Oasis of Calm in the Sub-Prime Maelstrom," Moody's Investors Service, July 23, 2007.

Mark Pittman and Elizabeth Stanton, "Subprime 'Tsunami' Hits Asset-Backed Commercial Paper Market," Bloomberg News, Aug. 8, 2007.

Mark Pittman, "Commercial Paper Yields Soar to Highest Since 2001," Bloomberg News, Aug. 9, 2007.

William Ackman, letter to Pershing Square investors, "Re: Second Quarter 2007 Performance," Aug. 14, 2007.

CHAPTER 18

PARTING THE CURTAIN

Ken Zerbe, "Financial Guarantors on the Knife's Edge: Can the Industry Survive?" Morgan Stanley, Nov. 2, 2007.

Merrill Lynch & Co. third quarter 2007 earnings conference call, Bloomberg transcript, Oct. 24, 2007.

MBIA Inc. third quarter 2007 earnings conference call, Bloomberg transcript, Oct. 25, 2007.

Testimony of William Ackman, "In the Matter of Gotham Partners Management Co.," Securities and Exchange Commission, Washington, DC, June 18, 2003.

Kathleen Shanley, "MBIA: Ghosts and Goblins," Gimme Credit, Oct. 31, 2007.

Zerbe, "Financial Guarantors on the Knife's Edge."

Tom Abruzzo and Keith Buckley, "Fitch Details Approach to Assessing Financial Guarantors' SF CDO Exposures," Fitch Ratings, Nov. 5, 2007.

Christine Richard and Cecile Gutscher, "MBIA, Ambac Downgrades May Cost Market $200 Billion," Bloomberg News, Nov. 15, 2007.

Elizabeth Hester and Bradley Keoun, "Citigroup, Banks Agree on 'Super SIV,' Person Says," Bloomberg News, Nov. 12, 2007.

ACA Capital third quarter 2007 earnings conference call, Bloomberg transcript, Nov. 8, 2007.

Karen Richardson, "How the Crunch Is Playing Out: Buffett Gets Opening as Bond Insurers Turn to Berkshire for Succor," Wall Street Journal, Nov. 13, 2007, section C, p. 1.

Christine Richard, "MBIA, Ambac Defending AAA Ratings, Consider Capital Raising," Bloomberg News, Nov. 7, 2007.

William Ackman, presentation at Value Investing Congress, New York City, "How to Save the Bond Insurers," Nov. 28, 2007.

Examination of William Ackman by the Securities and Exchange Commission, June 5, 2003.

Joe Nocera, "Short Seller Sinks Teeth Into Insurer," New York Times, Dec. 1, 2007, p. C1.

William Ackman, e-mail to the Securities and Exchange Commission, "The SEC's Enforcement Failures with the Bond Insurers and Other Issues," Dec. 2, 2007.

Letter to Mark Stein, Simpson Thacher & Bartlett LLP, from Cheryl J. Scarboro, Associate Director, Securities and Exchange Commission, "In the Matter of Gotham Partners Management Co., LLC," Dec. 19, 2007.

CHAPTER 19
RATINGS REVISITED

Doug Noland, "Wall Street Backed Finance," David Tice & Associates, Dec. 21, 2007.

William Ackman, letter to Rep. Barney Frank, Oct. 26, 2007.

David Einhorn, "The Curse of the Triple-A Rating," presentation at the Ira Sohn Investment Conference, New York City, May 27, 2009.

Karen Richardson, "Credit Crunch: MBIA Gets a Capital Pain Reliever," *Wall Street Journal*, Dec. 11, 2007, C2.

Martin Whitman, interview with Erin Burnett, CNBC, Dec. 21, 2007.

Jody Shenn, "Moody's Had $174 Billion in CDOs on Downgrade Review," Bloomberg News, Dec. 18, 2007.

Morgan Stanley, "Fourth Quarter 2007 Earnings," Bloomberg transcript, Dec. 19, 2007.

Ken Zerbe, "MBIA Discloses $8.1 Billion of CDO-Squared Exposure," Morgan Stanley, Dec. 19, 2007.

"MBIA Further Addresses Previously Disclosed $30.6 Billion Multi-Sector CDO Exposure," MBIA press release via Business Wire, Dec. 20, 2007.

Noland, "Wall Street Backed Finance."

Kathleen Shanley, "Gimme Credit Comments on MBIA's News," Dec. 20, 2007.

CHAPTER 20
THE PANIC BEGINS

Christine Richard, "Ambac Will Cut Dividend, Raise $1 Billion in Capital," Bloomberg News, Jan. 16, 2008.

"Comprehensive Plan to Strengthen Capital to Meet or Exceed Rating Agencies' Triple-A Requirements," MBIA press release via Business Wire, Jan. 9, 2008.

William Ackman, interview with Rhonda Schaffler on Bloomberg Television, Jan. 10, 2008.

Warren Buffett, interview with Becky Quick on CNBC's *Squawk Box*, Feb. 12, 2008.

Christine Richard and Pierre Paulden, "MBIA Pays 14 Percent Yield on Sale of Surplus Bonds," Bloomberg News, Jan. 11, 2008.

"AMBAC Announces Capital Enhancement Plan to Raise in Excess of $1 Billion," press release via Business Wire, Jan. 16, 2008.

James Eck and Jack Dorer, Moody's Investors Service, "Moody's Reviews Ambac's Rating for a Possible Downgrade," Jan. 16, 2008.

Kathleen Shanley, "Gimme Credit Comments on Ambac's News," Gimme Credit, Jan. 16, 2008.

Jim Cramer, "Cramer on Financials," *Squawk Box*, CNBC, Jan. 17, 2008.

David Wilson, "Bond Insurers' Fans, 'Negative Revenue,' Ill-Timed ETF: Timshel," Bloomberg News, Jan. 18, 2008.

"Evercore Asset Management Urges Ambac to Stop Capital Raising Effort and Accept Ratings Downgrade," PRNewswire, Jan. 17, 2008.

"Ambac Chooses Not to Raise Equity Capital Under Current Market Conditions," press release via Business Wire, Jan. 18, 2008.

William Selway, "Ambac's Rating Cut Alters Standing of 137,504 Bonds, Fitch Says," Bloomberg News, Jan. 18, 2008.

Christine Richard, "Ambac's Insurance Unit Cut to AA from AAA by Fitch Ratings," Bloomberg News, Jan. 18, 2008.

Doug Noland, "Daisy-Chain," David Tice & Associates, Jan. 18, 2008.

Heather Hunt, "Moody's Review and Share Volatility Don't Warrant Fresh Money," Citigroup Global Markets, Jan. 17, 2008.

William Ackman, letter to Raymond McDaniel, CEO of Moody's; Stephen Joynt, CEO and President of Fitch Ratings; and Deven Sharma, President of Standard & Poor's, "Subject: Bond Insurer Ratings," Jan. 18, 2008.

Ajit Jain, President, Berkshire Hathaway Group Reinsurance Division, letter to Gary Parr, Deputy Chairman, Lazard, Feb. 6, 2008.

Steve Rothwell, "Banks May Need $143 Billion for Insurer Downgrades," Bloomberg News, Jan. 25, 2008.

Paulson Credit Opportunities, letter to investors, 2007 Year End Report.

William Ackman, letter to Pershing Square investors, Nov. 21, 2007.

Christine Richard, "Ambac, MBIA Lust for CDO Returns Undercut AAA Success," Bloomberg News, Jan. 22, 2008.

CHAPTER 21

CATASTROPHE AND REVENGE

Alexandre Dumas, *The Count of Monte Cristo* (New York: Bantam Dell, 2003), p. 260 (originally published 1844).

Joshua Coval, Jakub Jurek, Erik Stafford, "Economic Catastrophe Bonds," April 2008, HBS Finance Working Paper No. 07–102.

Chua Kong Ho, "Asian Stocks Gain on Possible Bailout of U.S. Bond Insurers," Bloomberg News, Jan. 24, 2008.

"Security Capital Assurance Ltd. Provides Update on its Capital Plan," press release via PRNewswire, Jan. 23, 2008.

Thomas Abruzzo and Ralph Aurora, "Fitch Downgrades SCA and XLCA/XLFA; Ratings Remain on Watch Negative," Fitch Ratings, Jan. 24, 2008.

William Ackman, letter to Eric Dinallo, Superintendent of Insurance, State of New York; Sean Dilweg, Commissioner of Insurance, State of Wisconsin; Linda Thomsen, Director, Division of Enforcement, Securities and Exchange Commission; John White, Director,

Division of Corporation Finance, SEC; Mark Schonfeld, Regional Director; New York office, SEC; Leslie Kazon, Assistant Regional Director, New York office, SEC; Steve Rawlings, SEC; "Bond Insurer Transparency: Open Source Research," Jan. 30, 2008.

Dumas, *The Count of Monte Cristo*, p. 260.

Charles Gasparino, "Bond Insurers Face Downgrade Despite Call for Delay," CNBC, Jan. 30, 2008.

MBIA fourth quarter 2007 earnings conference call, Bloomberg transcript, Jan. 31, 2008.

Dick Smith, "S&P Lowers FGIC Ratings to 'AA' From 'AAA'; MBIA, XLCA Watch Negative," Standard & Poor's, Jan. 31, 2008.

William Ackman, letter to Federal Reserve Chairman Ben Bernanke, Federal Reserve Bank of New York President Timothy Geithner, Treasury Secretary Henry Paulson, and Under Secretary for Domestic Finance Robert Steel, Feb. 5, 2008.

Federal Open Market Committee, Board of Governors of the Federal Reserve System, Washington, DC. Meeting Notes for Jan. 29 and 30, 2008.

Dumas, *The Count of Monte Cristo*, p. 274.

CHAPTER 22
TIME RUNS OUT

Hearing of the Capital Markets, Insurance, and Government-Sponsored Enterprises Subcommittee of the House Committee on Financial Services, "The State of the Bond Insurance Industry," chaired by Rep. Paul E. Kanjorski (D-PA), Federal News Service transcription, Feb. 14, 2008.

Essex Equity Holdings USA, LLC v. *Lehman Brothers Inc.*, Financial Industry Regulatory Authority, Jan. 17, 2008.

MBIA Insurance Corp. v. *Merrill Lynch Pierce Fenner*, New York Supreme Court, New York County, Apr. 30, 2009. Docket 601324/2009.

In the Matter of UBS Securities LLC and UBS Financial Services Inc., Commonwealth of Massachusetts Office of the Secretary of the Commonwealth Securities Division, June 26, 2008. Docket 2008–0045.

Alex Crippen, "Buffett's Big Muni Bond Offer," CNBC interview transcript, CNBC.com, Feb. 12, 2008.

James J. Angel, Georgetown University, "The Municipal Bond Insurance Riddle," *The Financier: ACMT*, vol. 1, no. 1 (February 1994).

"The State of the Bond Insurance Industry" hearings, Feb. 14, 2008.

CHAPTER 23
BAILOUT

William Gross, "Rescuing Monolines Is Not a Long-Term Solution," FT.com, Feb. 7, 2008.

Vikas Bajaj and Julie Creswell, "Bond Insurer in Turmoil Turns to Familiar Leader," *New York Times,* Feb. 20, 2008, section C, p. 2.

Jay Brown, letter to owners of MBIA Inc., Business Wire, Feb. 25, 2008.

William Ackman, Pershing Square presentation, "Restructuring the Bond Insurers to Protect All Policyholders," Feb. 19, 2008.

"MBIA Says Ackman Proposal for Restructuring Guarantors No More Credible Than Flawed Open Source Model," MBIA press release via Business Wire, Feb. 20, 2008.

Doug Noland, "The Breakdown of Wall Street Alchemy," David Tice & Associates, Feb. 15, 2008.

Charles Gasparino and Steve Liesman, "Banks Attempt to Rescue Ambac, Other Insurers," CNBC, Feb. 1, 2008.

William Ackman, e-mail to Brian Leach, Vikram Pandit, and Robert Rubin, Feb. 24, 2008.

Christine Richard, "MBIA, Ambac Step Up Efforts to Keep Credit Ratings," Bloomberg News, Feb. 26, 2008.

Jim Bianco, president of Bianco Research LLC, interview with Pimm Fox on Bloomberg Television, Feb. 25, 2008.

Shannon Harrington and Christine Richard, "Moody's and S&P Say MIBA is AAA; Debt Investors Aren't So Sure," Bloomberg News, Feb. 27, 2008.

Christine Richard, "MBIA Removed from Review at S&P, Ambac May Be Cut," Bloomberg News, Feb. 25, 2008.

Jay Brown, letter to owners of MBIA Inc., Feb. 25, 2008.

Gross, "Rescuing Monolines Is Not a Long-Term Solution."

Jay Brown, letter to owners of MBIA Inc., Business Wire, Mar. 10, 2008.

Christine Richard and Elizabeth Hester, "Ambac Gets $1.5 Billion in Capital to Keep AAA Grade," Bloomberg News, Mar. 7, 2008.

Michael Callen, interview with Margaret Popper on Bloomberg Television, Mar. 7, 2008.

Jay Brown, letter to owners of MBIA Inc., Mar. 3, 2008.

Jay Brown, letter to owners of MBIA Inc., Mar. 9, 2008.

Eric Martin and Michael Patterson, "Ambac, Thornburg Reverse Last Week's Last-Minute Rise," Bloomberg News, Mar. 10, 2008.

CHAPTER 24
JUDGMENT DAY

Hearing of the House Committee on Financial Services, "Municipal Bond Turmoil: Impact on Cities, Towns, and States," chaired by Rep. Barney Frank (D-MA), Mar. 12, 2008.

Jonathan Laing, "Weapons of Mass Speculation," *Barron's,* May 12, 2008, p. W24.

David Einhorn, "Private Profits and Socialized Risk," Grant's Spring Investment Conference, New York City, Apr. 8, 2008.

Chrystia Freeland and Aline van Duyn, "View from the Top: Eric Dinallo, New York State Insurance Superintendent," FT.com video, Apr. 4, 2008.

Christine Richard, "MBIA Keeps $1.1 Billion Raised to Save Insurer Triple-A," Bloomberg News, May 7, 2008.

Rob Haines, "Ambac & MBIA: Sinking on Second Lien Slime," CreditSights, May 21, 2008.

Douglas Renfield-Miller, Executive Vice President, Ambac Financial Group Inc., presentation at the Keefe, Bruyette & Woods Diversified Financial Services Conference, New York City, June 4, 2008. Bloomberg transcript.

Ward Morehouse III, *Inside the Plaza: An Intimate Portrait of the Ultimate Hotel* (New York: Applause Books, 2001), p. 172.

Mark Lane and Rachel Carter, "Moody's Set to Downgrade Ambac and MBIA, All But Ends Any Hope of Revival; Assured Guaranty Appears Safe for Now," William Blair & Company, June 5, 2008.

CHAPTER 25

THE NUCLEAR THREAT

Rob Haines, "Ambac and MBIA: The Siege on the AAA Is Over," CreditSights, June 8, 2008.

Christine Richard, "Ackman Foresaw MBIA Drop, Is Short Financial Security," Bloomberg News, June 19, 2008.

Rob Haines, "Monoline Statutory Surplus: Levels Drifting Towards Regulatory Limits," CreditSights, June 8, 2008.

Jay Brown, letter to owners of MBIA Inc., Business Wire, June 11, 2008.

William Ackman, presentation, "How to Save the Policyholders," New York City, June 18, 2008.

William Ackman, letter to MBIA Inc. and MBIA Insurance Corp. board of directors, "Re: Bankruptcy," June 27, 2008.

Solomon Samson, "Playing Out the Credit Cliff Dynamic," Standard & Poor's, Dec. 12, 2002.

William Ackman, interview on *Squawk Box*, CNBC, July 15, 2008.

Martin J. Whitman, Third Avenue Value Fund, "Letter to Our Shareholders: Third Quarter Commentary," July 31, 2008.

Eric Dinallo, "Tackle False Rumours About Insurance Companies," *Financial Times,* July 31, 2008.

MBIA Inc. second quarter earnings conference call, Bloomberg transcript, Aug. 8, 2008.

Ambac Financial Group, second quarter 2008 earnings conference call, Bloomberg transcript, Aug. 8, 2008.

Christine Richard, "ACA Terminates $65 Billion of Credit Default Swaps," Bloomberg News, Aug. 8, 2008.

Merrill Lynch & Co. Inc. second quarter earnings conference call, Bloomberg transcript, July 17, 2008.

EPILOGUE

Charlie Munger, interview with Betty Liu on Bloomberg Television, May 4, 2008.

Jay Brown, letter to shareholders, MBIA Inc. 2008 Annual Report.

Martin J. Whitman, Third Avenue Value Fund, "Letter to Our Shareholders: Third Quarter Commentary," July 31, 2009.

ABN AMRO Bank N.V.; Barclays Bank PLC; BNP Paribas; Calyon; Canadian Imperial Bank of Commerce; Citibank, N.A.; HSBC Bank USA, N.A.; JPMorgan Chase Bank, N.A.; KBC Investments Cayman Islands V Ltd.; Merrill Lynch International; Bank of America, N.S.; Morgan Stanley Capital Services Inc.; Natixis; Natixis Financial Products Inc.; Cooperatieve Centrale Raiffeisen-Boerenleenbank B.A., New York Branch; Royal Bank of Canada; The Royal Bank of Scotland PLC; SMBC Capital Markets Limited; Societe Generale; UBS AG, London Branch; and Wachovia Bank, N.A. v. Eric Dinallo, MBIA Inc., MBIA Insurance Corporation and National Public Finance Guarantee Corporation, New York Supreme Court, New York County, May 13, 2009. Docket No. 6010475.

Financial Guaranty Insurance Co. v. IKB Deutsche Industriebank AG, New York Supreme Court, New York County, Dec. 29, 2008. Docket No. 600704/08.

Master File No. 07 Civ. 9901 (SHS) United States District Court Southern District of New York. In re Citigroup Inc. Securities Litigation. Citigroup's CDO Ponzi Schemes. 208.

Luke Mullins, "Waxman Digs Into Moody's, S&P with Internal Docs," *U.S. News and World Report*, Oct. 23, 2008.

Special Comment, "Structured Finance Rating Transitions: 1983–2008," Moody's Investor Service, March 2009.

Alexandre Dumas, *The Count of Monte Cristo* (New York: Bantam Dell, 2003), p. 272.

Index

About the Author

Christine S. Richard is a reporter with Bloomberg News. She has covered financial markets in Washington, Hong Kong, Singapore, and New York. Her reporting on the bond insurers received awards from the Society of American Business Editors and Writers, the New York Society of Certified Public Accountants, the National Association of Real Estate Editors, the New York Press Club, the Newswomen's Club of New York, and the Deadline Club. She lives in Frenchtown, New Jersey, with her husband, Dean, and their daughter, Sophie.